The Crisis of
American Foreign Policy

The Crisis of American Foreign Policy

The Effects of a Divided America

Howard J. Wiarda

with the assistance of
Esther M. Skelley

ROWMAN & LITTLEFIELD PUBLISHERS, INC.
Lanham • Boulder • New York • Toronto • Plymouth, UK

ROWMAN & LITTLEFIELD PUBLISHERS, INC.

Published in the United States of America
by Rowman & Littlefield Publishers, Inc.
A wholly owned subsidiary of The Rowman & Littlefield Publishing Group, Inc.
4501 Forbes Boulevard, Suite 200, Lanham, Maryland 20706
www.rowmanlittlefield.com

Estover Road
Plymouth PL6 7PY
United Kingdom

British Library Cataloguing in Publication Information Available

Library of Congress Cataloging-in-Publication Data

Wiarda, Howard J., 1939–
  The crisis of American foreign policy : the effects of a divided America / Howard J.
Wiarda ; with the assistance of Esther M. Skelley.
    p. cm.
  Includes bibliographical references and index.
  ISBN-13: 978-0-7425-3037-9 (cloth : alk. paper)
  ISBN-10: 0-7425-3037-X (cloth : alk. paper)
  ISBN-13: 978-0-7425-3038-6 (pbk. : alk. paper)
  ISBN-10: 0-7425-3038-8 (pbk. : alk. paper)
    1. United States—Foreign relations—2001– . 2. United States—Social conditions—
1980– . 3. Political culture—United States. I. Skelley, Esther M. II. Title.
  E902.W54 2006
  327.73009'045—dc22

                                                                2006011211

Printed in the United States of America

⊚™ The paper used in this publication meets the minimum requirements of American
National Standard for Information Sciences—Permanence of Paper for Printed Library
Materials, ANSI/NISO Z39.48-1992.

Contents

Preface   vii

Acknowledgments   xi

List of Abbreviations and Acronyms   xiii

Introduction: Rethinking American Foreign Policy   1

**PART I: AMERICAN FOREIGN POLICY—
CRISIS AND CHANGE**

1   American Foreign Policy: Politics and Paralysis   13

2   New Challenges in U.S. Foreign Policy   27

3   The Main Institutions of Foreign Policymaking   59

4   The New Powerhouses: Think Tanks and Foreign Policy   93

5   The Washington Social Circuit and Foreign Policy   117

PART II: HOT GLOBAL ISSUES

6   Ethnocentrism and Foreign Policy: Can We Understand
the Third World?   135

7   The Democracy Agenda in U.S. Foreign Policy   169

8   Human Rights Policy   183

9   Friendly Tyrants and American Interests   199

10   Globalization and Its Critics   217

PART III: REGIONAL RESPONSES

11 Asia and the Effort to Grow Civil Society   243

12 Democracy and Development in Sub-Saharan Africa   259

13 Benign Neglect: American Foreign Policy in Latin America
in the Post–Cold War Era   277

14 The Middle East and Islamic Society   295

Conclusion   311

Suggested Readings   317

Index   321

About the Author   329

Preface

This book argues that American foreign policy is in deep trouble. This trouble has not resulted from the actions of any one particular president or administration; the problems are much more basic and fundamental than that. The core of the problem is that the American political system is essentially not working, or working as intended, or working in such a way that enables us to carry out effective policy.

The American political system has become deeply divided and polarized. It is divided and polarized because the political parties, the overall political culture, and the country as a whole are divided and polarized. Those divisions are reflected in the workings (or nonworkings) of the political system. Congress is deeply divided along partisan lines. The divisions between the White House and Capitol Hill are deeper and more contentious than ever before. The State Department despises the Defense Department and vice versa, and both of them hate the CIA. They *all* hate the FBI and the new Homeland Security Department as horning in on their foreign affairs turf; they similarly resent the economics agencies like Treasury, Commerce, and Office of Trade Representative for elevating the increasingly important international economic agenda above the diplomatic and security ones.

When the country and the government are so divided, and the main foreign affairs departments are fighting with each other more than with their real foes, it produces gridlock and paralysis. The roots of this paralysis may be traced back to the Vietnam War, which divided the country, brought large groups of protesters into the streets, and democratized our foreign policy. Most of us will agree that democracy is generally a good thing and the more of it the better, but it remains an open question whether we can conduct a coherent foreign policy with thousands of interest groups now involved and both presidents and congresspersons constantly calculating foreign policy issues in terms of their own reelection possibilities. In addition, the country has become increasingly divided over what are called "the culture wars," and if the country is divided, it should not be too surprising that the government is too, and its foreign policy.

The discussion proceeds on three planes. The first examines the workings of the foreign policy machinery, the institutions of government, and the decision-making system, to explain how and why we are so divided and how these divisions are reflected in the rancorous, polarized debate over foreign policy. The second is the problem of American ethnocentrism, the condescending attitudes we have toward other countries and cultures, and our inability to understand other countries on their own terms rather than through our own rose-colored glasses. And the third plane is provided by a series of case studies—on Asia, Africa, Latin America, and the Middle East—where we have strong interests yet where our policy has often been ineffective and based on misunderstanding of the countries and cultures with which we are dealing.

This book is a serious, scholarly analysis of American foreign policymaking, but it is also informed by the author's extensive, over twenty years of experience in Washington policymaking. During that period he worked at the State Department and at the Defense Department, and was a foreign policy advisor to four U.S. administrations. He taught at the National War College and the Foreign Service Institute, served as a staff assistant to Henry Kissinger, worked for three of the country's leading think tanks, and functioned as an insider on many foreign policy issues. This author has seen firsthand how the American system works and fails to work, been through election campaigns with the candidates, and himself participated in the foreign policymaking process. He has seen the system up close and personal; he is very well-informed on the issues about which he writes.

This book would not have been possible without the assistance of many people. My wife, Dr. Iêda Siqueira Wiarda, once again provided invaluable insights based on her own experience in Washington policymaking; our three children, Kristy, Howard, and Jonathan, shared the Washington years with us; Doris Holden worked her usual editorial and word-processing magic on a manuscript that gave her many difficulties. Matt Hammon at Rowman & Littlefield had faith in the project and efficiently saw it through to completion. Esther M. Skelley, my superb research assistant, provided invaluable advice and editorial skills in helping me write, edit, and pull these materials together. The final product, however, is my own.

This book completes a four-volume set published by Rowman & Littlefield. All of the people named above had a strong hand in assisting me in preparing the set as well as its individual volumes. I owe all of them a deep debt of gratitude. The other books in the series, which reflect my own research and policy interests over the years, are *The Dilemmas of Democracy in Latin America: Crisis and Opportunity*; *Development on the Periphery: Democratic Transitions in Southern and Eastern Europe*; and *Comparative Politics: Approaches and Issues*.

Howard J. Wiarda
Bonita Hills
June 2006

Acknowledgments

The author wishes to express his gratitude to the following publishers and organizations for permission to include materials published earlier in preliminary form. All these materials have been thoroughly reworked, reorganized, rethought, updated, and rewritten for inclusion in the present book.

HarperCollins, for materials from Howard J. Wiarda, *American Foreign Policy* (New York, 1996) used in chapters 1, 4, 5.

Prentice Hall, for materials from Steven W. Hook, ed., *Comparative Foreign Policy* (Upper Saddle River, NJ, 2002) used in chapter 2.

American Enterprise Institute, for materials from Howard J. Wiarda, *Ethnocentrism and Foreign Policy* (Washington, DC, 1985) used in chapter 6.

Center for Strategic and International Studies, for materials from Howard J. Wiarda, *Cracks in the Consensus* (Washington, DC, 1997) used in chapter 7.

Frank Cass Publishers, for materials from Gabriel Marcella, ed., *Warriors in Peacetime* (Essex, England, 1994) used in chapter 8.

St. Martin's Press, for materials from Daniel Pipes and Adam Garfinkle, eds., *Friendly Tyrants* (New York, 1991) used in chapter 9.

Harcourt Publishers, for materials in Howard J. Wiarda, *Political Development in Emerging Nations* (Fort Worth, TX, 2004) used in chapter 10.

Westview Press, for materials in Howard J. Wiarda, *Civil Society* (Boulder, CO, 2003) used in chapters 11, 12, 14.

M. E. Sharpe, for materials in Jurgen Ruland et al., eds., *Benign Neglect* (New York, 2005) used in chapter 13.

Abbreviations and Acronyms

APEC	Asia-Pacific Economic Cooperation
BEMs	big emerging markets
CIA	Central Intelligence Agency
CIPE	Center for International Private Enterprise
EPA	Environmental Protection Agency
FDI	foreign direct investment
FSOs	foreign service officers
GNGOs	governmental-nongovernmental organizations
ICBMs	intercontinental ballistic missiles
IMF	International Monetary Fund
INS	Immigration and Naturalization Service
ISI	import-substitution industrialization
MFN	most favored nation
MNCs	multinational corporations
NAFTA	North American Free Trade Agreement
NED	National Endowment for Democracy
NGOs	nongovernmental organizations
NIPC	National Infrastructure Protection Center
NPOs	nonprofit organizations
NSA	national security advisor
NSA	National Security Agency
NSC	National Security Council
OPEC	Organization of Petroleum Exporting Countries
OSD	Office of the Secretary of Defense
OSS	Office of Strategic Services
OTR	Office of the Trade Representative

PACs	political action committees
SALT	Strategic Arms Limitation Talks
SALT II	Strategic Arms Limitation Talks
SOPs	standard operating procedures
USAID	U.S. Agency for International Development
USIP	U.S. Institute of Peace
WTO	World Trade Organization

Introduction:
Rethinking American Foreign Policy

American foreign policy is in very bad trouble. The problems are deep-rooted and systemic. They are not merely the product of some immediate crisis-of-the-moment, nor of any one president or administration, but go to the very fundamentals of who we are and what we stand for as a nation. Seen in this light, the many immediate dilemmas and difficulties of American foreign policy in Europe, the Middle East, Asia, Latin America, and Africa are merely symptoms of even larger, underlying problems. The fundamental problem is that, on far too many fronts, *the American political system is simply not working!*

The problems are both organizational and conceptual. Organizationally, the problem is that, as it is presently constituted, the American political system is so deeply divided, so partisan, so bureaucratic, so inefficient, and so inept that it is incapable of making clear, rational, well-informed decisions on a host of critical foreign policy issues, let alone implementing them. Conceptually, the basic problem is that the United States continues to view the rest of the world through our own rose-colored glasses (called "ethnocentrism"), assuming that the rest of the world can and wants to be exactly like us, with the result that we fail miserably to understand foreign countries and cultures and therefore stumble and blunder into innumerable mistakes of interpretation and policy.

When we say that these problems are "systemic," we mean that they are difficult, deep-rooted, and not easily or readily solvable. They are not the result of any single mistake, any one single party, or a certain administration or president. Rather, the problems have been accumulating for decades; they cut across party lines; and in some respects, such as separation of powers, they go back to the very foundations of the republic. Hence, if we ask why U.S. foreign policymaking is so divided, so polarized, and so often frozen in gridlock, the answer is because the *country* itself is divided, polarized, and uncertain of

1

the directions in which it wishes to go. Ultimately, a democracy's foreign policy reflects the kind of country it is and has become; and if the country is divided and uncertain, it should not be surprising that its foreign policy is similarly unclear, divided, and often unworkable. "The problem," Shakespeare perceptively wrote, "is not in the stars, it is in ourselves."

My students often ask me, "Why can't we just do the right thing" in Iraq, Cuba, Africa, Southern Asia, or wherever the issue might be? The answer is, "Because it all gets filtered through, influenced by, and shaped by the broader American political system and culture." And therein lies a long, convoluted, and very complicated story.

AMERICAN INSTITUTIONS

It used to be said (by Senator Arthur Vandenberg of Michigan) that "politics stops at the water's edge." By that he meant that it was acceptable to play politics with domestic issues such as the deficit, Social Security, or health care; but that when it came to foreign policy, politicians should refrain from the usual logrolling and patronage-based politics. The reason was, Senator Vandenberg argued, that the international world out there, with terrorism, nuclear weapons, and intercontinental ballistic missiles capable of raining massive death and destruction down on us on exceedingly short notice, was too dangerous for us to risk the country's future by the usual partisan politics. Hence, his catchy phrase that politics and partisanship should stop when we dealt with international security affairs.

Over the years, Vandenberg's injunctions were more or less adhered to by most politicians. But then came the Vietnam War of the 1960s and 1970s and its street demonstrations, massive protests, and what we can call the "democratization" of U.S. foreign policy. Now everyone had a say, and the discussion of American foreign policy took highly partisan, polarized, and sometimes violent directions. Then came the debates in the 1980s over Central American policy (El Salvador, Nicaragua, Guatemala), and the positions hardened and became even more intensely political and partisan. Finally, with the collapse of the Soviet Union in 1989–1991 and the end of the Cold War, the world was suddenly less dangerous and threatening. Without an enemy and seemingly with no foreign threat in sight, all restraints were off; politicians and interest groups felt free to say virtually anything, however bizarre, on virtually any foreign policy issue without fear of consequences. Both domestic *and* foreign policy would now be subject to partisanship, political squabbling, and the incredible hurly-burly and interest-group competition that *is* American politics.

And then suddenly came 9/11 and the terrorist attacks on the World Trade Center and the Pentagon. We had a new and very dangerous threat, a new and very frightening enemy, and in many ways we are in the worst of all situations. On the one hand, as in all crises, when the country is attacked or threatened, decision-making power tends to be concentrated in the White House, in the hands of the president, where the issue is most politicized and there is often the least expertise. On the other, the legacy of the last forty years, and continuing in the present crisis, is that politicians and groups on all sides feel free to criticize American policy with impunity. Now, even in crisis times, foreign policy has been politicized and is subjected to all the crosscurrents of American politics as is domestic policy. Can we carry out an effective foreign policy in this context? What are the present crosswinds in American society, culture, and politics that make a coherent, unified, effective foreign policy so difficult? Herewith an introductory list and analysis.

First of all (proceeding from the most general to the more specific), we are no longer as a country quite sure who we are or what we stand for. Our "political culture" (the values and beliefs on which the country is based) is no longer as clear or easily identifiable as it once was. Are we still, in Samuel P. Huntington's shorthand phrase, an "Anglo-Protestant country" ("Anglo" in the sense that so many of our political institutions derived from Great Britain; "Protestant" because that was, and maybe still is, the dominant religion of the country), or are we now so diverse, so pluralistic, and so multicultural that it is difficult to identify a single set of national values? We have become accustomed to (even if not in agreement over) dealing with these issues as regards prayer in public schools or displays of the Ten Commandments, but now we may have to deal with them in the foreign policy arena as well.

Obviously, these are enormously controversial issues over which Americans strenuously disagree. And with major implications for foreign policy. Are we interested in human rights, democracy, and the world's suffering poor only for secular political reasons? Or is there an especially American ethical or moral component to our interest in these issues—for example, the plight of Jews in Russia or of Christians in the Muslim world? Similarly, with alliances, should we have a "special relationship" with Great Britain and other Western countries because we and they share a common cultural (including religious) background, or should we simply maintain good relations with all nations regardless of history or cultural commonalities? Defining our own cultural norms and values is our first source of deep discord.

Second, and related, we are in fundamental disagreement over the future direction of the country. Look at the last two presidential elections: both disputed, very evenly divided, red states versus blue, fundamental differences between the candidates, hairline margins, no clear mandates. Even after

President George W. Bush's second election, the president's approval ratings hovered right at 50 percent, not exactly a sign of overwhelming support. Since then, they have continued to decline. Similarly, the country is evenly divided, 45–45 percent, over the question of whether the country is moving in the right direction, and those numbers are declining as well. Or take our most contentious foreign policy issue, Iraq: support for the war has steadily declined. It is hard to run a country, or its foreign policy, when electoral sentiment and public opinion are so evenly divided.

Let us turn, third, to the political party arena. We know already that our parties are very evenly divided at the national electoral level. They have also become much more ideological and polarized than in the past. American parties once represented a diversity of regions and viewpoints, but now they occupy much clearer—and farther apart—positions. The Republicans have become more conservative; the Democrats have become more liberal; and the moderate position in both parties is being squeezed out. It is hard to conduct foreign policy when the party differences are so deep, intense, and often downright nasty.

Fourth, the situation of interest groups in the United States is similar: deep polarization and testy relations. Business and labor are often at each other's throats over such foreign policy issues as trade, immigration, and outsourcing. Ethnic groups of *all* kinds and all nationalities are now mobilized on behalf of U.S. policy toward their countries, and frequently these loyalties come in conflict with other ethnic loyalties. In political Washington we have also seen the rise of a host of foreign policy groups dedicated to such "soft" issues as human rights, the environment, and disarmament, which are often opposed by those equally strong groups dedicated to a more hardheaded and military-based defense of the national interest. Many of these interest group conflicts are confined to the conference group meetings and congressional hearings of Washington and therefore we hear less of them, but they are often at least as equally intense as the party and electoral differences.

The media, it has become clear, is not just a neutral conveyor of the news but is also highly partisan and biased. The media not only reports the news, it *drives* the news, through its coverage of ethnic cleansing in the Balkans, starvation in Africa, or the tsunami tragedy in Southeast Asia, which then forces the world to pay attention and act. Reporters tend to be *overwhelmingly* (80–90 percent) on the liberal side of the aisle, which biases not only how stories are covered but *which* stories are covered; the liberal bias of the establishment press has triggered in turn an explosion of conservative media and talk shows. On many of these programs "good television" is defined as having a right-wing "nut" face off against a left-wing "nut," but meanwhile the pragmatic, centrist, consensual position that usually best serves U.S. foreign policy never gets heard.

A relatively new set of actors on the foreign policy stage are the Washington-based think tanks. The think tanks, staffed mainly by academic and policy wonks, tend in their presentation of policy positions and options to articulate and reinforce the partisan and ideological positions that already exist. Thus, we have the Heritage Foundation and the American Enterprise Institute on the right, the Brookings Institution and the Institute for Policy Studies on the left, and the Center for Strategic and International Studies in the center. Since the government is so big, bureaucratic, and often unable to do research, analyze options, and present policy positions clearly and articulately, the think tanks often do it for it. But since they are also partisan and ideological, they, too, reflect and reinforce the polarization already existent in American society.

Moving on to governmental level, we note first the role of Congress. Over the last several decades, Congress has similarly become more partisan, ideological, and divided. The roots of the division go back to the conflicts over the Vietnam War, Central America, and now Iraq. They also reflect the partisan, ideological, and cultural differences already discussed. Ask any congressperson or congressional staffer: Congress was once a wonderful place to work and serve, but now it is meaner, nastier, no longer enjoyable. The issues are more partisan and personal; the gaps, wider; and the capacity to compromise, more constrained. Congress both reflects and expresses the deeper partisan divides in the country-at-large.

Another feature of the American political system is the growing and entrenched rivalries among the main foreign policymaking agencies. The main rivalries are often between the State and Defense Departments: the former responsible for diplomacy; the latter for national security. During the Cold War it was frequently said in Washington, only half jokingly, that dealing with the Russians was easy; the real difficulty was bad relations between these two rival agencies facing each other across the Potomac River. But now we also see bitter rivalries between the CIA and the FBI and between all of these and the new Department of Homeland Security. And, as economics and trade have loomed larger in U.S. foreign policy in recent years, the Treasury and Commerce Departments and the Cabinet-rank Office of the U.S. Trade Representative have also loomed larger in American international relations. Similarly, as immigration and the environment have become major issues, the Immigration and Naturalization Service (INS) and the Environmental Protection Agency (EPA) have played bigger roles. The problem is that all these agencies compete with each other over foreign policy "turf" rather than working in a coordinated fashion to advance a unified American foreign policy.

As we get closer to the center of American foreign policy decision making, at the National Security Council (NSC) and within the Oval Office itself, the problems do not seem to get any better. The NSC is staffed mainly by bureaucrats from the agencies already mentioned so the rivalries existing in those offices are perpetuated within the NSC. Moreover, in recent years NSC positions have been filled by relatively weak individuals without the strength to do what the agency is supposed to do: knock heads if necessary between these rival agencies and produce coordinated policy for the president.

Finally, at the presidential level itself we have several major problems. Some of these have to do with weak staffing in the White House, some with the closeness and divisiveness of recent election campaigns, and others with the bitterness and fierce partisanship at the top levels of the U.S. government. But the main problem is the lack of knowledge of foreign affairs, foreign governments, and foreign countries on the part of America's top leadership. The American political system simply does not provide our elected officials with experiences of living in, knowing about, or functioning in global affairs. Neither Jimmy Carter, Ronald Reagan, Bill Clinton, nor George W. Bush (two Democrats, two Republicans) had any experience in foreign policy before coming to office. Of recent presidents, only George H. W. Bush had had prior experience in dealing with the outside world before being elected. The sad and dangerous fact is that our presidents must learn foreign affairs while on the job.

The result is that, from top to bottom, the American political system as it relates to foreign policy is riddled with problems. The greatest of these are division, bureaucratic rivalries, intense partisanship, and the incredible pluralism of America, which produces a cacophony of loud voices—all competing in the public sphere and producing a chaotic, fragmented, polarized, often paralyzed and gridlocked foreign policy. Note that all of these are deep-rooted, structural problems endemic in American society and politics that will not be changed by the mere substitution of one president or one administration for another. The wonder is not that our foreign policy is confused, chaotic, and frequently paralyzed but that, with all these problems, we still manage to have good, decent relations with so many countries around the globe.

AMERICAN VALUES AND POLITICAL CULTURE: THE ETHNOCENTRISM PROBLEMS

America's foreign policy problems as described above are structural and institutional, but they are also conceptual or ideological. The issue has to do with the values, ideas, and beliefs—or political culture—that Americans carry around with them in their heads. It is not just our institutions that stand in the way of a more coherent foreign policy; it is also our belief system and ideology that often lead us astray.

Even as a group of colonies, America thought of itself as different from other nations. The colonies often saw themselves in biblical terms as "God's people," set down in the "wilderness" that was America, a "special people" carrying out God's mission. After 1789 the noble United States was contrasted with those "evil" Europeans; we were a "nation on a hill," a "beacon of liberty," an example for all to emulate. Diplomatic historians have termed this ideology "American exceptionalism"; the United States viewed itself as different from other nations, pure of heart, singled out by God to play a special role in the world. Much of this ideology derived from America's Puritan, pilgrim, Christian, Calvinist background.

In foreign policy this background led America to attempt, missionary style, to export the blessings of its civilization to the rest of the world. In the twentieth century and onward, this missionary mentality came to be called "Wilsonian," after the twenty-eighth U.S. president. Democracy, human rights, anticommunism, the benefits of free market capitalism, sustainable development, and more recently the American war on terrorism are all American exports aimed at changing and improving the world. These policies are rarely discussed in religious terms anymore but the same missionary zeal to re-create the world in our image is still present. We want to bring the blessings of the American way of life to the rest of the world.

Public opinion surveys tell us that Americans really believe their democracy to be the best ever invented and the American free enterprise system to be responsible for our affluence and high standard of living. Those same surveys tell us that, since our system is so good and prosperous, we should export it wholesale to the rest of the world. Hence, this "missionary" or Wilsonian urge in our foreign policy to bring our advantages to poor, benighted peoples throughout the world, even in the poorest countries, such as Haiti, Somalia, Iraq, and Afghanistan.

There is much that is noble and self-sacrificing in these efforts. Americans can be very generous with their foreign assistance; willing to give up their lives for others to defeat fascism, communism, and tyranny; and dedicated to the spread of democracy and human rights. It is no accident that it was the United States that invented the Marshall Plan and the Alliance for Progress, came to Europe's defense in World Wars I and II, defeated the Soviet Union in the Cold War, and came up with the Peace Corps as a way to send idealistic young Americans into poor Third World countries to help.

There are two main problems with this agenda. The first is the American sense of superiority coupled with disdain for other nations and cultures. We really believe our institutions are superior and therefore that we have not only the right but the obligation to export them to other countries. Because we are successful and our institutions are superior, we have no need to learn how other countries do things. As a people, Americans pay little attention to other countries, seldom learn foreign languages, and expect other countries to emulate us. They must imitate our democracy and our free-enterprise economy if they wish to be successful. Almost never would we entertain the notion that we could learn from them. Hence, when Americans go abroad, their attitudes are frequently patronizing and condescending toward other peoples and countries.

A closely related trait is ethnocentrism, defined as seeing others' experiences only through one's own lenses. That is, when Americans do go abroad, they almost always see other countries through their own perspective. Because our institutions are, by definition, better and superior, it is hard for Americans to empathize (the opposite of ethnocentrism—seeing things as others see them) with other cultures and countries. Because American democracy, the American economy, our ways of doing things are always better, it is up to them to imitate us. So they must discard their own cultures, institutions, and practices and—an impossible task—imitate us. Sad to say, it is not just American tourists who hold such attitudes but often American foreign policy and foreign aid officials as well. The attitude is: *we* know what is best for you; you must imitate our ways (whether it be agrarian reform, family planning, sustainable development, or U.S.-style democracy), then you will be successful. Almost never would we contemplate that we could learn something from other countries instead of their always "learning" from us.

I would identify these as the country's two main foreign policy problems. The first is that the country's primary political institutions—parties, Congress, and the like—are not working very well. They tend to produce division, gridlock, and paralysis rather than effective foreign policy. The second is the ethnocentrism problem: our sense of superiority and condescension toward other countries, coupled with our inability to understand them in their own terms and languages, and therefore our need to impose our own institutions and ways of doing things on countries where (1) they do not fit and (2) the local or homegrown ways of doing things are probably better and more functional.

A LOOK AHEAD

The book has three main sections. In part I we discuss the main structures and institutions of American foreign policymaking. Part II analyzes some of the most important issues with which we must deal. In part III the focus turns to distinct regional areas and their relations to the United States.

Chapter 1 in part I returns to and elaborates the main themes of this chapter: discord in policymaking, producing gridlock and paralysis. Chapter 2 analyzes the new challenges in U.S. foreign policy. Chapter 3 focuses on the traditional sources of U.S. foreign policy: public opinion, Congress, political parties, interest groups, and the like. Chapter 4 analyzes the new actors in American foreign policymaking: the big Washington think tanks. Chapter 5 shows how foreign policy often gets made on the Washington social circuit rather than through the formal institutions we learned about in earlier civics courses.

Part II shows how a much more politicized American foreign policy produces often unforeseen results in dealing with major global issues. The specific issues dealt with here include U.S. efforts to export democracy abroad, U.S. human rights policy, the globalization issue—and globalization's critics, the ethnocentrism problem in American foreign policy, and the question of what to do about friendly tyrants: dictatorial or authoritarian regimes that support American policy abroad but are nevertheless gross human rights violators.

Part III shows how all these themes and conflicting crosscurrents of U.S. policy work out in different areas of the world. We concentrate here on Latin America, the Middle East and the Islamic world, Europe, Asia, and Africa. Obviously, we cannot cover all countries and all world regions in one book, so we have tried to pick out issues, countries, and areas that illustrate the book's main themes.

The conclusion summarizes the argument, pulls all the loose threads together, and wrestles with the question of where do we go from here.

Part One

AMERICAN FOREIGN POLICY: CRISIS AND CHANGE

Chapter One

American Foreign Policy: Politics and Paralysis

American foreign policy often appears to be in sad disarray—and sometimes it is more than just appearances; it *is* in disarray! The reasons for the fragmentation, for the increasingly common incoherence and creeping paralysis of American foreign policy, are deep-rooted and not just the product of the disintegration, prior to the war on terrorism, of America's historic enemy, the Soviet Union. Washington pundits have written about a certain "nostalgia for the Cold War"—at least during the Cold War we knew who the enemy was and what our purposes were, as compared with the present uncertainties. But the sclerosis and gridlock affecting American foreign policy are actually far deeper and more complicated than that. We are not sure whether the war on terrorism will fill that void.

More and more we are becoming aware that the ills, indecision, and division over American foreign policy are related to the kind of society that America has become. The reason our leaders cannot reach agreement on American foreign policy in such areas as Iraq, Iran, or the war on terrorism is that America is itself divided over these issues. And not only over these specific issues but also over the future direction of the country and where, precisely, foreign policy should fit in this new post–Cold War context. The public favors limited peacekeeping and a humanitarian role, but it is uncertain why U.S. men and women must always take the lead in solving problems in the world's trouble spots and if it is even in our interests to do so. Reflecting these public uncertainties, a nervous Congress, whose members are worried about their reelection possibilities, is debating about whether to set limits on U.S. intervention overseas.

Given the confusion and conflict over foreign policy issues, serious observers are questioning if America can have a coherent, rational, sensible, and long-term foreign policy. Over the years, especially since the Vietnam War and now accelerating again with the debate over the Middle East, U.S. policy has lacked focus; it has become more politicized, more partisan, and more conflicted. Foreign policy has also been greatly democratized, but that has not necessarily led to better foreign policy, only louder and more discordant voices. When Bill Clinton won the presidency in 1992, and both the White House and Congress were in the hands of the same party for the first time since the 1970s, political observers thought that the U.S. government gridlock would be ended; but it did not turn out that way. Similarly, in 2004, when the Republicans gained control of both the White House and Congress, partisan squabbles over foreign policy were not ended.

The divisions are basic, and they are deep. They have been growing for some time. There is not one single cause for our foreign policy problems but many. Moreover, such problems cannot be solved easily or quickly because they reflect the more divided, fragmented, and politically discordant society that America has become. The United States has always had disagreements over foreign policy—that is the price paid for living in a democratic and pluralist country. But now these differences are sharper and often more intense, and they frequently lead to paralysis of policy and nasty, mean-spirited polarization.

With all the multiple interest and veto groups out there, the conflicts between the president and Congress, and the rivalries and differences among foreign policy agencies (State, Defense, etc.), it is hard for the United States to get its act together and devise a coherent, workable foreign policy. While these conditions are certainly worrisome, they are not necessarily cause for total despair. The fact is that more often than not the United States manages, often quietly and on less controversial issues, to have a successful foreign policy. U.S. relations with most of the advanced nations, despite our differences over Iraq and other issues, are generally good and the United States has begun to put its relations with the developing countries on a more mature basis as well. Our historic enemy, the Soviet Union, has been vanquished, and American ideals—democracy, freedom, human rights, pluralism—seem almost everywhere to be triumphant. These have been successes in the war on terrorism. These represent major achievements.

But given the incredible pluralism of American society, our serious economic and budget problems, and our many discontents, the fashioning of a successful foreign policy now requires extraordinary skill, perseverance, leadership, and political coalition building. Foreign policy is no longer reserved for a small elite; rather, it now must be argued in the nation's town meetings, religious gatherings, universities, and media. Foreign policy is thus subject to, and must be carried out within, the same context of logrolling, political deals, conflict, and accommodation that has long been true of domestic politics.

The following section spells out in a brief and introductory way why the conduct of U.S. foreign policy has become so extraordinarily difficult. In subsequent chapters we will return to these main subject areas and discuss them in detail.

THE CAUSES OF OUR FOREIGN POLICY DIFFICULTIES

The causes of our current foreign policy difficulties are many and pervasive. The internal divisions that exist in the United States are reflected in a divided, uncertain foreign policy. Herewith in preliminary form is a list of the main causes of our foreign policy malaise.

The End of the Cold War

For forty-five years the United States knew clearly who its main foreign policy enemy was: the Soviet Union, which was also the center of international communism. The Soviet threat helped focus U.S. foreign policy, gave it a goal (containment of Soviet expansionism), and provided justification for a large military budget as well as a great variety of foreign policy agencies.

But the Soviet Union has disintegrated; its military alliance, the Warsaw Pact, has also collapsed. So who now is our enemy? Where is the threat? Why, or for what contingencies, do we need to keep such a large military budget and force? Do we still need agencies such as the Central Intelligence Agency (CIA) that were created in response to the Cold War with the Soviet Union? Is terrorism as big a threat as the potential of thirty thousand Soviet missiles raining down? Will the war on terrorism focus our attention and unify us as the Cold War did for many decades?

There are answers to these questions but they are not as clear-cut as they were when the Soviet Union was our main adversary. As for the issue of who is our enemy, no one knows for sure, but the Defense Department and others worry that one may emerge over the next twenty years and that we need to be prepared for a variety of possibilities. Germany or Japan? They are economic powers but not political, military, or global powers. North Korea, Iran, Iraqi insurgents, China? These may be hostile to the United States, but they are still Third World countries and are not able seriously to challenge U.S. power. Is the threat from terrorism, drugs, nuclear proliferation, or environmental damage? These are all *problems* or *concerns* but they may not constitute the same level of threat that the Soviet Union and its thirty thousand nuclear weapons did for so long. If we now say terrorism is the main threat, who and what precisely does that mean: al Qaeda, Islamic fundamentalism, who, what? Regarding the CIA, we probably do not need such a large agency spying on the Soviets anymore but we still do need a reformed and redirected CIA and good intelligence information on a variety of subjects and countries.

The point is that, even without the Soviet Union or even the war on terrorism, the world remains and will remain a dangerous place in many respects. Not *as* dangerous but still dangerous. The threats have been reduced, but there are still threats. We still need a military and an intelligence arm but their missions and purposes need to be redefined. The United States still has global interests to protect. But these days it is simply a lot harder to define our interests, locate *the* enemy, explain our foreign policy purposes to the public, or devise a coordinated policy than in the past.

Changing Demographics and Political Culture

The United States is a distinctly different country than it was thirty years ago. Its population is younger and far more ethnically, racially, and religiously diverse and multicultural than it once was. There is a greater variety of languages and peoples in the schools and workforce. The idea of the common melting pot is being replaced by greater ethnic pride in diversity and identity. At the same time, the ethnic makeup of the United States is also changing: Hispanics have become the largest minority group in the country.

All these forces are literally changing the face of America. The sheer diversity of the country and its separate ethnic enclaves make it harder to devise a single, unified foreign policy. If we look at Los Angeles or New York City, for example, and other cities, too, it is hard to define what constitutes the American community, as distinct from the many separate ethnic, racial, national, and religious groups. All this incredible diversity, coupled at a time when it is increasingly hard to define what still unites us as a nation, makes the devising and carrying out of a successful foreign policy even more difficult.

Political culture refers to the basic ideas, values, and beliefs of a people that shape their political attitudes. In its political culture, as in its ethnicity and religion, America is a more divided nation now than previously, separated by a great variety of conflicting values, ideologies, and partisan loyalties, and with little attachment to a common core of beliefs. Among the most important causes of this division have been the Vietnam War, the protest movements of the 1960s, Watergate, and several recent presidencies. Opinion surveys indicate not only that Americans are divided but that they have been losing faith in leading American institutions: the medical profession, Congress, the presidency, the judicial system, political parties, big business, labor unions, and so on. With cynicism and lack of faith in key institutions, it is not surprising that it is difficult to devise a foreign policy on which most of the public can agree.

Other broad cultural and social changes have worked to erode national confidence and unity. It has been argued, for example, that the self-centeredness of the "me generation," which has affected government officials as well as the broader society, means that Americans are mainly looking out for themselves rather than the common good of the entire nation. It may also be that the rising secularization of American society has served to erode common core values on which we all can agree. In addition, some of our leading cultural elites—for example, in the media, films, and universities—may have become more estranged from mainstream American society and its values. Red-state versus blue-state differences are deep and profound. Furthermore, our political discussion—on Vietnam in the 1960s and 1970s, Central America in the 1980s, Bosnia and Somalia in the 1990s, and Iraq recently—seems to have become more ideological, partisan, and often rancorous. We live in an era, it seems, when all institutions are under attack; we should not expect our foreign policy to be exempt from this tendency.

Economics and the Isolationist Temptations

One of the instruments by which the United States contributed to the decline of the Soviet Union was economic. We spent vast amounts on the U.S. military and on advanced military technology, knowing that the other superpower would have to match us; but since the U.S. economy was far stronger than the Soviet, we almost literally outspent them into surrender. In the process, however, we nearly bankrupted the U.S. economy as well. That gave rise to the bumper sticker: "We have defeated the enemy in the Cold War and the winner is . . . Japan!"

The U.S. budget deficit and continuing economic problems affect our ability to conduct foreign policy in many ways. There is less funding for all those agencies charged with carrying out foreign or defense policy: the State Department, Defense Department, CIA, United States Information Agency, and many others. There is also severe reduction in U.S. foreign assistance, which therefore gives us less leverage in dealing with many Third World countries. The fact that the United States has moved from being a creditor to a debtor (the world's largest!) nation means we have to borrow—and to seek investment capital from other nations, making us to some degree dependent on them. The weakening of the U.S. economy relative to other nations results in the United States having less relative economic clout in the world of today and therefore less political and foreign policy clout as well. We are still a rich country, but our share of the world's gross national product is less than it once was.

An additional result of our relative economic weakening is the temptation to isolationism. Isolationism has long been a strong force in America— roughly one-third of the electorate—but now, with U.S. industry and jobs threatened, it has gained added potency. Political candidates play on this frustration and urge us to turn our backs on the world, to throw up protectionist barriers to keep foreign-made products from competing with our own, and to withdraw into ourselves while shunning foreign affairs. But the United States is too big and powerful a nation to simply withdraw from the world. If we were to abdicate responsibilities as a superpower, the world would become hostile to us and our interests would suffer.

In addition, our economy and our political interests in democracy, human rights, narcotics, the environment, and other matters are now so interdependent and interrelated with the rest of the world—automobiles from Japan, VCRs from Taiwan, oil from the Middle East, shoes from Brazil, clothing and many other manufactured goods from Latin America—that we could not now withdraw from the rest of the world even if we wanted to. Movies, television, communications, supersonic jet travel, and the electronic movement of information as well as money have made all countries increasingly interdependent, rendering it impossible for us to throw up artificial walls to keep the rest of the world out. Nevertheless, our national frustrations plus the electoral and political strength of isolationist sentiment have made it harder to conduct a sensible foreign policy.

Public Opinion

Public opinion is playing an increasingly important role in foreign policy— mainly as a limiting factor. And all the polls tell us the country is almost evenly—and deeply—divided: red versus blue states, Republicans versus Democrats, liberals versus conservatives. President Ronald Reagan was the first president to have a full-time pollster right in the White House; his successors have continued the practice. Moreover, the technology of polling is now so sophisticated that, if it is done correctly, a president can know almost instantly how popular or unpopular his foreign policy initiatives are. In fact, on most issues a president now checks what the possible impact of his policies will be *before* he takes any action. For example, there is no doubt that opposition from the public was one of the main factors that kept U.S. military forces out of Bosnia for a time, forced the United States to reduce and cut short its mission in Somalia, for a long time prevented the United States from sending troops into Haiti, and limited President George W. Bush's options in Iraq.

A skillful president like Reagan, Clinton, or Bush can help educate and guide public opinion. But that can only be done so often or carried only so far. Public opinion thus sets parameters or boundaries on policy, beyond which presidents go only at their own peril. If they do go beyond the limits set by public opinion, they risk losing public support and probably their own re-election. And increasingly, in this post–Cold War era, the public is wary of foreign entanglements, wants to curtail foreign aid, and does not wish to see the United States involved in murky, sometimes deadly disputes in distant foreign lands, again Afghanistan or Iraq. A further complication, taken up later in this book, is that while opinion leaders in the United States (journalists, college-educated persons, government officials) are still strongly internationalist in their policy views, mass opinion is becoming more isolationist.

Interest Groups

Foreign policy was once largely isolated from the interest-group struggles that are characteristic of domestic politics. Foreign policy was made by a relatively small coterie of officials in the White House and the State Department who designed and carried out policy without—for the most part—worrying about the pressures of interest groups. No longer.

For one thing, the number of interest groups, foreign policy-oriented "think tanks," and money-raising PACs (political action committees) has enormously expanded in the last two decades. For another, many of these groups—religious organizations, business and labor lobbies, ethnic lobbies, human rights activists, think tanks—have increasingly taken stands on foreign policy issues. Foreign policy has thus become subjected to the same interest and pressure group lobbying and logrolling that marks domestic politics. In addition, many of these private groups are so powerful that they conduct their own foreign policies, or they write the policies that the government then adopts. A third new factor is that, since Vietnam, foreign policy has frequently become the subject of street demonstrations, marches on Washington, rallies on university campuses, town meetings, protests, teach-ins, and so forth. Such popular participation has led to greater public participation in U.S. foreign policymaking, but whether it has led to better or more enlightened foreign policy is a matter of great controversy.

The broader participation of the American people in policymaking forces the policymaking agencies to respond in mind. All the main Washington agencies now have large public affairs divisions (called "spin doctors"; they put a particular "spin" on events) that seek to present what they are doing in a favorable light. The democratization of policy also means that foreign affairs can no longer be the special province of a handful of government experts. Instead, the State Department and other agencies must now go out and "sell" their programs in the nation's churches, college forums, and town meetings. Government agencies need to build this kind of public support for their programs if they want them to succeed. In other words, the increasing democratization and interest-group struggle over foreign policy has produced a reaction from government agencies as well, who must now make a case for what they are doing and why. All this is probably good for the country in long-range terms, but it makes foreign policymaking much more time-consuming and complicated.

The Media

The media are now much more involved in foreign policy than previously—and not just as reporters of foreign affairs but also, frequently, as active participants in it. For example, there is no doubt that the gruesome pictures on television a few years back of starving and fly-covered children in Somalia were one of the key reasons President George H. W. Bush sent U.S. military forces into that unfortunate country on the initial humanitarian mission. It was also television—which showed bedraggled Haitians arriving in overcrowded boats on U.S. shores—that prompted the Clinton administration to refocus its policies on Haiti. Similarly, the televised reports of rape, genocide, and mass starvation in Bosnia-Herzegovina (part of the former Yugoslavia) forced the United States to consider intervention in that area. Pictures of possible weapons caches in Iraq stimulated our military intervention there.

Not only do the media sometimes *drive* U.S. policy in this way, they also often set the agenda and parameters of the debate. For example, when the media interview two persons on opposite sides of a foreign policy debate and then present them face-to-face on our television screens, or when anchor Charles Gibson arched an eyebrow and looked skeptical during an interview, or when Jim Lehrer's *NewsHour* or *Nightline*'s anchors present guests with different points of view, the media often serve to define the boundaries of the issue and the radically different positions taken. Other positions and viewpoints, including sensible centrist ones, may thus be excluded.

But the issue is not only whether the media at times drive and shape the issue but also whether they display political biases in presenting a story. The fact remains that in terms both of what they choose to cover and what they do not, the media frequently show some clear biases. At the same time various

U.S. government offices also try to *use* the media for their own, often similarly biased purposes.

Congress and the Executive

Fearing strong executive authority, the American founding fathers incorporated into the Constitution a system of checks and balances. Both Congress and the president have responsibilities in the foreign policy area, and their powers frequently overlap. The president is, for example, the commander in chief, but *all* appropriations for Defense, State, and other agencies, must be approved by Congress. The president has considerable appointment and treaty-making powers, but the Senate must concur on these matters. There are many unclear or gray areas where both branches have responsibilities. Most analysts agree that, in the absence of clarity on many issues, the Constitution provides an "invitation to struggle" between the executive and legislative branches.

When the White House and Congress are in the hands of different parties, as has mainly been the case since the 1950s, the conflicts between the two branches may become intense—as over Reagan's Central American policy and Clinton's interventions—and produce gridlock and paralysis. But even when the White House and Congress are both of the same party, as when Clinton was first elected or under George W. Bush, gridlock may not end, as we have seen in the debates over the North American Free Trade Agreement (NAFTA), on whether and how long to keep U.S. troops in Somalia, on whether and how much aid to give Russia's Boris Yeltsin, and over Iraq policy.

A handy rule of thumb in settling the executive–legislative tug-of-war is that the president "proposes" and Congress "disposes." But the world is often a dangerous place and what if the president is inexperienced in foreign affairs (as were Carter, Clinton, and George W. Bush) or allows his ideological commitments to get in the way of what others think is sound judgment? Then Congress is likely to play a more assertive foreign policy role. At the same time, even an inexperienced president is loathe to give up any real executive prerogative to Congress; no one can conceive that U.S. foreign policy could be effectively carried out by 535 "secretaries of state": 435 in the House and 100 in the Senate. That is why the executive–legislative battle goes on over foreign policy and will continue to do so. The system is one of checks and balances: good from the point of view of preventing too much power and authority from being lodged in any one place but not so good if one values efficient foreign policymaking, quick decision making, and an absence of conflict. Meanwhile, the nasty, testy, polarized relations between Republicans and Democrats within Congress and between Congress and the White House make an agreed-upon foreign policy all but impossible.

Bureaucratic Politics

Bureaucratic politics refers to the fact that the different agencies of the U.S. government charged with carrying out foreign policy (White House, State Department, Defense Department, Treasury, Justice, CIA, and others) frequently have different interests and points of view that work at cross-purposes and can lead to conflict. There are different "cultures" or "norms" that operate within each of these agencies, as well as different SOPs (standard operating procedures), and it is very hard to get these all coordinated. People who work within the system say (only half in jest) that it is often easier to deal with North Korea than with another agency of the U.S. government.

The State Department, for example, is frequently a guardian of continuity in foreign policy, whereas the White House, emphasizing change and seeking to get reelected, often wants to be more innovative. The Justice Department and its Drug Enforcement Agency (DEA), in pursuing a counternarcotics policy, often follows a vigorous law enforcement and arrest policy; while the State Department, wanting to have good relations with most countries and fearing a strong arrest policy might include another country's cabinet ministers or armed forces chiefs, resists. Another area of bureaucratic conflict is between State and Defense: the State Department often wants a U.S. military presence abroad—troops in the former Yugoslavia, Somalia, or Haiti—to back up its diplomacy; while Defense, concerned about the possibility of loss of life of its comrades and not wanting to be put in an indefensible position militarily, is usually more reluctant to go.

The importance of this bureaucratic politics factor is crucial but perhaps most difficult for persons on the outside to grasp. Their attitude often is that we should have a coordinated policy and anyone who operates outside of that should shape up or be let go. But these are powerful bureaucracies; they have their own ways of doing things; they are permanent and will be there long after the administration-of-the-moment is gone; and there are genuine differences of opinion and approach within these agencies as to how best to proceed. As one experienced foreign policy practitioner has commented, he would much rather have to deal with the murderous factions in the former Yugoslavia or Iraq than to go across town to deal with his counterparts in another U.S. government agency.

Partisan Politics and Ambition

It would be nice if we could believe that foreign policy options were decided solely on their merits. But they are not, and we might as well acknowledge that reality. In fact, foreign policy is now infused with political considerations, partisan politics, and the personal career ambitions of politicians in both Congress and the executive branch. The political factor needs to be figured into any consideration of foreign policymaking; moreover, if there is little or minimum threat, partisan politics become even more pronounced. Foreign policy issues sometimes get "used" to secure partisan political advantage. For example, during the 1980s debate on Central America, Democrats wanted to portray Republicans as insensitive to human rights, while Republicans sought to blame Democrats for "losing" Nicaragua and possibly El Salvador to communism. Both U.S. foreign policy and the countries in the region suffered as a result of this effort to secure partisan advantage from the issues. In the 1970s Jimmy Carter got the Panama Canal Treaties through Congress only by promising members of Congress lavish spending programs in their districts. In the Iraq crisis both sides tried to get political advantage from the conflict. In addition, congressmembers regularly posture over foreign policy issues for the sake of getting headlines and television coverage for themselves to help their reelection possibilities or to advance their political careers. Or they may trade their vote on a foreign policy issue (NAFTA) for a colleague's vote on a domestic affairs matter (health care). These and other political machinations often have little to do with the merits or demerits of the foreign policy issue at hand, but they are very important in foreign policy considerations—and becoming more so.

All this sounds rather discouraging, and it often is. But that is how the American system of politics and logrolling works, and there is relatively little we can do to change it. We cannot expect members of Congress to vote for a measure that is clearly in the national interest if doing so will harm their reelection possibilities; only rarely do we see such "profiles in courage." Instead, the key is to think in terms of what is both good policy *and* what is good for the congressperson. If issues can be framed so that they serve both these goals, then we may have the beginning of a successful policy.

Foreign policy, like other policies, does not get made in a vacuum. A variety of pressures, including partisan and political ones, operate upon any policy. The key to becoming a successful foreign policy maker in Washington therefore is to be able to advance a policy that not only can stand on its own merits but will also be politically and bureaucratically advantageous to the individuals and agencies affected. Students who can see this and are able to master the delicate juggling acts that are often involved in formulating policy in this manner are on their way to becoming successful foreign policy makers.

OVERCOMING PARALYSIS

The United States is internally divided; the partisan divide is wide; we are tired of the role of global policeman; the terrorist threat is frightening; and we would prefer to concentrate on our domestic agenda. It is not a happy time to be in charge of American foreign policy.

Sometimes we are tempted by isolationism: the real issue for us is not isolationism versus involvement in the world; we are and must be involved. The question therefore is can we design a prudent and sensible foreign policy that takes into account the new realities (including the threat of terrorism) in the world, the interrelations between a strong foreign policy role and a strong economic base at home, and the realistic limits on our willingness and power to act abroad. We are not equipped nor do we wish to be the law enforcers of the world; on the other hand, because so much is at stake, for the world as well as for us, we cannot withdraw. Hence, we must strike a balance, pick and choose when we get involved, and establish priorities. This is not an easy process and we should not be surprised that various factors such as interest groups, politics, and partisanship get involved. That, after all, is how we decide things in this uneven and sometimes messy process called democracy.

Nor do we as a nation do too badly at it over the long haul. We now have, after many years of debate, a quite prudent and sensible policy on democracy and human rights. We can reduce, but probably not entirely eliminate, the threat of terrorism. U.S. policy toward China, with some ups and downs, has been quite consistent over the years. By fits and starts, we are adjusting to the new role and power of Japan. NATO has redefined its functions now that it no longer needs to confront the Soviet Union. Many regional conflicts—in Southern Africa, Cambodia, the Horn of Africa, Central America, and perhaps even the Middle East—have been resolved or may be on the way to resolution. We are slowly adjusting to the reduced importance of Russia and Western Europe in our strategic thinking, and to the rising importance of East Asia, the Middle East, and Latin America. The process is often discordant and agitated—democracies take time to adjust to new realities—but overall it is not a bad record. More than that, this learning and adjusting process has taken place on both sides of the partisan spectrum; in the end, good politics and a good foreign policy are usually found in the middle, where we can agree and work toward a new, better informed foreign policy consensus.

Ultimately, American foreign policy is a reflection of American society itself. And the fact is that since the 1960s we are more divided as a nation, less sure of ourselves, torn over partisan and ideological issues, sometimes not quite certain of who we are as a nation and what we stand for, and hampered with severe budgetary problems. All this is reflected in our often unclear foreign policy, which has been further weakened by our lack of consensus and uncertainty of direction.

On the other hand, we did vanquish the Soviet Union. We may be getting a handle on the terrorist threat. Militarily and strategically, the United States now stands alone in the world as the only superpower left, and the power and influence of its ideals—not just Coca-Cola, jeans, and rock music, but also democracy, freedom, free markets, and human rights—have triumphed virtually everywhere. Furthermore, there is renewed hope in the air, great vigor, strong national self-confidence, and possibilities for greater prudence and centrism in American foreign policy. It is a strong base on which to build. But in the meantime, as the succeeding chapters make clear, the process by which we get to these goals is as messy, as clamorous, as complex, as endlessly fascinating as ever.

Chapter Two

New Challenges
in U.S. Foreign Policy

More than a decade after the Cold War ended, the United States remains the "lone superpower" in world politics. The country's military forces are unrivaled; its economy is still far larger than that of any of its competitors; and its political system—for all of its well-publicized faults—remains a model that many countries have sought to emulate. Yet, leaving aside the war on terrorism for the moment, the United States is still searching for a new set of foreign policy principles that reflects the changed conditions in the world, the altered post–Cold War U.S. global position, and the public's desire for greater attention to domestic issues. This search for a clear world role became a fixture of the presidency of Bill Clinton and continues today under President George W. Bush, who came into power in January 2001 after a narrow and controversial electoral victory over Vice President Al Gore and then defeated John Kerry in 2004.

Adapting to the post–Cold War era and to the newer terrorist threat has proven to be an elusive task for U.S. policy makers. The collapse of the Soviet Union, the primary adversary of the United States between 1945 and 1991, forced U.S. leaders to rethink their basic assumptions and strategies. The U.S. government itself, which had been geared to the Cold War struggle for nearly half a century, also required restructuring in order to meet the demands of the new era. The Defense Department, the State Department, and other agencies of foreign policy all were forced to adapt their sizes, structures, and missions in their own ways to the new global landscape. The war on terrorism forced all these agencies to adjust again.

The country's regional priorities also had to be rethought. During the Cold War, the Soviet Union and the Warsaw Pact were the main focus of U.S. strategic thinking. Since it was widely thought that the plains of Eastern Europe would be the main avenue of Soviet expansion, the political, economic, and military recovery and defense of Western Europe was the central objective of U.S. foreign policy. The Middle East area was also important, both for support of Israel (created in 1948) and because of fears of Soviet penetration of the oil-rich Persian Gulf. As the Cold War set in, East Asia was deemed crucial as a check on Soviet ambitions in this region. Africa, South Asia, and Latin America, by contrast, were thought of as "derivative" regions, important only when the Cold War extended to their shores, but largely ignored the rest of the time.

Since the Cold War, questions have been raised as to whether Russia should be as much a foreign policy preoccupation as was the Soviet Union. In this regard, the role of the North Atlantic Treaty Organization (NATO) has become ambiguous, along with U.S. relations with the major Western European states and the European Union (EU). Japan, China, and the rest of East Asia have remained priorities, but mainly for economic reasons rather than strategic ones. Meanwhile, turmoil in South Asia—particularly the emergence of India and Pakistan as rival nuclear powers—has demanded attention from Washington. Given that the perceived Soviet threat to the Middle East is gone, U.S. leaders have focused on the terrorist threat and on economic rationales (oil!) to justify activism in the region, along with ongoing concern for the security of Israel.

The U.S. government has looked toward Latin America with greater interest, given its growing economies and emerging democracies as well as its complex interdependence with the United States itself. Beyond economic relations, emerging priorities such as drug trafficking, immigration control, and environmental concerns resonate strongly in U.S.–Latin American relations. As for Africa, the United States has shifted its focus toward humanitarian concerns, largely in response to widening regional conflicts across the continent. Given its lack of strategic importance to Washington, however, Africa is likely to receive less overall attention by the Bush administration.

The experience of the post–Cold War period demonstrates that the United States, as the world's most powerful nation-state, continues to have global commitments, interests, and obligations that cannot be abandoned just because the Cold War is over. President Clinton came to recognize this central fact, as did his successor; the war on terrorism brought these facts home: the United States must be involved in the world if only for its own defense. But the U.S. government's approach toward all these issues and areas has yet to fully reflect the transformed global environment. A more coherent adaptation strategy thus remains vital, as does a clear articulation of U.S. interests and priorities.

In the midst of these uncertainties, U.S. leaders have been engaged in a sometimes vigorous, sometimes torpid discussion of what the shape and direction of its foreign policy should be. President George H. W. Bush welcomed the arrival of a "new world order" in 1990, but he lacked the strategic and conceptual vision that was needed to translate this cliché into a concrete strategy for U.S. foreign policy. His successor, Bill Clinton, first settled upon the concept of "assertive multilateralism," then shifted to "engagement and enlargement" when the earlier formulation was criticized as a result of perceived failures in such places as Somalia and Haiti. The enlargement theme begged the question "enlargement of and for *what?*" and also seemed awkward as a rallying cry.

Upon taking office in 2001, George W. Bush and his advisers also struggled to outline a grand strategy, citing only a need for the United States to remain strong and focus on its national interests. Bush's pledges to redirect U.S. foreign policy were reflected in his early appointments to key foreign policy positions: General Colin Powell as secretary of state, Condoleezza Rice as national security adviser, and Donald Rumsfeld as secretary of defense. Vice President Richard Cheney, who had served as defense secretary in the "first" Bush administration, quickly became the primary power broker in the White House. The president and his advisors signaled a rejection of the humanitarian interventionism of the Clinton administration and a shift toward more narrow concerns related to U.S. national security. They also called for greater defense spending, including the deployment of a nuclear missile-defense system, and promised a harder line toward Moscow and Beijing. However, given the slim margin of victory that brought the Bush administration to power in the November 2000 elections, and given the divided control of Congress between the Republican and Democratic Parties beginning in June 2001, a clear and cohesive statement of U.S. foreign policy goals and strategies remained out of reach.

The articulation of a coherent foreign policy was further hindered by the absence of a clear enemy to replace the Soviet Union or, more broadly, international communism. The United States initially identified several "rogue states"—including Iran, Iraq, Libya, and North Korea—but none of these could be considered a strategic threat to the United States in the same way the Soviet Union had been. Certain issues—illegal drugs, ethnic strife, nuclear proliferation, environmental decay, and illegal immigration—were also elevated in importance in the wake of the Cold War. But these problems did not threaten to destroy the United States, as Soviet nuclear weapons could, and proved fickle as leading foreign policy issues.

Until the September 2001 terrorist attacks on New York City and Washington, D.C., none of the rogue states, nor any of the issues noted earlier, sufficiently stirred the public imagination, secured the necessary congressional budget support, or demonstrated the staying power sufficient to replace "containment" as the focal point of U.S. foreign policy. The deadly assaults on the World Trade Center and the Pentagon focused the energies of the Bush administration toward an inescapable foreign threat, although its scope and the means required to counter the terrorist challenge were difficult to ascertain. Nor can we be certain how long the war on terrorism will last.

A more general debate has been revived in the absence of anticommunism as a basis of U.S. foreign policy. Clinton, who sought an expansive U.S. world role, criticized the "new isolationists" in Congress, which was controlled by the Republican Party for the final six years of his presidency. For their part, congressional leaders rejected the president's "romantic interventionism" in the absence of clear U.S. national interests. This struggle between Clinton and Congress remained unresolved as the United States pursued an inconsistent and often incoherent foreign policy. It remains to be seen whether the administration of George W. Bush will be able to reverse this trend and achieve a consensus with Congress regarding the ends and means of U.S. foreign policy.

In this chapter, we assess the foreign policy of the United States as it continues to adapt to the complex environment of the post–Cold War era. In our historical review, we first consider how the scope of U.S. foreign policy steadily broadened as the nation expanded from a regional to a global power. Specifically, we describe how a grand strategy based on detachment from the European powers ultimately gave way to a foreign policy of global activism that identified U.S. interests in virtually every corner of the world. Even as the United States adopted such global ambitions, however, many Americans resisted the government's growing involvement in "foreign entanglements" and favored a return to the "splendid isolation" of the nineteenth century. We then turn our attention to the many emerging issues confronting U.S. foreign policy makers after the Cold War. Finally, we consider the shifting sources of U.S. foreign policy at the global, societal, and governmental levels. We focus on the growing number of players in the foreign policy game, in particular, economic interest groups, government agencies, ethnic groups, and international organizations.

As we will argue, the more pluralistic policymaking environment of the post–Cold War era has pushed the United States in different directions—toward a more active world role in some cases, toward retrenchment in others—depending upon the foreign policy issue at hand. In this sense, the fragmented nature of U.S. foreign policy has greatly hindered the task of adapting to the post–Cold War era with a distinctive and coherent grand strategy, or of successfully waging the war on terrorism. The United States is not the only country with an increasingly democratic foreign policy; such a trend has become commonplace as more countries have adopted representative institutions and practices. The United States is, however, the world's most powerful nation, and the only remaining superpower with global responsibilities. Consequently, the outcome of these complex and overlapping struggles over U.S. foreign policy has profound implications not only for its own peace and prosperity, but also for the stability of the world and the international system.

U.S. FOREIGN POLICY IN HISTORICAL PERSPECTIVE

The foreign policy of the United States has evolved in many ways since the country's independence. The shifting balance between isolationism and internationalism has been among the most interesting of the changes in U.S. foreign policy. Throughout this history there have been periods when isolationist ideas dominated, and other times—primarily in the post–World War II period—when the United States pursued a distinctly internationalist agenda.

The isolationist impulse sprang from the foundations of the U.S. experience. The first settlers journeyed across the Atlantic Ocean in order to escape British rule, and their descendants fought to sever themselves completely from Great Britain. The presence of vast oceans that separated the United States and Europe served to further instill the sense that the United States was, and should be, separated from European affairs. As President George Washington observed in his farewell address, "Europe has a set of primary interests, which to us have none or a very remote relation. Hence she must be engaged in frequent controversies, the causes of which are essentially foreign to our concerns."

Throughout the nineteenth century, Americans generally kept their backs to Europe, concentrating on expanding their own borders westward. The United States acquired the vast Louisiana territory from France in 1803, then forcibly wrested control of Florida from Spain and the southwestern states from Mexico. In a major foreign policy pronouncement, President James Monroe declared in 1823 that the entire Western Hemisphere should be free of European interference. The Monroe Doctrine not only warned Europeans to stay out of the Western Hemisphere, but also shaped the U.S. relationship with its southern neighbors. Latin America and the Caribbean thus occupied a distinctive space within U.S. foreign policy. Although formally independent, they were considered to be within the "sphere of influence" of the United States.

This preponderant hemispheric role was further exemplified by the Spanish-American War of 1898, when President William McKinley felt justified in intervening in Cuba's war with Spain, acquiring Puerto Rico, and establishing a protectorate over Cuba. The war heralded a new phase in U.S. foreign relations, which soon assumed a global reach. The United States was quickly becoming a significant world power, with the economic and military might needed to back up such status. The United States, having also gained control of the Philippines from Spain, colonized the islands rather than grant them independence. Through its "open-door policy," U.S. leaders discouraged the European powers from dividing China into economic spheres of influence. As McKinley declared, isolationism had become "no longer possible or desirable."

In 1904, President Theodore Roosevelt added a new dimension to the Monroe Doctrine. In what has become known as the Roosevelt Corollary to the doctrine, Roosevelt asserted the right of the United States "to the exercise of an international police power" within the hemisphere. Wielding its "big stick," the United States intervened militarily in Colombia, the Dominican Republic, Haiti, Mexico, Nicaragua, Panama, and Cuba during the first decades of the twentieth century. Political leaders in Washington often justified these interventions on the normative grounds of promoting democratic order, but economic self-interests often lurked barely beneath the surface. Despite these interventions, isolationist sentiment remained strong. The United States entered World War I in 1917, three years after the conflict had begun in Europe and only after the German navy began to sink U.S. merchant ships. Once the war was over, the United States quickly demobilized. Despite President Woodrow Wilson's involvement in the design and creation of the League of Nations, the United States remained outside of this new international organization. The onset of the Great Depression during the 1930s furthered the revival of isolationism.

In the years leading up to World War II, the United States was determined to remain uninvolved in the developing conflict. The U.S. Congress enacted numerous neutrality acts in the mid-1930s that attempted to prevent future American engagement in Europe. Despite these efforts, the United States could not remain aloof from the conflict indefinitely. President Franklin Roosevelt recognized that the allies needed the United States' support and slowly chipped away at the isolationist wall built around the United States. The wall was toppled completely when the Japanese attack on Pearl Harbor on December 7, 1941, forced the United States to enter the war. This time, the United States intervened not just as another great power, but as a superpower intimately tied into the international system. The United States thus played a decisive role in both theaters of combat, the Western Pacific and Europe.

After the war, it was no longer possible for the United States to turn inward to return to isolationist "normalcy." The European powers and Japan were devastated. The war effort, on the other hand, had rescued the U.S. economy from the Depression while greatly strengthening U.S. military forces. As the Cold War set in, the United States remained the only power that could counter the aggressive behavior of the Soviet Union. Thus the U.S. war machine was not completely demobilized after World War II as it had been in 1918. To the contrary, by 1947–1948 the United States was party to a major expansion of its military forces in order to "contain" Soviet power.[1] As a result, the United States became a major power on a permanent basis.

The U.S. government embraced its role as the leader of the anticommunist alliance. "I believe it must be the policy of the United States to support free peoples who are resisting attempted subjugation by armed minorities or by outside pressures," President Harry Truman asserted in 1947. "The free peoples of the world look to us for support in maintaining their freedoms. . . . Great responsibilities have been placed upon us by the swift movement of events." The military aid programs approved under the Truman Doctrine were accompanied by a large-scale economic aid program to Western Europe, known as the Marshall Plan, and a major reshaping of U.S. military and intelligence institutions.

Polls taken at that time demonstrated that a majority of Americans supported their government's new international posture. The victory of communist forces in China's civil war, which resulted in the creation of Mao Zedong's People's Republic of China in 1949, further solidified the anticommunist consensus. In 1950, the United States led the United Nations-sponsored effort to repel North Korea's invasion of South Korea. Later in the 1950s, President Dwight Eisenhower ordered a buildup of U.S. nuclear forces, the creation of a global web of military alliances, and numerous covert interventions in such countries as Iran and Guatemala. The globalization of the Cold War reached its most dangerous point in 1962, when it was discovered that the new communist regime in Cuba was installing nuclear missiles that had been shipped secretly from the Soviet Union. President John F. Kennedy's refusal to permit such missile deployments prompted a head-on collision with Moscow, which withdrew the missiles.

Public support for the containment policy reached a turning point in the 1960s, when the United States intervened on a massive scale in Southeast Asia. Despite its military superiority, the United States was unable to prevent North Vietnam from taking control of South Vietnam and unifying the country under communist rule. American actions in Vietnam deeply divided the public. Despite the government's claim that the fall of Vietnam would profoundly alter the global balance of power, many doubted the "domino theory" and questioned why the United States was involved in this conflict, located thousands of miles away, in a region that was previously unknown to most Americans. Large-scale U.S. casualties—in addition to the even greater destruction imposed by U.S. forces on the Vietnamese people—prompted antiwar demonstrations and demands for withdrawal. Many Americans, who had previously viewed the United States as an "exceptional" world power, no longer saw it as a role model for others to follow.

As the U.S. involvement in Vietnam was winding down, President Richard Nixon sought to stabilize superpower tensions. In the view of his national security adviser, Henry Kissinger, the nation needed a new approach that would prevent future crises and proxy wars. The détente policy, designed to promote "a vested interest in cooperation and restraint," led to a series of summit meetings between U.S. and Soviet leaders and the beginning of negotiations to limit, then reduce, the size of the nuclear arsenals maintained by each superpower. The Strategic Arms Limitation Talks (SALT) represented a cornerstone of détente and provided a basis for deep cuts in nuclear stockpiles in the 1980s. The Nixon administration also established diplomatic relations with China as part of the détente policy, a move that exploited the break between Moscow and Beijing that had become apparent since the early 1960s.

Under President Jimmy Carter, the United States further shifted its foreign policy away from Cold War competition. Carter proclaimed that human rights would become a primary consideration in U.S. foreign policy, and he sought to improve relations between the United States and the dozens of developing countries that had been trapped in the Cold War cross fire. His efforts were frustrated, however, after the Soviet Union invaded Afghanistan in 1979 and after a neo-Marxist regime took control of Nicaragua in Central America. Most crippling to Carter's presidency, anti-American activists in Iran seized control of the U.S. embassy in November 1979 and held dozens of Americans hostage for more than a year.

The experiment with détente and the emphasis on human rights in the developing world largely ceased with the election of Ronald Reagan in 1980. Reagan's rhetoric—the Soviet Union had once again become the "evil empire"—was followed by on-again, off-again conflict and confrontation between the superpowers. Under the so-called Reagan Doctrine, the U.S. government pledged to support groups fighting Soviet-backed regimes worldwide. The United States launched a major military buildup during Reagan's first term, doubling the size of its defense budget, and vowed to escalate the arms race further through the development of a space-based, missile-defense shield, dubbed "Star Wars." Reagan sought to put maximum pressure on the Soviet regime in order to accelerate its demise.

By the mid-1980s, changes within the Soviet Union foreshadowed the end of the Cold War. The Soviet Union had been suffering from an internal economic crisis that was, in part, brought about by the escalating arms race. Soviet leader Mikhail Gorbachev realized that Moscow could no longer afford to match the United States in military spending. Through the glasnost and perestroika initiatives, Gorbachev sought to introduce political freedoms in the Soviet Union and to make its command economy more efficient. But by then the Soviet Union was showing increasing signs of crisis in multiple areas: economic, social, political, generational, ideological, and moral. By the end of the decade, the Soviet Union had withdrawn from Afghanistan, relaxed its internal political and economic controls, and allowed the rise of noncommunist governments in Eastern Europe.

Gorbachev's reforms led directly to the collapse of the Soviet Union. In 1989, the Berlin Wall, the long-standing symbol of the Cold War, came down amid cheers across Central Europe. With Germany reunited in 1990 and the Eastern European governments in the midst of democratic transitions, the territories of the Soviet Union demanded their own independence from Moscow. The secession of the largest territory, Russia, along with Ukraine and several Islamic republics, capped the Soviet Union's free fall. The Cold War had finally ended—peacefully, and on terms that exceeded the most optimistic expectations of U.S. leaders and their allies.

KEY CONCERNS AFTER THE COLD WAR

The end of the Cold War brought understandable relief to governments and mass publics throughout the world. The "doomsday clock" was set back. International security was no longer overshadowed by fear of a cataclysmic nuclear war. In the United States, long-neglected domestic problems could finally receive the government's attention. President George H. W. Bush welcomed the arrival of a "new world order," which, he presumed, would feature greater democracy, peace, and prosperity throughout the world. Yet in many ways the demise of the Soviet Union presented its own problems for U.S. foreign policy. As Soviet official Georgy Arbotov warned his U.S. counterparts in 1991, "We are going to do a terrible thing to you. We are going to deprive you of an enemy." The Soviet Union then followed through with this "threat" by disappearing from the map.

Not only had the Soviet Union vanished, but so had many Cold War–related issues. Suddenly a new grand strategy would be required. Bilateral and multilateral alliances would seek new missions, and the differences between allies and adversaries of the United States would become more ambiguous. Confusion resulted as the long-standing focus of U.S. foreign policy vanished. During the Cold War, when the enemy and threat were clear, policy makers were encouraged to put away their political and bureaucratic differences and to respond with single-minded purpose. Now that the threat was less clear, the domestic rivalries and political squabbles surrounding foreign policy returned to the surface.

All of this led foreign policy makers to seek out a creative adaptation strategy that suited the new international context. A central line of debate concerned the *extent* of U.S. involvement overseas and provoked familiar arguments between isolationists and internationalists. A second and related issue concerned the *nature* of U.S. involvement. This debate reflected long-standing differences between two contending schools of thought: idealism and realism.

The *idealist* position included conservative as well as liberal proponents. Among conservatives such as Joshua Muravchik of the American Enterprise Institute for Public Policy Research, the promotion of democracy emerged as a central priority in U.S. foreign policy. In his view, the United States should eschew other and sometimes contrary diplomatic, political, strategic, and economic interests (as in Kuwait, Saudi Arabia, and China, for example) in its effort to "export democracy." The liberal position, represented by such scholars as Larry Diamond and the journal *Democracy*, viewed the promotion of democracy less as an instrument of U.S. national interests and more as a moral imperative.

The *realist* position, represented most visibly by former secretary of state Henry Kissinger, had long been known for a hardheaded defense of the national interest, devoid of moralistic or idealistic concerns. To realists, a foreign regime's internal affairs (including human rights violations) should not interfere with the U.S. assessment of its power capability or usefulness to the United States in international politics. Importantly, however, even Kissinger came to recognize that the United States—perhaps uniquely among nations— could not operate on the basis of "power politics" alone, and that it needed moral purpose and a sense of doing right and good in the world to have a successful foreign policy.

Yet another dimension of the post–Cold War foreign policy debate pitted unilateralists against multilateralists. The unilateralists, otherwise known as "aggressive nationalists," believed that, with the collapse of the Soviet Union and the United States being the only remaining superpower, the United States must exercise its power aggressively to end world conflicts and impose a democratic stamp on other nations. This position was strongly argued by neoconservative columnist Charles Krauthammer, who termed the immediate post–Cold War period as the "unipolar moment." Krauthammer stated the following: "We are in for abnormal times. Our best hope for safety in such times, as in difficult times past, is in American strength and will to lead a unipolar world, unashamedly laying down the rules of world order and being prepared to enforce them."

This argument reflected the fact that, militarily and strategically, the United States was the only superpower in the Cold War's aftermath. But it ignored the fact that Congress and public opinion would not support an open-ended global policeman role, that the U.S. economy and its taxpayers could not afford such an ambitious international agenda, that the interests of such *economic* superpowers as Japan and Germany must also be taken into account, and that the more integrated international system of the 1990s and today placed far more restraints on U.S. power than the unilateralists were willing to acknowledge.

In response to budgetary as well as political restraints, the Clinton administration first proposed a foreign policy more heavily based on multilateralism. The strategy of "assertive multilateralism" called for strengthening the United Nations and other international organizations and for employing their forces and good offices in various local and regional conflicts rather than committing U.S. forces. But multilateralism also faced many problems, particularly in the late 1990s. Allies of the United States and other multilateral partners were often slow to act or had different interests, the United Nations and other international agencies were woefully ill-equipped in carrying out peacekeeping operations in far-flung areas, and many U.S. leaders opposed putting the nation's troops under UN commanders. As time went on, the public and the Republican-led Congress withdrew their support of the policy, and in the face of this opposition, the administration gradually withdrew its earlier faith in multilateralism.

Amid all of these intellectual debates, the primary agents of U.S. foreign policy struggled to find their way. The Defense Department, after concluding that no major power posed a serious threat to the United States, turned its attention to several "rogue states" (later dubbed "states of concern") that combined strong anti-American sentiments and a stated desire to acquire chemical, biological, or nuclear weapons. Iraq provided the Pentagon with an excellent example of the potential dangers presented by such states. Yet even after Saddam Hussein's forces were expelled from Kuwait during George H. W. Bush's presidency, the Clinton administration remained wary of Saddam's military capabilities and intentions. Despite harsh economic sanctions against Iraq that were sponsored by the UN and a protracted effort to block Iraq's effort to build weapons of mass destruction, Hussein remained firmly in power. He stayed there until George W. Bush launched a war to oust him.

The Uncertain Use of Military Force

The Persian Gulf War demonstrated that the "new world order" anticipated by U.S. leaders would be anything but orderly. The war also revealed that the United States might be tempted to confront other regional conflicts and consider resolving them through military force. Aside from Iraq's invasion of Kuwait, which clearly threatened U.S. economic interests, the United States became engaged in a variety of humanitarian interventions after the Cold War. American troops were deployed to Somalia in 1992 in order to provide food and other supplies to victims of a prolonged famine, which was made worse by the collapse of the Somali government and civil war. But the intervention failed after U.S. and UN peacekeepers launched an ill-fated effort to apprehend rival warlords and rebuild the Somali state. After U.S. troops were ambushed and the body of one soldier was unceremoniously dragged through the streets, public opinion that was fanned by television coverage demanded that the United States withdraw. Two years later, the United States intervened in Haiti, where a democratically elected government had been forcibly removed by military leaders. But again the intervention succumbed to challenges from indigenous forces.

In each case the United States seemed hesitant to intervene and only did so after much debate within and outside of Congress and the White House. Efforts by the United States in some cases actually hindered the resolution of these problems, which ultimately required the cooperation and reconciliation of the foreign governments and their peoples. By the mid-1990s, when the central African nations of Rwanda and Burundi descended into a genocidal conflict between the Tutsi and Hutu ethnic groups that claimed 800,000 lives, the United States remained passive and unwilling to stop the carnage.

Another casualty of the Cold War's end was Yugoslavia, which was deeply divided along religious and ethnic lines. Without a strong leader at the top, which Marshal Josip Tito provided for many years, and without the threat of Soviet military intervention, Yugoslavia disintegrated into civil war. At first the United States saw few of its interests affected by these conflicts.[2] But later, affected by gruesome television coverage of Yugoslav president Slobodan Milosevic's campaign of "ethnic cleansing" against Muslims, the United States and its NATO allies intervened. In Bosnia-Herzegovina, they sent peacekeepers to separate the contending factions in 1995 and began building a fragile new government. Four years later in the Yugoslav province of Kosovo, the NATO allies responded to Milosevic's latest atrocities by bombing his troops along with key targets in the heart of Yugoslavia, including the capital, Belgrade. The two sides eventually established a tenuous peace, which only the continued presence of NATO forces seemed capable of maintaining. These interventions were variously praised or criticized, but they did little to resolve the underlying questions regarding a U.S. grand strategy after the Cold War.

Foreign policy makers sought to maintain a sense of purpose by redesigning Cold War structures. The NATO alliance, formed to prevent Soviet expansion after World War II, lost its main purpose after the fall of the Soviet Union. Many politicians and academics predicted the dissolution of the alliance after its enemy had been vanquished. Not only did NATO survive, however, it also grew larger. This was done by redefining NATO as less of a collective military alliance and more as a political club of democracies with shared security concerns. In this spirit, Poland, the Czech Republic, and Hungary were the first three Eastern European countries to be admitted to the club. To other countries in Central and Eastern Europe, membership in NATO was dangled as a reward for good behavior, as a stepping-stone into the prosperous EU, and as a protective mantle against Russia's reemergence as a major power; NATO soon expanded to include *all* the countries of Eastern Europe. The alliance survived as a new kind of organization, but Russia continued to view NATO as a potential military threat.

A New Emphasis on "Geoeconomics"

Throughout history, political leaders have routinely utilized economic instruments to shape international relations in their favor. This practice of "economic statecraft"—involving the terms of trade, global financial flows, and the promotion of domestic firms—joined military defense as a central element of U.S. foreign policy after the Cold War.

All countries today are greatly influenced by economic decisions made outside their borders. Those states that are heavily dependent on export markets or on foreign investment are more vulnerable than others, but all are affected by international economic factors that, to an increasing degree, are beyond their control. Economic globalization—or the coming together of a single world market in addition to national and regional markets—is only the latest expression of international interdependence. The benefits of globalization could be immense for rich and poor countries alike. The integration of the world economy provides individuals with greater choice about where to shop, where to work, and where to invest. It has the potential to allow for specialization, improve efficiency, and spur economic development. But small farmers and others may be losers in this process.

The United States, which possesses the largest economy in the world, is increasingly sensitive to these machinations of international economic and financial pressures. According to the Central Intelligence Agency's *World Factbook*, the United States exported $663 billion in goods and services in 1998 while importing $912 billion in foreign products. The lessons from these statistics are clear. First, the United States is a major player on global trade markets and has a voracious appetite for foreign goods. Second, millions of U.S. jobs can be created or lost by foreign sales or competition.

Americans do not have the resources or inclination to produce everything they require, including many vital resources. In particular, the United States' dependence on oil has at times threatened to paralyze its economy. Twice during the 1970s the price of oil increased dramatically—in 1973–1974 after the Yom Kippur War and the creation of the Organization of Petroleum Exporting Countries (OPEC), and again in 1979 after the Iranian revolution. The impact of these two oil shocks on the United States, the world's largest consumer of energy, was dramatic. As a result, the vast amount of U.S. dollars spent abroad greatly enlarged the national debt and created a serious inflationary crisis. Long lines for gas were not uncommon and U.S. citizens everywhere felt the impact of these events occurring on the other side of the globe. President Carter alleged that the oil cartels were conducting "the moral equivalent of war" against U.S. consumers. As the twenty-first century began, fuel prices soared again, and power outages in California reminded Americans once more of their vulnerability to foreign energy sources.

Not only does this vulnerability affect Americans at home, it also affects U.S. foreign policy. For example, policy makers must balance their concern for human rights abuses in the oil-rich states of Saudi Arabia and Kuwait with the knowledge that these states control U.S. access to this vital resource in the Persian Gulf. The decision of the Bush administration to commit U.S. forces to defend Kuwait against Iraq during the Persian Gulf War was at least partially motivated by the need to secure continued access to Kuwaiti oil. The October 2000 terrorist attack against the USS *Cole*, which was refueling in a Yemenese port, later tested the country's resolve to keep the Persian Gulf open for business.

In terms of routine economic activity, the surge of Web-based business and "e-commerce" makes international purchasing more accessible to the average consumer, bringing exporting and importing to a new level and greatly increasing global economic connectedness. Consequently, U.S. prosperity is becoming even more reliant on international business. In addition, the United States has assumed a leading role in global financial markets. Through foreign direct investments (FDIs), which involve long-term development of companies overseas, and portfolio investments, which include U.S.-based investments in foreign stock, bond, and currency markets, the United States floods the world with capital on a daily basis. These largely private capital flows are accompanied by public funds originating from the World Bank and International Monetary Fund (IMF), to which the United States is the primary contributor.

Economic interdependence, in all its forms, has clear consequences for U.S. foreign policy. It has the potential to offer incredible rewards as well as possible problems. Many skeptics firmly believe that globalization represents a threat to global equality, the environment, and the cultural heritage of parts of the world that may be "swallowed up" by Western corporations and commercial media. The skeptics made this point clear repeatedly in 1999 and 2000 by disrupting the annual meetings of the World Bank, IMF, and World Trade Organization (WTO). If poorly managed, they argued, international economic interdependence has the potential to be damaging not only to the United States but also (and even more so) to less-secure economies in the developing regions.

Responding to globalization, the Clinton administration elevated foreign economic policy to a central position in its relations with other states. Clinton's agenda as president was primarily focused on spurring economic growth at home, and greater competitiveness in world markets emerged as a primary element of this "geoeconomic" strategy. Thus, Clinton was a strong supporter of the North American Free Trade Agreement (NAFTA), which more closely connected the U.S., Canadian, and Mexican trade and financial markets. The United States also helped create the grouping known as Asia-Pacific Economic Cooperation (APEC) to promote commerce among the North American and East Asian economies. Clinton also favored closer trade ties between the United States and China. His "engagement" policy was based on the assumption that Beijing's respect for human rights would improve as China developed economically and became more dependent on global trade to sustain its high rate of growth. Although the Chinese government continued to repress political opponents, workers, and religious movements, Clinton endorsed China's entry into the WTO. In September 2000, the U.S. Congress approved "permanent normal trading relations" with China. In the age of globalization, this marked a major foreign policy accomplishment for the Clinton administration as well as a great leap forward for the Chinese government.

A BROADER FOREIGN POLICY AGENDA

In addition to the key concerns of military intervention and global economic relations, the U.S. government broadened its post–Cold War foreign policy agenda to accommodate a variety of newer issues and problems. Narcotics trafficking, immigration pressures, terrorism, environmental decay, and energy "security" all preoccupied the first post–Cold War administration. These issues, described briefly in the following sections, further complicated the formulation and conduct of U.S. foreign policy.

International Terrorism

A critical problem facing the United States today is international terrorism. For many years, attacks by terrorist groups have posed a direct threat to U.S.

interests, both at home and overseas. By far the most devastating attack occurred on September 11, 2001, when hijacked U.S. airliners were turned into guided missiles that struck the World Trade Center and the Pentagon. The attacks killed thousands of civilians and traumatized the nation. These and other terrorist strikes have starkly demonstrated the extent of anti-American feelings overseas, primarily among militant Islamic populations.

Fighting terrorism has proven to be a difficult task. By their nature, terrorists are highly secretive and operate outside the traditional boundaries of international diplomacy. Their identities and whereabouts are often unknown, as is their direct involvement in specific terrorist incidents. The U.S. government identified one likely sponsor of international terrorism—the Saudi dissident Osama bin Laden. He was believed to be responsible for several terrorist attacks, including the cataclysmic 2001 strikes in New York and Washington, D.C., and the bombings of U.S. embassies in Kenya and Tanzania in 1998 that killed 224 people, twelve of them Americans. Bin Laden had long thwarted Western efforts to bring him to justice, hiding his militant followers in the remote, mountainous areas of Afghanistan and Pakistan.

The terrorist attack against the USS *Cole* in October 2000, leaving more than a dozen U.S. sailors dead, posed a similar challenge. The assault on the destroyer, which was bombed in a Yemenese port during a routine refueling stop, occurred on the same day that tensions between Israelis and Palestinians spilled over into widespread violence by both sides. The U.S. government thus confronted simultaneous military crises in both key subregions of the Middle East: the Arab–Israeli theater close to the Mediterranean Sea and the Persian Gulf area. But the September 2001 attacks on New York and Washington were the most devastating to the United States, leaving thousands of casualties, forcing the suspension of routine activities across the country for many days, and producing widespread fear and uncertainty. In response, the United States drove the Taliban out of Afghanistan, invaded Iraq to drive out Saddam Hussein, and launched the war on terrorism.

Cyberterrorism has also emerged as an additional problem for U.S. foreign policy makers. Questions of security now involve the protection of government and private computer systems. The U.S. government recently formed a new department modeled after the Centers for Disease Control. The National Infrastructure Protection Center (NIPC), located at the FBI headquarters, is an "information and warfare detection and response center" whose mission is to identify and respond to serious cyber-warfare threats, such as penetration of the banking sector or other critical industries. The Department of Homeland Security was similarly created to try to protect against terrorist threats.

It is not hard to imagine how a form of computer-based economic terrorism would be used as a weapon in a future war. According to General Kenneth Minihan, director of the National Security Agency in the late 1990s, there was evidence that recent Chinese government military exercises included the use of computer warfare. Computer hackers clearly demonstrated that this type of terrorism is possible. Internationally based hackers were able to halt business in a number of Internet-based companies in early 2000, demonstrating their ability to disrupt this new form of business and potentially inflict billions of dollars in losses. Keeping government and business sites secure will continue to be a priority as more of the world gets online.

America's "War on Drugs"

The international narcotics trade presented U.S. foreign policy makers with a new and difficult challenge. It has been estimated that the economic toll from drug abuse and related accidents reached $60 billion a year by the first part of the twenty-first century, not to mention the loss of life and personal tragedy that affected addicts and those who cared for them. As well as addressing the demand side of the problem, U.S. officials focused on the supply of drugs, treating this problem as an international relations issue.

Illegal narcotics mainly enter into the United States through Latin America. Bolivia, Peru, Ecuador, Colombia, Mexico, and the islands of the Caribbean are the major producers or transshipment points of illegal drugs that find their way into the United States through illegal smuggling. As a result, U.S. diplomatic relations with many of these countries have been dominated by this problem since the last stages of the Cold War. The official labeling of this effort as a "war on drugs" revealed the importance and international emphasis given to this issue in U.S. foreign policy. Accordingly, in December 1989, President George H. W. Bush sent U.S. forces into the Central American country of Panama to capture its leader, General Manuel Noriega, in part because of his ties to Colombian drug cartels. President Clinton appointed General Barry McCaffrey to lead his administration's drug policy and threatened to cut off aid to enlist cooperation from Latin American countries. Further, under NAFTA, the Mexican government agreed to strengthen its own domestic narcotics enforcement and expand efforts to prevent drug smuggling across the vast U.S. border.

The primary target of the "war on drugs," however, was the South American country of Colombia, which served as a primary source of cocaine production and worldwide distribution. As U.S. foreign aid programs to most other developing countries fell sharply in the late 1990s, the U.S. government steadily increased its assistance to Colombia. Its leaders were engaged in a virtual civil war against regional drug cartels, which were able to draw on their vast wealth in fending off the cash-starved Colombian government then led by President Andres Pastrana. The Clinton administration hoped to make more than $1.3 billion available to Pastrana between 2000 and 2002 to provide for military training; sixty U.S.-made helicopters; and funds for justice, agricultural, and human rights initiatives. Even with these funds, however, Colombian leaders would have a difficult time stopping the cultivation and export of coca, whose potential value in world markets exceeded that of Colombia's most lucrative legal cash crop: coffee. Thus, the civil war dragged on and limited the impact of U.S. financial aid.

Immigration Pressures

Another problem facing the United States today is immigration, both legal and illegal. Immigration levels in recent years reached a record pace of 1.1 million annually in the early 2000s, which exceeded the previous peak of about 700,000 annually between 1900 and 1920. The most recent surge went against the findings of the U.S. Commission on Immigration Reform, which in 1995 called for a one-third reduction in legal immigration and stronger efforts by U.S. firms to curb illegal immigration.

The mass movement of populations is certainly not a new issue in the United States, whose origin and rise as a world power were primarily driven by foreign immigration. However, with rising population pressures worldwide and within the United States, this issue has taken on greater significance in the past few decades. During the twentieth century, the source of immigrants gradually shifted from Europe to developing countries—mainly those in Latin America and the Caribbean, but also in East Asia.

The economic disparity between the United States and these regions intensified the immigration pressure on the United States to the point that many Americans felt threatened by the increased numbers of immigrants. The argument was that immigrants would take away the jobs of Americans. Since a significant number of these immigrants did not enter the United States legally, this perception of threat was increased. Further, high levels of immigration strained the political and economic resources—for schools, social agencies, courts, and law enforcement—available in many U.S. cities, particularly those close to the Mexican border in Texas and California. Thus, the problems faced primarily by local and state governments made illegal immigration a strong national concern. The terrorist threat added to these fears. According to a poll conducted recently by the Chicago Council on Foreign Relations, 72 percent of the respondents stated that "controlling and reducing illegal immigration" should be a "very important" goal of the United States.

During the Cold War, U.S. interventions in Central America and the Caribbean were justified in part on immigration grounds. President Reagan's first secretary of state, Alexander Haig, argued in 1982 that U.S. interventions to prevent the rise of totalitarian or communist states were necessary to avert mass migrations of individuals who would attempt to flee if such regimes were allowed to rule. As the threat of Marxist revolutions receded in the late 1980s, and as elected governments gained power across Latin America, U.S. leaders hoped improved conditions in the region would slow the tide of illegal immigration. Regional economic integration through NAFTA was also designed to improve living standards in Mexico sufficiently to encourage its workers to remain in their home country.

Many problems have remained, however. Among other examples, the mass exodus of Cubans into Florida in 1994 created serious problems for state and federal officials. These wide-scale movements of Cubans across the Florida straits were directly responsible for changes in U.S. policy toward Cuba. After the 1994 immigration wave, the Cuban government agreed to step up its restrictions against illegal emigration to the United States, and U.S. officials agreed to accept twenty thousand legal Cuban migrants each year. The Clinton administration also tightened other aspects of its Cuba policy.

The United States was also forced to take military action to stop another wave of illegal immigration from Haiti, the poorest country in Latin America, which fell into political and economic chaos in the early 1990s. President George H. W. Bush ordered the U.S. Coast Guard to forcefully return the hundreds of Haitian "boat people" who had constructed makeshift rafts to bring them to the United States. As a presidential candidate, Bill Clinton opposed Bush's policy, but he reversed his position after taking power in January 1993. The United States then used military force to restore the democratically elected government of Reverend Jean Bertrand Aristide. But in the years that followed, Haiti again succumbed to internal unrest and economic despair. Given the lack of another exodus of refugees, however, the U.S. government did not feel compelled to intervene again. Once again, the linkage between immigration pressures and U.S. foreign policy was clearly demonstrated.

Global Environmental Decay

Environmental problems have major implications for international relations and foreign policy. They do not respect man-made political borders, making them a shared problem requiring coordinated solutions. While some environmental disasters can be contained, most work their way through waterways and into the atmosphere to create health hazards in other regions. For example, in February 2000, poisonous chemicals from a Romanian mine reservoir leaked into the Vaser River and eventually into the Tisza and Danube Rivers, affecting Hungary and Ukraine. This crisis followed only weeks after a cyanide spill contaminated the same international waterway. These spills prompted urgent discussions among the governments involved, whose ecosystems had previously been degraded under more than four decades of communist control.

The United States has increasingly been engaged with its neighbors on environmental problems that cross national borders. In particular, environmental issues have often taken center stage in U.S.–Canadian relations since the 1970s. Air pollution originating in the United States causes acid rain that produces extensive damage to the Canadian environment. As a result, Canadian leaders and activists have insisted that a solution to the acid rain problem be incorporated in bilateral treaties and regional pacts such as NAFTA.

Since many environmental issues are global in scope, U.S. officials are also party to much larger multilateral discussions. Global conferences such as the 1992 Earth Summit have drawn much-needed attention to pollution problems and have been attended by thousands of national leaders, representatives of international governmental organizations, nongovernmental organizations (NGOs), and academic specialists. These meetings and the agreements they produce have not only influenced U.S. domestic environmental regulations, but have also shaped U.S. foreign policy in other areas. For example, protecting the environment became one of the key post–Cold War missions of the U.S. Agency for International development (USAID). The agency adopted many of the calls for "sustainable development" outlined in *Agenda 21*, the Earth Summit's concluding document, and pledged more than $600 million annually toward global environmental protection efforts in the late 1990s. The strategy of sustainable development, also adopted by other industrialized states, was designed to encourage economic efforts in less-developed countries that would not impose permanent damage on their ecosystems.

As the world's foremost source of toxic emissions, and as the world's leading consumer of nonrenewable resources, the United States bears a major responsibility for regulating the global environment. But in Washington, political leaders have been deeply divided over exactly how much of this burden should be carried by the United States. Despite strong evidence that growing emissions of fossil fuels have led to global warming, the U.S. Senate refused to ratify the Kyoto Treaty of 1997 that was approved by the Clinton administration and signed by the leaders of thirty-seven other industrialized countries. Under the treaty, these leaders agreed to reduce emission levels to 5 percent below their 1990 levels by 2012. Many state governors and members of Congress representing industrial states have argued that the strict environmental controls would jeopardize key U.S. industries and slow the nation's economic growth.

Such views were quickly accepted by the incoming George W. Bush administration, which openly declared the Kyoto Treaty unfit for further consideration by the United States. Bush further enraged environmentalists by declaring that carbon dioxide was not a primary cause of global warming and should thus not be strictly regulated, a reversal of his position as a presidential candidate. By this time, however, the United States was faced with a revived energy crisis, due largely to higher natural gas prices and record levels of demand for gasoline that exceeded the nation's refining capacity. Bush's proposed energy policy—to accelerate oil drilling and the opening of new coal- and nuclear-powered plants rather than encouraging energy *conservation*— clearly placed long-term environmental concerns behind immediate economic needs. Bush's critics also charged that the energy policy, drafted by Vice President Cheney, was designed to favor the oil industry in which both the president and vice president had worked before assuming power.

Beyond these changes, it was clear that U.S. "energy security" had become a central concern that crossed domestic and foreign policy domains. Meeting the nation's heavy demand for energy would no doubt require a favorable world market for petroleum and natural gas. Further, the balance to be struck between energy conservation and consumption would have real consequences for the global environment. The question of energy therefore became another "intermestic" (both international and domestic) issue that further complicated the task of foreign policy adaptation in the United States.

SHIFTING SOURCES OF U.S. FOREIGN POLICY

In many ways, the international environment today is as menacing to U.S. security as were the communist threats of the Cold War. Replacing the Soviet threat, the war on terrorism is *the* number one preoccupation. However, there is not just one overriding challenge today, but instead a number of potentially dangerous threats and issues that require effective foreign policies. More so than before, these issues often include a major domestic component. Economic globalization, illegal drug trafficking, immigration pressures, and environmental concerns have drawn attention far beyond the U.S. government. They have engaged a wide variety of individuals and groups in other areas as well, including state and local governments, international government organizations, and NGOs based in the United States and overseas.

The setting of U.S. foreign policy has therefore shifted from one in which policy was made by a relatively small group of elites to one that is the product of an enormous variety of domestic political, bureaucratic, and societal forces. Indeed, the most distinguishing feature of current U.S. foreign policy is the extent and variety of public pressures, the degree to which policy has become democratized, and how deeply divided the United States is. In most other countries, the formulation and conduct of foreign policy remain relatively insulated from these domestic political machinations. The foreign policy of the United States is unique in the degree to which its conduct in world affairs is shaped by domestic political considerations rather than by calculations of the national interest.

In this section we review the shifting sources of U.S. foreign policy. We begin by considering the effects of the transformed post–Cold War balance of power, an important *systemic* source of foreign policy. We then turn our attention to the altered *domestic* environment, which includes the traditional core elites within the U.S. government as well as nonstate actors such as the news media and NGOs. The more pluralistic nature of U.S. foreign policy today is one of its defining characteristics, one that helps explain the erratic performance of the United States in world affairs since the end of the Cold War.

The Balance of Power in Flux

Even the most powerful country in the world is not immune to the actions of states and other entities beyond its borders. In this respect, prominent realists of the Cold War period argued that a state's actions in the international system could be traced almost exclusively to external forces. To Hans Morgenthau, the struggle for power among nation-states represented the core of international politics; every state's primary goal was to increase its power, both on an absolute basis and relative to other states. Similarly, Kenneth Waltz claimed that the anarchic nature of the international system had the greatest influence over a state's actions within that system. In other words, the balance of power among states determined the actions of each.

Many U.S. leaders—from Alexander Hamilton to Theodore Roosevelt, George Kennan, Henry Kissinger, and now President George W. Bush and his key advisers—have viewed international politics through such a realist lens. Even though the United States was fairly secure from European attack for most of its history, the actions of other states played a significant role in U.S. foreign policy during its first century. Widespread concerns about the collapse of the Spanish empire, for example, contributed to growing U.S. involvement in Latin America and the Caribbean in the early 1800s. Fears that the European powers would attempt to fill the resulting power vacuum led directly to the Monroe Doctrine. From the realist perspective, U.S. entry in both world wars was necessary given that Germany was close to gaining control over Europe, a development that would have destroyed the balance of power within and beyond the region.

Of central concern to realists has been the number of "poles," or power centers, in the interstate system. As the two superpowers in the bipolar Cold War, the United States and the Soviet Union were destined to become enemies in this view. Realists of the Cold War era asserted that the Marshall Plan, the Truman Doctrine, and the presence of thousands of U.S. troops in Western Europe long after World War II stemmed not from idealism but from Washington's concerns about the balance of power in Europe. The United States, they argued, was compelled by the logic of bipolarity to prop up its European allies and prevent the expansion of Soviet power. To Waltz, "a war or threat of war anywhere is a concern to both of the superpowers if it may lead to significant gains or losses for either of them. In a two-power competition a loss for one appears as a gain for the other."

Both sides, therefore, attempted to gain as many allies as possible in order to increase their share of the balance. The U.S. government invested enormous amounts of resources worldwide and sought to persuade minor powers to join the Western alliance against communism.[3] American leaders adopted the "domino theory," which presumed that if one ally fell or changed loyalties, other states would inevitably follow. The potential fall of South Vietnam, deemed an important and delicately placed "domino," was therefore unacceptable. The seemingly illogical and disproportionate U.S. effort to salvage South Vietnam arose from this fear.

Since the end of the Cold War, realist thinkers have debated the nature of the system that emerged from the ruins of the old bipolar structure. Many, like Charles Krauthammer, argued that the United States remained the sole superpower in a *unipolar* world and challenged U.S. leaders to assume greater global responsibility. To other analysts, U.S. preeminence was challenged by other power centers such as the EU, Japan, China, and, to a lesser extent, emerging powers such as India and Brazil. These scholars foresaw a *multipolar* world and predicted the rise of many regional disputes within this system.

While power in the traditional realpolitik sense is understood to be rooted in military strength, the nature of power in the world arena has changed. Military might is no longer the sole predictor of international influence. Of course, political, diplomatic, and economic leverage have long been important. But today these and other ways for international actors to wield influence—by demanding democracy and human rights abroad, for example—have become more relevant. Robert O. Keohane and Joseph S. Nye recognized this development when they popularized the term *complex interdependence* in the 1970s. Its effects have profoundly shaped the agenda of U.S. foreign policy since the Cold War as nonmilitary issues such as economic globalization, environmental concerns, illegal drugs, and immigration have demanded sustained attention from policy makers and a greater degree of coordination with other governments. In this respect, not only is the balance of power widely considered to be in flux today, so are the *sources* of power in the post–Cold War international system.

Political Culture and Public Opinion

Increasingly, the external pressures noted earlier cannot be separated from domestic political or societal factors that shape U.S. foreign policy. In fact, most foreign policy decisions are heavily influenced by domestic factors, and some are ultimately determined by them. For example, while immigration pressures originate in foreign countries, how the U.S. government decides to deal with these pressures relates directly to public opinion, the condition of the U.S. economy, the existing concentration of immigrants in politically sensitive areas, and many other domestic issues. President George H. W. Bush's policy toward Cuba was not just affected by the arrival of Cuban refugees, but also by public opinion and electoral politics in southern Florida. Most, if not all, foreign policies are heavily influenced by these kinds of domestic considerations.

In this regard, U.S. political culture—the political values, norms, beliefs, and ideals held by Americans—has an important influence on foreign policy. Political culture is an elusive concept, but most scholars agree that U.S. political culture reflects the liberal tradition that emphasizes popular sovereignty, political equality, and freedom of expression. American "exceptionalism" is closely related to this tradition. Many U.S. citizens believe the nation's values and institutions should be adopted by other countries. Tellingly, both the Clinton and Bush administrations identified the promotion of democracy as a central foreign policy goal in the 1990s to today.

The ideas and values of political culture are often expressed through public opinion, which becomes translated into policy through interest groups, the news media, Congress, and political parties. Though generally more concerned about domestic issues, U.S. public opinion has a significant influence over foreign policy decisions. Democratic theory is based on the premise that a polity has a well-informed citizenry that cares about public affairs and is able to influence its leaders to make the correct policy decisions. However, in reality, most Americans care little about U.S. foreign policy and are woefully ill-informed. Two-thirds to three-quarters of U.S. citizens remain uninterested in developments beyond their borders. According to a 2002 Chicago Council on Foreign Relations poll, only 33 percent of the respondents were "very interested" in news about other countries; most were interested only in those issues that affected their economic situations. Subsequent surveys have offered similar evidence of scant public knowledge of, and interest in, important foreign policy issues.

Although most U.S. citizens do not have an extensive knowledge of, or even a strong personal opinion about most foreign policy decisions made by their government, public opinion does have an impact. Voting-behavior studies demonstrate that citizens do punish and reward candidates on the basis of their foreign policies. President George H. W. Bush was heavily criticized in the early 1990s for focusing too much on foreign policy at the expense of domestic concerns. This perception contributed to the election of Bill Clinton, whose campaign emphasized domestic (largely economic) issues. Thus, politicians who want to be reelected must respond to public opinion. But what if public opinion, as at present, is also deeply divided? Then, American foreign policy is also deeply conflicted.

Interest Groups and the News Media

Interest groups have been an important part of the U.S. political system throughout its history. The role and impact of such groups in shaping U.S. foreign policy, while rather limited until recently, will likely become stronger as the policy agenda widens. Yet increasingly, the role of interest groups in the policymaking process has come under attack. The sheer number of interest groups is considered problematic. Today there are over twenty-three thousand interest groups attempting to sway the U.S. government on nearly every foreign policy issue. The existence of so many groups, which frequently clash with each other over policy goals and choices, has often led to paralysis as decision makers fear offending groups that, collectively, represent a sizable segment of the voting public.

A vivid example of this problem was the outbreak of violence that occurred late in 1999 during the WTO's annual meetings in Seattle. Business groups advocating free trade were challenged by labor, environmental, and human rights groups that opposed the WTO's growing role. The showdown revealed deep divisions within Congress over U.S. foreign economic policy. In supporting the WTO, a coalition of congressional Republicans and conservative Democrats backed the Clinton administration, but they faced considerable opposition from a majority of Democrats with strong ties to organized labor. The threat that labor would retaliate in elections had many members scrambling for some midway position that neither fully supported nor opposed the trade body.

Powerful interest groups are also blamed for promoting narrow-minded policies that place their own self-interests above the national interest. For example, there are many questions about Vice President Richard Cheney's former firm, Haliburton, and its role in Iraq and other crisis spots. The largest and most powerful groups are charged with wielding virtual control over policy and drowning out dissenting opinion. In particular, business interests have become more active than ever in shaping foreign economic policy by contributing to election campaigns, lobbying Congress for favorable legislation, and acting as advisers to government agencies. Given that a growing share of the U.S. economy derives from international commerce, policy makers are inclined to do more than just listen to these business groups. To critics, the Department of Commerce has become a de facto advocate of U.S. business interests, which have used their massive resources to overwhelm less-affluent groups concerned with environmental degradation, human rights violations, and labor issues. Clinton's support for Chinese entry into the WTO, and Congress's subsequent agreement to normalize Sino–American trade relations, followed an intense lobbying effort that was dominated by business interests.

Agricultural interest groups have similar foreign policy goals. Since agricultural products account for approximately 15 percent of U.S. exports, these groups have wielded enormous influence in recent years. Indeed, the Department of Agriculture has become to farmers what the Department of Commerce is to business: an agency that often lobbies for large agribusiness concerns and not necessarily for public interests. Among other issues, agricultural lobbies have taken on the controversial embargo against Cuba, hoping to lessen the restrictions on the sale of food to Cuba. Agribusiness advocates estimated that U.S. sales of food to the island could total $1 billion. Their pressure on the Clinton administration was widely credited with the easing of export restrictions to Cuba in the summer of 2000.

Despite its waning numbers, organized labor remains a powerful interest group representing U.S. workers from every state. Today, organized labor is primarily concerned with the impact of foreign competition on jobs in the United States. When Clinton asked Congress to establish permanent normal trade ties with China in 2000, the labor unions intensified their lobbying, pressured the presidential candidates, and joined with environmental and student groups to protest further globalization. Vice President Al Gore, the Democratic nominee for president in 2000, and in 2004, John Kerry, relied heavily on support from labor and felt the pressure. Gore, traditionally supportive of free trade, declared that he would, if elected, renegotiate parts of the deal to address labor's concerns. Thus, even though the heyday of labor's power appears to be over, this interest group continues to wield significant power over U.S. trade policy.

Aside from the economic interests described earlier, there has been an enormous growth in the number of single-issue lobby groups, many of which exist mainly to shape U.S. foreign policy. Among the most well known of these groups are ethnic interest organizations, such as the American Israel Public Action Committee and the Cuban American National Foundation, which have contributed heavily to election campaigns and maintained aggressive lobbying efforts on Capitol Hill. Also, human rights groups such as Amnesty International, environmental groups such as the Sierra Club and Greenpeace, and religious organizations such as the National Council of Churches have all become visible in foreign policy. Increasingly, NGOs from all over the world have coordinated their efforts through public-information campaigns on the Internet and direct lobbying of political leaders. Although their direct impact on policy outcomes is difficult to measure, these NGOs have played a key role in shaping the foreign policy agenda and informing government officials and mass publics.

Finally, the U.S. news media also play an important role in foreign policy. The Cable News Network (CNN) has become a truly global medium, and major newspapers and wire services provide a crucial link in informing U.S. citizens about developments overseas. This link has tangible consequences for foreign policy, including the deployment of multinational peacekeeping forces to end regional conflicts and civil wars. Increasingly, however, news programs have bowed to ratings concerns, emphasizing the most shocking events rather than long-term problems. Furthermore, the major networks report less world news than during the Cold War and have closed many foreign news bureaus, which has made accurate and thorough reporting from overseas more difficult. As a result, foreign policy issues that U.S. citizens need to understand are often ill-reported, underreported, or not reported at all. Americans are thus becoming even less informed about international affairs issues, which impairs their ability to make thoughtful assessments of foreign policy. This is a paradoxical trend given that public opinion has more influence on U.S. foreign policy than ever before.

Struggles within the U.S. Government

The framers of the U.S. Constitution built a system of overlapping checks and balances. In so doing, they issued an "invitation to struggle" to Congress and the White House over U.S. foreign policy. For example, the Constitution designates the president as the commander in chief of the armed forces, but only Congress can declare war. Similarly, the president negotiates treaties, but they must be approved by Congress before they become law. Since Congress has the sole power over the appropriation of money, the president needs congressional support for his foreign policy initiatives or they will not become reality. This leads to much confusion within the government and also complicates relationships with foreign governments that do not always understand that the U.S. president cannot guarantee that his own government will honor a treaty he has just signed.

The balance of power between the president and Congress over foreign policy has waxed and waned over time. During the Cold War and during all wars in U.S. history, presidential control over foreign policy has been understood as necessary to prevent the appearance of disunity within the government and to facilitate quick decisions. Yet Congress has often imposed a very significant, perhaps even coequal, influence over foreign policy. After years of congressional acquiescence early in the Cold War, congressional involvement in foreign policy increased during and after the Vietnam War. The War Powers Act passed by Congress in 1973 required the president to obtain congressional consent for any long-term commitment of U.S. forces abroad. Over the next twenty years, as the Cold War slowly drew to an end, Congress continued to assert more power over the conduct of U.S. foreign relations.

Greater congressional power over foreign policy decisions also increases the impact of political parties on these issues. Congress is the most partisan branch of the U.S. government, in which votes are often cast along party lines. Traditionally, before World War II, the Republican Party leaned toward isolationism and the Democratic Party became more internationalist. But in the 1950s, the Republican Party became more assertive globally. These distinctions broke down in the last stages of the Cold War, and since its demise both parties appear to be mainly internationalist, but with isolationist factions. Despite these similarities, the parties still manage to disagree over foreign policy decisions. When Congress is controlled by one of the parties and the White House by the other, the chances for a stalemate are high. This situation, the product of divided government, is very common and increases the impact of partisanship on foreign policy.

President Clinton took office with a Democratic Congress in 1992, but in November 1994 the Republicans gained control of both houses of Congress. Not only were the two branches in different political hands but each tried to embarrass the other or gain political advantage from their positions. Thus the Senate held up Clinton's nominees to foreign policy positions, refused to grant Clinton "fast-track" authority in trade negotiations, and rejected the Comprehensive Test Ban Treaty that was previously signed by the president. In turn, Clinton sought to gain political advantage by criticizing Congress for its cutbacks in foreign affairs, foreign aid, and United Nations budgets. Domestic politics regularly took priority over a rational calculation of the national interest.

For a brief time after George W. Bush's arrival in the White House, both the executive and legislative branches were controlled by the Republican Party. This situation changed, however, when Senator James M. Jeffords of Vermont abruptly left the Republican Party in the spring of 2001 and declared himself an independent. His move, largely in frustration over the Bush administration's early foreign and domestic policies, shifted control of the Senate to the Democrats by a slim margin of fifty to forty-nine members (Jeffords would be the lone member of the Senate with no formal party affiliation). As a result, Democrats took over the leadership of the Foreign Relations Committee, the Armed Services Committee, and other Senate committees that were actively engaged in U.S. foreign policy. More broadly, Democrats were able to shape the Senate's foreign policy agenda, which contrasted starkly with that of the Bush administration on such issues as missile defense and environmental cooperation. Since Congress plays such an important role in the foreign policy process, the defection of Jeffords virtually guaranteed that Bush would not be able to achieve his stated goals in foreign affairs. Only the September terrorist attacks on New York and Washington, D.C., forced the two branches of government to cooperate, demonstrating the crucial role of international crises in shaping the domestic politics of U.S. foreign policy. From 2004 to 2006, the Republicans were back in control of both houses of Congress and the White House.

Also of note is the impact of bureaucratic politics. This dimension of U.S. foreign policy was first brought to the fore by Graham Allison's study of the Cuban missile crisis, which demonstrated how the recommendations of different advisers in the Kennedy administration reflected their bureaucratic roles within the government. Most foreign policy issues are of intense interest to many government agencies. The State Department, the Defense Department, the CIA, and the National Security Council each hold distinctive views toward U.S. foreign relations, as do the increasingly important economic agencies. Their views often reflect bureaucratic self-interests as much as, if not more than, objective assessments of the national interest.

The State Department, traditionally the main agent for carrying out U.S. foreign policy, has been losing power relative to the other agencies. Since the Cold War, as foreign economic policy achieved the status of "high politics," a growing number of federal agencies became key players in the formulation and conduct of U.S. foreign policy. Those formerly concerned primarily with domestic matters—such as the Treasury, Justice, and Commerce Departments—assumed a vital foreign policy role in the Clinton administration. Reflecting this change, the president created a National Economic Council to counterbalance the dominant National Security Council.

The effort to restrict the flow of drugs into the United States is a clear example of the complications involved when many agencies have an interest in a particular policy. No fewer than forty-three federal agencies are involved in this effort. The main responsibility in this area has been granted to the Drug Enforcement Agency (DEA), a division of the Justice Department. The DEA was primarily concerned with prosecuting drug traffickers, but this goal often conflicted with the mandates of the other agencies involved. Since the State Department first and foremost sought productive relationships with other countries, its officials opposed many tactics used by the DEA that threatened these relationships. Both the State Department and the DEA, by carrying out their legitimate roles, thus created interagency tensions that result in a sometimes confusing and incoherent policy.

Another problem is the lack of continuity in U.S. foreign policy. Each administration, for political reasons, seeks to discredit the policy of its predecessor and to strike out in a new direction. During the 2000 election campaign, for example, George W. Bush sought to emphasize the experience and realism that could be expected from his foreign policy in contrast to the perceived naiveté and idealism of the Clinton years. Still, Bush was unable to articulate a clear rationale of U.S. interests, objectives, and priorities any more than his immediate predecessors. Nor did he describe how his Cabinet officials would overcome the entrenched bureaucratic rivalries that had proven so disabling in the past. The deep divisions that existed within Congress as Bush took office in January 2001, combined with the persistent malaise and ambivalence among the general public toward foreign policy, prevented the "second" Bush administration from forging a widely accepted foreign policy until the terrorist attacks in September thrust the nation into a new sense of common purpose.

CONCLUSION

As we have seen, U.S. foreign policy has changed in profound ways throughout its history. The emergence of the United States as a world power early in the twentieth century, its successful interventions in both world wars, and the pressing demands of the Cold War forced the United States to abandon its isolationist tradition and to assert itself globally on a sustained basis. The end of the Cold War precipitated another shift, the direction and outcome of which remain unclear. While each of these periods was initiated by external events, they were also affected by parallel changes in the domestic environment. The greater impact of domestic influences is both a cause and a result of this shift in the foreign policy decision-making process. Increasingly, U.S. foreign policy reflects the incredible pluralism inherent in U.S. society. Today's foreign policy exemplifies the constantly evolving amalgamation of political alliances, interest groups, and government institutions that make up U.S. society. The power of each entity or interest shifts constantly, depending on the issue under review. All of this greatly complicates the task of adapting the nation's foreign policies to the new systemic context.

Moreover, in the absence of the Soviet threat, U.S. leaders have been able to play politics with foreign policy to a greater degree than was possible when the United States was immersed in the Cold War. In this environment, policy paralysis or confusion characterized much of post–Cold War U.S. foreign policy. Remarkably, it is a testament to the strength and resilience of the U.S. political system that, despite these problems, the United States has managed in many areas to carry out an effective and often successful foreign policy.

The need for a clear and coherent U.S. foreign policy was made painfully clear in the aftermath of the September 2001 terrorist attacks on the World Trade Center and the Pentagon. Although the source and intention of the attacks were not immediately known, the resulting sense of national anxiety and vulnerability was inescapable. Of immediate concern to the Bush administration, which viewed the assault as a declaration of war, was the need to create a worldwide coalition of states and international organizations. Such a coalition, Secretary of State Colin Powell observed, would be essential to counter the escalating challenge not only to the United States but also to "civilization." But whether the war on terrorism will serve as a unifying force or further divide the nation has yet to be determined.

No development since the Cold War so clearly revealed the intimate link between international security and U.S. foreign policy. Furthermore, the terrorist attacks highlighted the interdependent nature of the policymaking environment. Each U.S. bilateral relationship was tested, in some cases strained, by the crisis, and the need for multilateral cooperation through the UN and military pacts was on full display. Finally, the assaults battered the U.S. economy and disrupted economic activity around the world, reinforcing the sense of collective vulnerability.

In these trying circumstances, a new consensus on the direction or goals of U.S. foreign policy might yet be reached that would serve to unify the often contradictory forces of isolationism and internationalism, realism and idealism, and unilateralism and multilateralism. It is hoped that, in the years to come, U.S. leaders will ultimately adapt in creative ways to this new and fluid environment and learn how to incorporate the diversity of goals and opinions that emerge in the decision-making process. An effective and democratic foreign policy is not necessarily a contradiction in terms and should certainly be within reach of the world's "lone superpower."

NOTES

The author of this book acknowledges coauthorship of this chapter with Lana L. Wylie.

1. The containment policy was designed by George Kennan, a Russo-Soviet specialist in the U.S. State Department who became head of its policy-planning staff after nearly two weeks of intense negotiation.

2. As Secretary of State James Baker put it, "We don't have a dog in this fight."

3. Many states were able to play the Soviets and U.S. governments off against each other, obtaining arms and materials from both sides. For example, at the outset of the Somalia–Ethiopian conflict in 1976, the Soviets supported Somalia. But within a year, Moscow was aiding the Ethiopian side, which had previously received U.S. military aid. Somalia then turned to the Americans for support. Both sides thus used a combination of U.S. and Soviet war materials in fueling their deadly conflict.

Chapter Three

The Main Institutions
of Foreign Policymaking

In this chapter we look at the main institutions (Congress, president, State and Defense Departments, Central Intelligence Agency [CIA], National Security Council [NSC]) that are actually responsible for the *making* of U.S. foreign policy. We are moving from those groups, values, and interests that *influence* policy to those institutions with decision-making roles. Having previously examined the background, context, and interest-group pressures on policy, we now focus on the heart of the foreign policymaking system.

In treating Congress, we are dealing with only 535 persons (435 in the House of Representatives, 100 in the Senate). That number is considerably augmented if we include the several thousand staff persons who work on Capitol Hill, many of them well informed on foreign policy issues and a handful of them more influential than the congresspersons for whom they work. The tremendous growth of congressional staffs and the important implications of this increase are subjects to which we return later in the chapter. Nevertheless, it remains the case that at this stage we are dealing with a sharply reduced number of foreign policy influences and that Congress is one of the places in the U.S. system where foreign policy decisions are hammered out and made. By the time we get to the Cabinet, the NSC, and the White House staff, we are talking about even smaller numbers.

CONGRESS

From the Vietnam War to the present, Congress has moved aggressively, but also by fits and starts, to play a larger role in foreign policy. The causes of this new congressional assertiveness are complex, but there can be no doubt that Congress is playing a greater foreign policy role. First, during the Vietnam War, Congress began to grow increasingly uneasy over the conduct of U.S. foreign policy; then, during the 1970s, Congress moved on a variety of fronts to curb and check presidential authority in foreign policy. In the 1980s, Congress began to move to a position of virtually coequal status with the president on foreign policy, and in some instances, Congress seemed to be moving toward taking over various aspects of foreign policy for itself. The Iraq war emboldened Congress again to assert the role of critic of U.S. foreign policy. Because Congress enjoys playing a large foreign policy role and because its position as a major foreign policy actor has now been institutionalized in law and practice, it seems unlikely that we will go back to the older tradition of congressional quiescence and subservience in foreign policy anytime soon.

The assumption by Congress of a larger foreign policy role is part of the larger process of the democratization of foreign policy that has been occurring since the 1960s. While this process has made American foreign policy more participatory and responsive to the popular will, serious questions remain as to whether foreign policy can be effectively carried out on that more participatory basis and whether it is appropriate for Congress to play such a strong foreign policy role, to the extent of seeking to micromanage many areas of policy. Here are some of the key questions that arise out of the new congressional assertiveness in foreign policy and run through the discussion in this chapter:

1. Can we have a foreign policy run by a "committee"—Congress—of 535 persons without the central direction and coherence that only the executive branch can provide?
2. Will not a foreign policy run by Congress lead to a situation in which we have almost literally 535 secretaries of state, with all the fragmentation and political competition that implies?
3. Congress is a highly partisan body, even the embodiment of partisanship in the American political system. Won't such a body inevitably politicize foreign policy in inappropriate ways?
4. Congress is especially short-range and fickle in its attention span. It mainly follows the headlines on foreign policy issues, and part of its membership turns over every two years. Given these conditions, how can we have any continuity or long-range planning in foreign policy?
5. Congress has no intelligence arm, no diplomats, no foreign ministry, no embassies abroad, and no military department. Where is the institutional machinery to enable Congress to run its own foreign policy?

6. What then should be the role of Congress in foreign policymaking and
   what should be the proper balance between the executive and legislative
   branches?

These are the questions that frame our discussion of the role of Congress in
foreign policy.

Congress often vies with the president over the control of American foreign
policy. The Constitution gives considerable power in foreign affairs to both
the legislative and executive branches and is ambiguous and unclear on several issues where their powers overlap. Usually, the president leads on foreign
policy and Congress criticizes, but there are also times when Congress has
sought to lead. When the country is at war, Congress usually defers to the
president on foreign policy; in peacetime Congress is often more assertive.
But when the war itself is controversial—Vietnam or Iraq—Congress may
seek to limit the president's war-making authority.

During the long Cold War, as during all wars in American history, it was
the executive branch that dominated. Think back to George Washington, Andrew Jackson, Abraham Lincoln, Woodrow Wilson, and Franklin Roosevelt—
all wartime leaders and all thought of as among our greatest presidents. The
argument is that in wartime, when the nation is threatened, only the president
has the capacity to lead, to make the necessary quick decisions, to guide the
country, to serve as a symbol of unity and resolve. During wartime, therefore,
Congress usually yields to presidential authority. The Cold War was no exception to this rule; the only difference was it lasted longer than any of America's previous wars, and we got used to foreign policy leadership from the
president. Particularly during the nuclear age, it was felt that only the president had the resources, the intelligence information, the decision-making authority, and the informed and steady hand on the trigger to make the crucial
decisions that the Cold War called for. But it should be remembered that such
wartime (hot or cold) conditions calling forth presidential leadership were not
always the case in American history.

During many periods, Congress has played a large, close to coequal, role
in foreign policy. The debates in Congress over foreign policy have often
been spirited and rambunctious, with Congress frequently attacking the president, throwing roadblocks in his way, or even taking the lead. In the past,
such congressional involvement in foreign policy matters was often tolerated
or even encouraged because the stakes were usually low: America had no serious enemies on its borders, and the country was protected east and west by
thousands of miles of ocean. The advent of nuclear-equipped bombers, sub-
marines, and intercontinental ballistic missiles (ICBMs), however, changed
all the givens, requiring the kind of quick response to decision making that

only a president could provide. The Cold War altered the balance between Congress and executive in other ways as well, since it involved a situation of almost *permanent* (nearly half a century) conflict and crises at the international level that similarly demanded presidential leadership. Congress sometimes chafed at its subservient role, but until Vietnam it seldom challenged the president on foreign policy matters. There followed a period in the 1970s and 1980s, as the Cold War seemed to be winding down, when Congress gradually reasserted its power. During the 1990s, with the Cold War over and the threat to America greatly diminished, Congress seemed once again ready to resume its role as a coequal branch, including on foreign policy issues. But then came 9/11 and the war on terrorism, and decision-making authority was again concentrated in the president's hands, but not without Congress playing a role of overseer and critic.

The roots of this conflict between congressional and executive leadership in foreign policy date back to the founding of the American republic. It has its origins in the system of overlapping power and checks and balances that the founding fathers purposely built into the Constitution. For example, the president is designated commander in chief, but only Congress has the power to declare war. Is the sending of U.S. troops to Kuwait, Somalia, Rwanda, Bosnia, Haiti, Afghanistan, or Iraq an act of war that requires congressional approval or does it lie within the president's discretion as commander in chief? Who decides? Where do we draw the line? Therein lie some of the great controversies and conflicts of our day.

Similarly, the president may negotiate treaties, but Congress is required to approve them by a two-thirds vote. What therefore of "executive agreements" that look like, sound like, and take the form of treaties—must they also have congressional approval? Congress, of course, answers yes, while the president prefers the flexibility that executive agreements provide. The same situation occurs with appointments: the president nominates ambassadors and other high-ranking foreign policy officials, but Congress must approve these. What if the Senate—or just an individual senator—disapproves, on whatever grounds, and decides to hold up the nomination, often for months, years, or even permanently?

A key area, of course, is money. The president is in overall charge of foreign policy but *only* Congress passes on appropriations bills. The president may "lead" all he wants on foreign policy, but without money his initiatives will go nowhere. Without funding for foreign aid, or for the State or Defense Departments and the CIA or other agencies, the United States cannot have much in the way of an effective foreign policy.

The U.S. Constitution contains such a complex system of checks and balances, and many of its articles are sufficiently vague, that it is impossible to say definitively who is in charge of foreign policy. In addition, the relation between Congress and the executive varies over time, depending on a president's mandate and popularity, the national mood, the skills of the president or congressional leaders, the political party balance, and the international situation. Bill Clinton, for example, began his presidency with a Democratic Congress to back his initiatives, but with the victory of the Republicans in 1994 his foreign policy faced greater congressional scrutiny and opposition. George W. Bush faced strong Democratic opposition in his first term but had clear Republican majorities in his second.

What we can say about the Constitution therefore is that it provides an ongoing "invitation to struggle" between the executive and legislative branches; it provides for built-in conflict. Moreover, it is so vague on many issues that there is no way of completely resolving them or of stating definitively where the final power in foreign policy lies. Such tension and conflict between Congress and the president have long been present; nor should we expect these conflicts to be resolved soon. Tension and struggle over foreign policy should thus be looked on as the norm and not the exception.

Americans, as well as the country's friends and foes alike, will just have to live with the fact that U.S. foreign policy will always be less coherent, less unified, less consistent, and more conflict-prone than that of most other nations having different kinds of political systems. The uneasy relationship, even rivalry, between Congress and the White House will go on since it is built into the checks and balances of the U.S. government. There will *always* be competition and conflict between the two branches because the founding fathers designed the system that way. Hence, the numerous disputes that arise between them can, ultimately, only be resolved in the political process through elections, the interest group struggle, logrolling and political deals, and changes in national political sentiment. Such imprecision and uncertainty will leave many persons uncomfortable; but that is the nature of the American system. It is what the founders had in mind, and it is unlikely to change soon. Since we cannot do much to change this basic system, we will just have to live with and work through the system we have, however inefficient and conflict-prone that system sometimes is.

Congress: Politics and Partisanship

Congress is the most partisan branch of the American government. Here, parties matter; votes are often along partisan lines; appointments to key positions are determined on the basis of party affiliations; and loyalty, friendships, and alliances are often based on party criteria. Witnesses at congressional hearings are chosen on the basis of the "party lines" they represent—and all this endemic partisanship occurs frequently at the expense of merit considerations or achieving a truly sensible, reasonable, and *bipartisan* foreign policy.

There is abundant evidence that the public is becoming fed up with all the partisan posturing and the political gridlock that it produces. The low voting turnouts, the disillusionment with politics, the anti-Washington and antigovernment sentiment, and the sense of a "pox on both your houses" all point toward a sense of public disgust with partisan politics. The public wants efficient management and problem-solving programs to come from Washington, not the spectacle of one party constantly blaming the other, or vice versa, with both parties fleeing from responsibility. Congress is the embodiment of this partisan spirit, which helps explain why Congress is the lowest-ranking of the main American institutions. Hence, a disconnect has emerged between Washington (dominated by partisanship) and the rest of the country, which has other preoccupations.

Probably most of us are willing to acknowledge that partisan politics, as personified by Congress, will play some part in foreign policy decisions. But we may still much prefer a more rational system with its careful weighing of the costs and benefits of different policy options. We are still reluctant to admit that partisan politics—not merit, rational calculation, or the best and most compelling arguments—are what often drive foreign policy. But that is, in fact, one of the principal arguments of this book: that politics has frequently come to overwhelm sensible and rational considerations of the national interest, that partisan politics now takes priority in foreign policy decision making—and all this to the detriment of American foreign policy. Politics is no longer just *a* factor; in many cases it is virtually the *only* factor.

A good starting point for the discussion is to ask why members of Congress vote as they do on foreign policy and other issues. The answer, based on political scientists' quantitative analyses of congressional voting behavior, is clear: the desire to be reelected. That is, when we analyze congressional voting systematically and examine the variety of factors that might plausibly explain congressional votes—the gender of the congresspersons, their age, their religious affiliations, what part of the country they represent, whether their districts are primarily rural or urban, and so on—the one factor that best explains how they vote is their calculation of whether that will get them reelected or not. Sheer electoral self-interest (not necessarily the public interest) is the single best explanatory factor in telling us how and why lawmakers vote as they do.

Partisanship, self-interest, and the desire to be reelected—with all of these factors being closely interrelated—provide the key explanations as to why congresspersons behave and vote as they do. A few examples will be instructive. When Jimmy Carter negotiated the treaties turning over control of the Panama Canal to Panama in the year 1979, his administration determined that it lacked the votes to get the measure through Congress. So it invited the wavering congresspersons to the White House to see what they wanted, to determine what would win their votes. The answer often had little to do with the merits of the Canal treaties per se; instead, what the congresspersons wanted were new military bases, new federal buildings, and therefore vast construction projects that would translate into jobs in their districts that also mean votes at election time. It was "pork" that got the Canal treaties through Congress, not rational argument. The congresspersons supported the president on Panama and he, in turn, returned the favor on other matters. Votes were simply bought and sold (not literally for money) on the basis of a favor for a favor: you scratch my back on the treaties and I'll scratch yours on something else.

Or let us take another example of how domestic politics often overwhelms rational foreign policy considerations. In Central America during the 1980s, the Reagan administration was very much concerned with what it saw as a rising Marxist-Leninist threat within the region and took vigorous steps to prevent that from happening. Democrats in Congress were often less convinced of the communist threat; more than that, they thought they could embarrass Reagan politically by showing that he was insensitive to human rights and the plight of the poor in Central America. But then Reagan turned the tables: he indicated that, if Congress did not vote for assistance to the government of El Salvador and if the Marxists seized power as a result, the White House would not hesitate to blame Democrats for "losing" El Salvador to communism and would target them in the next election. Whereupon the Democrats similarly engaged in one-upmanship, voting just enough aid so that the White House could not blame them but not enough to ensure the guerrillas' defeat. The issue dragged on for years, with both parties playing the "politics of blame," both seeking to gain partisan advantage from the suffering in Central America, and neither working toward effective solutions. It has been estimated that 80 percent of the conflict over Central American policy had to do with domestic politics and only 20 percent with what was actually happening in such countries as Nicaragua and El Salvador.

A third example is Bill Clinton's efforts to get the North American Free Trade Agreement (NAFTA) through Congress. Despite the fact that the merits of the case for free trade were impressive and that most Americans would benefit, the Clinton administration found itself short of the needed votes for passage. In fact, it was reported that, in addition to those congresspersons who had legitimate concerns about the treaty because specific industries in their districts might be hurt, others who favored the treaty were nevertheless holding off from saying so publicly to see what kind of deal they could get out of the White House. So Clinton went to work on the holdouts, inviting them to the White House, wheeling and dealing, and promising them almost anything—more military bases in their districts, dams and public buildings, support for their pet projects later on—if they would support NAFTA. Eventually the treaty got enough support and passed, but the votes often had little to do with NAFTA and its merits; rather, partisanship, trade-offs, logrolling, and pure electoral self-interest were the deciding factors.

When George W. Bush sent military forces into Iraq, Congress was often in turmoil as to whether to support or criticize the action. The Democrats in Congress were opposed, but they didn't want to be seen as not supporting "our troops." So they waffled on the issue, trying to oppose the war but support the troops. Such "flip-flopping" may have cost John Kerry the presidency in 2004.

Some issues and geographic areas are more prone to this kind of logrolling and partisan horse-trading than others. For example, no congressperson would play politics with Israel the way they did with El Salvador or Nicaragua because the political consequences of antagonizing Jewish voters are much greater than those of antagonizing the few Salvadoran or Nicaraguan voters in the United States. Similarly with Saudi Arabia: because the stakes (oil) are so high, Congress largely ignores its internal politics and human rights abuses in ways that it does not do in Central America where the stakes are less and therefore Congress thinks it can afford to play politics with the issue. Because of the nuclear threat, the Soviet Union for a long time was similarly largely off-limits to U.S. domestic political posturing and interference in its internal affairs; but now that the Cold War is over and the threat is diminished, we have seen an increase in congressional meddling in Russian affairs.

Given the partisanship, political posturing, logrolling, and overwhelming congressional preoccupation with self-interested reelection calculation and Congress's low standing in the polls (lower than the president!), the fact that the United States still manages sometimes to carry out a sensible and rational foreign policy is little short of miraculous. But sometimes it does not, for which Congress often shares major responsibility. One can thus see why it is difficult to carry out foreign policy with the advice and consent of Congress but, on the other hand, you cannot govern without Congress either.

CABINET DEPARTMENTS AND "BUREAUCRATIC POLITICS"

Foreign policy is not just a "rational" process in which policy options are set forth and rationally decided on. Rather, politics in its broadest sense—

logrolling, partisanship, political deals and trade-offs, electoral posturing, the servicing of private political ambitions under the guise of serving the public interest—is also involved. In the discussion of public opinion, the mass media, political parties, interest groups, to say nothing of Congress, we have seen how intensely politicized the entire foreign policymaking process has become—even more so with the end of the Cold War and the disappearance of the Soviet threat.

But in addition to the political interests involved, bureaucratic interests and ways of doing things similarly affect foreign policy. The "bureaucratic politics" of foreign policymaking is the focus of this section. Here, we focus on the main, more traditional foreign policymaking agencies: the Department of State, the Department of Defense, and the Central Intelligence Agency; later, we discuss briefly those departments and agencies that have recently become important because of the New Agenda of foreign policy issues: Department of the Treasury (Third World debt, trade issues), the Department of Justice (drugs, immigration issues), the Department of Commerce and the Office of the Trade Representative (business, trade), and the Environmental Protection Agency (pollution, the environment).

Here are the bureaucratic-politics issues and why they are important. First, such agencies as the State Department (diplomacy), Defense (military), and CIA (intelligence) are supposed to perform separate but interrelated foreign policy functions, which are then supposed to be coordinated through the National Security Council and by the president. But, in fact, these agencies are not well coordinated; they have different standard operating procedures (SOPs) and subcultures that cannot easily be harmonized; they as often compete with each other as cooperate for common purposes; and they often go in separate foreign policy directions and are at loggerheads with one another in ways that produce conflict and gridlock. As one State Department official put it, "It has long been easier for us to deal with the Russians than to produce agreements with our own Defense Department."

Second, the *relative influence* of these often competing bureaucracies has changed over time with very important implications for foreign policy. The general consensus among foreign policy analysts is that since the 1950s the State Department has lost considerable influence in policymaking while Defense and the CIA have gained. However, with the war on terrorism and the creation of the Department of Homeland Security, we are likely to see a new reshuffling of power among the main foreign policy agencies.

A third important factor is the sudden emergence of a great variety of new agencies on the foreign policymaking scene. While State, Defense, and CIA have long been the main U.S. foreign policy agencies, in recent decades a large number of other departments have staked out a foreign policy role. The rise of these other agencies is related to the changing American position in the world and the rise of a variety of New Agenda issues. The Treasury Department, for example, only became a major participant in foreign policy about thirty years ago as international financial and trade issues loomed larger, as the issue of the unpaid (and unpayable) Third World debt emerged, and as economic issues for a time after the Cold War became more important than traditional strategic concerns. The same comments apply to the Justice Department and the issues of drugs and immigration, the Environmental Protection Agency and the rise of environmental concerns, and the Commerce Department and international business. After 9/11 the departments dealing with security issues gained more influence. Many of these, such as the FBI, are old departments or agencies, but they are new to foreign policy and lack experience in the international arena. Where Homeland Security will fit into this is still uncertain.

The rise of these agencies and their increased participation in foreign policy have added to the "bureaucratic politics" problem. Not only do these agencies compete with each other, but they are often viewed by the State Department as horning in on its domain. Immense problems of overlapping jurisdictions and coordination also arise. For example, on drug policy no less than forty-three agencies of the U.S. government have jurisdiction. Getting all of these agencies to act together in following common goals is an almost insurmountable task. Is it any wonder that our foreign policy often goes in many directions at once and lacks coordination?

Department of State

The Department of State is, ostensibly, the main agency for carrying out American foreign policy. But State has many problems, both internal and external—not the least of which is that it has been losing power over the years relative to other agencies and that it is frequently bypassed when the most important decisions are made.

Every recent American president has felt compelled to make a speech early in his term indicating that the Department of State will be his main instrument of foreign policy and the secretary of state his "single voice" on foreign affairs. As predictable and recurrent as is this speech, however, is the fact that presidents soon despair of the department, denounce it for foreign policy blunders, and come to rely increasingly on their own politically loyal White House foreign policy staff in the National Security Council. State then fades back into oblivion, used mainly for routine diplomacy and as a high-level messenger service. State is and can be a very creative agency, but all recent presidents have chosen to concentrate foreign policy decision making, especially on the big issues, in their own hands and to bypass State.

The history of the State Department may be divided into three distinct periods: before 1940, from 1940 to 1960, and 1960 to the present. Before 1940, reflecting America's isolationist tradition and lack of involvement in world affairs, the State Department was small, with few personnel and limited activities. Foreign service officers tended to come from the elite private colleges and universities and from socially prominent families on the East Coast. They were educated in the liberal arts, most often in history and law, and thought of themselves as pragmatists and generalists, able to step into all situations. They were assigned to problems as they arose, often on an ad hoc basis, and were frequently obliged to learn about countries, areas, and problems as they proceeded. While they were often intelligent and skillful, these diplomats tended to conduct foreign affairs unsystematically, impressionistically, and by the proverbial "seat of the pants." Although State is now a quite different department from what it was then, many of the traditions of the past—elitism, general versus specialized knowledge, unsystematic analysis—continue to haunt it today.

During and in the aftermath of World War II, as foreign policy struggled to catch up to the U.S. role as a superpower with global responsibilities, the State Department became a much more active player in foreign affairs. This is the second phase in State's development. World War II and then the Cold War meant the continuation and vigorous expansion of diplomatic activity. NATO, the Marshall Plan, the Soviet challenge, and threatened revolution in the Third World all demanded a larger foreign service. The State Department expanded from a few hundred foreign service officers (FSOs) to several thousand. Then, in the 1950s, as its activities expanded, several thousand civil service personnel were transferred to the State Department and given foreign service appointments. Meanwhile, State moved out of its cramped quarters in the Old Executive Office Building next to the White House to a large new building a half mile to the west, in an area of Washington known as "Foggy Bottom."

Even with State's rapid expansion, many of its historic problems continued. Its personnel still came mainly from the elite private schools and disproportionately from the East. It had few women or minorities in the ranks of the foreign service. It continued to prefer generalists to specialists, and it was not very good at conceptualizing. That is, State tended to see all problems and countries as discrete; it was notoriously poor at seeing general patterns. FSOs took pride in their pragmatism and problem solving—both useful skills—but that sometimes meant a reactive foreign policy without clear long-term goals or vision. Senator Joseph McCarthy's charges in the early 1950s that there were communists or "pinkos" in the department undermined morale and contributed to its discrediting in the public eye. State, which had long been mocked because of its "striped pants diplomats" and "cookie pushers," was now viewed as "disloyal" as well. Even with these mounting problems, however, the accomplishments—NATO, Marshall Plan, Point Four—were many; State Department officials tend to look back on this era from World War II until the 1960s as its most glorious.

The third era in State's history, its decline, dates from the 1960s. There is no one single event that precipitated this decline, nor can we say that it began in any one year. Rather, the causes derived from several factors and took effect gradually. First were State's own internal problems of reputed elitism and ineffectiveness. Second, the Defense Department and CIA began to take over more and more foreign policy for themselves. Third, State failed to adjust to the more democratic and participatory foreign policy process of recent decades. Fourth, many of State's planning and research functions were taken over by think tanks and interest groups. Congress and its staff also pushed in on State's functions. And fifth, a succession of presidents distrusted the State Department and were determined to run their own foreign policies; hence, they concentrated power in the NSC and took it away from State.

Recently the State Department has attempted to make a comeback. Under Colin Powell and Condoleezza Rice its budget increased. Presidents have given lip service to the idea that State will be dominant in foreign policy, but in reality little real power has devolved upon it.

Department of Defense

The Department of Defense is going through one of the greatest convulsions in its history—even greater than that which followed the Vietnam War. America's historic enemy, the Soviet Union, has been vanquished; now we have the war on terrorism. Therefore, virtually every strategic doctrine, weapons system, and policy built up over the last fifty years has to be reevaluated in the light of current needs.

Defense is seeking to redefine its role and mission: Will it be the traditional defense of U.S. security (but against whom or what foes?), or will it be a "menu" of new challenges that are often controversial and fall short of providing the clarity of purpose that the Cold War did: peacekeeping, counternarcotics, nation building, humanitarian relief, border patrol, counterterrorism, and law enforcement? Meanwhile, the department is trying to deal with a variety of internal problems, such as gays in the military and women in combat roles, that are reflective of broader issues in American society. At the same time, while seeking to answer all these challenges, the armed forces are going through major budget overhauls.

The Department of Defense is not well equipped to handle such a large restructuring. With about 2.6 million personnel (two-thirds military, one-third civilian), it is one of the world's largest bureaucracies and among its most cumbersome. Any agency that large is almost impossible to administer, let alone to reform. It is hard to change the institution from within and perhaps even harder to change it from the outside. In addition, there continue to be rivalries between the services (Army, Navy, Air Force, Marines) for increasingly scarce budget dollars, different assumptions and different operating procedures among them, and intense competition concerning which are best equipped to handle the new challenges. Moreover, unlike the State Department, each of the services and the department as a whole has its own domestically powerful "cheerleading" section—veterans' groups, retired officers' groups, the American Legion, and others—all ready to pour on the political pressure in defense of their military or service interests. Adding to the difficulties of restructuring is that virtually every state and congressional district in the country has a military base, which means jobs and a large payroll in that district and therefore makes the Pentagon's budget very difficult to cut.

Essentially, the strength of the U.S. armed forces provides a deterrent against an attack from a hostile outside power. During the Cold War, the nature of the threat was clear: the United States needed to deter the Soviet Union and its allies. And the logic of deterrence was also clear, if paradoxical: the United States required military strength of such magnitude that no hostile power would ever attack it, which therefore meant that it would not have to use the strength that it had. With the threat (the Soviet Union) and the logic (peace through strength) clear, the United States was able to justify a large military, highly advanced weapons systems, and immense spending for the military budget.

But in the aftermath of the Cold War, all this logic turned topsy-turvy. Who now is the enemy? Wherein lies the threat? Drugs, global warming, overpopulation are all *problems*, but not immediate strategic *threats* in the same way that thirty thousand Soviet nuclear weapons were. Whom are we seeking to deter? Japan, Germany, China, Libya, North Korea, Iran, Islamic fundamentalism, a revived Russia? All of these could be viewed as *potential* challengers to the United States. Some questioned why we need such a large military and such a huge budget for defense. But then came the attack on 9/11. Suddenly and unexpectedly the United States had a new and obvious enemy. The Pentagon's budget vastly increased to fight the Afghanistan and Iraq wars. Questions were raised about the capability of U.S. forces in dealing with complex terrorism issues, which involve cultural and political as well as military issues. Meanwhile, efforts to reform the department were often postponed. In its nation-building attempts in Iraq, the Pentagon seemed to be carrying out both political and military roles, again to the detriment of the State Department. New controversies swirled about American readiness, whether the draft should be reinstated, and the need for internal Defense Department restructuring. Many questions went unanswered.

In the long span of history the United States has not been a world military power, or a superpower, for very long. After the War of Independence, George Washington had warned against the dangers of keeping a standing army, and at first the new nation that was the United States in the late eighteenth century thought that, with immense oceans on both sides and far from the main powers of Europe, it would not need a large military establishment. But troubles on the frontiers; a succession of Indian wars; conflicts with Spain, France, and Britain on the North American continent; threats to American trade; the War of 1812; and then the Mexican-American War dispelled this early notion and led the United States to build up its army. Nevertheless, through the mid-nineteenth century the United States kept its military forces small, dispersed, and away from the seat of power in Washington. Only on one occasion (1860–1864) did the United States mobilize large military forces, and that was for a civil war, not an international conflict. Throughout most of the 1800s, the United States remained a small, weak power, isolationist, thinking of itself as different from other powers, and preoccupied mainly with continental expansion ("manifest destiny"), not foreign affairs.

As the United States became a major industrial power and more populous after the Civil War, it also acquired larger international ambitions and newfound military might. Admiral Alfred Thayer Mahan, the apostle of American sea power, laid the theoretical and strategic groundwork in the 1880s and 1890s for the United States to emerge as a major global power. During the 1890s, the United States began to challenge the dominance of British power in the Caribbean area, and in 1898 the United States defeated Spain and acquired the last remaining Spanish colonies in the Caribbean (Puerto Rico as well as a protectorate over Cuba) and the Pacific (the Philippines). The United States had emerged as a significant but not yet dominant global power.

Even with its newfound strength and ambitions, however, the United States was often a reluctant warrior. It intervened repeatedly in the Caribbean in the early twentieth century but in the larger global arena U.S. policy was still generally isolationist. Unlike the other great powers, the United States did not maintain a large standing army. Instead the American posture was to mobilize a large military force in times of genuine national crisis—and then demobilize once the crisis of the moment had passed. That is how the United States fought both World Wars I and II. The United States recruited a large army, fought for the defense of its principles and national interests, defeated its enemies, and then largely demobilized and went home. It did not maintain large standing armies after the war ended. And after World War I, the United States refused to get involved in the League of Nations, the predecessor of the United Nations, because it still wished throughout the 1920s and 1930s to stay out of foreign entanglements. The United States fought heroically in both world wars, but it had little desire to maintain a large peacetime military or to serve as the world's police force.

World War II was different, however, because the Cold War with the Soviet Union began in its immediate aftermath. President Truman had wanted to keep a sizable contingent in uniform after the war to serve as a check on Soviet advances, but the domestic pressures to "bring the boys home" and demobilize were immense. So the United States demobilized after the war and then quickly *re*mobilized again as the Cold War got underway.

With Great Britain, France, Germany, and Japan all lying in ruins after the war, the United States—along with the Soviet Union—emerged as a dominant superpower. In 1947 the United States reorganized its military forces, creating the Joint Chiefs of Staff, the Office of the Secretary of Defense, and the Department of Defense. During the Korean War (1950–1953), the United States was forced again to mobilize a large conventional army; during that period and on into the 1960s, the military buildup continued for the long, protracted, multipronged Cold War conflict with the Soviet Union.

The American defeat in Vietnam in the late 1960s and early 1970s, coming at the height of the Cold War, was a profound setback to the U.S. military. Out of that humiliation, however, came a rebuilt, reconstituted, modernized U.S. military that eventually helped to checkmate the Soviet Union and displayed awesome firepower, technology, and accuracy in the Gulf War with Iraq in 1991. During this period, the Defense budget climbed to $300 billion and the number of Defense personnel to three million, including two million in uniform. American military equipment, personnel, and doctrine were unsurpassed in the world. But precisely as the United States reached the height of its military power, all of this began to crumble as the Soviet Union disintegrated and the Cold War ended. Hence, as it had after Vietnam, the U.S. military would again require restructuring and reorientation, but this time on an even more profound basis—every strategic assumption and doctrine built up over the preceding forty years would need to be rethought as well.

It was precisely as this rethinking and restructuring were underway that the terrorists struck on 9/11. The United States was completely unprepared for the attack. The U.S. military, used to facing the threat of large, land-mass or ocean-going nations (Germany, Japan, the Soviet Union), was ill-equipped to deal with small, informal, cell-like terrorist groups that were not identified with any one particular nation. Not only was it hard to fight this new enemy, but it was hard to identify who, precisely, they were.

The task of the U.S. military at this stage is enormous. While fighting a war first in Afghanistan and then in Iraq, the Defense Department also had simultaneously to undergo fundamental internal reorganization to deal with the new terrorist threats. Its challenge was augmented by the fact that President George W. Bush trusted and relied on the officer corps more than he did the civilians in the State Department for peacekeeping and nation-building roles. But the U.S. military is a war-fighting machine; it is not well prepared or equipped for these new missions. A reflection of the shift in foreign policy influence in this era is the U.S. budget for 2005: more than $500 billion dollars (including war efforts) for the Defense Department, less than $20 billion (one twenty-fifth) for the State Department.

The Central Intelligence Agency

The CIA is one of the most maligned and least understood agencies of the U.S. government. The image many Americans as well as foreigners have of the CIA is that it is a secretive spy organization whose operatives are like the title character in James Bond movies: dashing, violent, ignoring or flouting the law, quasi out-of-control. CIA agents are widely thought to roam the world, undermining unfriendly governments, foiling anti-American conspirators, assassinating people who get in their way, and riding roughshod over international law as well as acceptable norms of moral behavior. This image of the CIA has its roots in many of the early books about the agency and in a number of popular movies (*Three Days of the Condor*, *State of Siege*, *Missing*, etc.) purporting to offer "factual dramatization" of CIA activities. The picture these books and movies portray is that of an agency operating outside of the law, using violence and assassinations, subverting "progressive" governments, and operating without proper oversight.

The actual situation is more complex and less dramatic. First, the CIA is a large bureaucratic organization like the others considered here; most of its activities, perhaps 80 percent, are normal, routine, administrative, and downright boring. Second, the main functions of the agency, though not so well known, involve the *analysis* of data, not James Bond derring-do. Most people who work as analysts for the CIA do research and write reports, not unlike their State Department colleagues; covert operations are actually quite a small part of CIA activities.

Third, the CIA rarely, if ever, initiates a significant action without presidential approval. It is not an agency "run amok" or with "rogue" agents operating on their own. Instead, CIA operations must be approved at the highest levels of the U.S. government (the NSC, the president, Congress), although elaborate pains are often taken to disguise that fact. This is the doctrine of "plausible deniability" by which a president approves an action but for which a "cover" is provided so that the president can plausibly deny responsibility if the operation goes awry. The rationale is that neither the president nor the U.S. government should be discredited because of some covert operation's failure. All of the most famous CIA operations—in Iran, Turkey, Italy, France, Guatemala, Cuba, Vietnam, Chile, Afghanistan, Iraq—had this kind of high-level approval, with a smokescreen provided in case they failed. "Plausible deniability," in which the president authorizes an operation but is given a means to deny U.S. involvement, is quite different from saying the CIA operates out-of-control. In the case of Iran-Contra, however, when lower-ranking officials (NSC directors Robert McFarlane and John Poindexter) were faced with the choice of going to jail for perjury or telling the truth by implicating higher officials, they chose not to go to jail. In these circumstances, plausible deniability was sacrificed for the sake of avoiding jail.

Congressional and executive branch oversight of CIA activities is stricter than it was thirty years ago, but a lot of gray areas remain. For example, while the president and the NSC must authorize CIA covert operations, implementation and the details of them are often at the discretion of the CIA director or of operatives on the ground. In addition, the directives signed by the president are often vague; not all contingencies are covered by them. Moreover, out in the field, CIA operatives may have to improvise, operate in emergency situations not covered by the directives, successfully complete the mission by cutting corners or operating at the margins of the law. Then too, some CIA directors like William Casey are more gung ho about covert activities than others and may stretch the presidential directives (called "findings") to accomplish their goals.

Tension will always exist in a democracy between the need for an open society and the need to conduct covert operations in order to protect U.S. interests. Although there are various proposals on the table at present to restructure and reform the CIA, few serious foreign policy practitioners would want to see intelligence activities ended altogether. The United States has a strong need for good intelligence on foreign countries and movements: terrorist groups, ethnic or breakaway movements, nuclear developments, impending revolutions, perhaps even economic intelligence. Nor do most practitioners want to do away entirely with covert operations. Covert operations should be viewed as one arrow in the archer's quiver, along with diplomacy, economic sanctions, and military action. Covert operations should be used sparingly, but we should not throw away that "arrow" entirely, for covert operations offer a range of intermediary policy options, stronger than diplomacy but not so large scale as a military invasion. One can think of numerous instances—to get rid of General Cedras in Haiti, to oust General Aideed in Somalia, to support Boris Yeltsin in Russia, to end ethnic strife in Bosnia or Rwanda, to end Taliban rule in Afghanistan—when covert activities would be enormously useful in assisting American foreign policy.

But the problems with covert operations are also numerous: Congress has put severe restrictions on them; U.S. intelligence agencies often lack the language and foreign area expertise to carry them out successfully; and America is such an open society that few covert operations stay secret for very long. Reporters and others relish exposing covert CIA operations, and copying and fax machines now make it very easy for a disgruntled employee or one who disagrees with the action politically to leak information about it and thus to spoil it. In the United States there are few secrets that can be kept that way for long, so that even the most successful covert operations often end up as overt operations. The covert arrow is often a useful one but one that also carries major risks. The terrorism threat poses additional challenges that the CIA, like the Defense Department, has not fully adjusted to as yet.

The United States does not have a long experience with intelligence operations and, by most accounts, is not very good at them. Part of the problem lies with America's Calvinist heritage, which insists that we should tell the truth and not engage in lies; another lies in democracy itself, which is based on open decisions openly arrived at. We also think of ourselves as different— more honest, less secretive—than other nations. Part of the problem stems from the sheer glee Americans get in exposing secret operations. All of these traits make it hard for America to be successful in covert activities or even to carry out any spy activities at all.

Before World War II, the U.S. had almost no intelligence system, and what we did have we felt uncomfortable about. As one secretary of state put it when the idea of an intelligence agency was put forth in the 1930s, "Gentlemen do not read other people's mail." But during the war, seeing the need to gather intelligence especially after the surprise Japanese attack on Pearl Harbor, the Roosevelt administration created the Office of Strategic Services (OSS). The OSS was headed by the legendary William "Wild Bill" Donovan; during the war it remained a small but quite successful operation whose activities were made into several movies. Many of the operatives who would later serve as directors of the CIA—Allen Dulles, Richard Helms, William Colby, William Casey—got their start with the OSS.

The Central Intelligence Agency was created by the same National Security Act of 1947 that created the National Security Council, the Department of Defense, and the Joint Chiefs of Staff. It was born at the beginning of the Cold War as the United States discovered that it could not completely disband its World War II intelligence operations and that the struggle with the Soviet Union would be long. The CIA was not meant to replace the existing military intelligence services, the Secret Service, or the FBI; rather, it was established to coordinate and disseminate intelligence information and to advise the NSC and the president. Additionally, the CIA was to perform "other functions and duties" related to national security that the NSC might direct, a vague phrase that was later used to justify covert operations.

During the 1950s the CIA flourished while also expanding its activities. President Eisenhower liked and used it to support U.S. foreign policy objectives. The CIA was used to prop up wobbly, bankrupt, postwar democratic governments in France and Italy; to restore at one point the shah of Iran against a populist challenge; and to defeat challenging communist movements in Turkey and Guatemala. Under Allen Dulles, brother of Eisenhower's secretary of state John Foster Dulles, the CIA bureaucracy grew rapidly. Ex-President Truman, however, under whom the CIA had been created but used sparingly, became critical of the agency because of its size and involvement in covert operations.

"The Company," as the agency was sometimes called, moved into a large new headquarters in the Washington suburb of Langley, Virginia. The leadership of the CIA, like that of the State Department at this time, tended to come from the "Ivy" (Yale) or "little Ivy" (Williams, Amherst) colleges; but given the focus on the Cold War and the perceived threat of the Soviets and the Warsaw Pact to Western Europe, a disproportionate share of the operatives and analysts in the CIA were recruited from among anticommunist Eastern Europeans. These orientations not only shaped the CIA and its internal culture in various ways but also led the agency for a long time to neglect the emerging issues in the Third World.

The 1960s was not a good decade for the agency—and then things went from bad to worse. The decade began with the CIA-sponsored anti-Castro invasion of Cuba in 1961 at the Bay of Pigs, an operation that ended in disaster and was called by one analyst a "perfect failure." Believing the CIA had given him bad information about Cuba, President Kennedy turned against it and concentrated foreign policy operations in the White House. In 1965 the CIA badly misjudged communist activities in the Dominican Republic as President Johnson sent in U.S. military occupation forces, leaving Johnson looking bad before the press and the public. Also in the mid-1960s came the revelations of the CIA's sponsorship of various U.S. and foreign foundations, and writer, student, and labor groups—revelations that forced the CIA to curtail these activities and also discredited the groups involved. The CIA was better at assessing the Vietnam War, but its dismal assessments were not acceptable to President Johnson, who opted not to listen to his own intelligence agency.

If the 1960s were bad for the CIA, the 1970s were even worse. Various efforts, some politically motivated, were made to blame the CIA for Vietnam or Watergate or both. In 1973 CIA attempts—most of them bumbling—to destabilize the leftist government of Salvador Allende in Chile resulted in a great deal of unfavorable publicity for the agency. The CIA, along with the U.S. armed forces, was also blamed for training despotic, repressive, military regimes in the Philippines, Iran, and throughout Latin America and therefore was held responsible for the widespread killings and human rights abuses practiced by these governments. On top of this came a series of critical books (see the suggested readings section at the end of this book) that portrayed the CIA in the worst possible light. In part because of such sensationalist books, the Senate, led by Frank Church (D-ID), held extensive hearings on the CIA and issued damaging reports indicting the agency for its participation in several assassination efforts and other dirty tricks. As a result of these hearings, both the House and the Senate established intelligence oversight committees requiring the CIA to report all its covert activities to Congress. The reports and closed hearings on these activities were then regularly leaked to the press, which, of course, ended their covert character and further eroded the trust between Congress and the CIA.

Nor was the CIA's leadership at the highest levels very helpful at either reforming or bolstering the agency. Director William Colby in the mid-1970s was roundly disliked by the agency's personnel because he had not stood up strongly enough to the congressional probes and seemed himself at times to be a party to reducing the CIA's activities and influence; he was eventually fired by President Ford. Then came the Carter administration, many of whose members and the president himself despised the agency. Carter's CIA director, Stansfield Turner, pared the CIA down, let go many of its ablest operatives, and all but terminated covert operations. This was in keeping with Carter's moralistic foreign policy, but it lowered CIA morale still further and severely weakened the agency.

Under Reagan and his CIA director, William Casey, the CIA began to recover. Its budget increased; Casey *loved* covert operations; morale went up; and, with both the State and Defense Departments often paralyzed by inertia, the CIA was viewed in Washington in the early 1980s as the only agency that could "get things done." But Casey recruited too many ideologues whose hasty conclusions were not always supported by hard facts, and in involving the CIA in Lieutenant Colonel Oliver North's "cowboy" arms-for-hostages operation ("Iran-Contra"), the CIA again suffered a setback.

In the post–Cold War era of the 1990s, the CIA's position was a lot like that of the Defense Department. Everyone understood that the agency needed to be reoriented and restructured away from Cold War concerns and in the direction of new issues, but there was little agreement on how or what form that should take. Should the CIA continue to do traditional foreign affairs intelligence or should it turn its attention to economic intelligence? With the Soviet Union gone, there was great confusion as to who should constitute the "enemy." Terrorists? Drugs? Ethnic strife? Political confusion and breakdowns? Nuclear proliferation? Should the CIA be eliminated altogether? Should its functions be given to other agencies (State, Defense) or should it be downsized and reorganized? Reform of the agency was long overdue, but this is a big bureaucracy and, again like Defense, it has powerful political allies, so any changes are likely to be slow, torturous, and controversial.

The September 11, 2001, attacks on the United States were a terrible blow to the agency. Neither it nor the FBI had been prepared for, nor were they able to predict, the attacks. Both these agencies suffered severe damage to their reputations; calls for reform were strong and prompted congressional action. But like the Defense Department, neither of these two agencies is as yet set up to handle the terrorist threat. They lack the language skills, the area expertise, the intelligence-gathering capabilities on the ground, and the ability to provide the sensitive, in-depth analysis that the president and his advisers need. The establishment of the Department of Homeland Security, in addition, gave them a new rival to compete with. Many Washington insiders despair that these big bureaucracies (State, Defense, CIA, FBI) can be sufficiently reformed to do their jobs effectively.

Treasury, Justice, Commerce, et al.

In recent years, a large number of other departments of the U.S. government have increasingly taken on major foreign policy roles. These include the Treasury Department (international finance, trade, Third World debt), the Justice Department (drugs, immigration), the Commerce Department (international trade and business), the Environmental Protection Agency (pollution, the environment), and a wide variety of other agencies (Labor Department, Interior Department, etc.) too numerous to analyze in a single chapter.

At least three major global phenomena explain the rise of these traditionally domestically focused agencies into foreign policy prominence. The first is increasing global interdependence or globalization, especially

in the economic sphere. Whether we are talking about Japanese cars and
technologies, Middle Eastern oil, Italian or Brazilian shoes, Chilean
grapes, a variety of goods manufactured in the Caribbean, Taiwanese or
South Korean products, Mexican fruits and vegetables, or Central American laborers—to name only a few—it is clear that the U.S. economy is no
longer self-sufficient and is increasingly interdependent with the rest of the
world in numerous complex ways. Up to *30 percent* of the U.S. gross national product is generated through international trade. Everything from
pajamas and industrial staples made in the Caribbean, to TVs and VCRs
manufactured in Asia are now imported into the United States. Meanwhile,
the goods that the United States exports abroad are increasingly important
to the U.S. economy. The rising significance of international trade, finance, and commerce has thrust such agencies as the Treasury and Commerce Departments and the OTR into the forefront of Washington foreign
policymaking.

The second global phenomenon is the emergence of new issues—human
rights, democracy, drugs, immigration, pollution, the environment, and now
terrorism—onto the front burner of foreign policy concerns. These are the
New Agenda issues that have begun to push the traditional strategic concerns
to the sidelines. These new issues, like the economic ones, have helped push
to the fore the agencies responsible for dealing with them: the Justice Department, the Environmental Protection Agency, the National Endowment for
Democracy, Homeland Security, and others. Each of these agencies has in recent years had to significantly expand its international division.

The third major international event that pushed these new issues and the
agencies that deal with them into the limelight was the end of the Cold War.
The end of the Cold War meant the United States no longer needed to concentrate so heavily on international strategic and military issues. While the
Soviet threat loomed large, the United States poured immense resources into
strategic and nuclear defense; with the Cold War over, the United States felt
it could afford to focus more heavily on economic, human rights, environmental, and other new issues.

It is not clear how much the war on terrorism will affect these newer foreign policy agencies. On the one hand, such issues as immigration, the environment, drugs, trade, and the international economy will be with us for
a long time to come and the United States will have to continue to deal with
them, regardless of the war on terrorism. On the other hand, particularly
with regard to issues like immigration, the international economy (trade and
energy supplies), and counternarcotics, the war on terrorism puts added
pressures on these agencies to reform, shift directions, and deal with the
new threats.

The emergence of more and more agencies of the U.S. government having international responsibilities has added a variety of new layers of complexity to American foreign policymaking. Two questions come immediately to mind. First, how well equipped in terms of personnel, language training, and foreign affairs experience are these traditionally domestically focused agencies to deal with the new international issues that have suddenly been thrust upon them? Second, how has the rise of these new agencies and issues affected the traditional foreign policymaking agencies and the bureaucratic competition and politics between them? How, if at all, is it possible to coordinate policy among what are often competing, noncooperating agencies? The involvement of all these other newer agencies in international matters has made American foreign policy even more complicated and divisive than before.

THE NATIONAL SECURITY COUNCIL

The NSC is a reflection and extension of the presidency. Located in the White House complex, the NSC consists of the president's own, personal foreign affairs staff. A president can—and all recent presidents did—change and shape it to suit his own plans and decision making. Along with the president himself, the NSC lies at the narrowest point of our decision-making funnel, in the innermost circle of our series of concentric circles.

The NSC has become one of the key agencies—if not *the* key agency—in foreign policy. First, since it is located in the White House complex, it is physically closer to the president than any other foreign policy agency. Second, since it is a presidential staff agency, the president can appoint his own trusted advisers and loyalists who will unquestionably carry out his wishes, in contrast to State, Defense, or CIA whose career officers may or may not share his political vision and are adept at following their own bureaucratic agendas, not necessarily the president's. The third reason the NSC has emerged as such a prominent and preferred agency is that presidents can reorganize and restructure it to their liking, molding it to their foreign policy styles in ways that they cannot reshape such big and impenetrable departments as State or Defense. *Every* recent president, while paying lip service to the State Department as *the* center of foreign policy, has come to rely more and more on his own foreign policy advisers in the NSC.

The NSC came into being as a result of the National Security Act of 1947—that same monumental piece of legislation that created the Department of Defense, the Joint Chiefs of Staff, and the CIA. The NSC was created, along with these other agencies, just as the Cold War with the Soviet

Union was getting underway. It was meant to solve a problem that had emerged during World War II: President Roosevelt regularly received numerous lengthy memos from the State Department, Department of the Army, OSS, and other agencies bombarding him with information, not all of it useful or accurate, requiring decisions, but without the president having the background himself or the staff to sort it out, absorb it all, present the options in concise form, or make informed decisions. Hence, the idea for a small foreign policy staff at the White House level that would take all this information from the different agencies, sort out the wheat from the chaff, summarize and coordinate it, and present it to the president in concise form and in a format that would facilitate decision making.

There is considerable confusion about the NSC and its acronyms. Technically, the formal National Security Council consists only of the president, vice president, secretary of state, secretary of defense, and others whom the president may designate—usually the director of CIA, the national security advisor, and the chairman of the joint chiefs, and sometimes the ambassador to the UN. This is a very small, high-level, interagency group that has responsibility for national security decision making. In actual practice, the term *National Security Council* is used to refer both to this group and the staff in the White House that serve under them. The NSC staff may number 100 to 150, depending on administrations, about half clerical and half professional. The NSC staff has a director, referred to as the NSA, who also is part of the formal high-level NSC. But do not confuse this NSA with the National Security Agency (which also uses the acronym NSA), which is a separate agency that specializes in monitoring global communications.

The NSC was originally conceived as a nonpartisan, nonpolitical, professional staff office designed to coordinate foreign policy options for the president. As the legislation creating the NSC stated, its purpose was to "advise the president with respect to the integration of domestic, foreign, and military policies relating to national security." As originally conceived, the NSC staff was meant to be a filter, integrator, and coordinator of foreign policy information coming from other agencies, not an independent policymaking body. With so much information coming into the Oval Office from so many different sources, someone needed to collect it all, boil it down and put it in readable form, and present it to the president for his decision. None of the existing departments could do that, it was felt, because they often had a biased, bureaucratic interest in the outcome and would present the information and options in such a way that favored their preferred solution. Hence, the NSC was to digest all this information and give it to a busy president in ways that facilitated rational decision making while also avoiding the problems of bureaucratic politics among the several foreign policy departments.

The NSC has gone through many incarnations. Early NSC staffs were largely invisible, remaining behind the scenes. Then with presidents Kennedy and Johnson, the NSA was called on to publicly explain and defend government policy, becoming more visible and also more political. In the 1970s Henry Kissinger and Zbigniew Brzezinski were strong figures, often overshadowing their own presidents on foreign policy. Presidents Reagan, Clinton, and George W. Bush had weaker NSAs, and the policy coordination function faltered since weak NSAs are not able to impose their policies in the face of opposition from strong department secretaries. President George H. W. Bush had a close relationship with his NSA, Brent Scowcroft, and conducted a quite successful foreign policy. It is generally agreed that the NSC system works best with a strong NSA who is close to the president, and is able to force the competing foreign policy departments ("bureaucratic politics" again) to work together and coordinate the policy.

THE PRESIDENCY

The presidency is *the* focal point, the epicenter, the hub of the American political and governmental system. Here is where real power lies. There is an unmistakable aura, a mystique, that surrounds the White House and the presidency. Part of it is the majesty, pomp, and symbolism of the presidency; part of it derives from the enormous power of the president almost literally to make or break nations, go to war, or determine the future course of humankind. It is not only America's most important job but, given the immense global power and responsibilities of the United States, also the most important in the world. As President Harry Truman once said, "The buck stops here"—in the president's Oval Office.

While the power and importance of the presidency and his staff are immense, there are also enormous limits on presidential authority. Ours is a system of elaborate checks and balances, and the president is frequently frustrated by his inability to get his agenda through Congress. He is also frustrated by his inability to get the various departments to actually carry out his policies, to line up a coalition of interest groups to support his initiatives, or to shape public opinion in his favor. The president must therefore constantly work at the job of building and enhancing his power. In addition, even with all his immense power, the American president is severely limited in his ability to change other countries in their fundamentals (Russia), create institutions where they do not exist (Haiti), stop bloody turmoil in societies that have long been killing each other (Bosnia, Rwanda), or deliver democracy to the Middle East. Every president soon discovers that even with all the levels of influence at his disposal, it is difficult to change and manipulate other countries' behavior from the confines of the Oval Office.

History and Background

Although Congress and the White House have long vied for supremacy in foreign policy, the general trend over the two-hundred-year history of the country has been toward executive predominance. Even with the reassertion of congressional authority in the last two decades, it is still the president who leads, directs, and provides the main initiatives. Congress may check, balance, and sometimes frustrate presidential initiatives, but in most cases it remains the executive who proposes the initiatives and provides the leadership. The presidency remains the main power in the American foreign policymaking system.

The Constitution, under Article II, provides that the president is the chief executive. He is also commander in chief of the armed forces. He is further granted the power to appoint officials and negotiate treaties, although for these actions he may be required to seek the advice and consent of Congress. With the powers of chief executive, commander in chief, appointment, and treaty making, the executive branch would seem to have sufficient constitutional power to prevail in most foreign policy decisions.

It was clearly the intention of the founding fathers to enhance the powers of the presidency, including that over foreign policy. The Constitution of 1787 stood in marked contrast to the earlier Articles of Confederation in which Congress dominated foreign policy through a Committee on Foreign Affairs. But the earlier system had proved unworkable, as both Congress and the writers of the Constitution realized; hence, the vesting under the Constitution of broad powers in the executive branch. As Alexander Hamilton noted in *Federalist No. 70*, the presidency was made into a more powerful office because that way "decision, activity, secrecy, and dispatch" would all be enhanced. These were qualities that the founders associated with sound government and effective decision making, especially in the field of foreign affairs. The broad powers granted the president in the Constitution as well as the writings of the founders made it clear that the executive was expected to be the main agency for carrying out foreign policy. Congress was supposed to check, balance, and oversee his authority and to share in some important responsibilities, but not to take the lead itself.

Over the course of the next two centuries, the power of the presidency in foreign affairs was generally strengthened. At least five factors are involved: new precedents, Supreme Court decisions, congressional delegation and deference, growth of the executive office, and emergency factors such as wars or threats of war.

Some of the initial precedents were set by President George Washington, who made it clear that *he* would be the one to represent the United States abroad, negotiate international agreements, recognize other states, and initiate the conduct of foreign policy. President Jefferson negotiated the Louisiana Purchase without congressional involvement, and President Polk forced the hand of Congress in declaring war on Mexico. President Lincoln blockaded the port cities of the South during the Civil War; and presidents McKinley, Roosevelt, Taft, and Wilson all sent U.S. forces abroad without congressional authorization. The sending of U.S. military forces to Korea by President Truman was done without a congressional declaration of war (but not without controversy), and recent American presidents have sent U.S. forces abroad on numerous occasions to protect American citizens, restore order, feed starving people, or patrol international waterways—all without congressional authorization, although usually with some congressional grumbling. Executive agreements are another way in which presidents have used precedent to give themselves greater flexibility in conducting foreign policy.

A second factor in explaining the enlargement of presidential leadership in foreign policy is Supreme Court decisions. For example, in *United States v. Curtiss-Wright Export Corporation et al.*, a 1934 case involving the sale of machine guns by a private company to Bolivia, the Court ruled that Congress could delegate power to the executive, the president was *the* representative of U.S. sovereignty in foreign affairs, and the president's leadership prerogatives went beyond the actual constitutional listing of his powers. In *Missouri v. Holland* (1920), the Court upheld the supremacy of the president in making foreign policy over against the powers of the states. In *United States v. Belmont* (1937), the Court held that executive agreements were the law of the land even if they had not received congressional approval. In these and other cases the Court has often reinforced and enhanced presidential authority in foreign policymaking. The War Powers Act enacted by Congress during the Vietnam War to limit presidential war-making authority may be unconstitutional but it has not been tested as yet.

A third factor is congressional delegation and deference. For example, in the Formosa Resolution of 1955, Congress delegated to the president the power to use American armed forces to defend Formosa, as well as some smaller islands near mainland (Communist) China, *as he saw fit*. The Gulf of Tonkin Resolution of 1964, which passed the House by a vote of 416–0 and the Senate 89–2, authorized President Johnson to deploy U.S. military forces in Southeast Asia without a congressional declaration of war.

Congress also supported President Bush's war efforts in Afghanistan and Iraq, but without ever making a formal declaration of war. In these ways Congress delegated its war-making power to the executive. In many other instances Congress has simply deferred to presidential leadership. Whether talking about U.S. entry into the United Nations, the Marshall Plan, the formation of NATO, or the sending of U.S. forces abroad on numerous occasions, Congress has—until recently—been willing to defer to presidential leadership. Even now, with a more partisan and assertive Congress, it is not clear how much Congress wishes to challenge presidential foreign policy leadership over Iraq or other issues.

A fourth factor contributing to rising presidential influence in foreign policy is institutional growth within the executive branch. Most media attention has focused on the growth of congressional staffs but, in fact, staff growth in the executive branch has been even faster. All the main executive departments—State, Defense, Justice, Treasury, CIA—experienced significant growth from the 1960s to the present. The White House staff has similarly experienced major growth, including the addition of public diplomacy, polling, and liaison offices. These increases have given the president an enormous staff and expertise, all of which enhance the knowledge base, political and bureaucratic clout, and operational capacity of the executive.

A fifth factor has to do with the actual practice of foreign affairs and its effects on the presidency. Every single war—including the war on terrorism—that the United States has fought in the last two hundred years has served, inexorably, to increase presidential power in foreign policy. Wars are national emergencies, and in emergencies we have felt it necessary to allow and trust broad presidential discretion. War also necessitates quick decisions and flexibility; only the presidency is thought to have those capacities. The forty-five-year Cold War, during which the Soviet threat loomed constantly, particularly increased the independent foreign policymaking power of the presidency, as has the war on terrorism. It is doubtful if this trend will be reversed anytime soon.

The Powers of the Presidency

The president has broad formal power in the area of foreign policymaking. In addition, he has wide informal power that will vary over time depending on his particular personality and political skills and the context of the times. The president is similarly limited both by formal, constitutional checks and balances and by informal and dynamic factors.

The Constitution states that the president is commander in chief of the army and navy; by extension, this means the more recently created air force and Marine Corps as well. Although there is room for dispute over what the term *commander in chief* means, most presidents as well as Congress and the public have interpreted it widely to give the president vast power over military mobilization, deployment, budget, strategy, and missions.

The president's role as commander in chief is checked by the power of Congress to declare war. But the United States has been involved in more than 130 hostilities in its history and in numerous smaller episodes or near-hostilities, of which Congress has only declared war on five occasions. These were the War of 1812, the Mexican War of 1846, the Spanish-American War of 1898, and World Wars I and II. All of the others—the vast majority—have been undeclared wars (Korea, Vietnam, Iraq), "police actions" (sending U.S. troops to occupy the Dominican Republic in 1965, to Lebanon in 1982, or to Haiti in 1994), patrol operations, or lower-level engagements. The large number of actions in which Congress did not declare war and yet American forces were committed illustrates the vast power of the presidency under the commander-in-chief clause.

In addition to the power to deploy American forces, the position of commander in chief has been interpreted in ways that give the president even stronger power. First, it is the president along with the Joint Chiefs and the Office of the Secretary of Defense (OSD) who decide overall military strategy: Roosevelt in World War II, Truman in Korea, and Johnson in Vietnam. But during the Iraq War, President George W. Bush carefully avoided getting involved in detailed military tactics and let the generals do the fighting. The president may make decisions concerning the deployment and patrol functions of the military that may actually increase the possibilities of a wider war: for example, Kennedy's blockade of Cuba in 1962 or Reagan's decision to escort tankers through the Persian Gulf in the face of Iranian hostility. It has been the president's assumed responsibility to plan for the "end game" of hostilities: to decide on the when, where, and how of war termination or the withdrawal of troops. In all these areas the president's power as commander in chief is vast. But during the Vietnam War, as well as over Central American in the 1980s and Haiti, Somalia, and Bosnia in the early 1990s, more recently the Middle East, Congress began to challenge some of the actions of the president. So far, however, that has consisted mainly of chipping away at presidential prerogatives, not of undermining the president's role as commander in chief.

A second major power of the president is treaty making. The Constitution gives the president the power to sign treaties "by and with the advice and consent of the Senate, provided two-thirds of the Senators present concur." It is not clear from this language whether the president should seek the advice and consent of the Senate *after* the treaty is negotiated and signed or during the negotiation itself. Historically, the president has sought Senate concurrence only after he negotiates and signs the treaty; but in recent decades, as Congress reasserted its foreign policymaking power, the requirements of politics and the need to ensure ratification have meant the involvement of Congress at earlier stages. Jimmy Carter consulted with over seventy members of Congress in the process of negotiating the divisive Panama Canal treaties; during the Strategic Arms Limitation Talks (SALT II), over sixty-five congresspersons went to Geneva at various times to sit in on the negotiations; and during the formulation of the NAFTA agreement with Mexico, Bill Clinton was forced to consult, negotiate, and bargain with virtually everyone in both houses. The treaty-making process has thus become more complicated and politicized, with the president oftentimes having to engage in two sets of negotiations simultaneously: one with the other country (or countries) involved, and the other with Congress.

Treaty making is not a cut-and-dried process; a considerable political process is often involved. First, the treaty is negotiated and signed by the parties involved, a process that is often lengthy, may involve the media as well as strong interest groups and public opinion, may be controversial, and may involve numerous compromises. Once signed, the treaty is submitted to Congress, where it may by approved, rejected, amended, or approved with reservations. These congressional changes may make the original document unacceptable to the other country (countries) involved, in which case it will have to be renegotiated and then resubmitted again. The president also has considerable influence in this process. He may withdraw the proposed treaty from consideration, ask for further changes from the other party, bargain with Congress, or refuse to sign it if it comes back from Congress in an unacceptable form. While the political process thus unfolds, the treaty may acquire a political life of its own: approved by other nations, which puts added pressure on the United States, or caught up in emotional public opinion (such as Central America, the nuclear freeze movement, or antiwar sentiment), which may oblige a president to sign a treaty he is uncomfortable with. All these and many other complications make it understandable why presidents prefer executive agreements (which do not require congressional approval) over treaties.

A third power of the president is the appointment of high-level foreign policy officials. These include the secretaries of state and defense, the director of the CIA, UN representative, NSC staff, all ambassadors, and undersecretaries and assistant secretaries. While the national security advisor and the NSC staff do not require Senate confirmation, all the other positions do, and in recent decades it has also become customary for Senate approval to be sought for the security advisor. In the past, Senate approval of high-level presidential appointments—even if the president and Congress were of different parties—was largely routine, the assumption being that a president was entitled to have the team of his choosing. Other than for obvious malfeasance, incompetence, or criminal behavior, the Senate rarely rejected a presidential nominee; and even when there was opposition, a determined president could usually have his way.

But now the system of appointments has become much more politicized. Appointments that used to be routine are now closely scrutinized. A president can still get most of his appointments through the Senate, but now there are greater barriers, more litmus tests, and intense public debate, especially if the media gets hold of something controversial. For example, when Carter attempted to appoint former Kennedy speech writer Theodore Sorensen as director of the CIA, he was told not even to submit the name to the Senate because Sorensen was considered too liberal. When Reagan wanted to name Ernest Lefever to head the human rights bureau in the State Department, an office Lefever had vowed to abolish if he was confirmed, opposition was such that the president was forced to withdraw the nomination. The NSA now gets a thorough grilling by Congress even though that is not one of the positions for which congressional approval is required.

Ambassadorial and other appointments are now routinely held up by the Senate, often for months and even years, because of political or ideological differences—delays that leave important embassy posts open. "Senatorial courtesy" now means that just a single senator can hold up an appointment indefinitely, frequently leaving the nominee in limbo and without salary for months at a time. During the last year of Reagan's presidency, Democrats in the Senate held up all his nominees, assuming that the Democrats would win the 1988 election and be able to name their own ambassadors. Republicans got their revenge in the election of 1994; thereafter, with a Republican-controlled Senate, Clinton nominees would be given much tighter scrutiny and some persons who had already been waiting for *two years* to be confirmed had their names withdrawn. Many of George W. Bush's appointments were similarly held up by Senate Democrats who threatened to filibuster unless the president obtained a super-majority (sixty votes) instead of the usual fifty-one. Partisanship seems to know no bounds in these matters even if it comes at the expense of U.S. foreign policy.

Fourth, the president has the power to grant, withhold, or withdraw recognition from other nations. The Constitution says that the president "shall receive ambassadors and other public Ministers," from which is derived the recognition power. By hallowed custom, the president is the head of state and foreign diplomats are accredited to him personally. He has the power to receive them or not, to allow them into the United States or to ask them to leave.

Recognition of other states has also taken on increasingly political overtones. Most other countries grant or withhold recognition of foreign governments simply on the basis of whether a government is in effective control of the national territory. But the United States has introduced other criteria for recognition. Is the state democratic? What is its human rights record? Did it come to power by electoral means or through a coup d'état? Is it communist or fascist? These criteria for recognition often give the United States leverage over the *internal* affairs of other nations. If the human rights record is abysmal or there are no democratic elections, the United States may refuse to recognize the regime. Nonrecognition may also serve as a lever by which the United States can get a nonelected government to hold elections and become democratic. These criteria for looking at the domestic behavior of other nations also add new layers of political considerations to our own domestic foreign policy debate as well. Nonrecognition is like economic sanctions: sometimes it works to push another government toward democracy, sometimes it does not.

Fifth, the president may be said to have certain inherent powers. He is, by common agreement, the chief decision maker on foreign policy. He is also the nation's chief spokesperson on foreign policy, and the only *official* voice. As head of state, he is the person with whom foreign governments have official contacts. The president travels abroad to summits and is the symbol and representative of the United States. When he goes abroad, the power and image of the United States go with him; when he speaks, the whole world looks for clues to future policy directions. Both the real and the symbolic power of the presidency have been enhanced in recent decades by modern communications, jet travel, and television.

A sixth power of the president is the use of the "bully pulpit" (speeches, now television) to convince the public that his policy is the correct one. But the power of persuasion is limited—increasingly more so among a skeptical electorate. The conventional wisdom is that a presidential speech can change public attitudes (for example, on whether to send U.S. troops to country X) by about 5 percent; a concerted White House public relations campaign can maybe alter public opinion by 10 percent—enough in many cases to get a working majority of support for the president's policies. However, in recent years, the capacity of the president to "move" public opinion has shrunk; surveys indicate that both before *and after* major presidential speeches the percentage of people who support the president's policies on Haiti or Somalia or Iraq has not changed much if at all. President Clinton's popularity, for example, had fallen so low or skepticism concerning his credibility was such that, despite massive lobbying by the White House for his positions, public opinion was not moving at all. This may be the reflection of a particular president going through hard times in his administration; more likely it reflects a more deeply cynical public unwilling to be moved by presidential speeches. President George W. Bush similarly encountered skepticism and cynicism over his policies in Iraq.

If we examine carefully the six areas of presidential power analyzed above, one theme stands out clearly: how politicized the process of presidential foreign policy decision making has become. In each area it is clear that politics infuses and is at the heart of every one of them. The president cannot just "announce" foreign policy decisions and expect the rest of the country to line up in agreement. Instead, as on domestic policy, the president must get out and lobby for his program. He must guide, instruct, convince, and cajole. He must meet with members of Congress, go on national television, mobilize public support, line up a supportive coalition of interest groups, secure international support, be willing to compromise. He must send his spokespersons out into the universities, town meetings, churches, synagogues, and mosques to rally domestic backing. On foreign policy the president can no longer simply offer his recommendations and expect automatic support; instead, the modern president must engage in political lobbying activities of the kind that in the past were largely confined to domestic politics. For a president to be successful in the changed circumstances of the new millennium, he needs to become actively engaged in the whole political process.

This is what political scientist Richard Neustadt meant in his celebrated, if somewhat demeaning notion that the president must function essentially as a "clerk." All the power and majesty of the presidency notwithstanding, Neustadt's research indicated that, to be successful, a president must bargain, negotiate, twist arms, and compromise. In the American system of checks and balances, the presidency is not all-powerful—now, in foreign policy matters as well as domestic ones. The president cannot simply give marching orders the way a general would. America, including Congress, the various foreign policy bureaucracies, the interest groups, public opinion, and so on, is too diverse, too independent, and too pluralistic for that to work. As foreign policy has become increasingly politicized, the president must "go into the political pits" to gain allies and support if he wishes his policies to succeed.

CONCLUSION

These are the main institutions of American foreign policymaking. Two main themes run through our analysis. One is the sheer power and influence of the United States, and particularly of the American presidency. The other is the immense amount of conflict, politics, and potential for conflict built into the system, all of which seem to have gotten worse in the last two decades. These include the conflicts between the president and Congress over a wide range of issues, the rivalries and intense competition (bureaucratic politics) between the various agencies of the U.S. government (State, Defense, Treasury, Justice, CIA, FBI, Homeland Security, etc.), and the equally intense and increasingly bitter conflict between Republicans and Democrats and within the electorate.

The question we need to wrestle with is whether this is just the normal workings of the checks and balances that the framers built into the Constitution, or is it more than that: a sign that the country is dividing and/or polarizing, and that its political system is no longer working. We return to this theme later in the conclusion.

Chapter Four

The New Powerhouses: Think Tanks and Foreign Policy

Think tanks are major new actors on the foreign policy scene, and they have become increasingly influential. The phenomenon of the think tank and its role in international affairs is a new one (the last thirty years) and therefore has not so far been adequately treated in the literature on American politics and foreign policy. Yet it can be argued that the major United States think tanks are every bit as influential in shaping American foreign policy as the political parties, interest groups, and other institutions surveyed in this book. The think tanks have taken their place among the most important foreign policy actors in Washington, D.C. Plus, they are fun, fascinating places to work.

WHAT ARE THINK TANKS?

Think tanks are unlike other institutions with which we are more familiar. Think tanks are centers of research and learning but, unlike colleges or universities, they have no students (but do have student research interns), do not offer courses (but do hold lots of seminars and forums), and do not try to offer a smattering of expertise on all subjects but rather concentrate preeminently on key public policy issues. Nor are think tanks like foundations, because they do not give money away; instead, they try to raise money for their studies from the foundations and other sources. They are not corporations because, while they have a product (research), think tanks are not profit-making organizations. And they are not like interest groups because their primary purpose is research, not lobbying—although some think tanks do that as well.

Think tanks are research organizations that have as their primary purpose *public policy research*, and which are located in or have close connections

93

with (at least the more important ones do) Washington, D.C., where they can more effectively influence the public policy debate. Think tanks contain no departments of English, art, or chemistry—although one of the more prominent "tanks" has a division of religion, philosophy, and public policy. Rather, think tanks focus chiefly on economic, social, and political policy issues and recently have concentrated on defense, security, and foreign policy issues as well. They seek not just to do research and write about these issues, however, but to influence the policy debate toward their point of view and to put forth their solutions to public policy problems.

What members of think tanks do is *think* (and write, and publish, and also disseminate their products) about public policy issues; they also serve as *advocates* for their public positions. It is the think tanks—not so much the parties, the interest groups, Congress, the White House, or even the media—that have come increasingly to set the public policy agenda and define the issues. It may sound ludicrous upon first hearing, but the fact is that these days neither congresspersons nor presidents, nor secretaries of state, have the time or specialized knowledge necessary to think about, do the research, and fashion recommendations on major public policy issues. So the think tanks often do it for them. It is the think tanks that have the ideas and expertise, can do the necessary background work and research, and are able to put their ideas into attractive form that is translatable into public policy proposals.

Think tanks have come essentially to do the government's thinking for it. The persons who work at the think tanks are experts in various areas of public policy analysis: housing, health care, education, the economy, or foreign policy. Think tank scholars either come up with new ideas themselves, based on their own research, or they rationalize and put into articulate, public policy form the ideas and conclusions that other academics, politicians, and government officials had already arrived at but were unable for various reasons to put in a framework that policy makers can use. The think tanks tend also to perform an integrating role when the national bureaucracy is divided or when too many parts of it are involved in a policy issue and no coherence among them is possible. Then the think tanks may step forward and provide the integrating perspective that is necessary.

The think tanks provide an essential service. In an era when many books, statements, and speeches are ghostwritten by persons other than their purported authors, when the budgets of various government agencies are prepared not by the agencies themselves but by private contractors, and when even the testimonies of Cabinet secretaries are often written not by the secretaries or their staff but by outside consultants, we should not be surprised to find think tanks performing public policy work and not necessarily the government agency we would assume to be responsible for such work. The activities performed by the think tanks are part of what we will call the privatization of the American public policy process. Such privatization is widespread in the government and is a result in part of the bigness, inefficiency, and sheer lack of time to do long-range planning in the public bureaucracies. The work the think tanks do is essential; and if the government cannot or will not do it, then these private agencies will have to fill the void.

Implied in the above is the suggestion that there are risks and dangers involved in such privatization, as well as advantages. There is almost no public accountability or oversight of the think tanks' activities, a particularly risky situation when the think tanks start to perform quasi-public policy roles. Moreover, the proliferation of think tanks in recent years (there are now six or seven big ones but literally hundreds of more specialized ones) has meant that each think tank wants its point of view to be the dominant one. The proliferation of think tanks and their strong positions all along the political spectrum from extreme Left to extreme Right means that the world of the think tanks is often as partisan, ideological, and divisive as is the nation as a whole. It is one of the main theses of this chapter that the think tanks both reflect and add to the politicization, fragmentation, and creeping paralysis that we have repeatedly seen as among the main—and dangerous—characteristics of contemporary American foreign policy.

WHY THINK TANKS HAVE SO MUCH INFLUENCE (IN CONTRAST TO MOST ACADEMIC SCHOLARS)

Many of us who teach foreign policy courses are frustrated policy makers. Here we are, knowing quite a bit about foreign policy issues and having written extensively about our areas of expertise, and no one calls on us for our advice! Many foreign policy instructors believe that, if only given a chance, they could do infinitely better at foreign policy than the present administration—whatever the administration. Many would much rather be making American foreign policy than teaching it, but no one has ever tapped them for a position. Hence, many teachers are often caustic, and sometimes bitter, in their criticism of American foreign policy—especially knowing that they are frequently better informed than the government officials responsible.

There are good reasons, however, why scholars and intellectuals from our colleges and universities, and their expertise on foreign policy issues, are not often tapped by policy makers. These reasons have to do mainly with the contrast between how foreign policy issues are discussed on campus and how they are dealt with in Washington, D.C. A person who wishes to join this debate, or become a policy maker, should understand and realistically come to grips with these differences.

1. The writings of academics tend to be too abstract and theoretical for most policy makers to deal with. For policy makers, academic writing is usually too far from political realities to be of much use. Hence, they don't pay much attention to academic foreign policy writings.
2. Academics tend to be concerned with developing models and discovering general laws of behavior; policy makers tend to emphasize the concrete and the particular, and to be suspicious of "grand theories." Policy makers don't have the time, or the inclination, to wrestle with grand theories like "dependency analysis" or "state–society relations"; they need to know how to vote or decide *today* on military aid to Pakistan.
3. Contemporary academic writing is often too far on the Left for policy makers to feel comfortable with. Policymaking and policy makers, almost of necessity in a democracy, must stick close to the center of the political spectrum, to the mainstream. Otherwise they will lose public support and votes, and their policies will fail. By contrast, academics who do not have to face the task of explaining and gaining support for their recommendations among a skeptical public or of having to face the voters every two years tend to write in an ideological vein that is not always supported by domestic public opinion.
4. Academics are not usually aware of the bureaucratic limits that face the policy maker. The policy maker's range of choices is usually quite constrained and he or she must operate within a bureaucratic matrix of diverse interests and responsibilities. Options and freedom to chart new paths are very limited. Hence, the advice the policy maker receives from the academic, who is not ordinarily aware of these bureaucratic pressures and constraints, is not often very useful.
5. Nor is the academic analyst always aware of the everyday political crosscurrents in Washington: who's up and who's down, who has whose ear and when, what the different factions in the administration are and their current jockeying for power, and the rivalries between the different foreign affairs bureaucracies. Without such knowledge, the academic's "rational actor" advice is likely to be of only limited utility.

It is precisely these flaws that the Washington-based think tanks, and the academics who serve on their staffs, can avoid. That is also why the think tanks have such influence and most college- and university-based academics do not. The think tank scholars tend to produce concrete analyses and recommendations, not abstract ones; they are seldom preoccupied with general models; they do know the bureaucratic ins and outs; and they keep current on the everyday political and bureaucratic changes as their academic counterparts outside of Washington cannot possibly do. The think tanks know how to plug into the system in ways that academic scholars generally do not.

Three brief illustrations of these points make them more concrete:

At a recent conference on defense strategy that brought together academics, military officials, and foreign policy planners, a naval admiral was saying what academics have long known but are often reluctant to admit. "You academics should have no illusions that you have any influence on policy," he said. "The Navy *knows* what it wants; the policy papers you prepare have not one iota of influence on policy." He continued, "However, if we can use your papers in our fights with the Army or the Defense Secretary or with Congress over the appropriation for the Defense Department, then we will use your arguments. But don't think you have any influence on real policy because we have already decided which way we want to go."

The moral of this story is that academic writings may be used as rationalizations for decisions already arrived at, or in internal bureaucratic battles, but seldom to present a series of options to policy makers. Knowing that will shape the kind of policy papers that academics, or in this case denizens of the think tanks, will send to policy makers.

During the revolution in Portugal in 1974, the U.S. ambassador to Portugal and the U.S. secretary of state were in strong disagreement about the nature of the revolution and what should be done about it. The secretary of state was convinced Portugal was lost to communism and that the American response should be to mobilize the CIA or send in NATO forces. The ambassador, in contrast, did not believe the revolution was hopelessly lost to the Communists and wanted to give the Portuguese a chance to work out a democratic solution to their own problems. An academic who knew Portugal, and who was also acquainted with this bureaucratic struggle between the ambassador and the secretary of state, helped influence the outcome by feeding information about Portugal and its institutions to the ambassador, enabling him more strongly to argue his case. The ambassador won the argument—unusual because an ambassador does not usually take on his boss, the secretary, in this way. And the outcome was also favorable: Portugal is today a flourishing democracy and faces little if any Communist threat.

The moral of this story, again, is that academics can influence policy, but only if they know the bureaucratic struggle going on within the foreign policymaking system and how and in what format to channel information into the system.

Two academic colleagues, friends as well as specialists on Africa, sought to influence the policy debate on that troubled region. One stayed on campus, gave flaming speeches, issued ideological diatribes, and fulminated against the administration. He gained some student following, but his shrillness and ideological attacks had no influence on policy whatsoever. The other scholar also favored a more enlightened approach toward Africa. He went to Washington, joined a leading think tank, studied the statements of the administration to understand its concerns, wrote reasoned and sensible articles about the region, and eventually was recruited as a consultant into the State Department where he helped work on African issues.

Here the moral is obvious: shrill criticism does not work (except maybe on campus) and may produce among the general population the opposite effects of those intended; but a person who takes the time to learn the system and to understand what motivates policy makers can be quite effective.

This discussion of how scholars can and do influence policy is also relevant to our discussion of think tanks and what they do. The think tanks are largely staffed by scholars who are public policy oriented, are often Washington insiders, and know how to influence the debate. In contrast to their academic colleagues in the universities, they know where the pressure points are, who's in and who's out, when the appropriate moment is to get their viewpoint aired, and how to go about doing so.

The think tanks play an especially important role in linking research to policy. In addition to their own independent research, the think tanks serve as a transmission belt, a broker, a link between academic work and policymaking. The think tanks thus perform liaison functions. They sift and filter the academic research for ideas that are useful and will "fly" in a policy sense. The think tanks often invite the best academic minds on the subject to Washington to the numerous conferences they put on. Then it is the job of the think tank scholars to translate the generally abstract prose in which academics write into terms that a policy maker can deal with. They must cut out the theory, the "conceptual framework," and the models, and put the knowledge and information contained in the scholarly papers into concrete, practical language and recommendations.

Think tank scholars make the academic research realistic and down to earth. They know the bureaucratic infighting; the political constraints; which ideas have a chance and which do not; and how, where, and when to feed these ideas in. In this way the think tanks can help make academic research look useful, reasonable, and workable to the policy makers. They define the options, give the arguments for them depth and sophistication, provide rationales for policy or help steer it in new directions. The think tanks can thus define the parameters of the debate, educate the public and Congress, show what will work and what will not, and demonstrate how to get from here to there. Such work may not always be in accord with the "purity" of academic research, but it is infinitely more practical and certainly has a far stronger effect on policy.

In the analysis so far, we have drawn the lines rather sharply between campus-based academic research and the public policy research and dissemination done by the think tanks. While the general points made still hold, the argument needs to be qualified in certain ways. First, some academic scholars—primarily at the Ivy League universities but often those with specialized knowledge at other universities as well—*do* have an influence on policymaking. Second, at some institutions (Harvard's Weatherhead Center for International Affairs is the best example), specialized foreign policy research centers exist that represent hybrids between the university world of pure research and the think tank world of policy-oriented research—and which not only serve to bridge the gap between these two but are also influential policy centers in their own right. Third, the case can be made that, while university-based academics usually have little influence on everyday policy, through their students as well as their writings they may have influence in longer range terms. Finally, many of the new recruits to top-level posts in the Defense or State Departments and the CIA are former academics, often frustrated ones who want to *make* policy rather than just write or lecture about it. That is another way in which the line between academic work and actual policymaking is being increasingly blurred.

THE COUNCIL ON FOREIGN RELATIONS AND THE THINK TANKS: FROM AN OLD ELITE TO A NEW ELITE IN FOREIGN POLICY

For a long time in the post–World War II period, the Council on Foreign Relations was the dominant private organization in the foreign policy field. The council had actually been formed earlier, right after World War I, to help generate public support for the Fourteen Points of Woodrow Wilson's Versailles peace treaty. Centered in New York, the council attracted elite establishment figures. It was not so much a think tank (although the council now does have its own research staff) as a gathering place for wealthy, well-placed New Yorkers who had an interest in foreign policy. During the period before and right after World War II, when the United States still had strong isolationist tendencies, the council was a center of internationalist sentiment. It put on programs, listened to speakers talk about various parts of the world, and published the leading journal in the field—*Foreign Affairs*.

Membership in the council is by election only. Membership was thus kept select and limited. It consisted mainly of prominent Wall Street bankers and lawyers as well as diplomats. During the 1940s and 1950s, a large portion of the foreign policy leadership was recruited out of the council: Dean Acheson and John Foster Dulles, David Rockefeller and C. Douglas Dillon, Averell Harriman and John McCloy, and a large number of ambassadors and assistant secretaries. Although there were partisan differences, most council members thought of themselves as moderates and centrists. They were the backbone of the consensual, bipartisan foreign policy that prevailed up to the Vietnam War.

By the 1960s, criticism of the council began to be widespread. Economist John Kenneth Galbraith denounced it as "irrelevant" and resigned. It was said to be too WASPish, too old-fashioned, and with too few women, minority, and younger members. As a New York–centered organization, it was denounced by conservatives as a part of the "Eastern liberal establishment." And as a bulwark of post–World War II foreign policy, it was held responsible by leftist critics for the assumptions that led to American intervention in Vietnam.

In the 1980s and to today, the council vigorously moved to refurbish its image and its position. It recruited new members among women, minorities, and younger persons. It opened a branch in Washington and sought to recruit members from other parts of the country besides the East Coast. It has a more vigorous research program and expanded activities.

In the meantime, however, a fundamental transformation in foreign policy-making influence has been taking place. The center of foreign policy influence has shifted from the New York–based Council on Foreign Relations to the Washington-based think tanks. The council has lost its place as the dominant, or virtually only, private influence on foreign policy. That role has now been filled by the think tanks, with major impact on United States foreign policy.

Let us sum up the changes that this shift from the council to the think tanks implies:

1. Power in foreign policy has definitely shifted from New York, which once was dominant not only in banking but also in foreign affairs, to Washington.
2. It has shifted from Wall Street bankers and lawyers to the scholars and public policy specialists who inhabit the think tanks.
3. It has shifted from an older generation whose assumptions were based on the experiences of the 1930s, World War II, and the emerging Cold War to a new generation shaped by the 1960s, Vietnam, and the war on terrorism.
4. It has shifted from the middle-of-the-road and bipartisan elements who were predominant in the council to the much more partisan, ideological, and political elements who are in the think tanks.

It is this last change that is particularly worrisome from the point of view of the main theme of this book. For if American foreign policy appears already to be divided, fragmented, and often in disarray, then the think tanks, with the divisions between them and their more partisan and ideological approach, may well be further instruments of this divisiveness. That at least is the hypothesis with which we begin.

THE WORLD OF THE THINK TANKS

The world of the think tanks is fascinating and ever changing. Think tanks come in a variety of forms and locations. Some are located on or near university campuses; others are independent. Some serve basically as research centers for the U.S. government; others do not accept government contracts at all. Some are large and some are small. Some have a single focus or issue for which they are known; others work on a variety of subjects. Here we will be concerned chiefly with the large and influential Washington-based think tanks, since that is where considerable power lies.

First, let us look at what may be termed the "minor leagues" of think tanks, or what is sometimes referred to as the "feeder system"—so-called because they often feed ideas and budding personnel into the larger think tanks. This league includes the Mershon Center at The Ohio State University, the Foreign Policy Research Institute in Philadelphia, and the Institute for Foreign Policy Analysis in Cambridge, Massachusetts. These are all small "tanks" with staffs of ten to twenty people and budgets usually in the neighborhood of $1 or $2 million. They specialize in foreign policy and national security issues. However, because they are outside of Washington and therefore can neither know about nor directly influence the everyday insides of policymaking in the nation's capital, these think tanks tend to concentrate their efforts on publishing scholarly books and articles—on longer-range policy analysis—in order to influence the scholars, editorialists, and others who *do* have a direct influence on policy.

A second category is the think tank that does most of its work for the government. Examples include the RAND Corporation, which used to be an air force think tank and now is more independent; CNA (Center for Naval Analysis), which does research for the navy; or the BDM Corporation, a multimillion-dollar private firm whose business is chiefly with the Defense Department and has recently been bought out by the even larger Ford Aerospace Corporation. But because these think tanks do chiefly contract research for the government and are not independent, general foreign policy think tanks, they are not our chief focus here.

A third category is major think tanks that have influence but are nonetheless (and almost a contradiction in terms) outside of Washington, D.C. The Hudson Institute was located in New York and headed by Herman Kahn, a visionary thinker who specialized in futuristic studies. Kahn became famous for "thinking about the unthinkable"—that is, a rational, calculating approach to nuclear war strategy rather than a purely emotional one. He was practically a one-man think tank, although he did vastly increase the staff and budget of Hudson. But Kahn has since died and the institute moved to Indianapolis; it keeps up its influence through a branch office in Washington, D.C.

Another one of the "biggies" outside of Washington is the Hoover Institution on War, Revolution, and Peace. Centered in three beautiful buildings on the lush Stanford University campus in Palo Alto, California, Hoover is one of the most influential and well-funded of the think tanks. It has a marvelous library (begun by President Herbert Hoover), wonderful facilities, a first-rate research staff, and aggressive, top-flight leadership. Although Hoover is known as a conservative think tank, its scholars are about equally divided between Republicans and Democrats and include many centrists, which means that its relations with the more liberal and often left-leaning Stanford faculty are often tense. Hoover sent many of its personnel into the Reagan and George W. Bush administrations and is most famous for its research on economic and social policy as well as foreign affairs. Like the Hudson Institute, it has a Washington office; its California staff keeps in touch by frequent long plane rides between the West Coast and the East.

Our main concern here, however, is with the five major, independent, Washington-based think tanks. They are, going from Left to Right on the political spectrum, the Institute for Policy Studies (IPS), the Brookings Institution, the Center for Strategic and International Studies (CSIS), the American Enterprise Institute for Public Policy Research (AEI), and the Heritage Foundation.

Institute for Policy Studies

The IPS is the most left-wing of the major think tanks. It was founded in the early 1960s by dissident government employees Marcus Raskin and Richard Barnett, who advocated a "radical critique" of American foreign policy and a dismantling of the capitalist system. It has an office in Washington, D.C., several affiliates abroad, and a staff of under fifty. IPS was funded chiefly by the Samuel Rubin Foundation, Mr. Rubin being a founder of the Faberge cosmetics firm and, at one time, a registered member of the American Communist Party. The Rubin family kept a strong hand in IPS through daughter Cora Rubin Weiss and son-in-law Peter Weiss, chairman of the Board of Trustees. The institute says its budget is about $2 million.

IPS represents the "hard Left" in American politics. It is not just liberal but often Marxist, with some of its associates veering off to full-fledged Marxism-Leninism. IPS pictures the United States as "the most evil society in history" and blames the United States and "capitalism" for virtually all of the world's ills. It sees its own mission as liberating people from their "colonial" status and reconstructing society along socialist lines. It is against all defense measures and has consistently sided with countries hostile to the United States. Because of its activities and the suspicion that it was supported by the Soviet Union, IPS was the object of repeated FBI and Internal Revenue Service probes. In turn, IPS is suspicious of and hostile toward outsiders who make inquiries about its funding and internal affairs.

IPS reached the height of its influence during the Vietnam War protest years; some of its stalwarts even found their way into the Carter and Clinton administrations. But during the administrations of Presidents Reagan, George H. W. Bush, and George W. Bush, and the more conservative turn of the country, IPS became the think tank that time forgot—at least in Washington, although not on some college campuses. IPS was especially effective in getting its personnel invited to speak at many American colleges and universities, and while its influence on Washington policymaking is small, it does have some support among radical students and faculty.

Brookings Institution

On the moderate and eminently respectable Left is the Brookings Institution. Brookings was founded in 1927 by a St. Louis businessman, Robert Brookings, although its roots may be traced back as early as 1916. Brookings occupies a splendid building on Massachusetts Avenue in the heart of Washington, D.C.; its budget is between $20 and $30 million (ten times larger than IPS's budget), which places it right up there with the Hoover Institution and ahead of any of the other Washington think tanks. Brookings became famous largely on the strength of its economics "faculty," who were champions of Keynesian economics as early as the 1950s and whose viewpoints triumphed during the Kennedy administration. Only later did Brookings begin to expand its foreign policy activities, focusing on nuclear strategy, the Middle East, and general foreign policy issues.

Over the years Brookings has moved steadily toward the center. That is where the money to support its research is and where the bulk of public opinion lies. Brookings had for a time a Republican president and a Republican vice president, is recruiting more centrist scholars, and raises the bulk of its money from the same corporate sources as do the more conservative think tanks. Its current president is former journalist and Clinton administration official Strobe Talbott. Brookings has moved away from a strong ideological posture, and its foreign policy activities and publications are also serious, scholarly, and middle-of-the-road. Most observers, in fact, have not seen very many ideological differences in recent years between Brookings's foreign policy positions and those of the Center for Strategic and International Studies (CSIS). But as Brookings moved to the center, a hole opened on the liberal Left.

Former Clinton administration chief of staff John Podesta filled it by organizing a new think tank, the Center for American Progress, built on money from financial guru George Soros. Podesta recruited scholars and political activists from IPS as well as the left wing of the Democratic Party. It aimed to unseat President George W. Bush in the 2004 election. But Bush won; Democratic Party candidate John Kerry lost; and, thus, in the absence of a track record of producing serious policy studies, the future of this new think tank is uncertain.

Center for Strategic and International Studies

The CSIS was founded in the early 1960s as a foreign policy offshoot of the American Enterprise Institute by two of its former associates—Richard Allen, who was President Reagan's first national security advisor, and David Abshire, who later became an ambassador and presidential troubleshooter. CSIS was different from the other Washington think tanks (and more like the Mershon Center or Hoover Institution) in that from the beginning it was associated with one of Washington's leading universities, Georgetown. But the relations between Georgetown and CSIS steadily worsened (the Georgetown faculty was more liberal and faculty members were seldom brought in on the more lucrative research opportunities available at CSIS) until in 1987 they formally separated, a divorce that was probably detrimental to both institutions.

For a long time CSIS had only a limited staff and resources, but in the 1980s and 1990s it steadily grew until its budget reached $20 million. The affiliated staff includes a number of highly visible foreign policy specialists of Cabinet-level rank: Henry Kissinger, Harold Brown, James Schlesinger, and Zbigniew Brzezinski. CSIS, unlike Brookings, has only a limited endowment and must raise virtually all of its operating funds every year, and therefore the staff often spends upward of 70 to 80 percent of its time raising money for its various projects. Despite this time spent in money-raising, the CSIS staff still manages to produce an impressive amount of research and publications.

CSIS has been aggressively courting larger donors and expanding its seminar, publication, and outreach activities. It stands for a "realist" position in foreign policy, which probably defines it as centrist and somewhat conservative. Its foreign policy positions are not all that much different therefore from the AEI—at least until recently.

The American Enterprise Institute

The American Enterprise Institute for Public Policy Research was founded in 1943 as an advocacy agency for free enterprise; it later emerged as a full-fledged but still conservative think tank. During the 1950s, when Brookings took up the Keynesian cudgels, AEI remained committed to a free market approach. It is largely because of their orientation toward the role of government in the economy (broad for Brookings, limited for AEI) that Brookings was baptized the "liberal" think tank and AEI the "conservative" one. For a long time, in fact, AEI and Brookings were the two major (and virtually only) think tanks in Washington; both of them had large budgets approaching $30 million by 2005.

In the 1970s and 1980s, AEI began to build up its foreign policy staff to match its already stellar economics staff. It concentrated on defense policy, NATO, general foreign policy, Latin America, and the Middle East. The foreign policy staff was made up largely of centrists, liberal Republicans, moderates, and serious scholars. Although there continued to be differences between AEI and Brookings in their economic policy recommendations, in the foreign policy field AEI's research products were hardly distinguishable from those of Brookings and CSIS.

But that is what turned out to be precisely the problem for AEI. By the mid-1980s, AEI was in serious financial trouble. It was deeply in debt and plagued by major management problems. Some donors complained that, with its increasingly centrist and pluralist foreign policy orientation, AEI had lost its mission and sense of purpose. In addition, AEI was outflanked on the right by the aggressive Heritage Foundation, which began to draw the conservative money that used to go to AEI. Its budget shrank to $8 million, and its president was fired.

In a series of purges in the 1980s and 1990s, AEI let go or pensioned off almost its entire foreign policy staff. In their place it hired a number of neoconservatives. Some analysts feel that AEI's foreign policy team is presently even more conservative than that of the Heritage Foundation, which has long been thought of as the major think tank on the political Right. Meanwhile, AEI's research productivity and publications, and its reputation as a major center for foreign policy research and influence, plummeted as well—until it regained influence under President George W. Bush.

Heritage Foundation

The Heritage Foundation is a relative newcomer among the leading Washington think tanks. It is also the most conservative. Founded in 1973 by two former congressional aides, Edward Feulner and Paul Weyrich, Heritage represented the far Right or most conservative wing of the Republican Party. A number of its early leaders and associates had been part of Barry Goldwater's losing presidential campaign in 1964, and they sought to keep the conservative flame alive. By the mid-1970s, they had become followers of Ronald Reagan, later of George W. Bush.

Heritage's initial funding came from wealthy sponsors like Joseph Coors, the beer manufacturer. It also tapped into "the movement," the large number of ideologically committed conservatives in the United States. Alone among the think tanks it used direct mailings to raise funds among small donors— 130,000 persons who give perhaps $10 or $25 per year.

Heritage grew slowly in the 1970s but expanded meteorically in the 1980s when its man, Reagan, was elected president. It vastly expanded its staff to about 120, bought its own building on Capitol Hill, and began a vigorous program of seminars and publications. Its *Mandate for Leadership* volume provided a blueprint of policy proposals for the Reagan and Bush administrations and, like the Hoover Institution and AEI, twenty to thirty of its personnel went into each of these administrations. As a kind of clearinghouse for young committed conservatives of "the movement," Heritage found jobs for many others hot off the college campuses and eager to serve.

Heritage also benefited from the decline of AEI during this period. The foundation had staked out a frankly conservative position to the right of AEI and began to attract more and more of the conservative financial support that had previously gone to AEI. Moreover, it was noticeable that after the mid-1980s, when foreign ministers, heads of state, and other visiting dignitaries came to town, they often went to Heritage to visit or hold a seminar. That was a measure of the fact that their embassies in Washington had adjudged Heritage to be a rising and influential power in the Reagan and Bush administrations.

Heritage is still viewed by the other think tanks as often superficial and a Johnny-come-lately, however. It is seen as more of a lobbying organization committed to advancing its own policy agenda than a serious research institution. Unlike the other think tanks, Heritage has hired few academic stars, but lots of ambitious young people whose scholarly credentials are not yet established and whom it therefore does not have to pay very much. They are worked very hard producing what the other think tanks refer to derisively as "instant analyses"—hastily prepared reports culled from newspaper files that Heritage can place on the desks of congresspersons within twenty-four hours. Many of these reports are heavily loaded ideologically and politically. For that reason, Heritage's research products in the past have had a dubious reputation among scholars. But it should be recalled that Heritage's main purpose has not been to produce original research; rather, it wants to shape and influence the policy debate, and by that measure it has been phenomenally successful.

In many ways, sad to say, and although scholars have not yet faced up to this reality, the fact is that most congresspersons and their aides, as well as journalists, White House officials, and policy makers in the executive agencies, do not have the time to read the weighty, scholarly tomes that independent researchers or Brookings or AEI prepare. What Heritage does successfully is to produce short, pithy papers on very short notice that tell too-busy congresspersons and their aides how they should vote. Congresspersons and other policy makers cannot be expected to be informed on the complex details of all the issues that come their way, so the brief, direct, and straightforward Heritage papers and recommendations are often a godsend to them.

While AEI and Heritage have long dominated the conservative side of the political spectrum, the Cato Institute has recently emerged as a major influence as well. Cato is the libertarian think tank, and for a long time its policy pronouncements were not taken very seriously. But now the country is more conservative; Cato's research reports have also improved greatly. On foreign policy it is against most U.S. alliances (like NATO) and in favor of free markets and free trade. Cato's foreign and defense policy analyses are now taken seriously by Washington policy makers.

HOW THINK TANKS EXERCISE INFLUENCE

How do think tanks go about exercising their influence? Why do their books and studies have an influence on policy while so many of the studies produced by academic scholars do not?

Let us take the second question first. So many books and studies are being produced on so many foreign policy subjects these days that even scholars cannot keep up with the writings on their country, area, or issue of expertise. Government officials, who are very busy and do not usually have the academic background in a field that scholars have, are far less able to keep up. So they pick and choose very carefully what they read.

Also, there is a pecking order, a set of presumptions about who or what is worth reading. Whether it is a mistaken presumption or not, the fact is that the scholars who inhabit the Washington think tanks—especially Brookings, CSIS, and AEI—are presumed to be at the top of their fields, higher even than the Ivy League institutions. Parenthetically, we should say that in actuality such a rank order is probably exaggerated, that a good university department is probably as strong in terms of its research as the contingent of scholars at any of the leading Washington think tanks. But in Washington and in the country-at-large, it is often thought that the think tanks represent the top rung. And, of course, in this area as in so many others, what people think is often as important as what really is. So if you're a too-busy government official with only limited time to read, where do you turn first? The answer is, to the think tanks, because that's where it's believed the real expertise lies. And because you often know personally the people involved.

How do the think tanks actually go about influencing policy? There are several methods, and the think tanks have become very adept and clever at getting their research products and message out there.

1. Lunches, seminars, dinners. Virtually every day the think tanks have programs on one subject or another. To these meetings are invited congresspersons and their aides, White House and State Department officials, journalists, and other opinion leaders. Not only are the food and drinks free, but if you are a policy maker and don't attend, you might miss something and then someone else will be one-up on you. Usually these forums offer an opportunity for scholars from the think tanks to showcase their ideas or a new study that they have just produced. For example, at AEI, lunches and seminars on the Middle East were de rigueur for persons wanting to have a say or influence policy on that area.

2. Television and media. Think tank scholars regularly appear on such programs as *Nightline*, *The NewsHour*, CNN, FOX, or the evening news. They are not necessarily better informed than scholars in Berkeley or Ann Arbor, but they are known to the media programmers; their offices in Washington are practically next to the television studios; and it does not cost the networks anything to bring them in compared with flying their own crews out to some college campus. For many of those same reasons, think tank scholars are often quoted in the press.

3. Public appearances. Think tank scholars have virtually daily opportunities (if they wish) to speak before college and university audiences, seminars and forums, professional associations, State Department or other training programs, foreign exchange groups, or the audiences of fellow think tanks. This exposure makes them well known nationally and even internationally; hence, at some future time when a policy maker is looking for someone to give advice, he will most likely call on the speaker he heard at one of these forums.

4. Access to policy makers. Think tank scholars have direct access to policy makers. They are in the White House, the State or Defense Departments, and other government agencies for meetings on, again, a virtually every-

day basis. Because of the presumption noted earlier that they represent the top ranks of scholars, think tank personnel are able to get through doors and see people where others are not able to do.

5. Congressional testimony. Think tank scholars often know personally the congressional staffers who schedule hearings, or are known to those staffers. Hence, when a committee or subcommittee is looking for testimony on a particular subject, it will usually call on persons from the think tanks. Also, since Congress is itself a very partisan institution, its members know that by calling on representatives of the several think tanks they can get testimony that supports the conclusions they have already reached, which is always comforting to congresspersons.

6. Advisory panels. Think tanks have high-level advisory panels for virtually all their programs. These consist of outside persons, usually prominent in the worlds of business, banking, and industry. In this way the think tanks can list many more important persons of wealth and influence on their letterheads and in their annual reports. These same persons help them raise funds and get their studies into the right hands.

7. Personal contacts. Think tank scholars, because of their presence in Washington, ordinarily have a vast range of personal contacts. These include not only fellow scholars from other think tanks and the universities, but also journalists, government officials, business executives (who often sit on the boards of directors of the think tanks), labor officials, foundation heads, representatives of foreign governments, and so forth. The range of people with whom think tank scholars come in personal contact is far broader and at a much higher level than that of most university-based academics. Think tank scholars are able to take advantage of these contacts to get their message across.

8. Government experience. The think tanks are prime recruiting grounds for new government talent. Many longtime think tankers have gone in and out of government service several times. They go in when their preferred party comes to power and back to the think tanks when the other party is in power. There are few things more heady for think tank scholars than a chance to put the ideas they have been writing about and nurturing for so long into actual practice in government. And, of course, because they are already in Washington, are well connected, and have probably signed up to be on one or another of a presidential candidate's advisory teams far in advance, their chances of getting an interesting position at State, the National Security Council, or another agency are far greater than those of a university scholar who may be just as knowledgeable on the issues.

9. Studies and publications. The think tanks are very good at getting their products out to where they are read and paid serious attention. They

maintain vast and highly specialized mailing lists that are constantly up-dated and that enable them to reach quickly virtually every well-known person in the country on any particular issue. They have publications and public relations offices that prepare press releases about the study, or-ganize press conferences for a new book, do summaries that then appear on the op-ed pages in leading newspapers, get their authors on the talk shows, and send out endless free copies. After all, no study will have in-fluence unless important people read it. The think tanks have facilities for bringing their scholars' work to the attention of opinion leaders and decision makers. On Central America policy, for instance, the workings of CSIS and AEI scholars were important in returning the Reagan ad-ministration to a more moderate and centrist position. Quite a number of these scholars even have their own syndicated newspaper columns.

An informal but useful way to measure the influence of the think tanks (or of other scholarship) is the following. Government runs, in part, on the basis of memos. If a State Department or Defense Department official or an analyst at the CIA or the National Security Council has your study in front of him and open at the time he is writing his own memo to the sec-retary or the director or perhaps the president himself—if, in short, he is using your ideas and analysis at the time he writes his own memo—then you have influence. If your study is not open in front of him or, worse, you do not even know who the responsible official is, you do not have influ-ence. It is as simple as that.

THINK TANK DYNAMICS

If you are a scholar, think tanks are very nice places to work. They are like universities in their dynamism and intellectual excitement, but they have no students and, hence, no teaching obligations, very few of those endless com-mittee meetings that plague university faculties, and no heavy layers of bu-reaucracy. Despite the fact, as we know, that most professors love their stu-dents, with no teaching, no committees, and no bureaucracies—what, the scholars of the think tanks often ask, could be better than that?

The staff salaries at the think tanks also tend to be far higher than in col-leges or universities. There is an almost unlimited photocopy, postage, and long-distance telephone budget. Think tank scholars have research assistants (often several of them) and usually a private secretary. The larger think tanks have their own dining facilities, kitchen staff, editorial and publications staff, conference and travel staff, administrative staff, and fund-raising offices. It is far easier to be a productive scholar when all these facilities are at your dis-posal and when a friendly editor is right down the hall. Think tanks are nice places for student interns, too.

But there are some drawbacks as well—although on balance the benefits seem to greatly outnumber the disadvantages. Foreign policy issues in Washington (Korea, the Middle East, India–Pakistan) are very fickle; they often rise and fall with the headlines; and there is no permanent tenure at the think tanks. For example, one of the think tank presidents justified the expansion of Latin America programs at his institute by referring to Central America as a "growth industry." Crudities aside, this means it was great for the scholars in that program as long as Central America was seen as a critical policy arena; but once the attention had passed on to other issues—Iraq, Iran, Afghanistan—the program and the scholars associated with it could expect to be cancelled.

Some scholars will also feel uncomfortable doing public policy research (as distinct from value-free research), since public policy research is almost inevitably partisan, political, and somewhat one-sided. In addition, there is a growing tendency within the think tanks for management, not the individual scholars, to decide what topics are to be researched. The scholars may also be required to do fund-raising, an activity with which some of them may feel uncomfortable, and the management system in most think tanks tends to be top-down rather than grassroots and participatory as in most universities. And, as in most Washington agencies, the public relations officials tend to have more say than their talents or abilities would seem to indicate—sometimes more power in their think tanks than do the scholars.

Now let us turn to the issue of think tank influence in different administrations. If we position the main think tanks on a political spectrum, the picture will look something like this:

Far Left	Moderate Left	Center	Moderate Right	Far Right
IPS	Brookings	CSIS	AEI	Heritage

If we next consider which of the think tanks have influence (measured in terms of receptivity to their ideas or the number of scholars who enter government) in a liberal-Democratic (Carter, Clinton) administration, the loop would look something like this:

Far Left	Moderate Left	Center	Moderate Right	Far Right
IPS	Brookings	CSIS	AEI	Heritage

That means that, within a liberal-Democratic administration, Brookings will occupy the center, CSIS the right, and IPS will be given a few positions on the far left. AEI and Heritage will be excluded; however, AEI will be thought of as the "responsible opposition" and Heritage as "far out"—too far to have any influence at all.

In a conservative-Republican administration (Reagan, George W. Bush), the loop of influence will look as follows:

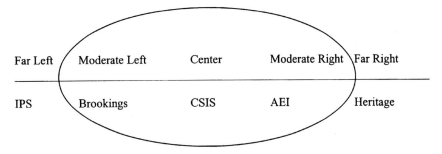

Note that here AEI is the center, CSIS the left, and Heritage the right. Brookings is now thought of as the "responsible opposition" and IPS thought of as the "nuts," the "bomb throwers," or worse.

In a centrist administration (Ford, George H. W. Bush, Johnson), the loop would look like this:

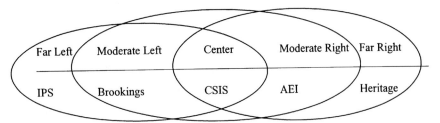

Thus, CSIS becomes the center, AEI the right, and Brookings the left. IPS and Heritage are both excluded from influence in such a centrist administration.

Now, finally, if we superimpose these three loops, we also see some interesting things:

Note that, as in a multiparty political system, the "party" of the center, CSIS, has influence in all administrations—just because it is in the center. AEI and Brookings have power in two-thirds of the cases and are thought of as being influential even when their favorites are out of power. On opposite sides of the political spectrum, the situations of IPS and Heritage are also analogous: two-thirds of the time they are out of the loop and not taken very seriously. It takes special circumstances for either of these two more radical think tanks to exercise power: a sharp swing to the left of the Democratic Party to bring IPS into influence, and a sharp swing to the right of the Republican Party to bring Heritage to power. There is a political science maxim in all of this and that is that the center groups have power all of the time (usually out of proportion to their actual vote or strength), the moderately partisan or ideological groups have influence most of the time, and the radical elements are chiefly left out in the cold. Democratic politics and pluralism of necessity mean centrist politics.

This configuration and these loops of influence should not be thought of as immutable, however. The power and influence of these think tanks rise and fall. For a long time Brookings and AEI, the two great liberal and conservative antagonists (the "thinking man's think tanks," as they were sometimes called) had the field pretty much to themselves. Then along came IPS and CSIS in the 1960s and Heritage in the 1970s. All of the "big five" seemed for a time to be booming in terms of larger staffs, more activities, and ever larger budgets. But IPS seemed to suffer a precipitous decline; AEI went into a downward slide from which it has since recovered; and CSIS has also had intermittent budget difficulties.

In the meantime, a variety of new think tanks, like CATO and the Center for American Progress, stand ready in the wings, hoping for a growth spurt in funding or a new idea that will propel them to prominence. Other smaller, more specialized think tanks may also have influence on particular issues.

THINK TANK FUNDING

The question we raise in this section is the degree to which the sources of think tank funding bias the research work and product that come out.

Few of the think tanks raise much money "democratically"—that is, from the general public. Among the big think tanks, only Heritage has been able to develop and use effectively the device of direct mass-mail solicitations. But, of course, Heritage appeals to a special ideological clientele, persons who have strong conservative views and support the foundation with small donations.

"Contract research" is another touchy matter. Brookings and CSIS accept a limited amount (about 15 percent of their budgets) of contract work from the government. But AEI has consistently turned down all contract work because it wants to maintain complete independence in deciding what topics to research and because it fears its research will be tainted if it agrees to accept government money.

Among the think tanks, only Brookings has a large endowment—that is, money donated to the institution with the understanding that it will be invested and only the earned interest will be used to fund current projects. Its large endowment makes Brookings virtually immune to ups and downs in other forms of giving. All of the other think tanks are trying similarly to build up a sizable endowment, but this requires time and the careful cultivation of large donors.

Support from the major foundations is also important for the think tanks, accounting for about 20 percent of their budgets. The think tanks tend to draw support from like-minded foundations according to ideological criteria: the more liberal Ford, Rockefeller, Mellon, and MacArthur foundations give mostly to Brookings and sometimes to IPS and CSIS, while the more conservative Scaife, Pew, Olin, Bradley, and Smith Richardson foundations give chiefly to AEI and Heritage. This pattern of ideologically based giving is clear, even though by their charters—to say nothing of the tax laws—the foundations are supposed to be "nonpolitical."

The biggest source of support for the think tanks is private business and business foundations. Such gifts are, of course, tax exempt. Upward of 60 to 70 percent of the several conservative think tanks' support comes from business's largesse because those are the think tanks most in accord with business's point of view. But now even the liberal Brookings is raising more and more of its money from the business sector, which is also having the effect of drawing its ideology more toward the center. IPS is antibusiness and anticapitalism, so it does not attract much support from big business, but it does get funds from some of the sons, daughters, and grandchildren of the earlier scions of industry who, although very rich, are often committed to capitalism's demise.

The relationship between the think tanks and big business is changing, however. First, there is an increasing tendency for business firms and foundations to designate their gifts for specific research projects rather than for general budgetary support as they had done in the past, thus muddying the distinction between contract and noncontract research. Second, the tax laws have changed, making it less attractive for companies to give money to the think tanks. And third, there is a tendency among business firms to give more money to local charities (the opera, the orchestra, parks, playgrounds, educational opportunities) and thus get back immediate credit for their generosity in their own "neighborhoods" rather than to give it to the think tanks where the returns are not so immediate or so obvious.

Above and beyond these issues is the question of bias. If so many of the think tanks are so heavily dependent on big business for such a large share of their support, doesn't that necessarily bias their research products? Money does talk, after all. And so the answer is "yes," but not in blatant and obvious ways. That is, none of the larger think tanks is really a lobbyist for big business, nor can business really "buy" a research result that it desires. But at the same time all the major think tanks (IPS is the exception, and it has little influence) tend to champion open, market, capitalist economies and to be suspicious of, if not in some cases hostile to, statism and central planning—all of which serves the interests of big business. While they do not lobby for specific business interests, the think tanks do refrain from criticizing big business and provide an overall intellectual climate in which business can flourish. Indeed, one can explain the Brookings Institution's move toward the ideological center as a reflection of its efforts to attract business financial support.

CONCLUSION

The analysis presented in this chapter tends to confirm the hypotheses with which we began:

1. Power in foreign policy has shifted from New York to Washington.
2. It has shifted from the Wall Street bankers and lawyers who were in the Council on Foreign Relations to the scholars and academic professionals who inhabit the think tanks.
3. It has shifted from an older to a newer generation.
4. It has shifted from middle-of-the-roaders to much more ideological and politicized analysis in the think tanks.

This last point especially deserves elaboration because it relates to a more general point raised in this book: The Council on Foreign Relations was an agency of bipartisan consensus in an earlier time, but the think tanks tend to be partisan and fragmented. They range up and down the political spectrum, from extreme Left to extreme Right. Hence, the think tanks have become still one more set of agencies contributing to our foreign policy fragmentation and divisiveness. The point should not be exaggerated, since the several major think tanks often work together on various projects; their scholars tend to be personal as well as professional friends who attend each other's conferences; and at least among AEI, Brookings, and CSIS—the more centrist tanks— there has long been a considerable degree of consensus, especially in the foreign policy area. But at present even this may be changing.

Hence, we are left with a situation in which, instead of the single, bipartisan, consensual voice on foreign policy that we once had, five major and hundreds of minor think tanks are competing for attention and trying to get their viewpoints across. This has led often to a more contentious, more partisan and ideological, and more fragmented and polarized foreign policy debate. The older unity has broken down and in its place has come a myriad of rival, often squabbling, voices. The think tanks have been both a reflection and a further agency of this greater divisiveness and disarray. This divisiveness will undoubtedly continue, even though under recent administrations an effort was made to recruit centrist foreign policy advisers and the influence of the Council on Foreign Relations seems once more to be on the rise.

The think tanks represent a whole new range of voices on foreign policy; in recent years they have also become very influential, providing ideas and publications as well as feeding their people directly into important government positions. At the same time their influence, while considerable, should not be exaggerated. The think tanks are only one of a great variety of sources (interest groups, political parties, and many others) that feed options, information, policy positions, and people into the U.S. government. Nevertheless, the think tanks have the power in some cases to alter perspectives, affect policy decisions, and exercise direct influence. They help define the boundaries of public policy debate; they offer agendas and options; they confirm changes already afoot in some areas and lead them in others; they catalyze and popularize new ideas; they help bridge the policy gaps between the executive and legislative branches and among a variety of agencies; they also bridge the gap between academic and Washington research; they are effective in formulating the position papers between administrations; and they serve to educate the media, congressional staffers, policy makers, and the general public. These are all important functions and, hence, in the shifting kaleidoscope of influences that is our foreign policy, the think tanks have assumed a major role.

Chapter Five

The Washington Social Circuit
and Foreign Policy

Not all of Washington policymaking takes place within or through formal political institutions, of course. We know that such institutions as political parties, interest groups, think tanks, Congress, and the presidency all have an important influence on policy, including foreign policy. These are some of the main institutions that our laws and Constitution, as well as the textbooks that we read, designate or point to as key actors in the policymaking process.

But all of us know, deep down, that the process also works through other, less formal means. The formal institutions are important, to be sure, but they are not the only way that foreign policy influence is exercised. Also important are the informal contacts, the lunch and dinner get-togethers, the social networks, the interpersonal relations, the clans, cliques, and friendships that Washingtonians maintain. Some would maintain that these informal gatherings are as important as—or even more important than—the formal institutions. We cannot here resolve that issue once and for all, but we can say that most Washington insiders tend to believe that *both* the formal institutions and the informal contacts are useful and therefore take considerable pains to cultivate both.

The present chapter serves as a beginning guide to some aspects of the social scene in Washington, D.C. It contains some gossip, some travel information, and some tips about Washington social life. Some readers may feel that the treatment of these informal aspects is too breezy, reads too much like a travelogue, or treats serious subjects (foreign policy) at the level of party gossip. But in fact: (1) a great deal of *serious* foreign policy discussion *does* take place at this informal level; and (2) a great deal of Washington political life, including foreign policy, *does* revolve around gossip and interpersonal relations, as well as parties and informal get-togethers. This is not a chapter on foreign policy as it might be taught by a society columnist, but it does suggest that the Washington social circuit is far more important as a *serious* subject for discussion of how the foreign policy process works than most books have been willing to acknowledge.

WASHINGTON, D.C., AS A CITY

Until the 1960s, Washington was considered a bit of a provincial southern capital. The real centers of power and influence in the United States were New York, Boston, Philadelphia, Chicago, and, eventually, Detroit and Los Angeles, but not Washington, D.C. Washington was a small town by comparison with these others, with little to recommend it: little industry, little commerce, little banking, no stock market, limited power. In addition, the climate is terrible (steamy, muggy) in the summer; before the widespread use of air-conditioning, Washington and its institutions (Congress, the Supreme Court, the presidency) used to close down in June, flee to cooler climes, and resume again in the fall.

While Washington was and is a southern city, it is also a city of enormous contradictions. It has a large middle class, consisting chiefly of persons employed by the government or by government-related private organizations, but it also is a city of enormous poverty, with a large underclass. Some of its African Americans are well off and highly educated, but Washington also has large ghettos within sight of the Capitol where poverty and malnutrition are present. Washington, the capital of the greatest and freest nation on earth, is also a center of grinding poverty in which over half the population may still be subject to racial discrimination.

Nor did Washington have in these earlier days much in the way of a cultural life—no opera, one theater (the National), and a poor orchestra. However, it did have excellent chamber music and, since the 1920s, the truly great museums built along the Mall. The restaurants were not very distinguished nor was there much in the way of international cuisine. Educational excellence was concentrated in the prestige universities of Philadelphia, New Jersey, New York, and Cambridge, not in Washington. Real money and social status were similarly concentrated in these other centers—Boston's Beacon Hill, New York's Park Avenue, Philadelphia's Main Line, Grosse Pointe outside Detroit, and Lake Forest outside Chicago. Washington was not a center of wealth or a very impressive social life. Elite social life was active but dominated by old families and less easily penetrated by newcomers and outsiders than today. And by international standards, Washington as a capital could hardly compare with London or Paris.

Even politicians did not stay in Washington any longer than they had to. They looked on Washington as a temporary assignment, not a place to live. Often they stayed in downtown hotels like the Willard or the Mayflower, and left their families in their real homes in their congressional districts. They got out of Washington as soon and as often as possible; few thought of settling permanently in the city once their period in office was over.

But now all this has changed, making Washington one of the most attractive places to live in the entire country—if not *the* most attractive. Washington has even better museums than before and, by now, a rich cultural life. Its theater and music are outstanding. Air-conditioning has made it livable all year round. Many areas of the city feature beautiful parks and stunning architecture. Washington now has many fine restaurants; the underground Metro system is superb; and condos and apartments abound, although housing is very expensive.

There is now real wealth in Washington to rival and surpass that of other cities. The government, the think tanks, as well as the Washington universities have made it one of the nation's main centers of intellectual life—maybe *the* main center. Because its economy is diversified and intimately tied to government, which continues to grow even with antigovernment conservatives (Reagan, Bush) in the presidency, Washington—unlike Detroit or Houston, for example—is virtually recession-proof. Despite these positive changes, however, Washington remains a city where there is widespread poverty, oftentimes tense race relations, a high crime rate, and social conditions that are sometimes akin to those in less-developed nations.

There is an aura of power about Washington that is especially attractive to persons interested in public policy. Washington is, after all, where government authority and decision making in the United States are concentrated. It is, in many ways, a wonderful place to live: vibrant, alive, exciting, stimulating. Every summer thousands of our best college and university graduates flock to Washington, looking for both personal advancement and an opportunity to serve. The social, intellectual, and, of course, political life is virtually nonstop. The opportunities, the capacity to exercise influence, the chance to meet new friends and interact at the highest levels are enormously attractive.

Living and working in Washington give one a sense of importance and power. The White House and Capitol Hill act like magnets to the bright and the ambitious. It is a booming, vibrant, and dynamic city. It is fun to walk down the sidewalk and cross paths with persons that before one saw only on television: former Secretary of Defense Robert McNamara hurrying to work down Connecticut Avenue, ABC newsman Sam Donaldson berating his camera crew right there on the street, or a famous congressperson who by chance shares an elevator ride with you.

Washington not only attracts thousands of young people every year, but more senior people have come to love the city and seldom go back to their old home districts once their appointments or terms in office are up. They find jobs as lobbyists or consultants and thus remain influential. They also serve as teachers of the young people coming in, showing them the ropes of how Washington works. Plus, with its abundant cultural life, its never-ending social life, and the rich network of opportunities for retired or out-of-office politicians and officials, Washington is a wonderful city in which to retire.

All these changes have made Washington a very attractive and seductive city. In addition, although now far more pluralistic than before, it remains a *Southern* city with the elaborate social graces, the importance of family connections, the clique and clan rivalries, and the informal ways of operating that are the focus of this chapter. The *Washington Post* understands the importance of all these social activities—it is often said that the real news in Washington is reported in the Style (or society) Section, not on the front pages—but our other great national newspaper, the *New York Times*, does not. The *Times* takes Washington politics deadly seriously at the policy level and in terms of the formal institutions of government, which is also where many of our early civics courses and government textbooks concentrate, but it does not cover well and often fails to understand the strenuous social life of the capital, which many are convinced is just as important as the formal institutions.

INSIDE AND OUTSIDE THE BELTWAY

The Washington Beltway is a sixty-three-mile, circular stretch of the interstate highway system that wraps completely around the District of Columbia. Inside the Beltway are located the White House, Congress, the Pentagon, the State Department, virtually all other federal government agencies, as well as the headquarters of the political parties and almost all important interest groups. This is where the seat of government power in the United States is located.

But "inside the Beltway" is more than a geographic location; it is also a metaphor, a symbol, for a whole way of thinking. Washington, D.C., although now a diverse city, is the nation's political capital. Politics remains its main "industry" (that is chiefly why people go to Washington); politics is the chief subject of conversation and for many Washingtonians is an all-important and even consuming preoccupation. It is not so much literature or art or even the Redskins football team that people talk about in Washington but politics, politics, politics. Day or night, at work or at home, socializing or just riding to work, politics is the passion and the consuming interest.

There are endless stories, rumors, and gossip to pass around and discuss. Such political talk goes on virtually nonstop. All this constant political talk is not the preoccupation in most of the country, where jobs, schools, family, and the local community are the main topics of conversation. But in Washington, politics is the main and almost only subject of conversation. That is, after all, what Washington people do, not only in their jobs but also in their lives.

People who work inside the Beltway thus have a set of understandings, jokes, stories, even a language—almost all of it focused on politics—that is all their own. That is what being "inside the Beltway" means: being "in" on all this political gossip and information, loving it, and participating in it. People who live in other parts of the country are seldom aware of all these insider jokes and stories, nor do they care all that much. Outsiders tend to believe that things in Washington do, or ought to, work the way their textbooks, their civics classes, or the Constitution says. But persons who work inside the Beltway know better: it is informal or personal connections that count as much as the formal institutions. Further, they are not always willing to share this insider information with those who live outside the Beltway. The insiders prefer to maintain their own monopoly of information and thus to keep the rest of the country, so much as that is possible in our open, democratic society, somewhat in the dark. Such secrecy, they argue, helps maintain the mythology and legitimacy of the overall system. But it also helps keep outsiders out; it enhances the power of those who *do* know how the system really works, who do know all its skeletons and secret closets; and somewhat cynically we can say that it also enhances the insiders' speaker fees.

This insiders-versus-outsiders mentality breeds certain resentments. Outsiders frequently resent it when insiders keep them in the dark and refuse to give them full information. Insiders can be rude, patronizing, and condescending to outsiders. Because of these resentments, some politicians (Jimmy Carter, Ronald Reagan, George W. Bush) choose to run *against* Washington, D.C., against the bigness, bureaucracy, and arrogance of Washington, knowing they could gain votes by this strategy. Jimmy Carter, however, maintained his hostility to Washington insiders even after his inauguration and refused to learn the ropes of how to get along in the city; it is no accident that his is usually considered a failed presidency. Reagan also ran against Washington; but once there he made his accommodation with the Washington establishment, worked and consulted with it, fit right in, and himself became a consummate Washington insider. The moral is: as a politician it is OK to run against Washington, but once you're in Washington you had better make your peace with its power centers and ways of doing things or yours will not be a successful administration. George W. Bush has mixed feelings toward Washington.

Why are these considerations so important? First, Washington does not always operate strictly by law and Constitution; informal channels are also important; and to tap these channels a new president or administration must rely on Washington insiders who do know how things work. Second, to get your agenda passed, you've got to do more than just deliver formal messages to Congress; you must socialize with them, share a bourbon at the end of the day, take time to listen to their stories, learn their personal problems and the pressures upon them. Third, a similar approach is required with the bureaucracy: you have to work with it to be successful in implementing your program, sympathize with its problems rather than just criticizing its inefficiencies, attend its functions, join the social swirl. Fourth, a successful administration also needs to cultivate the press, to be well liked, to project a favorable image—and once again socializing and becoming a Washington insider is enormously important for the success of your program. It is not by merit alone but also by the ability to get along and go along that administrations succeed or fail.

A fifth and very important reason for becoming a Washington insider and participating vigorously in the Washington social circuit is to learn new information. All those Washington parties that go on night after night (and by now, lunch after lunch and even breakfast after breakfast) are not just for the fun of it. Rather, that is where you pick up information, learn who is rising or falling in the power hierarchy, find out what kinds of pressures operate on whom, and catch up on the insider news that does not get in the papers or on the evening television broadcasts. It makes a difference to know who is falling out with whom, who is having a fight with whom and whether it's irreconcilable, who has begun a love affair with whom, who's changing to what job, who's coming to Washington and who's leaving, and what that all means. For example, if you know that a certain NBC reporter has begun an affair with a high-ranking member of the White House National Security Council (NSC) staff, not only do you expect that this will probably bias her reporting but you also begin to watch her broadcasts for insider information about the White House that only her NSC friend could have provided. All this becomes grist for the Washington gossip and informal news network, providing tidbits of information that you store in the back of your head for use at some future time.

Perhaps the differences between a Washington insider and a Washington outsider can best be illustrated as follows. Outside Washington, people tend to say that the Clinton administration did this or the Bush administration did that—as if there were a monolithic, unified, single-minded administration in office. When Washington insiders hear such blanket statements, however, their eyes tend to glaze over. They want to know if it is the White House or the State Department that is the doer, if it is Donald Rumsfeld or Richard Cheney, which *faction* in the administration, and whether that is a sign that that faction is rising or falling in power or favor. Only a Washington insider knows all these factions, who's in them, what they stand for, and where the pressure points are. And only by being *in* Washington, on the social circuit, can one have the knowledge to know all these pressure points and, more than that, what they mean and how policy operates within and through them.

It may take a year or more (depending on the level) for a newcomer to become acclimated to this Washington social circuit, get on the mailing and invitation lists, learn how the system operates and who's in it, and begin to operate effectively within it. It takes time to learn the ropes, build up one's file of phone numbers and addresses, and acquire the expertise and knowledge that make people in Washington want to invite you to their functions.

The reverse process is much quicker, however. That is, once one leaves Washington, one loses touch with "the system" very quickly. Not only does the phone ring less and the invitations come more infrequently, but one's "inside" knowledge and understanding of how things work fades rapidly as well. Even for people with long Washington experience who do understand the system in general terms, it takes only about a month away from Washington for their understanding and analyses to begin to suffer. Once they're out of the Washington circuit, they very quickly lose touch with all the details of who's rising and who's falling. Once they leave Washington, they're cut off from the Washington information network, and their analyses and judgments reflect that cutoff. One almost *has* to attend those constant receptions and dinners to stay well informed and to remain current with what is really going on in Washington beneath the surface.

That has important implications as well for scholarship and for our understanding of how American foreign policymaking works. Many books are written on foreign policymaking by persons who have not spent adequate time in Washington. These books may cover some, mainly institutional, aspects of the process well, but they often leave one dissatisfied. They frequently lack the nuance and the understanding of the details and the informal processes that are also very important in policymaking. A more complete analysis can only come from trying to blend an understanding of the more formal aspects with more informal processes. That is our intention here.

LEVELS OF SOCIAL LIFE

Washington social life—and the political news and gossip that go with it—operates at many different levels. At the highest level are the White House state dinners, often for a visiting head of state—formal, quite stiff, often glitzy affairs. These are, of course, by invitation only, usually for sixty to one hundred persons, mainly persons of wealth and/or prominence, high government officials, and a handful of experts in the visitor's country. Such dinners may be fun once or twice because it is, after all, the White House and there is a lot of pomp and circumstance involved. They are also important because they may add to your knowledge about a visiting president or his country but guarded as well and not the kind of gathering where a lot of informal conversation can go on. These are quite stylized affairs with severe limits on what one can say or do—although sometimes some of the guests may slip away for a private conversation of substance.

At the lower levels are the wine and cheese parties that college-age interns may attend. Most of these take place in private houses and apartments; but if you are a smart and ambitious intern and you work on Capitol Hill, you learn after a while which interest groups throw the best receptions and where you can get practically a full meal before you go home at night. Some interns and low-level employees on the Hill have a whole network of friends and contacts who report to each other during the day where the best receptions are going to be that evening. Sometimes congresspersons as well as the lobbyists who host them also attend these events. But congresspersons are persons of importance and they, of course, expect more than wine and cheese: they expect ham, roast beef, lobster, shrimp, and other niceties. Congresspersons also learn which interest groups or which political action committees (PACs) put on the best spreads; the interest groups, in turn, learn that, if they want to attract congresspersons and important members of the administration to their parties, they had better make quality food and drink—and lots of it—available. Important persons are often invited to several dinners and receptions every day; hence, they can afford to choose carefully among the invitations, or try to put in a brief, "political" (handshaking) appearance at several functions.

The Washington social circuit is important not only for its good food and drink (the "lubricators") but also for the rich information and gossip that are exchanged there. It is on the social circuit that you catch up with the news of the day, find out who's doing in whom, exchange ideas and impressions, establish new interpersonal relationships as well as cementing old ones, talk about programs as well as personalities, discuss how programs are faring in Congress, hear about the latest administration moves or appointments. This is also where new books are discussed, ideas evaluated, and personalities dissected. All this is essential information that every Washington mover and shaker must have. Hence, everyone who is anyone or wants to become someone *must* attend—whether such a vigorous social life is your cup of tea or not—because that is where the action is and if you're not there, your rivals and competitors will be. And as a result, they will be better informed than you.

Most of Washington social life thus takes place somewhere between the high-level glitter of the White House and the down-and-out reception with wine and cheese. It is important to remember that the kind of hosts is also changing, which similarly tells us something about Washington and the organization of power there. The analysis that follows is thus not meant simply as a set of social tips but, more importantly, as an analysis of the levels of social life, what goes on there, and how these relate to the informal channels of foreign policy.

First, let us focus on the institutions that are becoming *less* important. These are often the kinds of gatherings portrayed in movies made by producers who don't know or understand Washington. For example, embassy cocktail parties are on the way down. The embassies often have lavish food and parties (especially the Middle Eastern and some Latin American countries); but they are seen as stiff and formal and, except for a few embassies (British, French) and a few occasions, they are not viewed as places of lively conversations. These are often large and sometimes noisy affairs; but some news may be exchanged in a brief encounter, and the important guests may at times slip away to a private room for further conversation.

Washington's famed hostesses have also largely faded away. These were usually wealthy women (the stereotype is Perle Mesta), often widows of important persons, who had the money, servants, and large houses that enabled them to throw elaborate dinner parties for several score of persons. Such hostesses thrived in an earlier era (the 1950s) when Washington was still a small town and all of its important people could be fitted into one party. But the big-time hostesses have died or "retired"; the town has changed (no longer can all its movers and shakers fit into one room); few persons have servants or mansions anymore; and no longer do such gatherings attract many of the city's real powerhouses.

The famed Georgetown dinner party is also in decline. It has not disappeared and never will, but there are far fewer than there used to be. Many Washington people still entertain at intimate dinner parties (no longer necessarily in Georgetown; wealth has spread to the suburbs), but seldom at the pace of once a week or once a month as in earlier times. The size is now eight or ten people (what most dining rooms will hold) rather than twenty or more as in the past; it costs a great deal to have even that many people over on a frequent basis; spouses are unwilling or unable to spend two days cooking and cleaning in preparation; maids and cooks are in very short supply; caterers are very expensive; and most persons are too busy to do this more than a few times a year. Plus, many Washington families now consist of *two* working, professional persons, and cleaning, cooking, and entertaining thus become more difficult. It should be said that at very wealthy and high-prestige levels (the Cabinet or agency heads), small and intimate dinner parties are more frequent since these people have both money and "help," but among the majority of upper-middle-class persons who have important positions in Washington, the "Georgetown" dinner party is no longer an everyday or every week event.

Another reason for the decline in importance of the private Georgetown dinner party is that the ten-or-so most important foreign policy "wise men" who could be expected to gather at one of these dinners are no longer around. Up through the 1950s American foreign policy was dominated by a handful of experienced persons with vast backgrounds abroad and who knew each other well: Dean Acheson, George Kennan, Robert Lovett, Charles "Chip" Bohlen, John J. McCloy, Llewellen Thompson, Averell Harriman, and a few others. The nation's foreign policy expertise could not only all be gathered in one room but literally at one dinner table.

But now this has changed as well. Along with the Washington hostesses, this older generation of foreign policy generalists has passed from the scene. Foreign policy knowledge has become so detailed and specialized that it is impossible now for a half dozen men to hold it all in their grasp. Specialized knowledge as well as the elaboration of a broad framework of foreign policy has passed to the think tanks and the executive agencies. And all these persons cannot be included in a single Georgetown dinner party as was the case with the smaller corps of generalists in the old days.

Nor have government agencies picked up the slack. In an age of budget restraints, the agencies do not have surplus funds, and among the first items to be cut are their entertainment budgets. The State Department is especially known for its cheapness. At the conferences it hosts, guests must go out and buy their own coffee and doughnuts as well as their own lunches. When the State Department hosts a reception, someone else—usually a private interest organization—must usually pay for it. Nor do the CIA and Defense Department entertain lavishly, although they do at least provide coffee and doughnuts to their conference participants—and sometimes even lunch.

As individual entertaining has declined, institutional entertaining has increased. That is, in fact, where most of Washington's social life now takes place. It is no longer in the homes of the few or the wealthy but in and among some of the new Washington institutions. Here we have in mind Washington-based interest groups who, to get their message across effectively, do a lot of entertaining; the think tanks, who also have a message to deliver; the PACs; and such research cum action agencies as the Carnegie Endowment for International Peace and the Council on Foreign Relations.

One or another of these agencies holds a reception, dinner, sit-down lunch, or breakfast virtually every day. They bring together persons from the think tanks, from the administration, congresspersons and their legislative assistants, lobbyists, media people. What attracts these people is not just good food and drink but usually a presentation by a high-level policy maker, the launching of a new book or research project, a seminar or conference, or the visit of a foreign dignitary. In other words, Washington social life is intimately tied to political and policy discussions. That is what makes Washington go around: good entertainment *and* policy discussions and ideas. Just as these agencies (think tanks, PACs, research organizations, lobbying agencies) have become major new actors in the city's political life, they have also become the primary centers of social life. Moreover, with the cost of food and drink to entertain lavishly so high, only institutions (no longer individuals) can afford to put on these sorts of meetings. The power structure in Washington has changed since the 1960s, and so has its entertainment.

What happens at these events? First, there is usually a social hour or half hour. That is where you greet your friends, have a drink, and start to catch up on the news. Then usually there is a speaker, or a panel of persons dealing with a certain subject—for example, NATO or U.S. policy in the Middle East. That is often followed by dinner and more chances to converse informally. Then comes a period of questions and discussion. If it is a dinner meeting, it will usually begin at six o'clock and be over by nine o'clock. And remember, this goes on virtually every single night.

Who comes to these meetings? They are almost always by invitation only. But new members are also welcome and brought in if they are occupying positions of influence in Washington. Power, position, and influence are what count, not family background or social position. The guest lists usually include persons from the government, congresspersons, ambassadors and State Department officials, former presidential candidates, scholars and think tank personnel, lobbyists of various kinds, and journalists. It is a diverse group but often very high level, made up of highly intelligent and experienced persons, whose discussions tend to be factual and noninflammatory rather than intensely ideological. Washington insiders quickly learn, despite their political or ideological disagreements, to get along with persons of all points of view and not to insult them, because the person you insult one day may be the same person you need a favor from, or will have to work with, the next.

Even though the United States is a large country and Washington a big city, the actual number of movers and shakers in various policy fields is quite small. Everyone who counts almost literally knows everyone else who counts. For example, in the areas of Middle Eastern or Latin American affairs, the number of key policy influentials in each area is no more than sixty or seventy persons. These lists of area specialists often overlap the ranks of overall foreign policy generalists in Washington who have influence, whose number is probably not more than five hundred. That is a very small number. It means also that through these frequent social gatherings the members of the foreign policy community in Washington get to know each other very well. It is also from these ranks that the foreign policy personnel of the next administration — whatever the party — are likely to come.

These considerations return us to the broad purposes of all this social life. It is not just food, drink, gossip, and the exchange of ideas. Other important purposes are also served. For example, in these frequent informal gatherings bad ideas are often winnowed out from good ones, and solid and sensible personnel from the opposite kind. A political process is at work here by which the Washington foreign policy community sorts out people as well as programs. Persons who regularly attend these get-togethers know who would be a good person in what key government positions and who not, what ideas will work and what not. That is why, when a new administration (Clinton or Bush) comes to power after having run against Washington, and brings with it foreign policy advisers whom the Washington community does not know, Washington starts to shudder. Neither these people nor their policies have gone through the Washington winnowing process. Thus, we are likely to get all manner of inexperienced people with some "nutty" ideas — and we usually do, to the detriment of our foreign policy. But after a while, the newcomers also get acclimated to Washington's ways.

The Washington foreign policy community can be seen as an "establishment." It is centered in the think tanks, the interest groups, the journalistic community, the research agencies, and the Council on Foreign Relations as well as in the government itself. Since it is an establishment, that breeds resentment on the part of those who are not members of it. On the other hand, it is not a closed establishment and is always open to new members and new ideas. But in the winnowing process we have described, this establishment does tend to force policy back toward the middle of the road. Individuals with highly partisan or ideological points of view have to compromise with those whose assumptions are different, and the result is a tendency toward centrism in foreign policy. It is no accident that recent administrations that started off very ideologically eventually — as this foreign policy establishment reasserted itself — gravitated toward the center. Democratic politics, we have seen, is almost by definition centrist politics. By pushing foreign policy back toward the middle while also being open to new ideas, this foreign policy establishment and its web of informal interconnections perform a useful service.

WASHINGTON "FRIENDSHIPS"

If you want a friend in Washington, you should buy a dog, or so says an old adage.

Washington is a city of fickle tastes, fleeting friendships, and passing policy preoccupations. South Africa is "it" one day, Central America the next, the Middle East the third, then Japan, NATO, China, or Russia. In addition, Washington is a city of recent arrivals: few people have deep roots there or strong family ties. Most people are newcomers to Washington who migrated to the city because a job, a cause, or a political campaign brought them there. Washington is not usually where you grew up, where your strongest friendships are, where your family is, or where people accept you (warts and all) just because you are you.

Washington is a friendly city, a Southern city, a city of often gracious hospitality; but friendships there tend to be based more on your political position than on anything else. You are important for the power and position that you hold, not necessarily for your intrinsic worth as an individual. That means that friendships tend to be temporary, politically connected, and usually short-lived.

This is disconcerting to many Washington newcomers who are used to the warmth, serenity, and permanence of *real* friendships. Such newcomers, if they are elected or appointed to important positions, are often lionized at first, leading them to believe that they have many "good" friends. They are flattered, invited out to dinner often, cultivated by the press, and played up to by other persons. What such newcomers forget is that in Washington such expressions of friendship are more political than personal. People make friends with you because of the important position that you hold or the influence you are thought to wield, and not always because they genuinely like you. They like you because you are important and they need or want to get something from you—or simply to get along with you out of necessity. Genuine friendship, however, is very rare.

The acid test of real friendship in Washington comes when you fall from or lose power. *Then*, count the number of friends you have, the calls you receive, the number of persons who flatter you, the amount of attention you are paid. The answer is: almost none. Because as soon as you leave, another person will fill your position, and that person will begin receiving all the attention. Once again it is the position that is all-important, not so much the person occupying it. True friends are those who still call after you've fallen or are on the outs; but in Washington, D.C., with its emphasis on position more than person, such friendships are rare indeed.

Now this is not an altogether bad system—as long as one knows ahead of time what the givens are. But many Washington newcomers mistake the flattery that comes with their new position for genuine friendship, and they often turn bitter toward former colleagues who do not call them anymore once they no longer occupy their old posts. If one understands the givens ahead of time, however, one can avoid the bitterness that ensues after a political friendship has gone by the boards. One simply comes to accept the fact that some friendships are real, some are political, and the two types should not be confused.

OTHER CHANNELS

In addition to the parties, social circuits, and informal channels already mentioned, several other channels of influence need to be noted here. Few of these have received the scholarly attention that they deserve, but their importance makes it necessary for us to discuss them briefly even in the absence of detailed information.

One of the most important of these new influences is the large Washington law firm. Many of these firms now are home to several *hundred* lawyers (the three- or four-person partnership has largely gone by the boards) and have branches in several American cities and abroad. The fees for these Washington firms are very high, and the firm's business may exceed $100 million yearly. These are big outfits with major influence, doing important work. As the United States in recent decades has become a more legalistic and litigious nation, and as our legislation and regulations have become more complex, the role of these large firms has grown enormously. Many have clients (including governments) abroad, which means they tend to become lobbyists as well as counselors. In fact, that is one of the new features of Washington that is worth further study: the merger of lobbying and legal activities within the same gigantic firm. In one notorious case, for example, the law firm of Arnold and Porter took the lead in trying to arrange the overthrow of dictator Manuel Noriega in Panama; sometimes the firm worked with the U.S. government, but at other times it went ahead on its own. Most large Washington law firms, however, try to wield their considerable influence quietly and behind the scenes.

American (and sometimes foreign-based) interest groups are a second major informal influence. Virtually every American interest group worth its salt now has a Washington office. In addition, most foreign governments have both law firms and public relations agencies to represent them. Some of these are large organizations employing scores of persons and, as indicated, often overlapping in many complex ways with the large Washington law firms. The fact that these interest groups now concentrate far more strongly on foreign policy issues reflects the growing interdependence of the United States with other nations. Representatives of these interest groups prowl the corridors of Congress and the executive agencies, keeping track of legislation as well as new regulatory rules and interpretations that affect their or their clients' interests. Oftentimes these interest groups are better informed than the congresspersons or executive agency personnel who are supposed to keep tabs on them, and between them and their regulators a complex, symbiotic relationship has grown up. An "iron triangle" connects the interest groups, executive agencies, and congressional subcommittees. The interest groups want and require government help, while the government could not function well without these groups' expertise. Many areas of public life have thus been "privatized," while numerous private activities are carried out in conjunction with public agencies. In these ways the public and the private domains have often merged. The results of this "corporatization" of the American polity are not yet certain, but of the increasingly important role of these interest groups there should be no doubt.[1]

A third category of informal power wielders is individual operators who know Washington intimately and have a knack for getting things done, for making the wheels turn. Examples include the late Clark Clifford, the debonair lawyer who had served virtually every president since Truman; Robert Strauss, a Texas entrepreneur, lawyer, and consummate wheeler-dealer; and Joseph Califano, a former Cabinet member under Lyndon Johnson. These men are power brokers: when their (usually high-priced) clients have a problem, they know whom to call, what buttons to press, how to get the bureaucracy to move and take action. Usually these individual power brokers are lawyers, lobbyists, ex-campaign chairs, ex-congresspersons, and former high-ranking government officials—or all of these at once. They know how to "fix" things; they maintain good connections in the press and in government; and they have friends in all the important agencies whom they can turn to for assistance.

The fourth category of informal influences to be mentioned here is a catchall category. It includes patronage networks, usually government officials who brought their own former students or underlings into government with them and who maintain contact with them in the form of a system of ongoing interpersonal relationships even after they leave office. It includes alumni associations, such as the University of Michigan Alumni Association, which was particularly strong and active when one of its own, Gerald Ford, was president. And it includes other networks: women's networks, old school ties, political networks, religious connections, ethnic linkages, and the vast web of associations that is so much at the heart of American pluralist democracy.

CONCLUSION: IN FRONT OF AND BEHIND THE CURTAIN

Most Americans understand the role of the formal institutions in American politics, what the Constitution says, and the role of the president, Congress, and the political parties. Often more vaguely, they also understand that there are interest groups "out there" that similarly play a role. What is often

completely unknown to outsiders, however, is the role of informal, interpersonal connections and of the Washington social circuit. These influences
are not often reported on; they are the hardest to learn about; and many
Americans are unaware of their vast importance. For, as emphasized here,
all these social gatherings are not just fun and games; they are intimately a
part of the broader political process. As Max Friedersdorf, a former legislative assistant in the Reagan administration, once put it, "You have to go to
parties to stay informed."

The image that should be used to try to understand Washington policymaking is that of a stage in a theater production. In front of the curtain is what
we all see: the actors (president, Congress, parties, and so forth) carrying out
their roles, publicly, visibly, according to the script (the Constitution). But behind the curtain, backstage, all kinds of other things are also going on: stage-
hands and production managers running around, improvisation as some of the
actors forget or botch their lines, informal meetings by some of the actors
who are temporarily offstage, advance meetings with or phone conversations
to reviewers and critics. What goes on behind the curtain is often not at all the
same as what the public sees in front of it.

So with Washington policymaking. What goes on in front of the curtain is
visible, public, plain for all to see. But behind the curtain may lie an even
vaster range of activities: plots and counterplots, endless telephone calls, private meetings upon private meeting, snippets of usually incomplete information filtering in, and all kinds of personal and political considerations and networks coming into play. In all this, the Washington social circuit plays a
major role, for it allows policy makers to unwind at the end of the day, catch
up on the latest news, exchange stories and gossip, hear some new ideas, size
up people and policies, forge new coalitions or cement old ones. The president's life is too public for him to engage in all these activities, but his aides
certainly do—and virtually every day. In this way the Washington social circuit, which remains almost completely unstudied in the political science and
foreign policy literature, begins to acquire an importance that rivals—and
maybe even surpasses—that of the formal institutions with which we are far
more familiar.

NOTE

1. "Corporatization" here means the incorporation of the private interest groups
into the public or governmental structures, by formal or informal means, so that the
private and the public domains become virtually inseparable. For more on this subject, see Gerhard Lehmbruch and Philippe C. Schmitter, eds., *Patterns of Corporatist
Policy-Making* (Beverly Hills, CA: Sage, 1982).

Part Two

HOT GLOBAL ISSUES

Chapter Six

Ethnocentrism and Foreign Policy: Can We Understand the Third World?

The Third World, viewed collectively by regional blocs (Africa, Asia, Latin America, the Middle East) or in terms of individually important nations (Argentina, Brazil, Egypt, India, Indonesia, Iran, Mexico, Nigeria, the Philippines, Venezuela), has become increasingly important to the United States in the past fifty years and a major focus of U.S. foreign policy. Yet it is also the area that we know and comprehend the least and where American policy has produced its most notorious gaffes and failures.

The Third World has become increasingly important to us economically. We now trade more with the Third World, including the Middle East and Latin America, than with Western Europe and Japan *combined*. In addition, most of our foreign policy crises in recent years have involved the Third World: Southeast Asia, the Middle East, the Horn of Africa, Southern Africa, Central America and the Caribbean, Afghanistan, and Iraq. Militarily, politically, strategically, we now need the Third World almost as much as it needs us.[1]

The thesis of this chapter is that at the heart of our foreign policy problems in the Third World, explaining why policy so often flounders or ends up on the shoals, is a fundamental lack of understanding and empathy about the Third World and Third World areas and countries. More specifically, we suggest that at the root of our foreign policy dilemmas in these areas is a deeply ingrained American ethnocentrism, an inability to understand the Third World on its own terms, an insistence on viewing it through the lenses of our own Western experience, and the condescending and patronizing attitudes that such ethnocentrism implies. Embedded deeply in the American ethos, this ethnocentrism is part of our educational system and is reflected in the social science literature on development. It is also inherent in virtually all our policy initiatives: economic aid, military assistance, human rights and democracy, and the effort to initiate and implement agrarian reform and other social programs. The questions explored here are why this American ethnocentrism is so deeply ingrained, how that ethnocentrism affects foreign policy, and what—if anything—can be done about it.

Although the critique of American policy offered here is strong, it is meant to be nonpartisan. Both Democratic and Republican administrations have frequently exhibited the same ethnocentrism, the same appalling ignorance of Third World areas, the same patronizing and superior attitudes, the same inability to countenance models of development other than our own, and the same insistence that we know best for the Third World. At times a more liberal or a more conservative approach to development may prevail, but what is striking to longtime observers is that both these approaches derive from a uniquely American model that has but limited utility and applicability in the Third World.

These ideas are controversial and challenge numerous established beliefs and call for a fundamental reexamination of major U.S. foreign policy programs. Many such programs are so closely based on the North American-West European model of development that they are largely inapplicable in the Third World, where the conditions, culture, institutions, and practices are quite different from our own.

Not only is our own developmental model of limited relevance in these areas, but it may be downright harmful to the basic goals of U.S. policy in securing stable, functional, and friendly democratic governments. The United States must be receptive to the growth of indigenous Third World institutions, developmental models, and ways of doing things, and we must encourage such growth. There are not one or two (capitalist or Marxist, democratic or statist) but many routes to development; however inchoate, the theme of "finding our own path" is becoming universal throughout the Third World. Furthermore, it behooves the United States to comprehend, perhaps show some sympathy for—maybe even accommodate and assist—these new trends. We should not stand unalterably opposed to them or insist our way is the only way and thus be surprised and humiliatingly defeated, as in Iran, Iraq, and other countries, when our own preferred model and route to development are faced with new alternatives.

The ideas presented here are controversial not only because they challenge many deeply held assumptions of the social sciences and of our development assistance programs, but also because they seemingly run counter to many long-established American beliefs. We really believe, as a nation and a political culture, that our institutions are the best and most developed that mankind has devised, that we can export our institutions to less-favored lands, and even that we have a moral duty to do so. That missionary spirit of bringing the benefits of our civilization to the developing nations is very strong in America. It goes back to our Puritan and Judeo-Christian forebears; it was strong among the Founding Fathers who wanted to export American republican ideals to Latin America; and it is expressed in Woodrow Wilson's naive faith that we could "make the world safe for democracy." That spirit is also reflected in John F. Kennedy's Peace Corps and Alliance for Progress, in Jimmy Carter's campaign for human rights, in Ronald Reagan's effort to promote democracy and laissez-faire economic enterprise in Central America, and in George W. Bush's faith in ending tyranny and exporting democracy to the entire world. This ethos is deeply ingrained; it is of historic duration; and it crosses all partisan and ideological lines.

Another American ethos, however, is also deeply ingrained. It suggests that pragmatically we take local institutions realistically on their own terms, rather than through our own rose-colored glasses; that we respect existing institutions rather than try to sweep them away and thus create the potential for confusion and chaos; that we seek not to impose our preferred (but in their context not always entirely appropriate) ways on others; that we have some Burke-like respect for history, including other people's histories. And that finally, in accordance with this attitude, we practice a considerable degree of restraint, tolerance, and laissez-faire toward other nations' institutions—as we have long done with regard to our domestic economy and politics. We may still be able to assist in Third World areas and to suggest and even push for the democratic, free market outcomes we prefer. That can be done, however, not by imposition but only with some modesty and deference, genuinely respecting the nations and local institutions with which we deal. We can suggest and prod, but heavy-handed interventionism and an attitude that we know best or that our institutions are superior simply will no longer do in most of the Third World.

This chapter suggests that the crux of our difficulties in understanding Third World nations is our Eurocentrism—our belief that the developmental experience of Europe and North America can be repeated, even initiated (albeit belatedly) in the Third World. The models that we use, with regard to economic development, social change, or political modernization, all derive from this Euro-American experience. Hence, we are ill-equipped to comprehend other regions whose ethos, institutions, and history (Islamic, tribalist, Buddhist, Confucian, or patrimonialist in various forms) are fundamentally different from our own.

Not only do policy prescriptions based on our own developmental experience and often applied indiscriminately to Third World nations go frequently astray, but our educational system does not prepare us to grasp fully why that is so. To a considerable degree the United States remains (about 30 percent of our population, the surveys tell us) an isolationist nation, and our experience abroad or training in foreign languages and cultures is quite limited. Our educational system is based almost exclusively on the liberal arts, which, of course, means the Euro-American tradition. In this tradition we generally only touch in limited ways on the Third World. This is not to condemn a liberal arts education—far from it—but it is to note the biases that this focus builds into our understanding of the world. If the liberal arts are, as suggested here, really a Western area study, lending themselves to assumptions that have particular rather than universal application, and if those assumptions are the ones on which we base much of our development literature as well as public policy, then it is small wonder that our initiatives in the Third World so often produce unanticipated consequences. It is not just our general educational system, however, that leaves us ill-prepared to understand Third World areas, but the kind of narrow training provided our diplomats sent abroad, which is also woefully inadequate for them to comprehend the cultures, societal mores, and political dynamics of the countries to which they are sent.

The problem is not just an educational system that fails to equip us to understand non-Western areas; the problem lies deep in the American ethos and political culture. We are fundamentally a liberal, republican, and democratic nation and, with some qualifications, have always been so. The question, as posed by Louis Hartz,[2] is whether a country born free as we were—that is, without a feudal or strongly patrimonialist past—can *ever* understand other nations not so blest. The answer, unfortunately, seems to be "no," or only with great difficulty.

This chapter calls for a thorough reexamination of many social science assumptions about the way nations change and modernize, about the development literature with which a whole generation and more of scholars and foreign affairs specialists have grown up, and about the policies based on these assumptions and literature. For example, a great deal of our economic assistance program aimed at developing nations is still based, more implicitly than explicitly by now, on the 1960 book by W. W. Rostow, *The Stages of Economic Growth*,[3] which helped shape the Alliance for Progress and all subsequent U.S. aid efforts. Rostow's position was strongly reinforced in other economic and sociological writings of the time, chiefly Kennedy administration officials who had a strong hand in designing the Alliance for Progress—John Kenneth Galbraith, Robert Heilbroner, Lincoln Gordon, C. E. Black, Max Millikan, and Seymour M. Lipset.[4]

At this point, several decades later, the Agency for International Development (AID) is no longer quite so mesmerized by the Rostow categories, and its emphases have gone through various ups and downs: infrastructure growth, community development, basic human needs, sustainable develop-ment, civil society, and the like. But what is striking is the degree to which the Rostowian assumptions still hold: that there are "stages" of growth; that Europe and America provide the model; that the process is inevitable, unilin-ear, universal, and irreversible. All our experience in Third World countries in the past half century, however, leads to quite different conclusions: that the process is not necessarily inevitable, that decay and disintegration as well as growth may occur; that the Euro-American experience is not global but par-ticular; that there are many routes to development and not one; that the social and political concomitants that are supposed to follow from economic growth do not, in fact, often follow; and that our experience is only of limited utility for the rest of the world.[5] Hence, we have this curious situation where the old assumptions no longer hold, yet policy continues to be based in large part on them because of both bureaucratic and intellectual inertia and because we can find no suitable substitute.

This chapter suggests that foreign policy toward the Third World in virtu-ally all its aspects requires a fundamental reexamination. One can go down the list of U.S. policy initiatives, literally from top to bottom, and find that virtually all items are based on a Euro-American model of dubious applica-bility in the Third World. This is not to say one should be against all these policies but only that their assumptions need to be reexamined, their rele-vance and prospects for success carefully weighed, and, where necessary, changes introduced.

Agrarian reform, for example, is based on the model of a medium-sized, middle-class, family-based, civically conscious yeoman farmer that may still apply in rural Wisconsin but seems of limited usefulness in Latin America. Our efforts to instill professionalism in many Third World armed forces are also based on an American model, one of strict segregation between the civil-ian and the military spheres, which simply does not apply in most Third World nations. Community development has been superimposed on highly centralized code-law countries where the entire history has been to look to the central government for direction. The model of labor relations brought by the AFL-CIO to the Third World is based on a U.S. framework of nonpolitical collective bargaining that applies only partially in these other areas.[6]

The list of wrong, misleading, and ethnocentric assumptions can easily be expanded. Much of our economic assistance derives from the idea that greater affluence will lead to a larger middle class and that this new middle class will be moderate and pragmatic just like our own. The evidence, however, indi-cates that the middle classes in Latin America and elsewhere behave and act differently from that in the United States and are not likely to be a bastion of stability, democracy, and progress. Our efforts to forge a strong human rights policy in recent years, however laudable, have been based wholly on Western criteria and definitions, which are not always universally accepted except in a ritualistic sense and which do not convey the same meanings or hold the same importance in many Third World nations. Likewise, our recent efforts to export democracy are grounded entirely on U.S.-European understandings and institutional forms of democracy. Even terms like *capitalism*, *private enterprise*, and the like carry connotations in Japan, as well as in many Third World areas, quite different from our own.[7]

Understandably, we may have to use these terms politically in very simplified form because that is how policy proposals are able to get public support and pass Congress. But such usage often involves a trap as well. Let us take U.S. policy toward Mexico or Pakistan as an example. We are in favor of democracy in these countries, not only because it is intrinsically good but also because that helps the administration defuse congressional opposition and gain popular support for its policies. The trap for policy, however, is that our democracy agenda may not work, democracy may be overthrown; it may lead to instability; and we may have to face the reality of another repressive authoritarian regime. But if our democracy efforts fail or if democracy is overthrown, we might still have to support the succeeding government, however undemocratic or repressive, because our nation's interests are affected. Favoring democracy is thus both an opportunity and a potential trap for policy. My own view is that we can favor a strong human rights policy and a policy in support of democracy, but that we must be very sure of what we are doing, accept the requirement to adapt our categories and prescriptions to particular Third World situations, and recognize the need to exercise restraint, prudence, and considerable forbearance in these matters.[8]

The proposal put forth here is that we must not only adapt our Euro-American models and understandings to quite different Third World contexts, but that the models derived from our Western experience and used in part are not universal. They have limited applicability in the Third World. Hence, we must be prepared to accept and deal with an Islamic model and social science of development, an African model and social science of development, a Confucian model, a Latin American social science of development, and so on. At the least we need to be very careful in suggesting what of the Euro-American experience of change is universal and what is not. More ambitiously, we need to know whether we can blend and reconcile what is useful, relevant, and *global* in the Western experience with the newer ideologies and developmental formulas, largely indigenous, originating in the Third World. The Frank Sinatra-like cry of "Let us do it our way" is virtually unanimous in the Third World, and the insistence by these nations on fashioning their own models of development and democracy—as well as our response to this—is likely to be the next great frontier in policy and the social sciences.

THE ETHNOCENTRISM OF THE SOCIAL SCIENCES

Western modernization has been accompanied throughout by a particular intellectual construction of that experience, prompted by moral or reforming impulses often presented in the guise of scientific generalizations.

—Reinhard Bendix

The proposition advanced here is that the vast bulk of our social science findings, models, and literature, which purport to be universal, are, in fact, biased, ethnocentric, and not universal at all. They are based on the narrow and rather particular experiences of Europe (actually a much smaller nucleus of countries in central and northwest Europe) and the United States, and they may have little or no relevance to the rest of the world. A growing number of scholars, particularly those who have had long research experience in the so-called developing nations, have now come to recognize this fact. Among others, new efforts are being made to reexamine the very "Western" experience on which so many of our social science "truths" and models have been based. Because these verities are still widely believed, however, by many scholars and policy makers alike, the ethnocentric biases and assumptions undergirding them need to be examined and their implications for research and policy explored.

Not all the social sciences, of course, are equally guilty of the biases and ethnocentrism when confronting foreign cultures that we have ascribed to them. Sociology, with its universalist assumptions and the way in which most sociology departments are staffed, by subject area rather than by geographic or cultural area, seems to be the worst offender, giving rise to analysis that is often more wishful than based on the actual processes or institutions of the society or culture studied. Political science and economics may be only slightly less ethnocentric, however; and it is on these three disciplines that the following analysis concentrates. Anthropology, particularly cultural anthropology, has been more sympathetic to the need to take foreign societies on their own terms and in their own contexts rather than through the supposedly universalist perspective derived from the Western European and U.S. experience. Anthropologists, however, also have their biases and particularly as they, too, have turned to the examination of whole national systems and international links, the familiar prejudices have appeared there as well. While there are thus degrees of bias and ethnocentrism in the social sciences, itself a topic deserving further careful research, all of them seem sufficiently narrow, particular, and parochial to profit from a re-examination of their basic assumptions.

To most of us a liberal arts education is something familiar, comfortable, an integral part of our intellectual upbringing. It shapes our thinking, attitudes, and intellectual preconceptions. However much our liberal arts heritage is celebrated, we must also recognize the biases inherent in that approach. Indeed, it may be that it is the very nature of our liberal arts focus that lies at the heart of our present dilemma and of our incomprehension of Third World nations. For as now structured, liberal arts education is essentially *Western* education, the Greco-Roman and Judeo-Christian traditions and European history, from which derive a set of concepts, ethics, and governing norms and experiences that have their basis in the Western background and that may have little reference to or applicability in other global areas. Although it is understandable that those who inhabit the West should structure their educational system as an appreciation of their own history and culture, we must also recognize such training for what it is: traditional liberal arts education is essentially the original "area study" program.[9]

Our concepts of justice, fair play, good government, progress, and development are similarly Western concepts. The latter two terms imply a certain unilinearism and inevitability in the evolution of man's social and political institutions. The former three imply some shared expectations about the social and political institutions and concomitants that are supposed to follow from industrialization and economic development. So long as we could divide the world into two parts, Western and non-Western, and so long as we assumed that the non-Western world would inevitably follow the same developmental path as the West ("the developed world shows to the less developed the mirror of its own future"),[10] our social science assumptions rested easily and comfortably. By this point, however, it is abundantly clear that these conditions no longer, if they ever did, apply. The world cannot be so simply divided, and it seems obvious that the developmental experience of today's emerging nations and transitional democracies cannot repeat or mirror the experience of Western Europe. Our social science assumptions, based so heavily on the European experience therefore require close reexamination as well.

Not only are our liberal arts traditions and, hence, our social science assumptions Western, they are also based strongly on metaphorical concepts. The great danger in the present context is that we have both reified our metaphorical constructs, failing to keep clear the difference between metaphor and reality, *and* extended what are essentially Western metaphors to the rest of the world where they neither fit nor have much meaning. Concepts like progress, development, stages of growth, or modernization are metaphors, poetic devices that have some relation to reality but are not to be confused with the real thing.[11] Among AID administrators and many students of social and political change, however, development and modernization have been given real, flesh-and-blood attributes and have become measurable and quantifiable—so much so that in some writings on the subject and in many U.S. assistance programs, these concepts and the models derived from them have been treated as actually existing realities and as concrete policy programs. What are at best abstractions and ideal-type creations have been given real-life characteristics with precise indicators for their measurement.

One of the contentions here is that such concepts as development or modernization must be re-recognized for what they are: metaphors, poetic figures, shorthand tools, abstractions that have some importance in defining, outlining, or describing reality but that should not be mistaken for reality itself. Not only are they metaphorical devices with all the limitations for describing reality that implies, but they are *Western* metaphors, which may or may not (most likely the latter) have relevance to the non-Western world. Let us examine these propositions in terms of three major disciplines of particular importance, both to the study of development and to our understanding of the Western biases therein: political theory, political sociology, and political economy.

Political Theory

As offered in our usual history-of-political-thought courses and seminars, political theory, particularly as taught to an older and still influential generation of scholars and policy analysts, demonstrates all the biases previously mentioned. It is prejudiced in favor of exclusively Western perspectives; it is narrowly ethnocentric and particularistic rather than universalistic; it seeks to show a unilinear and "progressive" development toward "modernity"; it favors some theories and is opposed to others; and it has little relevance to the developing nations.[12]

Although most U.S. universities now have courses on multiculturalism and non-Western areas, political theory remains true to an older canon that is almost exclusively Western. Most political theory courses spend a week or two on the pre-Socratics and then move quickly to Plato and Aristotle. The Romans are studied chiefly for their contributions to Western law and governance. The texts and courses move then to medieval political thought and the Catholic-Christian systems of Augustine and Aquinas. Toward the end of the first semester, several rays of light are often perceived in these otherwise "dark" ages: early glimmerings of the ideas and concepts that will come to undergird the "secular" nation-state, nascent justifications for the separation of church and state, and arguments in favor of limited government. All this with a purely Western orientation.

The big break comes with Machiavelli. Political scientists tend to like Machiavelli (although not countenancing all he advocates) more than Aquinas because he is perceived as the first real modern, a thoroughly rational, secular, pragmatic, and realistic thinker, who coolly analyzes political power and how to achieve and exercise it, presumably without the religious and ethical inhibitions of his predecessors. It is probable that political scientists admire Machiavelli because in these traits he conforms closely to our own notions of ourselves and our discipline. But while admiring Machiavelli, we typically forget the explicit repudiation of his ideas elsewhere in Italy and France, and in the writings of a prolific influential group of Spanish theorists—Suárez, Molina, Vitoria, and Mariana—who rejected the sharp distinction between politics and ethics and continued to advance theories of a polity based on the credentials of logic, rightness, relation to abstract justice, and the continued integration of the social and the moral.[13] But owing to the prejudices that social scientists often hold and the way we structure our courses, this important strand in the history of Western thought has been conveniently ignored. Nevertheless, it remained the dominant tradition in Spain, Portugal, and Latin America.

After Machiavelli we turn generally to Hobbes, another purely secular analyst of political power, and then to the basis of liberal-democratic rule in Locke. The Protestant Reformation is similarly viewed positively, on balance, because of its break with Catholic orthodoxy, the pluralism of ideas it helped usher in, and its rationalizations for individual initiative, local self-rule, the rise of capitalism, and democratic choice. Our point here is not to question these as values but to show that they represent one set of values among several and that, by our celebratory treatment of them and lack of attention to other traditions, we inevitably prejudice our understanding of the history of Western thought.

Beginning with the eighteenth-century Enlightenment, our typical political theory courses become even more narrowly circumscribed. It is during this period that many of our modern notions of progress, rationality, popular government, and secularism flourish; but these concepts are again based on the experience of a very small, select group of countries and experiences. Our attention focuses on Rousseau, Voltaire, and the French Revolution; Hume, Bentham, Smith, Ricardo, Mill, and perhaps T. H. Green and the development of British liberalism and utilitarianism; and the tradition of German idealism in Kant, Hegel, and eventually Marx. We may then present an analysis of the great alternative ideologies of the early twentieth century: socialism with its democratic and communist variations, liberalism, and fascism—as if these were the only contemporary alternatives available.

Several criticisms may be leveled regarding the organization of this more or less representative political theory course. These concerns seem especially important because there are remarkable parallels in the structuring of our "History of Western Civ" and other courses that form the core of our liberal arts curriculum and because, it seems apparent, these concepts learned in college by generations of students have powerfully conditioned our social science understandings, our assumptions about the world, and the foreign policies flowing from them.

First, these courses have an almost exclusively Western focus. From beginning (Greece, Rome, and the Judeo-Christian tradition) to end (the alternative twentieth-century ideologies), it is only the Western and European historical theater of ideas and experiences that receives attention. Nowhere in these courses is there any examination of Taoist, Confucian, Buddhist, Hindu, Islamic, or African ideas, institutions, or concepts of change; worse, there is seldom mention that such exist or that they are worthy of study. One supposes that when we believed, as we once did (and many still do) that development inevitably meant Westernization, that in order for Third World nations to develop and enter the mainstream of history (recall both Hegel and Marx claiming arrogantly and ethnocentrically that the non-Western nations had "no history" or were locked in "prehistory"), they first had to overcome their traditional indigenous institutions and shuck off their historical cultures and beliefs, then such omissions might have been rationalizable.

By this time, we know: (1) development does not, automatically or inevitably, imply or produce Westernization—many forms of modernization are possible (in Japan or the Islamic countries, for example) that do not necessarily mean Westernization; (2) the Western–non-Western or traditional–modern dichotomies are in any case misleading and far too restrictive of the range of possibilities open;[14] (3) traditional beliefs and institutions, rather than being swept aside or superseded as modernization goes forward, have proved to have remarkable staying power, flexibility, and adaptability;[15] and (4) many Third World nations have by now rejected, in whole or in part, the models of the already developed world and are searching in their own histories and cultures for indigenous frameworks more in keeping with their own customs and realities.

These changes have left a whole generation and more of social scientists and policy makers at a loss. Their assumptions of universal and inevitable Westernization and modernization no longer wash; yet that is the only model they know since very few have the advanced and specialized training in non-Western frameworks to conceive of development in any other way. The absence, for example, of more than a handful of persons in the U.S. Department of State, CIA, or Defense Department, as in academia or the nation-at-large, who know anything about the Islamic tradition—from an empathetic rather than a hostile viewpoint—not only helps us understand why our foreign policy has been so inadequate but also reflects a broader malaise: our continued belief in the superiority and inevitability of the Western way and our ignorance and disparagement of all others.

Even within the Western tradition, however, our history-of-political-thought courses may be criticized for the selectivity involved in stressing certain ideas and concepts as opposed to others. Once past the feudal period, these courses are highly discriminating in focusing on what are perceived as modernizing ideas or focuses or, conversely, in consigning to obscurity those seen as nonprogressive or traditional. Among the latter, in addition to the Catholic-organic conception already noted, are elitism, social hierarchy, mercantilism, corporatism, familialism and kinship, authoritarianism, ascriptive criteria, patrimonialism, localism, divine right, and so on. Those in the former category include an emphasis on (and implied admiration for) secularism, pluralism, democracy, rationalism, pragmatism, equality, and so forth. These are admirable values, of course, but they also represent political choices or cultural gives, and one may question whether these values ought to be emphasized to the exclusion of all others.

Nor should history be presented as if one particular set of desired values is universal, inevitable, and the end point toward which all nations aspire. Even the sharp distinction we draw between traditional and modern is itself a product of our Western historical experience and would not be so sharply drawn in other cultural areas. It seems likely these values and interpretations of history are stressed because they represent what we think of as the Western tradition as well as the political preferences and ideology of the political science profession or some segments of it, and the belief that one's own values are both superior and inevitable is always pleasant. But such an approach is not good history, fails to square with the empirical facts, and renders a disservice to our understanding of numerous alternative currents in both Western and non-Western thought. The fact that many social and political analysts are now reexamining not only their assumption about the Third World but also the biases in the Western tradition itself, and the way it is taught, would seem to be a healthy step in the right direction.

Another criticism concerns the selectivity used in determining which parts of the West are to be studied. For once in the modern era our attention focuses almost exclusively on three countries—England, France, and Germany—their developmental experiences, and the major intellectual figures who have chronicled or rationalized these changes. Obviously, these are important traditions out of which many of our families come, but unless one can make the increasingly doubtful argument that the developmental processes of other nations *must* follow the path of these three—especially the paradigmatic cases of the French Revolution of 1789 and the social and political crosscurrents to which it gave rise, or the English experience of industrialization, 1760–1830, and its accompanying effects—the patterns of change in these nations should not be treated as the only or even most advanced model. Left out in such a view are the quite distinct experiences of northern Europe (the Scandinavian countries), eastern Europe, and southern Europe (Greece, Italy, Portugal, and Spain). If one is to speak of a Western model, after all, then it is incumbent that all, or at least most, Western nations, not just a select few, be included.[16]

The social science "out" has been to consider England, France, and Germany as the leaders or "norm" (whatever that means, given their diverse histories), the models others must emulate, and the rest as somehow deviant or less developed. Eventually, Scandinavia and the Benelux countries came to approximate the model and were thus deemed acceptable and worthy of study, but Eastern Europe and Southern Europe still did not. That fact was seldom upsetting to social science theory, however, since if some countries failed to fit the paradigm it was the countries and their social and political systems that were condemned or deemed exceptional, not the paradigm that needed assessment. That plus the fact that the nations of southern Europe, especially, still exhibited many traditional features such as persistent authoritarianism, elitism, and corporatism enabled much social science to continue labeling these nations as retarded or underdeveloped, perhaps someday capable of catching up with the West once they had rid themselves of these nefarious features. That, after all, is what the Western model had comfortably suggested, that such changes or catching up were inherent in development and inevitable.

Little thought was given to the possibility that the organic-corporatist or mixed liberal-corporatist systems of Spain and Portugal, for instance, might represent an *alternative* route to modernization rather than just backward deviations from the progressive Western (actually, only northwest European) model. Because of our democratic biases and our identification of corporatism with fascism, we remain hostile to the theory of corporatism and its ideological background.[17] Pareto and Mosca also seldom find a place in our political theory courses both because they do not fit our preconceived notions and because we do not like elitist and undemocratic theories, particularly those that are unabashedly so. From this and other factors stem the dislike and incomprehension that both the social sciences and policy makers sometimes harbor toward southern European nations, especially those "damnable and unstable" (as if the two were synonymous) countries, as Henry Kissinger once put it scornfully, that lie over the Alps or Pyrenees ("beyond the pale of civilization," as Metternich said). Let us not take this argument further for now except to say that it is not just in the non-Western world where the European-based model, ideology, and dominant political beliefs fail to apply, but they may also be only narrowly applicable in significant parts of the very European context where the model was born.[18]

To assert that the great Western tradition of political thought with which we are familiar is of less than universal applicability and that there are major geographic and cultural areas, including some within the West, that are entirely neglected in our political and social theory courses is to imply that there is something worth studying in these other areas and traditions. That is a difficult proposition to demonstrate to those who have always thought in Eurocentric terms, and it helps explain why so many of those studying other areas spend much of their professional careers defensively seeking to justify to their colleagues why their areas may be just as profound and complex, with as many important research implications, as Britain, France, Germany, or the United States. It is a long, uphill battle, which is still only partially won but seems to be gaining added momentum due to the growing malaise within these core areas in recent years and the corresponding increase in importance of such previously neglected nations as Brazil, China, India, Iran, Egypt, Indonesia, Mexico, Nigeria, and Tanzania.

In my own research and writing, I have tried to show the continued importance of Iberian and Latin American organic-corporatist thought and sociopolitical organization, to present this as a viable alternative to the usual liberal-pluralist models with which we look at these areas and to understand Latin America, in the words of novelist Carlos Fuentes, as a distinct *civilization* and not as a series of agreements about tomatoes (or coffee, sugar, or bananas). In other quite distinct cultural and national settings, comparable studies are now appearing or being rediscovered of traditions of thought, law, and social and political organization that were previously ignored and remain largely unknown but that are probably at least as important as the European ones for analyzing these nations' unique developmental processes. It is not our purpose here to describe these alternative traditions in any detail but merely to note that they exist and to point readers toward some of the literature.[19]

Political Sociology

Political sociology demonstrates many of the same biases as does political theory. Indeed, an entire generation and more grew up with the development sociology literature of the past four decades, a body of literature that is as narrow, particularistic, ethnocentric, and Western-biased as the theory just analyzed.

Since Durkheim, sociologists have generally assumed that the processes of modernization are more or less universal. Once industrialization begins, a number of concomitant changes occur in the structure of society, class organization, social mobility, behavior patterns, division of labor, and the like. These alterations occur regardless of cultural context: indeed, their very power as motor forces of change tends to erase cultural, linguistic, or geographic differences.[20]

It is not our purpose here to offer a detailed critique of Durkheim's seminal work or of Marx's analysis of the social and political effects of industrialization, on which so much of modern sociology is based. We grant the general utility of some of these conceptions at the level of broad abstraction and as heuristic devices. It is our contention, however, that these are starting points of explanation, not end points, necessary explanations but not sufficient ones. Durkheim (Marx is treated later) was, of course, a European writing of a particular time and place, a philosopher of the French university, a spiritual descendant of Auguste Comte and the Enlightenment, and a believer in social consensus and progress, shaped by both the intellectual climate of France at the end of the nineteenth century and by the social changes then under way in Paris.[21] He had little knowledge of events and cultures outside Europe, and his research dealt chiefly with the Western European (actually French) concomitants of economic growth.

Obviously, the conditions of the present-day emerging nations, the timing and sequences of their development, and the international context are quite different from that of the European countries a century ago. With our more extensive research in non-Western areas, we now know how distinct cultural contexts and institutions can filter, screen out, and mediate, if not determine, the social and political effects of industrialization. Moreover, while Durkheim limited himself to outlining only some of the broad and general societal concomitants of industrialization (increased specialization and the division of labor may well be universal, for instance), latter-day sociologists went considerably beyond his findings to identify very specific changes in political party organization, middle-class behavior, governmental organization, trade union and military behavior, and the like, as also following necessarily from modernization. It is at this level of quite specific indicators and predictors of the sociopolitical concomitants of modernization, again and inexcusably all derived from the Euro-American experience, that ideal types became confused with reality and the biases and ethnocentrism of political sociology became most apparent.

The empirical evidence does not support the claims to universalism and inevitability put forth by the major Western theories of sociopolitical development concerning the impact of industrialization on the broader social system.[22] The transition from an agrarian society to an industrial one and such
factors as increased population, urbanization, the separation of place of resi-
dence from place of work, coupled with rising occupational differentiation
and specialization have tended *in the West* to have brought specific kinds of
changes in familial, religious, political, and all other major areas of social organization. It is for this reason, and because at that time the sociologists and
political economists who analyzed these changes were themselves exclusively from that area, that the specifically Western social and political concomitants of industrialization came to be incorporated into theoretical con-
ceptualizations of the change process per se. Given the historical context (the
mid- to late nineteenth century) and the fact that northwest Europe experienced these mammoth changes first (and particularly at that time the lack of
any non-Western experience with the transition to an industrial society), one
might well say that the Western social adaptations occurring then almost *had*
to be closely associated with a more general and presumptively universal theory of development and modernization.

Not only are the timing, sequences, and international context of development different, but non-Western societies have generally been quite selective
in accepting what is useful from Western modernization while often rejecting
the rest. Of course, this is a mixed situation, for while some elements associated with Western modernization are kept out, other aspects enter regardless
of the barriers erected. But the process itself is one of filtering and not simply of imitating and inevitably following. Japanese modernization under the
Meiji, for example, came about through the cooperation of government and
powerful family groups. The tenacity of such traditional family elements and
their persistence were not the result merely of nostalgic attachment to the past
or to some vague tradition; rather, there were valid economic reasons—
Japan's abundance of manpower as opposed to capital, her traditional family
handicraft industry that could be used to generate the needed capital—for
their retention. As a result, the Japanese pattern of modernization has indicated significant differences from that of the West (and it obviously continues
to do so). The social and political concomitants that in the West followed
from industrialization have not necessarily followed.

The Japanese evidence and parallel findings from other regions of the
world suggest that the forms of Western social and political organization are
not the inevitable consequence of the replacement of feudalism, traditionalism, and agriculturalism by a modern industrial technology. Instead, the capitalistic individualism, secularism, the particular role of the middle classes

and middle "classness," the growth of liberalism and interest group pluralism, and a host of other features that are so much a part of the northwest European and U.S. religious, familial, social, and political system should be seen as only one of numerous possible alternatives in the urban-industrial transition, and not necessarily a more developed or ethically or morally superior one. Other, *alternative* routes to modernization also command our attention.

Modern political sociology and the development literature derived in large measure from the perspectives outlined above and from the "pattern variables" of Talcott Parsons.[23] Parsons advanced three (occasionally four) measures to gauge the transition from traditional to modern, whether in society, polity, or even individual personality. Thus, whereas traditional society is functionally "diffuse," modern society is functionally "specific"; whereas traditional society is "particularistic," modern society is "universalistic"; whereas traditional society is based on "ascription," modern society is based on "achievement." In the words of such prominent scholars as Sutton, Shils, Deutsch, Lerner, Riggs, Lipset, Almond, Levy, and Black, who wrote on developmental themes, these pattern variables became a key means to distinguish between traditional and modern, underdeveloped and developed. The industrialized, modern, and developed society is thus characterized by law, regular procedures, merit, and the like, while the agrarian, traditional, underdeveloped society is characterized by custom, status, and ascription.[24] The Western model's relevance in explaining the transition from the latter to the former was assumed to be global. Armed with the "certainties" this assumption and the pattern variables provided, waves of graduate students and well-meaning Peace Corps members and AID staffers fanned out to the Third World to find development and advance it.

The problems with the pattern variable and Western-oriented developmental approach are numerous. In the first place, the pattern variables imply a sharp dualism between traditional and modern that in actual fact does not exist. The sharpness of the breaks ushered in with the English, French, and Russian revolutions lent support to this view, but it was not relevant to most non-Western areas. The more sophisticated developmentalists recognized that the pattern variables represented continua, not either-or situations, and that most societies consisted of diverse mixes and fusions of traditional and modern, and further that these were ideal types, heuristic devices, or shorthand terms with no necessary correlation with reality. However, many forgot this distinction, confused approximations of reality with the real things, became so used to the shorthand that it came to have real substance, even reified these artificial concepts and applied them to actual, existing institutions. One of the most dangerous tendencies was to treat the developing countries not only as less developed economically and sociopolitically but psychologically and morally as well. More often implicitly than explicitly, underdeveloped countries became underdeveloped peoples, and the implications of that are so racist, condescending, and obvious that the argument need not be detained by further details.

Especially presumptuous was the expectation of a single, unilinear path to development. There was only one acceptable route along with certain common signposts—all derived from the Western experience—along the path. Traditional society was seldom further differentiated, leaving the impression that all Third World nations had evolved from a common background and had begun at the same starting point; and, once started, they had embarked on a single path that led them to shed their traditional features and proceed irreversibly to modernization. Almost no thought was given to the fact that not only were the starting points and the natures of traditional societies immensely different, but that the paths to development and the end products were certain to be vastly dissimilar as well. The image that should have been used was not that of a single path or route to development but that of a much more complex *lattice*, with numerous, diverse beginnings and multiple, criss-crossing channels.[25]

A key reason developmental sociology went astray—and a major cause of its attractiveness—is that a close identification was made between development as a process and development as a moral and ethical good. As social scientists or foreign policy analysts, we could analyze development and identify with it as well; development was seen as a desirable normative goal toward which all "right-thinking" people should surely work. Particularly as development was closely identified with the values that social scientists hold—secularism, rationalism, pluralism, and the like—and as it implied the destruction or replacement of the values and institutions social scientists tend not to like (authoritarian and traditional structures; religious beliefs and institutions; familial, tribal, or clan ties), it carried enormous appeal.

There is certainly something we can analyze as *change*; "development" and "modernization" are probably too Western, too loaded, to be of much use in describing Third World events. But change should be regarded as a neutral process and not involve the intrusion of ethical, political, or moral judgments—unless we are willing to abandon all pretense to objectivity and assume that our private values are or ought to be everyone's values. That is highly conceited and pretentious. Certainly it is difficult to be against development and modernization. The mistake was that social science presumed to *know* what a developed society looked like (liberal, pluralist, democratic: our idealized image of ourselves) and that it assumed that the values of Western civilization were or had to become everyone's values. Hence, if traditional societies or institutions—African tribalism, Indian caste associations, a host of others—failed to develop in terms of prevailing social science theory, they had of necessity to be uprooted and obliterated in favor of new modernizing ones; and if in the process the modernizing institutions such as political parties and trade unions failed to develop, it was again the societies that were dysfunctional rather than the theory that needed reexamination.

Seen as an ethical good in accord with narrow Euro-American perceptions, development also closely served U.S. foreign policy goals. One treads cautiously here to avoid engaging in verbal overkill or to make the ludicrous claims that some fringe-radical critics of U.S. policy have. One need not be on the fringes to recognize that the development literature and strategies served as a convenient means to expand immensely the U.S. presence in the developing world. Development helped rationalize the large number of labor officials, tax specialists, agrarian reform technicians, businessmen, AID administrators, academic experts of all sorts, Peace Corps members, and others sent abroad during the heyday of both U.S. power and concern for development. The sheer amounts of money and U.S. personnel involved converted many smaller and weaker Third World nations into quasi dependencies of the United States—whether that was part of a conscious design or not. The effort to bring development to the Third World succeeded in pulling many of these nations into the U.S. orbit, increasing our influence and levers of manipulation there, making them dependent on us, imposing our preferred solutions on them, and thus strengthening our hand in a global Cold War struggle. In the post–Cold War global order, it is precisely the nationalistic reaction against these influences, against American economic, cultural, military, and political domination, that we are now reaping in the Middle East, Latin America, and throughout the globe.

Such nationalistic or cultural-area (as in the Islamic world) reactions against the Euro-American development model make it doubly ironic that the bulk of the literature saw such development both as an ethical good and as an inevitable process. Ultimately, all societies, it was argued, had to go through the same or similar modernization. It is, of course, enormously comforting to social scientists to know that what they are studying is not only scientific, ethically good, and supportive of the national interest, but also inevitable. Development studies had strong elements of both moral self-righteousness and absolute certainty, while also serving our foreign policy objectives. We were comfortable in knowing that what we studied and advocated was morally just and that in the long run, despite occasional coups, revolutions, and other dysfunctional reversals, our developmental formulas were bound to be correct and that the emerging nations would ultimately conform to our preferred model.

There are, certainly, universals in the development process, and perhaps Western Europe and the United States provide us with a model of how this occurs. Economic development and industrialization *are* occurring in virtually all areas of the globe; class transformations are under way; people are being uprooted and mobilized; urbanization is accelerating; traditional institutions are changing and new ones are being created; specialization and differentiation are going forward. The mistake of the development literature was in ascribing specific social and political concomitants to these changes based on a model that was not universalistic, as it claimed, but particularistic and narrowly Euro-American. Because all economic and class transformations are, after all, filtered through and shaped by distinct, indigenous cultural, social, and political institutions, no less so in the Third World than in Western Europe, the timing, sequences, context, and character of these changes are also quite varied. What the social sciences did, however, was to generalize inappropriately from the sociopolitical institutional concomitants of modernization in the United States and Western Europe, which they knew best and assumed to be desirable, to other nations, which they knew less well and with whose traditional institutions they felt uncomfortable. Generalization from a single unique case to the rest of the world is not unusual among policy makers or social scientists: in the case of the development literature, however, the assumptions were widely shared, and the results for developing nations have often been particularly unfortunate. We have recently begun to pay the costs of this myopia in terms of unstable regimes and even terrorism.

Political Economy

Economics as a discipline is, along with sociology, most explicit in its claims to universality. Therein lies one of the world's great problems.

Two grand traditions exist in economic thought: the Marxian and the non-Marxian. Both are based on the Western European experience. Neither, in their classical forms, or taken without qualification or without appending major amendments, is of great utility in dealing with the realities of the non-Euro-American world.

What Marx had to say about the non-Western or Asiatic nations, disparaging their cultures and condemning them to prehistory, was not very flattering;[26] but that is not our chief concern here. What does concern us is the selective use of history by Marx to argue his famous case, and the oftentimes mindless and unqualified application by his latter-day disciples of his major categories to societies where they fit but imperfectly and incompletely. It is common knowledge that the national sources for Marx's philosophic and empirical work were mainly three: philosophically, it was German thought and idealism that strongly shaped his concepts; he took most of his political illustrations from French history; and his understanding of industrialization and its effects was principally derived from the English experience. Certainly, no one would deny the importance of these histories or of Marx's influence. The questions center on the small size of the sample, its representativeness, whether the experiences of these three early modernizers are relevant to the situation of Third World nations today, and whether the mid-nineteenth-century European context may not have been so unique as to carry but limited lessons for the non-Western world. Marx himself, after all, consistently cautioned his followers that his analysis derived from and was meant to apply to Western Europe.

Economic and class changes are obviously occurring in the Third World, but we make a mistake if we think that social and political institutions in these nations are or will be the exact mirror of underlying class structure—or that they will everywhere be the same. Nor is it the case that political forces in these societies can always be subordinated to economic variables; rather, the reverse process often occurs, with class structure and economic change shaped by cultural, social, or political institutions. Nor is it accurate or even realistic to expect that the experience of a highly select group of countries in the nineteenth century will be repeated in exact or even similar form in the developing nations today. One must question whether England really provides *the* paradigm case of the capitalistic mode of production. Nor can we assume as Marx did that the same organization of production will necessarily generate the same class and political changes, the same developmental epochs or typical sequences. Nor should we think that the social and political changes that accompanied these transformations in northwest Europe will inevitably reappear in non-Western areas in parallel form. The international contexts of dependence and interdependence are so different, the cultural and institutional milieu so varied, and the social and political filters governing the way these changes take place or are perceived are so distinctive that it is preposterous to think that the developing nations will repeat, albeit much later, the experiences of economic development of Western Europe or the United States. Not only has Marxism-Leninism collapsed in the Soviet Union, Eastern Europe, and elsewhere, but Marxian economics and analyses have been generally discredited as well.

Non-Marxian developmental economics is often as Eurocentric as the classical Marxian variety. The famous aeronautical stages in the "non-Communist manifesto" of W. W. Rostow ("drive to take off," "take off," etc.), which so strongly shaped—as did Parsons and Lipset in sociology and the Almond and Coleman volume on "The Politics of the Developing Nations" in political science—whole generations of development-minded economists, were based almost exclusively on the Western European and U.S. experiences. The logic of the Rostow analysis (and of the Alliance for Progress and U.S. foreign assistance since, as head of Policy Planning at the State Department and then as National Security Adviser, Rostow was also the chief influence in shaping these programs) was that if only the United States could pour in sufficient economic aid, "take off" would occur and the following social and political effects would be felt: organized labor would become less extremist and revolutionary and more professional, and, hence, less political; armies and bureaucracies would grow; a large middle class would emerge as a bulwark of stable, middle-of-the-road rule; the peasants would become yeomen, middle-class family farmers; and radical ideologies such as communism and fascism would diminish in attractiveness.

These assumptions, originating in the literature on European and U.S. economic history (Japan fit uncomfortably in Rostow's analysis) undergirded both much social science theory and the U.S. foreign aid program during the 1960s and 1970s. It was an application of the Marshall Plan, successful in Western European *recovery*, to Third World nations where the cultural conditions and economic and political givens were fundamentally different. The assumption was that, if we provided economic aid, sent our technical experts, promoted agrarian reform, trained the local army, reformed the tax system, encouraged local community development, pushed family planning, provided for administrative reform, and all the other developmental panaceas that have had their own life histories during the past two decades,[27] modernization would certainly take place and these "aspiring nations" could be recast in our own image.

Large numbers of developmentally trained academics were enlisted during this period to assist the U.S. government and a host of quasi-public though ostensibly private foundations and other agencies with this effort to bring modernization to less-favored lands. Few questioned the assumptions of the Western-derived developmentalist model and not just because travel expenses and an honorarium were involved. We really believed our models were universally relevant. If difficulties arose, whole programs wasted, or unanticipated consequences produced, these were consistently viewed as problems to be overcome or dysfunctional aspects that could be solved by more aid and technical expertise. Little consideration was afforded the idea that indigenous social and political institutions might represent the givens to work with rather than merely problems to be overcome. If a particular program misfired (there are some spectacular cases) or had little or no effect (the less-spectacular fate of most of the U.S.-conceived programs), it was the Third World country that required reform, seldom the program itself.

Less sanguine observers of these programs were often amazed that the experts really expected a land-reform program appropriate for Wisconsin to work in Peru, a system of local government modeled on the New England town meeting to take root in the centralized code-law nations of Latin America, or a progressive income tax as in the United States to be applied where the expectations regarding the fairness and impartiality of the state were quite different. Watching with wonder as program after program failed or produced meager results and yet where the major assumptions still went unexamined, one came to question if the social scientists and AID administrators were so naive as to believe that they really could work, so unimaginative as to see no other solutions besides the Western ones, or if they continued to push these programs simply because that was their job. Perhaps they did not want to rock the boat or become a naysayer of programs that enjoyed such wide consensus and came wrapped in the mantle of academic social science. Perhaps no one was willing to say that the developmentalist emperor had on no clothes. Doubtless, all these explanations have some validity.

By this point it should be abundantly clear that the Rostowian stages do not necessarily follow one another, that there is no unilinear and inevitable path to development; that with the oil price increases, interdependence, and globalization, the condition of the Third World nations today is fundamentally different from those prevailing a century or more ago; that the development process in these nations, hence, will not and cannot be a mirror of the Western European experience; that there are numerous culturally conditioned routes to modernization and not just the West European one, and therefore that the social and political concomitants that, based on the West European experience, are supposed to follow from modernization may not, in these quite different temporal and spatial contexts, follow at all.[28] Rather, development will take directions that reflect both imported and indigenous traditions and institutions; and it is time that we recognize this fact rather than continue to dismiss these processes and institutions as dysfunctional or try to interpret them through a Western social science framework that has only limited relevance in non-Western areas. As David Apter reminded us some time ago, industrialization in the West is only one form of industrialization.[29] The dilemma for most developing nations is, hence, not Westernization or even modernization but how to gain and employ Western capital and technology while preserving what they see as valuable in their own cultures and traditions.

POLICY CONSEQUENCES OF THE WESTERN BIASES

The northwest European and North American biases on which so much of our political theory, sociology, and economics are based have produced major consequences, many of them unfortunate so far as a better comprehension of the developing nations goes. Our ethnocentrism has led not just to continued misinterpretation, however, but also to immense and often negative practical consequences for these nations. In this realm the ideas of academics and policy makers *have* had an impact, unfortunate though that has frequently been. After all, social scientists and policy makers generally spend at best a year or two in their countries of specialization and can fly off at any time when their theories or programs prove wrong; left behind, however, are the people of the developing nation who have no choice but to try to cope as best they can with the misfortunes wrought upon them. We propose here to examine briefly only a few of the results of our social science biases, under three categories: those topics to which we have unwarrantedly given too much attention, those we have afforded too little, and the damage we have wreaked upon the developing nations because of our ethnocentrism.

The theory and assumptions we have applied to the developing nations have often led us to expect certain trends to occur and institutions to develop that have, in fact, not consistently developed. We have expected, and perhaps hoped, that modernization would produce more pluralist and secular societies when, in fact, in Iran and the Middle East generally powerful religious revivals are taking place that are monistic and theocratic and that proclaim a single right-and-wrong way to do everything, which seems appallingly oppressive to most Westerners. We celebrate pure versions of democracy and pluralism in our theories in the political sphere as well, when the reality in virtually all developing nations is a mix of authoritarianism and usually quite limited forms of democracy.[30] We have expected more universalist criteria to take hold when in fact particularism seems everywhere on the rise. We applaud merit and have elevated it to a universal norm of modernity when the fact is ascriptive criteria seem ascendant, perhaps increasingly so even in our own society. Obviously, differentiation of labor, specialization of function, and rationalization and bureaucratization have occurred throughout the developing world, but rather than producing much democratization in countries where a strong imperious central state has been either the norm or the aspiration, these trends have in many cases produced more efficient and centralized forms of statism, authoritarianism, or mixed regimes.[31]

Our social science and policy assumptions have also led us to look for the growth of an increasingly more prosperous working class and, hence, a more apolitical trade unionism when, in fact, in Brazil, Argentina, and elsewhere the latter does not seem necessarily to follow from the former. We expected an increasingly professional and, thus, apolitical military when, in fact, increased professionalism leads many militaries in developing states to become more political rather than less. We hoped for stronger local government when, in fact, the dominant tendency even of our community development programs has been toward greater concentration of state power. We predicted mass-

based political parties that would perform the interest aggregation and articulation functions when actually most parties in the developing nations are that
only in name and may not at all be inclined to perform the functions Western
political science assigns to them.

We believed that the middle class would be moderate, democratic, and inclined to assist the less-favored elements in the society when, in fact, the divided middle sectors in most Third World nations are inclined to ape upper-
class ways and use the instruments of the state (armies, labor ministries, and
the like) to keep their own lower classes subservient. We expected elites and
businessmen to recognize their social responsibilities to the poor in a more pluralist setting, when the real situation is that the elites are intent not on sharing
but on getting more wealth and monopolizing it. We thought that greater respect for civil liberties and democracy would evolve, rather than the increased
statism, authoritarianism, and corporatism that seem to be the real-life situation
increasingly in much of the Third World. The list of misapplied theories and
programs goes on and on. In short, few of the social and political concomitants
of modernization that our Western experience would lead us to expect to see
developing are, in fact, developing. The problem lies not in the developing areas since they are often merely continuing preferred and traditional practices;
rather, the problem lies in the Western-based concepts and often wishful social
science with which we have sought to interpret these nations.

At the same time that too much attention has been devoted to those institutions that, based on the Western experience, social scientists expected or
hoped to develop, too little has been afforded those not in accord with these
preferences. It seems obvious, for example, that in the Islamic world and elsewhere religious beliefs and institutions cannot simply be relegated to the ash
cans of history under the "inevitable" onslaught of secularism, nor can the
former be dismissed as part of traditional society certain to be superseded.
The same applies to tribal and caste associations: these are not just traditional
institutions certain to give way under modernization's impact. Behind much
of the ideological skirmishing in Africa, for instance, is a tribal or ethnic context, one that should not be denied or wished away as much social science
does but taken as a given and perhaps as a base for social and political associations other than the preferred Western ones. Similarly, India's caste associations are now viewed as adaptable institutions capable of serving as modernizing agencies.[32] There is a refreshing degree of realism now on the part
of political leaders and intellectuals in the Third World to take such institutions as givens and potential developmental building blocks rather than as
symbols of backwardness that had to be destroyed. The functioning and
changes in such institutions during epochs of transition ought also to be a primary focus of social scientists and should not be easily dismissed.

With the strong social-democratic bias that undergirds much of the development literature, social scientists have disregarded a variety of other institutions either because we do not like them politically or because they do not fit our preferred models. Most social scientists, for instance, are uncomfortable with, and often quite hostile toward, the Catholic, elitist, and authoritarian assumptions of traditional Latin society. Because we do not like elite-structured societies, we have seldom studied the dynamics of elite strategies and elite networks, preferring to dismiss these out-of-hand or apply the familiar traditional label, which seemingly helps make the problem go away. There is abundant literature on labor and peasant movements but very little on elites, both because of practical research problems and because social scientists, like most Americans, are ill at ease with elitist assumptions. We do not like theocratic societies either and especially despise the Islamic mullahs and fundamentalists for seeking to resurrect one, but our understanding of events in Iraq and other nations will not be advanced by complete hostility or the dismissal of such popular movements as irrational.

Military coups provide another illustration of the familiar biases. Most Western social science, with its favoritism toward democratic and civilian government, treats coups as aberrations—irregular, dysfunctional, and unconstitutional—thus ignoring their normality, regularity, workability, often legal-constitutional basis, the reasons for them, their functional similarity to elections, and the fact the former may be no more comic opera than the latter. Our antimilitary bias, however, often prevents us from seeing these events neutrally and scientifically.[33]

If these errors of both commission and omission by social scientists and policy makers were merely benignly neutral, there would be little to worry about. Unfortunately, such errors and oversights are not benign, neutral, or harmless. The subject merits much fuller attention; here let it simply be said that (1) based on the ethnocentric developmental assumptions of the social sciences and of policy makers, enormous amounts of money and effort have been wasted on a variety of misguided and misdirected programs; (2) confirmed in the modernity and, hence, superiority of our own institutions, we have continued patronizingly to dismiss or disparage as traditional or primitive a large number of beliefs, practices, and institutions in the Third World; (3) because our models and perspectives are so narrow and Eurocentric, our comprehension of the real dynamics of change and continuity in these nations remains woefully inadequate, based more on prejudice or romance than on actuality; (4) grounded on this same particularistic and ethnocentric northwest European and U.S. experience, the policy measures we have sought to implement have produced hosts of backfires, unanticipated consequences, and sheer disasters; and (5) in the name of advancing modernity, we have helped undermine a great variety of quite viable traditional and transitional institutions, thus contributing by our policies to the breakdown, fragmentation, and instability of many developing nations that we had ostensibly sought to avoid.

All these charges are serious, but the last one may have the gravest long-term consequences. By helping destabilize their traditional institutions and by erecting ephemeral modern ones cast in our own image to replace them but often entirely inappropriate in the societies where we have sought to locate them, we have left many developing nations neither with the traditional and indigenous institutions that might have helped them bridge the wrenching transition to modernity nor with viable new ones that have any basis or hope of functioning effectively in the native soil. By forcing some wrong and falsely dichotomous choices on the developing nations (traditional *or* modern democracy *or* dictatorship), social scientists and policy makers have contributed strongly to the institutional vacuum that plagues these countries and to the hopeless cases that, in the absence of genuinely homegrown institutions, some of them are certain to become.[34]

CONCLUSION AND IMPLICATIONS

The development literature, whether in political science, sociology, or economics, assumes that the path to modernization in the Third World can be explained by reference to the past or the present of the already industrialized nations. Development in Africa, Asia, Latin America, and the Middle East is seen, in Glaucio Ary Dillon Soares's words, as specific instances of a general course of events already studied and fully comprehended in the experience of the Western European countries and the United States.[35] Such an approach assumes that quite distinct cultural areas and historical epochs can be understood using the same terms and concepts as in the West. It assumes a single unilinear path to development and also the universality of what is a far narrower and particular European or Western experience and set of institutions. The ethnocentrism of this interpretation and the absurdity of reducing a great variety of histories and sociopolitical formations to the single matrix of the Western European-U.S. experience are patent. This approach has stultified the creation of new concepts and prevented us from understanding the realities of the developing nations. It has wreaked positive harm upon them and cast the developing nations in an inferior position vis-à-vis both the developed countries and those who study them.

A growing chorus of voices in recent years has asked why the United States fails to comprehend and, hence, anticipate the profound, revolutionary, and sometimes anti-American changes sweeping the developing world, particularly in the Islamic world, and why our policy response to these changes has been and remains so inadequate. Why did we not see these occurrences coming; why did our policy makers fail to foresee the consequences of their actions; why are there so few scholars or policy makers who have a thorough understanding of Islamic law, institutions, and social change so that we might comprehend Middle Eastern events properly? Iran and Iraq are not the sole countries where such changes are, or are about to be, happening, however; in many Third World countries similar revolutionary winds are blowing. This chapter hints at answers to some of the questions posed above.

The problem is that we neither understand nor *have wanted* to understand movements that run counter to the Western conception of change. We *really believe* in both the inevitability and the universality of the Western conception of how change, properly, should go forward. The Eurocentric ideas that we as social scientists and policy makers carry around in our heads and that we studied in college, where we learned all those Parsonian, Rostowian, Almondian, and Lipsetian theories of development, are still the concepts on which our assumptions regarding modernization and development in the Third World are based. The generations grounded so strongly in this tradition are now precisely the generations that are governing us—those in their thirties, forties, and fifties who went to college during the heyday of the developmentalist concepts.

The higher one goes in government, moreover, and, hence, the more generalists one finds (the president and his advisers, the secretaries and undersecretaries of State and Defense, national security advisers, and CIA directors, etc.), the less the expertise on particular nations and cultures is brought to bear and, hence, the more policy makers tend, usually only half-consciously, to fall back on the simplistic, narrow, Western, Eurocentric conceptions inculcated in earlier years. How many of these leaders have spent the years outside this country that are required to comprehend fully foreign cultures and institutions? The answer is very few. Indeed, it is in the nature of the American system of politics and career advancement that those spending too long abroad are punished in terms of their possibilities for professional and political advancement at the highest levels. A partial reason why we failed so utterly to comprehend Middle East events, as well as those posed less dramatically for now in scores of other nations, is that our biases and prejudices prevent us from doing so. In fact, our entire educational, socialization, and career system, so heavily European- and U.S.-based, is weighted toward demeaning and denigrating the values and institutions of cultural areas other than our own.

The universals in the modernization process include economic growth and industrialization, class and societal changes, division of labor and increased specialization of functions, rationalization and bureaucratization of society and polity, and the impact of what Lucian Pye once called the "world culture" (not just jeans, Coke, and rock but also outside political ideologies and forces).[36] The difficulty is that the presumed more specific social and political concomitants of these changes—modern political parties, armies, and the like—have not in fact developed simultaneously. The problem is not just "lag" or "uneven development" but that we have failed to appreciate sufficiently the present era's changed circumstances and also the strength and workability of many traditional institutions and how these may shape, mold, and even determine the impact of these larger, more universal changes. We have dismissed as "traditional" the role of tribes, caste associations, mullahs, religious and fundamentalist movements, elites and family structures, patron–client systems transferred to the national level, and a host of other local and particularistic institutions, rather than seeing them as persistent, flexible, perhaps viable structures on which an indigenous process of development might be based. By now it is clear that such institutions will not necessarily disappear or be superseded as modernization proceeds, nor should they be easily dismissed, as our social science literature is wont to do, as dysfunctional. We must recognize the diversity of societies and developmental experiences.

Social scientists and policy analysts must begin with a renewed awareness of their biases, societal likes and dislikes, the Eurocentric basis of so many of their theories, and their particularistic rather than universalistic nature. This will require a fundamental reexamination of most of the truths social scientists, especially North American social scientists, hold to be self-evident. It will also require a new and stronger dose of cultural relativism. Cultural relativism need not be carried so far as to accept or remain neutral toward a Hitler, a Bokassa, or a Saddam Hussein. But it does imply a much more empathetic understanding of foreign cultures and institutions than before, an understanding of them in terms of their own cultural traditions and even languages, rather than through the distorting, blinding prism of Western social science.[37] The social sciences have been guilty of too-hasty generalization; hence, we require more modesty than before concerning the universal applicability of our social science and foreign policy notions, greater uncertainty in our assertions of global social science wisdom, more reluctance to apply the social science findings (apples) of our culture to the realities (oranges) of another, where they neither fit nor add up.[38]

To say that much social science theory we took as universal is somewhat less than that implies that future theory about development and democracy ought probably to be formulated at a lower, cultural-area level. We shall probably have to develop an African social science, an Islamic social science, a Latin American social science, and so on, and a region- and country-specific foreign policy as well. It may be that such middle-range theory at the cultural-area level will eventually yield again some more general, even universal findings about the development process. This will be a long-term process, however, and we may well find few universals on which to hang our social science hats. Many social scientists will be uncomfortable with this fact; a more useful approach may be to take the absence of very many such universals as a given and proceed from there. Some prominent social scientists are already saying that theory and research at the cultural-area level, the examination of more particularistic, culturally unique, perhaps regionally specific institutions and processes, will probably be the focus of future comparative development studies.[39]

The necessity of analyzing indigenous institutions on their own terms and in their own cultural contexts rather than through Western social science frameworks seems particularly appropriate in the present circumstances, given both the assertion of indigenous and nationalistic ideologies and movements in many development nations and the corresponding rejection of European, American, and Western ones. The emergence and articulation of distinctive Latin American, African, Islamic, and other cultural-area-based sociologies and political sciences of development raise a host of intriguing issues for scholarship and for policy. Implied is that we now take the developing nations and their alternative civilizations seriously for the first time, and on their own terms rather than through the condescension and superiority of U.S. or Western European perspectives. It means that the rising sense of nationalism and independence throughout the Third World is likely also to be reflected in a new insistence on indigenous models and institutions of development. It requires the formulation or reformulation of a host of new concepts and interpretations. It also implies that if the West, particularly the United States, can no longer be the world's policeman, it must also exercise restraint in seeking to be its philosopher-king, in terms of its assertion of the universality of its particular developmental experience.

This chapter has been something of a broadside. Its claims and criticisms are sweeping. Essentially it says the social sciences of development must start all over. So must U.S. policy in many areas. Of course, one purposely overstates the case to make it more forcefully. We have seen that there are universals in the development process, and we need to sort out more carefully what non-Western developing societies allow in and what gets winnowed out. We need sharper distinctions in the present critique between cultural definitions of concepts that implicitly influence social science theory construction, ethnocentrism as a distortion of perception, lack of research in specific culture areas, and simple analogy to the Western development experience, instead of analysis of the respective dynamics of given cases, political shortsightedness, and interest politics. We require qualification and refinement of the arguments. Nonetheless, the criticisms leveled here are fundamental and far-reaching.

The policy implications of these comments are also major. They mean the reexamination and likely restructuring of most of our aid and foreign assistance programs directed toward developing nations. They imply the short-sightedness and impropriety of seeking to apply European and North American strategies and institutional paraphernalia to societies and cultures where they simply do not fit. They imply that U.S. and international agency decision makers be much more circumspect in their assertion that they know best for the developing nations. Even more fundamental, these comments imply a considerable reeducation, in nonethnocentric understandings, of at least two generations of social scientists, policy makers, and the informed public, indeed of our educational focus, national ethos, and career system.

NOTES

1. For elaboration, see Howard J. Wiarda, "Cancún and After: The United States and the Developing World," *PS* 15 (Winter 1982): 40–48.

2. Louis Hartz, *The Liberal Tradition in America* (New York: Harcourt, Brace and World, 1955).

3. W. W. Rostow, *The Stages of Economic Growth* (Cambridge: Cambridge University Press, 1960).

4. See, for example, Robert Heilbroner, *The Great Ascent: The Struggle for Economic Development in Our Time* (New York: Harper & Row, 1963); Seymour M. Lipset, *Political Man: The Social Bases of Politics* (Garden City, NJ: Doubleday, 1960); C. E. Black, *The Dynamics of Modernization: A Study in Comparative History* (New York: Harper & Row, 1966); and especially Max Millikan and W. W. Rostow, *A Proposal: Key to an Effective Foreign Policy* (New York: Harper, 1957), which had a major impact on policy at the time.

5. Some other writings by the author on this theme include *Politics and Social Change in Latin America: The Distinct Tradition* (Amherst: University of Massachusetts Press, 1982) and *Corporatism and National Development in Latin America* (Boulder, CO: Westview, 1981).

6. For a fuller discussion, see Howard J. Wiarda, "At the Root of the Problem: Conceptual Failures in U.S.–Central American Relations," in Robert Leiken, ed., *Central America: Anatomy of Conflict* (New York: Pergamon, 1984), 259–78.

7. Chalmers Johnson, "The Institutional Foundation of Japanese Industrial Policy," in Claude Barfield and William Schambra, eds., *The Politics of Industrial Policy* (Washington, DC: American Enterprise Institute, forthcoming); see also the collected essays in *Human Rights and U.S. Human Rights Policy* (Washington, DC: American Enterprise Institute, 1982); and Howard J. Wiarda, "Can Democracy Be Exported? The Quest for Democracy in United States Latin American Policy," in

Kevin Middlebrook and Carlos Rico, eds., *The United States and Latin America* (Pittsburgh, PA: University of Pittsburgh Press, 1985).

8. For further argument, see Howard J. Wiarda, *In Search of Policy: The United States and Latin America* (Washington, DC: American Enterprise Institute, 1984).

9. William P. Glade, "Problems of Research in Latin American Studies," in *New Directions in Language and Area Studies: Priorities for the 1980s* (Milwaukee: Center for Latin America, University of Wisconsin at Milwaukee for the Consortium of Latin American Studies Programs, CLASP, May 1979), 81–101.

10. G. W. E. Hegel, *The Philosophy of History* (New York: Dover, 1956), 87; Shlomo Avineri, ed. *Karl Marx on Colonialism and Modernization* (Garden City, NY: Anchor, 1969); W. W. Rostow, *The Stages of Economic Growth: A Non-Communist Manifesto* (Cambridge: Cambridge University Press, 1960).

11. Robert A. Nisbet, *Social Change and History: Aspects of the Western Theory of Development* (Oxford: Oxford University Press, 1969).

12. See virtually any text, such as those by Hacker, Sabine, Wolin, etc.

13. Bernice Hamilton, *Political Thought in Sixteenth-Century Spain* (Oxford: Oxford University Press, 1963); Guenter Lewy, *Constitutionalism and Statecraft during the Golden Age of Spain* (Geneva: Droz, 1960); Howard J. Wiarda, "Corporatist Theory and Ideology: A Latin-American Development Paradigm," *Journal of Church and State* 20 (1970): 29–56.

14. For more details, see Bendix, "Tradition and Modernity Reconsidered," *Comparative Studies in Society and History* 9 (April 1967): 292–346; and Howard J. Wiarda, "Corporatism and Development in the Iberic-Latin World: Persistent Strains and New Variations," *Review of Politics* 36 (January 1974): 3–33.

15. See especially the writings of S. N. Eisenstadt, e.g., "Post-Traditional Societies and the Continuity and Reconstruction of Tradition," *Daedalus* 102 (1973): 1–27; and "Tradition, Change and Modernity: Modern Society and Sociological Theory" (unpublished).

16. For a volume that does encompass the smaller nations and advances an alternative, "corporative" European polity model, see Martin O. Heisler, ed., *Politics in Europe* (New York: McKay, 1974).

17. Frederick B. Pike and Thomas Stritch, eds., *The New Corporatism: Social-Political Structures in the Iberian World* (Notre Dame, IN: Notre Dame University Press, 1974); Howard J. Wiarda, *Corporatism and Development: The Portuguese Experience* (Amherst: University of Massachusetts Press, 1977).

18. See Howard J. Wiarda, "Toward a Framework for the Study of Political Change in the Iberic-Latin Tradition," *World Politics* 25 (January 1973): 206–35; *From Corporatism to Neo-Syndicalism: The State, Organized Labor, and the Changing Industrial Relations Systems of Southern Europe* (Cambridge, MA: Harvard University, Center for European Studies, 1981).

19. To start, see Paul E. Sigmund, ed., *The Ideologies of the Developing Nations* (New York: Praeger, 1972); W. A. Beling and G. O. Totten, eds., *Developing Nations: Quest for a Model* (New York: Van Nostrand, 1970); Howard J. Wiarda, *Politics and Social Change in Latin America: The Distinct Tradition* (Amherst: University of

Massachusetts Press, 1982); Wiarda, *The Soul of Latin America* (New Haven, CT: Yale University Press, 2001).

20. Examples include Daniel Lerner, *The Passing of Traditional Society* (New York: Free Press, 1964); Wilbert E. Moore, *The Impact of Industry* (Englewood Cliffs, NJ: Prentice Hall, 1965); Clark Kerr et al., *Industrialism and Industrial Man* (Cambridge, MA: Harvard University Press, 1960); and Alex Inkeles and David H. Smith, *Becoming Modern* (Cambridge, MA: Harvard University Press, 1974).

21. Raymond Aron, *Main Currents in Sociological Thought: Durkheim, Pareto, Weber* (Garden City, NY: Anchor, 1970).

22. The analysis here derives in large measure from Thomas O. Wilkinson, "Family Structure and Industrialization in Japan," *American Sociological Review* 28 (October 1962): 678–82; and his *The Urbanization of Japanese Labor* (Amherst: University of Massachusetts Press, 1965).

23. Talcott Parsons, *The Social System* (New York: Free Press, 1951); *The Structure of Social Action* (New York: Free Press, 1937); (with Edward Shils) *Toward a General Theory of Action* (Cambridge, MA: Harvard University Press, 1951).

24. Gabriel A. Almond and James S. Coleman, eds., *The Politics of the Developing Areas* (Princeton, NJ: Princeton University Press, 1960). The other authors cited are so familiar as to require no specific references to their work.

25. The image is that of Philippe C. Schmitter, "Paths to Political Development in Latin America," in *Changing Latin America* (New York: Columbia University, Academy of Political Science, 1972), 83–105.

26. Avineri, *Karl Marx*, Introduction; Bendix, "Tradition and Modernity."

27. The parallels in the rise and decline of such U.S.-sponsored programs as agrarian reform, community development, family planning, and sustainable development would make an interesting study.

28. These considerations of "historical space-time," a concept that has often confused U.S. observers, lay behind the efforts of Haya de la Torre and the Peruvian *Apristas* to develop an indigenous ideology for Latin America.

29. David Apter, *The Politics of Modernization* (Chicago: University of Chicago Press, 1965).

30. Anthony James Joes, *Fascism in the Contemporary World* (Boulder, CO: Westview, 1978); James Malloy, ed., *Authoritarianism and Corporatism in Latin America* (Pittsburgh, PA: University of Pittsburgh Press, 1977).

31. Claudio Veliz, *The Centralist Tradition of Latin America* (Princeton, NJ: Princeton University Press, 1979); A. James Gregor, *Italian Fascism and Developmental Dictatorship* (Princeton, NJ: Princeton University Press, 1979); David Collier, ed., *The New Authoritarianism in Latin America* (Princeton, NJ: Princeton University Press, 1979).

32. Lloyd I. Rudolph and Susanne Hoeber Rudolph, *The Modernity of Tradition: Political Development in India* (Chicago: University of Chicago Press, 1967); Randall Stokes and Anthony Harris, "South African Development and the Paradox of Racial Particularism: Toward a Theory of Modernization from the Center," *Economic Development and Cultural Change* 26 (January 1978): 245–69.

33. Howard J. Wiarda, *Critical Elections and Critical Coups: State, Society and the Military in the Processes of Latin American Development* (Athens: Center for International Studies, Ohio University, 1979).

34. For one such example, see Howard J. Wiarda, *Dictatorship, Development, and Disintegration: Politics and Social Change in the Dominican Republic* (Ann Arbor, MI: Xerox University Microfilms Monograph Series, 1975).

35. Dillon Soares, "Latin American Studies in the United States: A Critique and a Proposal," *Latin American Research Review* 2 (1976): 51–69.

36. In Lucian Pye and Sidney Verba, eds., *Political Culture and Political Development* (Princeton, NJ: Princeton University Press, 1965).

37. For such a *verstahen* approach and its effect *both* on the region studied and the researchers, see Jean Duvignaud, *Change at Shebika: Report from a North African Village* (New York: Pantheon, 1970).

38. Peter Winch, *The Idea of a Social Science and Its Relation to Philosophy* (London: Routledge & Kegan Paul, 1960).

39. Samuel P. Huntington, in a personal conversation with the author; see also the volume edited by the author, *New Directions in Comparative Politics* (Boulder, CO: Westview, 2002), which grew out of a faculty seminar with the same title organized at the Center for International Affairs, Harvard University.

Chapter Seven

The Democracy Agenda in U.S. Foreign Policy

The United States has long proclaimed that it is "different" from other nations, both in domestic politics and in foreign affairs. In domestic politics, stretching back to the founding of the republic, America has stood for life, liberty, equality, and, as the Declaration of Independence proclaims, the "pursuit of happiness." American politics has, over the centuries, tended toward greater democracy, openness, pluralism, and transparency. America has long believed in limited government, a weak state, checks and balances, and, as John Locke, the founding oracle of Anglo-American republicanism put it, "estate," by which he meant the right to acquire, hold, and dispose of private property. In all these ways, America sought to set itself apart from the Old World of European nations, which did not regularly practice these traits and from which most of the early colonists in America had come.

But right from the beginning America believed in and practiced exceptionalism in its foreign affairs as well as in its domestic politics and beliefs. In the famous doctrine that bears his name, President James Monroe compared the Old World of European powers with the New World of the Americas. *They* are mainly monarchies and practitioners of absolutism and autocracy, he said, while *we* practice republicanism. *They* believe in domination and tyranny while *we* practice liberty. Moreover, *they* practice the European strategies of colonization and empire while *we* believe in freedom. And *they* utilize the Old World techniques of diplomatic secrecy, balance of power, and Machiavellianism while *we* are the apostles of openness, moral precepts, and honor. These contrasts between Old World practices *and* the stated goals of the new United States could not have been portrayed more starkly.

Moreover, in actual conduct of its foreign affairs the United States continued to practice and proclaim its distinctiveness—even while later skeptics expressed doubt as to the purity of American motives. For example, in the wars of Texas independence (1836) and with Mexico (1846), when the United States deprived Mexico of roughly 40 percent of its national territory, the United States justified its land and power grabs with the nobler language of "manifest destiny," "self-determination," and "Westward expansionism"—to say nothing of anti-Mexican, anti-Spanish, anti-Catholic racism; xenophobia; and prejudice.

When the United States defeated Spain in the War of 1898 and seized Puerto Rico and the Philippines while establishing a protectorate over Cuba, there is no doubt the American public believed it was operating morally in behalf of the peoples affected, not just in self-interest. When the United States "stole" (Teddy Roosevelt's words) Panama from Colombia in 1902 in order to build the Canal, and subsequently sent military occupation forces to Cuba, the Dominican Republic, Haiti, Nicaragua, and Panama, no one can question that Americans genuinely *thought* they were bringing the benefits of a superior civilization (democracy, elections, Protestantism, free enterprise) to "less fortunate" lands and peoples.

America has thus always justified its great power or national interest pursuits with the *language* of moral superiority and purpose. The need for high moral purpose both reflects American beliefs and reinforces the sense of American distinctiveness from other powers that practice realpolitik. This need for high moral purpose in U.S. foreign policy extends to today: when George W. Bush sent U.S. troops into Iraq to find and destroy what were thought to be weapons of mass destruction, it was not sufficient for him to proclaim that the United States was operating from the principle of self-interest. Instead, he first had to demonize Saddam Hussein as a new Hitler and then proclaim our mission was to spread democracy, not just to Iraq but throughout the Middle East and to tyrannies everywhere. Similarly, current U.S. efforts in China or Russia cannot be set forth as simply balance-of-power politics or the effort to check and contain former or future rivals and adversaries but as a campaign to bring democracy, free enterprise, and human rights to these nations.

In most cases throughout history—such as World Wars I and II—American statements of moral purpose and the pursuit of hardheaded national interests went hand in hand. That is, the United States went to war against Germany and the Axis powers in both instances both to defend threatened U.S. interests globally and in Europe, as well as to "make the world safe for democracy" or to defeat fascism. The Cold War for all those decades was both a strategy to contain the Soviet Union and to defeat "Godless communism." In these cases there was generally little contradiction between morality and self-interest and, hence, comparatively few problems in the conduct of U.S. policy. But occasionally, as in Vietnam, and perhaps more recently in Haiti, Somalia, Bosnia, and Iraq, U.S. moral rhetoric and national interest goals seem not in harmony. Or the facts on the ground belie the rhetoric, which then proves hollow. Or the United States begins taking literally or too seriously the moral goals, elevating them to a vaunted position above its national interest goals. Policy often becomes a prisoner of and paralyzed by our own rhetoric. It is then that U.S. foreign policy gets in trouble, for ends and means do not match up, the goals come to appear unreachable and unrealistic, and the public, Congress, and the media stop supporting the policy.

This chapter argues that, with the newest expression of American high moral purpose, the democracy agenda, the United States is currently verging on such a disjuncture. The lofty goals of the policy and the limited means Americans are willing to use to achieve it appear at times to be out of balance. The rhetoric and ideology of the democracy agenda have come to overshadow the national interest concerns involved. Even worse, the strategy seems not consistently to be producing friendly, stable regimes but too often results in the opposite consequences. The results, for example, of recent democracy efforts and the election strategy in such diverse areas as Haiti, Mexico, Algeria, Pakistan, Russia, Bosnia, Afghanistan, and Iraq may be to produce instability rather than stability, chaos rather than order, national breakdowns deleterious to U.S. interests instead of happy, peaceful, friendly, democratic regimes.

At the least, the issue merits serious review and reconsideration. I should say that I myself am a strong believer in democracy and human rights as a part of U.S. foreign policy—both because they conform to my own beliefs and because I do not believe it is possible to have an effective *American* foreign policy unless it can be justified on moral and idealistic grounds. But to be successful the policy needs to be carried out effectively; the moral and self-interest motives need to be kept in accord; and the policy needs to produce concrete, positive results that the public can see and appreciate. Because these features, I believe, are now out of kilter, this chapter explores the dimensions of the problem and suggests new solutions.

THE DEMOCRACY AGENDA

The democracy agenda suggests that the pursuit of democracy and human rights is and ought to be at the heart of U.S. foreign policy purpose. Almost no one disagrees with that focus anymore. Even such hardheaded apostles of realpolitik as George Kennan and Henry Kissinger, who in the past criticized America's moralistic crusades in foreign policy and called for a policy based

exclusively on national interest considerations, came to recognize that for an
American (as distinct from those still Machiavellian Europeans) foreign policy to be successful, it must have a strong democracy/human rights component to it. If the policy lacks this moral dimension, then the public, Congress,
religious and human rights groups, labor unions, and even now, the foreign
policy establishment are unlikely to support it, and the policy probably cannot succeed.

But if there is a consensus by now on the need for a democracy/human
rights component to U.S. foreign policy, that still leaves open the question of
how strong that component should be. Should it be the only or clearly the
most important element in our foreign policy, or should it be but one consideration among several? Therein lies the current rub—and the policy conflict.
For while almost no one disagrees anymore that democracy and human rights
should form *some part* of the foreign policy agenda, the question remains as
to the degree, the relative importance of the democracy component, as compared with other considerations.

A few preliminary comments and distinctions will help frame the debate.
First, although most of us want a democracy/human rights component in U.S.
foreign policy, we also accept the maxim that no rule needs to be 100 percent
pure in order to serve as an effective basis for policy. For example, other than
an occasional embassy démarche on the national palace, Americans have not
talked very much about democracy and human rights in such countries as
Kuwait and Saudi Arabia. The reason is obvious: although we would obviously prefer democracy in these two countries, our and the rest of the world's
(Japan as well as Western Europe) absolute dependence on Persian Gulf oil
for the health of our national economies means that in practice we have opted
to largely ignore the democracy-advancing aspects of our policy in favor of a
stable (we hope) but nondemocratic regime that provides us with a reliable
source of oil. There are relatively few dissents from this policy; we do not
proclaim it publicly but informally almost everyone agrees that U.S. prosperity and the health of our economy and jobs—all of which depend on Middle
East oil—are simply more important in these two cases than a too vigorous
and potentially destabilizing democracy/human rights policy.

National security issues are approached similarly. Because of the long Cold
War with the Soviet Union and the threat posed by Soviet armaments and
missiles, the strategic dimensions of that relationship took overwhelming
precedence over democracy or any other dimension. The defense of U.S. security and the threat posed by the Soviets was *the* number one priority; all
other considerations were secondary, for without national security, it was argued, there could be neither democracy nor human rights. Moreover, as with

the oil issue in Kuwait or Saudi Arabia, few questioned the ultimate priority of the security relationship vis-à-vis the Soviet Union.

Questions arose mainly on the periphery where, in fact, some of the most intense Cold War battles were fought out: Southeast Asia, the Middle East, Sub-Saharan Africa, Central America. There the issue was often whether the Cold War security issues ought to take priority or whether local conditions of poverty, human rights abuses, and *lack* of democracy had caused the problems. In general, however, as long as the Cold War was being waged in all its intensity, whenever the security aspects of U.S. policy conflicted with the "softer" or pro-democracy facets, the security considerations won out. The policy became known in the 1960s and 1970s as the "lesser evil doctrine": when faced with a choice between a strong autocrat who is anticommunist and protects our interests (Marcos, the shah, Diem, Sukarno, Batista, Trujillo, other military-authoritarian regimes) *and* a wobbly democrat who may coddle the Left and prove unstable, the United States would almost always opt for the lesser evil of the stable autocrat.

But now let us introduce some complications into what has been a fairly clear-cut case:

The United States discovered in the Cuba case that supposedly stable authoritarians like Batista, rather than preserving stability and anticommunism, may actually prepare the ground in which radical revolutions like Castro's may flourish. This dawning realization prompted a reevaluation of U.S. policy toward such dictators as Trujillo, Marcos, Diem, Somoza, and others.

The United States began to realize in the early 1980s, following Jimmy Carter's earlier romantic and idealistic policy of human rights that was often self-defeating, that a hardheaded democracy/human rights agenda could be used as a way of destabilizing the Soviet Union and the Warsaw Pact countries. In other words, instead of the perpetual conflict between strategic and human rights considerations in foreign policy, the Reagan administration sought to utilize democracy and human rights as a strategic weapon to weaken, delegitimize, and undermine the Soviets and their allies.

Similarly in El Salvador in the early 1980s—and then in many other countries—U.S. human rights policy acquired a practical as well as an idealistic dimension. Instead of being hammered for its focus on the strategic as opposed to the democracy, human rights, and socioeconomic dimensions of the several Central American conflicts, the administration discovered that by standing for democracy and human rights it could defuse the critics in Congress, the media, and the religious and human rights groups; provide internal bureaucratic unity to its policy; get otherwise critical allies to support the policy; secure a more centrist government in El Salvador (as distinct from the unhappy choice between a rapacious military and a guerrilla triumph); and actually carry out its security strategy more effectively. The positive benefits from the El Salvador experience served as a model for similar strategies elsewhere in Latin America, Asia, Eastern Europe, and eventually the Soviet Union.

In general, the arguments between advocates of the primacy of the strategic dimension in U.S. foreign policy and the advocates of other dimensions have been largely static and dichotomous: either one or the other. But in the 1990s debate over China policy a more dynamic dimension has been added: that emphasis on the trade and economic side of the relationship would, in the long run, improve both human rights and the strategic relationship. The issue was the renewal of most favored nation (MFN) status to China. Human rights groups opposed the measure on the grounds it would be rewarding China for its various human rights abuses, mainly the crushing of the student democracy movement in Tiananmen Square. But business groups wanting to trade with China argued that the economic growth generated would improve living standards and the human rights situation in the long term, and would also serve to anchor a more prosperous China as a stable and responsible international participant in the world economy. In this way, instead of the usual conflict and zero-sum trade-off between democracy/human rights and trade/strategic considerations, the latter was pictured in a dynamic and positive relationship to the former.

 The end of the Cold War altered all these givens—including in the China case above. With the disintegration of the Soviet Union and the Warsaw Pact, and with no powerful strategic threat looming immediately on the horizon (until the war on terrorism), the United States could now pay more serious attention to democracy/human rights concerns, and less to strategic issues, than in the past. The equation or trade-off, always delicately balanced, between the democracy/human rights agenda and the strategic one had now been tipped definitely toward the former. China provides an example—which is what made the ongoing debate over MFN so close. As long as the Cold War was still on, the United States needed to use China in a strategic sense ("the China card") to counterbalance and play off against the Soviets. But with the Cold War over, the United States no longer so strongly needed China's strategic presence on the Soviet border and could afford to emphasize human rights issues more than in the past.

We need to worry whether the war on terrorism changed these policy givens. On the one hand, because of the 9/11 attacks, the United States felt justified in putting in place limits on personal freedom that would not have been permitted had there been no attacks. These antidemocratic steps (the Patriot Act, torture of prisoners, restrictions on travel and immigration) were criticized both at home and abroad. But then President George W. Bush proclaimed a crusade in favor of abolishing tyranny and expanding democracy to hitherto nondemocratic regions and countries. Which will win out, the restrictions on freedom or the democracy crusade?

One further new factor merits mention here—the growth of pro-democracy/human rights lobbying groups and of a "cottage industry" of organizations, both private and public, aimed at furthering the democracy/human rights agenda. When the human rights issue first came up as a major issue in foreign policy in the early 1970s, there were few human rights lobbies; but now there are a *host* of general and specialized religious and human rights groups, foundations, and constituencies dedicated to advancing that agenda. In addition, we now have the National Endowment for Democracy (NED), the Democratic and Republican international affairs institutes, agencies for democracy and human rights in the Agency for International Development (AID), the State Department, the CIA, the Defense Department, and the White House, and again a variety of public, private, and public–private election observer agencies (such as the Carter Center). In other words, the debate between the strategic and the democracy/human rights aspects of policy is no longer just a "rational-choice" process among policymaking elites of carefully weighing alternatives and options; rather, it is now the "stuff" of intense lobbying, street (and church, synagogue, town meeting, etc.) activity, pressure politics, congressional interest and posturing, partisan disagreement, and significant bureaucratic interests and rivalries. These activities have also forced a change over the past twenty-five years in the strategic democracy/human rights equation.

THE WILSONIAN TRADITION IN FOREIGN POLICY

We often speak of democracy and human rights as if these were new (the past thirty years) items on the U.S. foreign policy agenda. But in fact, the United States has long had this moralistic, idealistic strain as part of its foreign policy. Indeed, one could say that the United States, founded on the ideals of liberty and freedom, has *always* had these elements as part of its foreign policy. As former UN ambassador Jeane Kirkpatrick once remarked to the author, "What are we as a nation if we do not stand for democracy and human rights?"

Of course, motives are almost always mixed, and diplomatic history is full of examples where U.S. territorial or power grabs were covered over with the language of high-sounding principles. Or, where moralism and self-interest overlapped and got mixed together. Nevertheless, there is—perhaps unique among nations: "American exceptionalism" again—a strong streak of wanting to do good in the world, as distinct from naked self-interest. Even the fact that America feels compelled to justify its power politics by the use of moralistic argument—and then often becomes a prisoner of its own rhetoric—is itself an indicator of the importance of idealism in policy.

When the Monroe Doctrine was promulgated in 1823 at the height of the Latin American independence movements, there is no doubt that most Americans favored the cause of the new republics—even while Henry Clay cautioned a national interest strategy of wait-and-see. When Andrew Jackson acquired Florida from Spain, and then subsequently when the United States took Texas and the Southwest from Mexico, there is no doubt most Americans believed these territories would be better off, better blessed, and more productive under American than Mexican rule. And who can doubt the sincerity of William McKinley who allegedly prayed for divine guidance the night before seizing the Philippines?

Similarly with Panama in 1902: we may have nefariously "stolen" Panama from Colombia but at least we did so, in former Senator Hayakawa's immortal words, "fair and square." When Woodrow Wilson sent U.S. Marines to occupy a half dozen countries in Central America and the Caribbean, he and others doubtless believed they could "teach" the Latins to use the ballot box instead of the coup d'état. Nor should one doubt his sincerity in entering World War I not just to protect and enhance U.S. interests but to "make the world safe for democracy." World War II was similarly fought not just on national interest grounds but as a crusade against fascism; even today that campaign is often thought of as the last "good" war. And John F. Kennedy's Alliance for Progress should be seen as a way not just to check Soviet and Cuban expansionism in Latin America but also as a reflection of the liberal idealism of Kennedy's supporters.

In all of these instances it seems clear that hardheaded realism (expansionism, territorial aggrandizement, economic gain, bases, military victory) went hand in hand with moral purpose and justifications. Moral purpose and self-interest seem inseparable in the American tradition and must be wedded to achieve a successful foreign policy. Or else, moral purpose was used, concurrently or after the fact, to rationalize and justify self-interest considerations. But seldom did the moral imperative get in front of or begin to drive national interest considerations. That, in the American system, is a formula for trouble: when we begin to believe literally our own rationalizations and to conduct policy on that basis. But that is precisely what began to occur under President Jimmy Carter.

It is not the purpose here, nor is there space, to review the entire history and record of President Carter's foreign policy, particularly his human rights agenda. Suffice it to say that Mr. Carter began his presidency on a high moral plane, indicating that he would not lie to the American public and that human rights would constitute the foundation of his foreign policy. Some of Carter's appointees went even farther than the president himself, elevating human rights into virtually the *only* foreign policy consideration. In the Department of State, when there were conflicts between the idealistic human rights bureau and the more realistic regional bureaus, human rights considerations, thanks to the decisions of a mediating committee headed by then undersecretary Warren Christopher, consistently sided with the human rights advocates. In a number of difficult cases—Iran, Nicaragua, Argentina, Brazil—the human rights policy seemed to run so far ahead of national interest considerations, or to ignore these altogether, that the administration was accused of "losing" these countries or else of promoting such nationalism and anti-Americanism that the human rights policy was self-defeating. That is, in the latter two cases mentioned, the policy *strengthened* military-authoritarians in power for a time by enabling them to rally nationalistic public opinion against the United States.

President Ronald Reagan's foreign policy advisers set out to change the Carter emphasis. At first they appeared to be abandoning the human rights policy altogether; soon they evolved a more sophisticated position. The strategy involved two different kinds of targets. In right-wing and authoritarian regimes such as El Salvador and others in Latin America and Asia, the policy involved pressures for democratic elections, assistance to civil society groups, and the gradual nudging of these regimes back toward the political center so as to defuse domestic discontent, make the government more stable, and deprive far-left or communist groups of their support base. In the communist regimes the strategy was to use the democracy/human rights agenda (such as aid to Poland's Solidarity) to embarrass these regimes, deprive them of legitimacy, and ultimately undermine them. As added bonuses, the administration soon found that, by standing for democracy and human rights, it could defuse U.S. domestic discontent, get Congress and the human rights lobbies to support the policy, garner allied support, and provide unity and coherence to the foreign policy bureaucracy.

President George H. W. Bush largely followed the Reagan strategy of combining democracy/human rights concerns with hardheaded realism. But he was criticized by candidate Bill Clinton in the 1992 election campaign both for earlier mistakes in dealing with Iraq (the first Gulf War) and for giving insufficient attention to democracy/human rights issues in China and elsewhere. President Clinton vowed to reverse that course and brought with him into office many of the earlier advocates (Warren Christopher, Anthony Lake, Madeleine Albright) of Jimmy Carter's original human rights policy. He filled many assistant secretary, deputy assistant secretary, and office head positions with a new generation of policy activists more "progressive," even radical, than the generation that had designed Mr. Carter's early policy. The result during President Clinton's first two or three years was a policy emphasizing (in Albright's words) "aggressive multilateralism," sometimes at what seemed to be the cost of hardheaded U.S. national interests; "enlargement" (Anthony Lake's term), which begged the question of enlargement for or toward what—presumably greater democracy and human rights—and interventions in Haiti, Somalia, and Bosnia that often seemed motivated considerably more by television coverage, unchecked idealism, domestic politics, and the desire to do "good" in the world than by considerations of the national interest. For these incursions the Clinton administration was roundly criticized, even by Democrat supporters, as following a "Mother Teresa foreign policy."

Part of this renewed idealism involved a refocusing on democracy and elections in a variety of nations that had seldom, if ever, had democracy and elections before. Now, of course, no one can argue against democracy and elections; that is akin to arguing against God, apple pie, and motherhood. But in numerous countries—Russia, Bosnia, Haiti, Mexico, among others— the democracy/elections policy seemed to take on aspects of a moral crusade, a "missionary" effort similar to those undertaken early in the century often under U.S. Marine occupation forces to bring the benefits of U.S.-style practices and institutions to poor, presumably benighted lands. The same patronizing, condescending, even racist attitudes present early in the century were visible in this campaign. No one asked if democracy was really possible in countries that lacked the social, economic, cultural, or historical base for it. Once again the moral crusade seemed to be running ahead of realistic considerations and to be proceeding regardless of other U.S. policy considerations in these countries.

Obviously the United States prefers democracy in Iraq, Russia, Bosnia, Haiti, and Mexico. That is not the issue. The issue is whether democracy is possible or likely even with U.S. efforts in these countries. And whether an ethnocentric, moralistic, heavy-handed, and excessively idealistic democracy-through-elections policy might not have the effect of destabilizing these countries rather than stabilizing them. These are countries, recall, in the cases of Russia, Haiti, and Mexico, that America would *least* like to see destabilized because the consequences both for foreign policy (in the case of Russia) and for domestic politics (Haiti, and especially Mexico) would be disastrous. For instance, even the slightest hint of instability in Mexico will send millions of Mexicans streaming toward the U.S. border rather than the "mere" tens of thousands as at present. With the best of intentions, the democracy/elections policy has the clear possibility of destabilizing Mexico—the *last* country in the world Americans should wish even inadvertently to see destabilized.

Complicating the issue is the institutional apparatus of election technicians, AID and other personnel, political party assistance by the NED and the Democratic and Republican Parties' international affairs institutes, and networks of election observers (themselves often politically biased and/or ethnocentric) who now appear to spring *automatically* into action whenever an election is called and without the larger U.S. national interest (again, who could ever be "against" democracy?) being considered. The complications, missteps, and potentially disastrous consequences stemming from this unexamined *and virtually unexaminable* policy lie at the heart of this critique.

Much the same needs to be said regarding President George W. Bush's announced campaign to end tyranny and spread democracy. No one disagrees with these goals. But when the president mentions Saudi Arabia, Iran, and Egypt as candidates for democracy, warning signals should go up. Are these countries ready for democracy? Do they have the foundations to support it? Where are the institutions on which democracy could be built? And what if, by pushing too hard or too fast for democracy, we destabilize some very important countries in the world (Saudi Arabia for oil, Egypt for the Middle East peace process) whose stability it is in our interests to preserve?

THE EMERGENCE OF CONSENSUS ON THE DEMOCRACY/ELECTIONS POLICY

The consensus on democracy and elections, as one of the three pillars of the so-called Washington Consensus (the other two pillars were free trade and open markets), emerged slowly during the 1980s and 1990s. At first, President Carter's democracy/human rights policy was very controversial. As secretary of state under President Richard Nixon, Henry Kissinger had followed a more hardheaded balance-of-power policy and had frequently testified in congressional hearings against the introduction of a moral agenda into foreign policy. He argued that the United States should look solely at a country's foreign posture and not pay significant attention to its internal politics. President Gerald Ford and the Department of State had also resisted the human rights agenda when it first appeared as a serious policy issue in the mid-1970s. But a purely realistic, balance-of-power approach aligned the United States with some fairly unsavory characters: Somoza, Marcos, the shah, Suharto, human rights–abusing Latin American militaries. Moreover, it soon became clear that, in terms of U.S. domestic politics, foreign policy could not turn a blind eye to the plight of nuns who were raped and murdered in El Salvador, blacks in South Africa suffering under apartheid, or Jews and Baptists who wished to emigrate from the Soviet Union. It may be that other countries—France, for example with its nuclear tests in the South Pacific—could conduct foreign policy completely devoid of domestic public opinion, but in the United States of America, with its long moralistic and Wilsonian tradition, that was not possible.

The democracy/human rights agenda had begun during the Vietnam War at the initiative of a handful of liberal congressmen: Senators Tom Harkin of Iowa, Edward Kennedy of Massachusetts, Alan Cranston of California, and James Abourezk of South Dakota, and Representative Donald Fraser of Minnesota. The proposal to focus U.S. foreign policy strongly on human rights also came from a coalition of anti–Vietnam War groups led by the innocuous-sounding Clergy and Laity Concerned. In 1972, in addition, Senator Henry ("Scoop") Jackson had sought to tie U.S. trade policy toward the Soviet Union to a willingness on the part of the Soviets to allow dissident Jews, Christians, and others to emigrate. The human rights agenda was generally supported by liberal Democrats and opposed by the Republican administrations then in power (Nixon and Ford) as constituting unwarranted congressional interference in the president's foreign policymaking authority and as meddling in the internal affairs of other nations. The policy remained very controversial during President Carter's administration.

But succeeding Republican administrations discovered that the democracy/human rights agenda, which they had previously denounced as romantic idealism, could be used as an effective instrument in the Cold War. In El Salvador, the democracy initiative helped bring to power centrist democrat José Napoleon Duarte, which gave the United States a moderate, elected government with which it could effectively deal, as opposed to the earlier "evil choices" of supporting a rapacious military regime or allowing the leftist guerrillas to win. In Poland through Lech Walesa and Solidarity and in Russia as well, the administration discovered that it could use democracy and human rights as a way to delegitimize and help destabilize communist regimes. Plus the policy had the added bonuses noted earlier of defusing congressional criticism, reducing allies' criticism, and providing domestic policy coherence. In other words, Democrats often supported the policy for one set of reasons (humanitarian concerns) and Republicans for another (strategic), but they both supported the policy. This was the beginning of the domestic consensus on the democracy/human rights agenda.

By the 1990s, with the collapse of the Soviet Union and the end of the Cold War, two additional features of the emerging consensus became apparent. First, the failure and eventual collapse of such economies as the Soviet Union, Eastern Europe, Cuba, and Nicaragua revealed the bankruptcy of Marxist-Leninist ideas for managing national economies. With distinct variations, capitalism, free markets, and the idea of neoliberalism emerged triumphant in the economic sphere, just as democracy had clearly triumphed in the political sphere. In addition, armed with the arguments of professional economists that showed a multiplier effect from lowering tariff barriers, and spurred on by the realization that both Europe and Asia seemed to be moving in the direction of regional trading blocs that might at some levels exclude the United States, the United States itself began to advocate a free trade bloc encompassing North and Latin America. The older high-tariff, Third World model of ISI (import-substitution industrialization) underwent severe criticism for having outlived its usefulness or for having produced deleterious consequences. In its place came a new economic model—one that had earlier been championed by Margaret Thatcher, Helmut Kohl, Ronald Reagan, and others but that now, with the end of the Cold War and the discrediting of both Marxism-Leninism and ISI, triumphed seemingly *everywhere*—that emphasized both open markets and free trade.

Hence, by the early 1990s, and certainly by the time of the Miami Summit of December 1994 that brought together the heads of state of all the Western Hemisphere countries save Cuba, what was now being called the "Washington Consensus" was firmly in command. The consensus consisted of three interrelated goals: (1) *democracy* (mainly meaning elections) and human rights; (2) *open markets*—coupled with privatization, state downsizing; and (3) *free trade*, within a larger common-market arrangement. The interrelations of these three harked back to a long tradition of U.S. policy and foreign assistance and bore a striking resemblance to the 1960s ideas of economist, architect of the Agency for International Development, and national security advisor W. W. Rostow. That is, open markets and free trade will help improve the economy, raise living standards, create a larger middle class, and ultimately promote stability and democracy. In turn, democracy was seen as the best way to ensure stability and moderation that would guarantee a propitious climate for investment, open markets, and free trade. In addition—again in keeping with a long tradition of American thinking— all three of these pillars—democracy, open markets, free trade—were seen as complementary and as going hand in hand; no thought was afforded the possibility that open markets and free trade could upset stability and democracy, or that democracy might not always be the most conducive political system to a functioning, efficient economic program, particularly in developing nations' early stages of growth.

After all the disputes over U.S. foreign policy between idealists and realists during the course of the 1960s, 1970s, and 1980s, achieving a consensus on policy in the 1990s was nothing short of remarkable. With only slight variations, that consensus has largely held from the Clinton through the George W. Bush administration. Moreover, because it is so difficult and time-consuming bureaucratically for the U.S. policymaking system to reach closure, make a decision, let alone reach consensus on *anything*, one can understand why, once reached with so much difficulty, decision makers would be reluctant to reopen the issue.

Yet reexamination is necessary, because in many key countries the policy is not working. It is often producing discord, division, and even disintegration in many societies rather than harmony, consensus, growth, and stability. In country after country—Russia, Mexico, Bosnia, Haiti, maybe Iraq—both the policy and the assumptions that undergirded it are faulty, producing unintended consequences. It is not just that the glass of policy accomplishments is both half empty and half full, which would be a comfortable belief on which to rest and go forward. Rather the policy itself is flawed because a number of its assumptions are either erroneous or mistakenly applied.

Democracy is a worthwhile goal for the United States to pursue. That is our history and that is what we stand for as a nation. But the democracy agenda needs to be pursued carefully. We cannot impose it on countries that are not prepared for it; we also need to be prepared to adjust our policies to fit the cultures and societies of other countries. We cannot ride roughshod over local practices and impose our preferred political formulas on countries where they don't fit and won't work.

We need to be careful to balance democracy concerns with other U.S. interests—economic, strategic, diplomatic. Democracy is not our only concern or interest. We need to balance our democracy advocacy with our need to pursue a variety of foreign policy goals. In important countries like Russia, Mexico, Egypt, or Saudi Arabia, we had better be very careful that our pushing for democracy does not destabilize countries on whom we depend for other reasons. The goal needs to be to establish democracy. That should be articulated strongly and forcefully. But we also need to be prepared to compromise, be pragmatic and selective. A pro-democracy policy need not be 100 percent pure to be a good policy. China and Saudi Arabia may be too important for other reasons for us to push too hard on the democracy front. In Africa, the Middle East, and Latin America we need to be prepared, for now, to settle pragmatically for various mixed or halfway solutions. Later, when the conditions are more favorable, we can push again and harder for democracy. A prudent U.S. policy for democracy will thus combine idealism with a careful, balanced, case-by-case treatment.

Chapter Eight

Human Rights Policy

The movement in the last twenty-five years of many countries away from authoritarianism and toward democracy, and the impetus and applause that U.S. policy has given to this movement, should not blind us to the very real difficulties accompanying a pro-democracy, pro–human rights policy. By this time there is near universal, even bipartisan, support for a democratization/human rights policy, but it has not always been so. Democracy and human rights are now right up there with God, apple pie, and motherhood (assuming that we still support all *those* institutions!); no one (and certainly not this author) could be opposed to them. But while the democracy/human rights agenda has provided a marvelous opportunity for U.S. foreign policy, it also has the potential to be a trap as well. We need to explore how and why this may be so, and to be apprized of the pitfalls.

Latin America was the main venue, the living laboratory, where U.S. experimental policies in support of democracy and human rights were first tried out. But now the policy has become a global one encompassing Russia, Eastern Europe, the former Soviet republics, China, Africa, and even the Middle East. As the United States attempts to pursue a global foreign policy in support of democracy and human rights, it needs to keep in mind the warning lights that continue to flash from the Latin American experience, as well as the go-ahead signs. We need to be aware of the sensitivities, the flashpoints, and the policy dilemmas involved in the democracy/human rights policy, as well as the promises.

The issue is particularly acute as the United States armed forces are now increasingly involved in democracy-building programs for Iraq, Afghanistan, and other countries. On one level, the end of the Cold War implies that such nontraditional defense and security issues as democracy and human rights will receive greater attention from defense planners. On another level, democracy, human rights, and nation building are often viewed at high political levels in the Pentagon as a way, like counternarcotics, of continuing to justify military budgets and missions. At still a third level, the Defense Department—like other agencies—has been directed to support and enhance a pro-democracy/ human rights foreign policy in Iraq and elsewhere. The war on terrorism makes it imperative that the United States be seen as supporting human rights as a way of undermining the appeal of radical elements. All of these pressures make it incumbent that policy planners on both the defense and civilian side understand clearly the history and unresolved dilemmas of this policy, as well as its obvious advantages.

HISTORY

The United States, we have seen, has always had a foreign policy grounded on human rights. The United States achieved its independence from Britain on the basis of its struggle for representative self-government; we sympathized with the ideals of liberty, equality, and fraternity of the French Revolution; and most Americans supported the efforts of Latin America to achieve independence and democracy in the early nineteenth century. The United States "liberated" Texas as well as the American Southwest from Mexico in the name of democracy; fought Spain in 1898 to bring freedom to Cuba; sent the Marines to numerous spots in the Caribbean in the early twentieth century to bring the presumed benefits of democracy to, as President William H. Taft put it, our "little brown and black brothers"; and, of course, President Woodrow Wilson involved the United States in World War I in order to "make the world safe for democracy." Diplomatic historians have been quick to point out that democracy was not always the real goal, let alone the outcome in all of these cases, but the U.S. ethos and history have nonetheless led the nation more or less consistently to justify its policies in terms of seeking democratic ends.

Critics of this emphasis—Hans Morgenthau, George Kennan, and Henry Kissinger—have urged the United States to eschew moralism in its policy and to embrace a policy based on realism and the national interest. The debate waxed in the 1950s, 1960s, and 1970s. On the one side stood the idealists who argued that the United States was a special nation, a "city on a hill," a case of "exceptionalism." It was, they argued, America's duty and moral responsibility to provide leadership in an amoral world, to set an example, to stand firmly for our ideals of freedom and democracy. On the other side were the realists who advocated a hardheaded and pragmatic foreign policy, free of moral restraints; as one realist put it, "we have no friends in the world, only interests."[2]

As part of the Alliance for Progress, John F. Kennedy had supported new democratic openings in Latin America. His administration had even tried for a time to stem the wave of military-authoritarian takeovers that began to occur in the early 1960s. Yet these efforts were insufficient to hold back authoritarianism. In fact, when faced with the choice, at the height of the Cold War, between a weak and often wobbly Latin American democrat who might allow full freedom for the Left *and* a strong, authoritarian regime that vigorously pursued anticommunism, the Kennedy and Johnson administrations invariably chose the strong authoritarian over the wobbly democrat. The policy was known, somewhat derisively, as the "lesser evil doctrine."

It was during this period of seeming U.S. preference for authoritarians, coupled, of course, with the Vietnam War protests, that a manifest human rights lobby and policy-in-preparation began to be formed. It is to be emphasized that this was different from the typical, historic, and generalized American *preference* in support of democracy abroad; this was a narrower group, a lobby, a political point of view with a specific policy position. And therein lay the first problem with U.S. human rights policy: it was not entirely clear if human rights were really the agenda or if it was a particular and partisan political agenda whose aim was to use the human rights issue for other purposes.[3]

The answer to that question is unclear and will probably always remain so. The impetus to Congress on human rights issues during the late 1960s came from an amorphous coalition known as the "human rights movement" or "community." The movement's activities were coordinated by the Human Rights Working Group of the Coalition for a New Foreign and Military Policy, which was headed by anti–Vietnam War activists. The movement brought together a variety of antiwar groups, including the innocuous-sounding Clergy and Laity Concerned; its ranks included such antiwar and left-wing stalwarts as Jane Fonda, Tom Hayden, Jacqui Chagnon, Staughton Lynd, and Ramsey Clark. The driving force within the movement was the peace groups as well as the New Left and the Old Left. In Congress these groups found sympathetic ears among such persons as Senator Tom Harkin, Congressman Ron Dellums, and the left-wing of the Democratic Party. Within the movement—and that is what makes our interpretation difficult—were numerous people (clergy, students, citizens) who genuinely wanted to promote human rights. Yet others wanted to use the human rights issue to promote their own, generally left-wing political agenda. These "other agendas" of several groups that call themselves human rights defenders remain a part of the problem of human rights policy still today—even though the essentials of the human rights policy have by now been incorporated and co-opted into official U.S. policy.[4]

The first legislation systematically linking U.S. foreign policy to human rights issues was the Jackson-Vanik amendment to the 1972 trade agreement with the Soviet Union, which tied trade concessions to the USSR to greater opportunities for dissidents to emigrate. In the next four years other pieces of legislation were put in place, making U.S. bilateral assistance conditional on the recipients' human rights performance. Efforts were also made to extend human rights "conditionality" to the major international lending agencies such as the World Bank.

The policy was controversial from the beginning and was strongly opposed by the White House, the State Department, and then national security advisor Henry Kissinger. Presidents Richard Nixon and Gerald Ford opposed the policy as constituting unwanted and unwarranted congressional interference in their foreign policymaking prerogatives. The State Department took the position that human rights were a domestic matter of the countries with which Washington had relations and in which the United States ought not to interfere. Kissinger saw the policy from his realpolitik perspective as causing potentially immense problems for his budding balance-of-power policy in such important (and human rights–abusing) countries as China, Iran, the Soviet Union, Brazil, and the Philippines. The debate was fierce; but through the mid-1970s, while the legislation calling for human rights observance continued gradually to expand, the White House and State were still able generally to pursue their grand strategies without the constraints of a body of human rights restrictions.

All of this changed under President Jimmy Carter. During the 1976 campaign, but especially in his May 1977 speech at Notre Dame University (Indiana), Carter elevated human rights into *the* number one priority of his administration. His transition team at the State Department brought in several officials at the assistant secretary and deputy assistant secretary levels who were recruited out of the human rights movement. In addition, at the deputy assistant secretary level and on the policy planning staff were some key but often lower-level and therefore obscure individuals from the antiwar, McGovern, left-wing of the Democratic Party who were strongly committed to the causes, including human rights, of "the movement." Carter did not closely supervise appointments below the Cabinet level so a significant number of persons who emerged from what were considered fringe movements of the 1960s were recruited into his administration and placed in charge of official policy.

The institutional apparatus for a vigorous human rights policy was also put in place. At State, what had been an "office" of human rights was now elevated into a full-fledged "bureau." Patt Derian, a former civil rights activist in the U.S. South who thought that that noble but particular struggle could be carried over into other cultures and societies, was made assistant secretary for human rights and humanitarian affairs. Increasingly, policy in various regional areas had to be in conformity with the norms laid down by the human rights bureau. When there were conflicts between the regional bureau (such as for Africa or Latin America) and the human rights bureau, the dispute was settled by a special committee led by then undersecretary of state Warren Christopher. Invariably, the Christopher committee sided with the human rights bureau and against the regional bureaus who, after all, knew far better the circumstances in the individual areas or countries of dispute.

The Carter foreign policy record and failures are too well known to be discussed at length here. These include Iran, where the Carter human rights policy helped undermine the shah and led to the Ayatollah Khomeini's rise to power, Islamic fundamentalism, and the imprisonment of U.S. Embassy hostages. The cases include the important South American countries of Argentina, Brazil, and Chile, then governed under military regimes but in which historic close relations with the United States were sacrificed for the sake of a futile and self-defeating human rights policy. Derian's approach in dealing with these critical countries was to rant and rave and condemn the entire nation or its armed forces as "fascist" (as distinct from condemning the individual bad apples in it), thus forcing the rest of the population to defend the regime or the rest of the officers to defend the military institution on nationalistic grounds. Another case was Nicaragua where, as Professor Anthony Lake showed, the Carter administration was torn between its desire for human rights and its (contradictory) unwillingness to sanction intervention, which resulted in disastrous indecision and temporizing thus enabling the Marxist Sandinistas both to seize power and to consolidate their hold on power while progressively excluding other, democratic groups.[5]

In long-range terms, Carter's human rights policy did help undermine the legitimacy of these authoritarian regimes and helped lead to the reestablishment of democracy. In short-range terms, however (other than a handful of people being released from jail), the policy was often a failure. Not only did it not improve the human rights situation in these countries, it hardened the resolve of the military regimes to stay in power and to resist Washington's pressures. Moreover, it produced such strong anti-American sentiment in these countries that it led to a permanent estrangement, which, despite the surface manifestations of agreement on open markets and democracy, has not fully healed to this day. From this point on, in contrast to the previous 150 years of history that had even in its darkest moments at least paid lip service to the pan-American ideal of hemisphere cooperation, the two parts of the hemisphere, North and South, seemed destined to go permanently in their own separate, distinct directions. Hence, despite some notable diplomatic accords over Panama and Israeli–Egyptian relations—both of which looked increasingly threadbare as time went on—the Carter presidency is almost universally thought of by the experts as a foreign policy failure.[6]

The Carter human rights policy was very controversial and came under strong attack from presidential candidate Ronald Reagan and his foreign policy advisers during the 1980 campaign. The Reagan people accused Carter of having "lost" Iran, Nicaragua, Afghanistan, Ethiopia, Grenada, Angola, Mozambique, and perhaps El Salvador, Guatemala, and others during his watch. They blamed the Carter human rights policy for helping to lose most of these nations to Marxism-Leninism since the Carter policy had undermined erstwhile allies (however tyrannical) and paved the way for takeovers by parties hostile to the United States.[7] It should be emphasized, since the point is frequently misunderstood, that the criticisms were not against human rights per se. Rather, the criticism centered on the following points:[8]

1. Carter's elevation of human rights to a position of virtually the *only* consideration in U.S. foreign policy, to the exclusion of economic, commercial, diplomatic, security, and military interests.
2. The double standard involved: right-wing regimes who were allies of the United States were picked on far more than left-wing regimes such as the Soviet Union or Cuba that constituted the real threats to U.S. interests.
3. The policy was applied inconsistently, incoherently, and with no agreed-upon criteria; even the definition of *human rights* was changed several times.
4. The persons charged with carrying out the policy were often incompetent and knew appallingly little about the countries where the policy was applied.
5. The policy was unsophisticated and indiscriminating; it used too-blunt instruments; and it was unable to distinguish between the often mild repression practiced by authoritarian regimes and the massive abuses of communist or totalitarian regimes.
6. The policy was often counterproductive for the reasons already indicated; it led frequently to a hardening of attitudes in the countries involved rather than reform.
7. The policy was unrealistic. It could not sort out the possible from the merely desirable or the desirable from the impossible. It often verged on the romantic and wishful rather than having a strong base in international realities.
8. The policy was ineffective in terms of human rights goals. It produced few changes. A few people were helped but basic policy in the offending countries was unchanged. There was a lot of noise over very little.

The Reagan administration was determined to change this orientation. However, the administration was not monolithic on the issue: not only were there different points of view but the administration also changed dramatically over time.

Some of the Reagan foreign policy team were so incensed by the Carter human rights policy that they were determined to abolish it. For example, Reagan's first nominee for the post of assistant secretary for human rights and humanitarian affairs, Ernest Lefever, avowed that, if confirmed, he would abolish the very office for which he was being considered. It was not that Lefever was against human rights; in fact, he had a long history as a fierce human rights activist. But he believed human rights was a domestic issue of each country and should have no place in foreign policy. Lefever, however, failed to win Senate confirmation; meanwhile, cooler heads and a different view began to prevail.

In spring 1981 and continuing into 1982, two themes began to come together. The first was a new view of human rights policy in general; the reasoning, quite different from the Carter approach, was as follows:

1. There is a close relationship between democracy and human rights. Democratic governments are more likely to respect human rights and therefore a policy in favor of democracy is also in favor of human rights.
2. There is a close relationship between Soviet expansionism and the loss of human rights. There is also a close relationship between U.S./Western influence and the protection of human rights. Therefore, a policy of opposition to Soviet expansionism and of strengthening the United States is also a pro–human rights policy.
3. The United States must sometimes work with friendly authoritarian regimes that are resisting communism. Because such regimes can be nudged toward democracy, and because a communist takeover will make human rights even worse, that is also a pro–human rights stance.
4. A government (like Cuba's) that provides some social and economic benefits but denies basic political and human rights is not a pro–human rights regime.

This was obviously a Cold War/ideological position that could be used to berate the Soviet Union and its allies. Yet meanwhile, another case was being decided that would have a profound effect on U.S. human rights policy: El Salvador. The El Salvador case provided not theoretical arguments as above, but hardheaded practical lessons about the political consequences of human rights. We cannot review all of this history here but in 1981 U.S. policy in El Salvador was on the ropes, faced with the unhappy choice between allowing the Marxist guerrillas to triumph, which was clearly unacceptable to the goal

El Salvador (cont.)

of preventing "another Cuba" or "another Nicaragua" in the region, and supporting an exceedingly repressive military regime that raped and murdered nuns and many others, which was clearly unacceptable from a moral and a domestic politics viewpoint. Hence, the United States helped engineer a series of elections and reforms that eventually brought moderate, democratic, civilian, elected Christian-Democrat José Napoleon Duarte to power, and thus provided a third and quite attractive alternative—democracy—to the unacceptable other two.

Out of this experience Washington learned some critical lessons that it then applied to other countries and to human rights policy in general:

1. Congress will support the policy if you stand for promoting democracy instead of allying with a repressive military.
2. Ditto the media.
3. Ditto the religious groups and human rights lobbies.
4. Ditto the public.
5. Ditto our allies.
6. Standing for human rights and democracy gives unity and justifiable purpose to the government and the diverse foreign policy bureaucracies.
7. Democratic governments do not start wars that cause no end of trouble, à la Argentina in the Malvinas/Falklands.
8. Democratic governments do not (à la Nicaragua) aid guerrilla campaigns in other people's countries.
9. Democratic governments do not send terrorists into neighboring countries or seek to destabilize those countries. (This became the theme and policy of George W. Bush.)
10. Democratic governments do not ally themselves with the Soviet Union or allow themselves to be used as bases for Soviet machinations.
11. Democratic governments simply cause much less grief than either right-wing regimes (Somoza, Pinochet, Marcos) or left-wing ones (Cuba, Nicaragua, North Korea).

A careful reading of this list reveals that these are all very *practical* reasons to be in favor of human rights, not romantic or idealistic ones. Moreover, what the Reagan administration discovered—gradually, by fits and starts, and without being planned in advance—is that with this policy it had an opportunity to blend and fuse both idealistic (democracy, human rights) concerns and very realistic ones (anticommunism, defense of the national interests), and thus to erase once and for all that historic conflict between idealism and realism that had long bedeviled American foreign policy. The policy is both popular domestically (who could be against democracy and human rights?), but it is also effective internationally by helping to undermine communist regimes and enabling the reform of authoritarian ones. What could be better than this?[9]

It is no surprise that a policy that combined so many good things would quickly become very popular. Both Congress and the White House could support it. It not only "saved" foreign policy chestnuts in El Salvador, Guatemala, Nicaragua, Chile, and numerous other Latin American countries, but it also helped usher in the greatest foreign policy triumphs of the post–World War II era when both Eastern Europe and then the Soviet Union disintegrated and moved toward democracy. It is small wonder that this new, updated version of human rights policy came to enjoy widespread bipartisan support; indeed, the support for this policy is so strong that it is inconceivable that any future administration would abandon it. George H. W. Bush clearly followed this revamped Reagan policy; Presidents Bill Clinton and George W. Bush have done the same. There are really no alternatives anymore. But will it work in the Middle East?

UNRESOLVED DILEMMAS OF HUMAN RIGHTS POLICY

While it is easy to wax hyperbolic over this unaccustomed consensus on the democracy/human rights agenda, we need to recognize the pitfalls, limitations, and possible traps in this approach as well. American policy pronouncements tend to slide over and avoid these problems, and just to say "democracy" and "human rights" has become an incantation that by expression alone seems to leave no further doubts or room for discussion. Yet, in fact, things are more complicated than that; particularly as the U.S. military is called upon to take on new missions including the furtherance of democracy and human rights, it needs to know the potential problems involved.

1. *Diverse meanings of democracy and human rights.* Clearly in China, the Islamic world, and Africa, democracy has different meanings than it has in the West. Even in Latin America, which is a predominantly Western area, democracy has always been more centralized, "organic," and Rousseauian, as contrasted with the Lockean, Madisonian version of the United States.[10] No democracy/human rights policy can be successful unless it recognizes both the universals of democracy *and* the subtle differences. Not every nation can or will be forced into the U.S. mold; rather, each must adapt the universals of democracy and human rights to its own particular culture, society, and circumstances. Iraq and Afghanistan are cases showing how difficult it is to implant democracy in a very different culture.

2. *Distinct categories of human rights.* Human rights may be divided into three categories: prevention of torture and crimes against the person, political

and civil rights (free speech, assembly, etc.), and social or economic rights (housing, health care, education, etc.). The experience so far has been that there is more global consensus on the first two of these than on the third and therefore better chances for success. In addition, the third category is very expensive to implement and most countries have been unwilling to take up very much of the burden of paying for such "rights" in countries other than their own.

3. *Evenhandedness.* China (as a check on the Soviet Union) and Saudi Arabia (oil) have long been considered so important that they have largely been exempted from human rights considerations. But with the end of the Cold War, China seems no longer to be free from criticism. Besides Saudi Arabia and Kuwait, are there other nations of such overriding importance that we should be careful in pushing human rights there because to do so might destabilize them?

4. *Intervention versus nonintervention.* As an aggressive human rights policy is pursued, it must be recognized that it entails interfering in the internal affairs of other nations. How can one best reconcile (which the Carter administration failed to do as did the Clinton) nonintervention on the one hand, which is generally supported, with human rights advocacy, which is also supported? How far should one go and how hard can human rights be promoted before the policy becomes counterproductive?

5. *What instruments?* Human rights and democracy are important U.S. interests, and they have recently become even most important. But they are not the only interests, and in some circumstances they may not even be the most important—although that discussion is likely to set off alarm bells in the U.S. domestic debate as El Salvador and South Africa did in the 1980s. Saudi Arabia is the most obvious case: oil takes precedence over human rights considerations. In Peru, the U.S. interest in counternarcotics may have a higher priority than human rights abuses by the Peruvian government. In Mexico the desire for continued stability in a large neighbor may take precedence over greater democratization. In Iraq and Afghanistan we may be more interested in eliminating terrorism than in protecting human rights. Hard choices!

6. *Backsliding.* The United States has been euphoric over the transition to democracy in so many countries in recent years that it has paid insufficient attention to the policy responses it should have if democracy is overthrown or reversed. Haiti is the most obvious case, and while Haiti is not typical or representative of Latin America, the debate over U.S. policy there has been deeply divisive. Yet what if democracy were reversed or destroyed in a large and important country: Peru, Venezuela, India, Colombia, the Philippines, Indonesia, Brazil, or Argentina? What if it is reversed in Poland or Russia? The prospect is so distasteful that contingency plans have not been sufficiently

thought through and formulated should democracy be overthrown. What precisely should the U.S. response be? If sanctions do not work, are the American people willing to intervene militarily to restore democracy? What if democracy is reversed not in some isolated, small, and unimportant country but there is a whole *wave* of reversions to authoritarianism as in the 1960s? What could or should the United States do?

(7.) *Democratic consolidation.* During the 1980s and now in the Middle East, the United States concentrated on *establishing* democracy: creating the conditions for and then holding elections. Yet a genuinely functioning and long-term democracy requires more than a single election; it requires an institutional infrastructure (political parties, interest groups), a climate of opinion ("civic political culture") conducive to a workable democracy, and public policies that enhance and support democracy in the long run. The tasks of democratic *consolidation* may well be even more demanding, and certainly imply a far longer commitment than the initial establishment of democracy. Haiti is a case in point: even if the United States succeeds in reestablishing a democratic government, does anyone believe that in the absence of any viable institutions or infrastructure in that country that democratic consolidation—and, hence, the need for a continued U.S. presence—will not require a *very* long time and a mammoth commitment of resources? Somalia may be at an even less politically developed level in these regards than Haiti. How about Palestine, Iraq, or Afghanistan? Are we willing to commit the resources in this time of budget cutbacks, declining foreign aid, military reductions, and popular impatience with long-term foreign commitments? It must be acknowledged that democracy building is a very long, hard, and expensive process.

(8.) *Democracy and socioeconomic development.* An even harder question is whether democracy is even suitable and supportable in these countries. We tread on dangerous ground here because a widespread assumption of popular opinion is that American know-how and influence can succeed in democratizing even the poorest country. Yet a wealth of social science literature suggests that, with some exceptions, democracy is likely to prosper and become consolidated in countries that have a sufficiently high level of socioeconomic development (and, hence, a large middle class, etc.) where representative institutions can be supported and develop firm foundations.[11] Those who would have U.S. forces rush into Haiti, Somalia, or Afghanistan, for example, or into other very poor countries in order to secure democracy, should know that would likely require a forty- to fifty-year occupation at enormous political and financial costs.

(9.) *Creating versus preserving democracy.* The first implies starting from scratch (again Haiti or Iraq), creating something out of nothing, building democracy where none had existed before—an almost impossible job. The second involves supporting an already existing but now troubled and politically unstable democracy (Indonesia, the Philippines), bolstering a possibly fragile democratic regime that is already in place, where the political culture is already supportive of democracy and where democratic institutions already function albeit imperfectly. This second task is not only far easier but it is likely to produce successful foreign policy that enjoys popular support. The first strategy is far more difficult, less likely to be successful, and Americans lack the skills to implement it.

Now if these complex issues can be resolved—and there are signs that in recent years policy *has* managed to accomplish some of the goals or at least blur and fudge over the difficulties—one can have a successful human rights/democratization policy that goes beyond the apple pie and motherhood level. In short, more than rosy incantations in support of democracy and human rights is needed; there also needs to be hard thinking on these tougher and more complicated issues before a successful and long-term policy can produce effective results.

GLOBAL IMPLICATIONS

The programs from the 1960s (even earlier if one goes back to Presidents William McKinley, Theodore Roosevelt, and Woodrow Wilson—or even to James Polk!) in support of democracy and human rights grew initially out of the Latin American experience. The Soviet Union, Eastern Europe, China, and the Middle East were thought to be either too volatile for a successful human rights policy, or else too dangerous, or with the stakes too high for other reasons—for example, Soviet missiles or Saudi oil. Latin America, because the stakes and/or costs of a mistake were assumed to be lower, and because it is close to home and subject to American pressures, was the venue where a variety of programs were experimented with, from agrarian reform and community development in the 1960s, to family planning and human rights in the 1970s, to democratization in the 1980s. In this sense, Latin America has been a guinea pig, a political and sociological laboratory for all manner of U.S. reform programs from time immemorial, but mostly from the 1960s.

The successes, mostly unanticipated by foreign policy specialists, of the democracy/human rights program in Latin America have by now helped elevate this aspect of U.S. policy to a global dimension. The United States now has a set of institutions (the National Endowment for Democracy, Republican and Democratic international institutes) for the spread of democracy; a democracy office in the Agency for International Development; a democracy/

human rights bureau at the State Department, CIA, and Defense Department; a variety of agencies for observing elections; and a host of special interest groups to further the democracy/human rights agenda. President Clinton and Secretary of State Christopher proclaimed—and no longer just rhetorically—that the promotion of democracy abroad was at the heart of their foreign policy. President George W. Bush made it into a global campaign. Democracy and human rights have become *the* central unifying theme of the diverse foreign affairs bureaucracies, one of the few issues on which they agree. When one asks what now is U.S. policy in Russia, the former Soviet republics, Eastern Europe, Latin America, Cambodia, Vietnam, Africa, and the Middle East, the answer invariably is *democracy and human rights*.

This emphasis received added impetus because of the end of the Cold War. The cessation of the Cold War not only terminated the superpower competition between the United States and the USSR but it also led to the fall of the Berlin Wall and the unification of Germany, the freedom and democratization of Eastern Europe, the breakup of the Soviet Union, and the easing and negotiations for the ending of various regional conflicts in Cambodia, Southern Africa, the Horn of Africa, and Central America. Not only did these momentous international events flow from the withering or atrophying of the Cold War; the Cold War's end also stimulated immense domestic changes in the countries with which the United States has long been concerned. Among other things, it has led to the declining popularity of communist parties worldwide, the decline of various guerrilla movements, the discrediting of the Left in various countries, and the bankruptcy of such regimes as Castro's Cuba as models of Third World development.

All these post–Cold War changes made the democracy/human rights agenda even more attractive than before. We could now afford to talk about human rights in countries like China that during the Cold War was considered too sensitive and because other, more important stakes were concerned. During the forty-five years of the Cold War, security issues could often be used to override all other concerns. In a sense, many "idealistic" agenda items like democracy and human rights have flourished only in times of peace, as luxuries, not in times of crisis or war—even Cold War. In the post–Cold War era there was that peace; there was that luxury. So it could be expected that human rights/democracy issues would achieve even greater importance than before and on a global scale. President Carter was premature in elevating human rights to *the* central position in his foreign policy before the Cold War had ended; but after it did end, one could anticipate far greater democracy/human rights emphasis.

The post–Cold War decade, 1991–2001, was especially propitious for promoting human rights. Without a major enemy anymore, the United States could afford to devote much of its foreign policy energy to supporting democracy and human rights. But with the attack of 9/11 the old issues are open again. Do we continue to focus on human rights or will strategic concerns (fighting terrorism) take precedence? Can we balance the two? George W. Bush believes that expanding freedom and democracy will also help defeat the terrorists. It is a risky gamble. But in the long tradition of American foreign policy, it is a new way of combining idealism with hardheaded realism.

This emphasis on democracy and human rights is therefore not without its problems. First, although there has been progress in some areas, the ten dilemmas discussed in the preceding section have by no means been resolved—or even addressed in some areas. Second, the policy may still be selective in some cases: witness the dispute in the Bush administration over applying human rights criteria in Iraq, the question of how far (if at all) Washington should push Kuwait or Saudi Arabia on democracy/human rights issues, or the longtime dispute over how hard the United States should push Israel to implement Palestinian rights. Third, what of countries like Russia, Iraq, and others where Washington has put so many of its foreign policy eggs in the democracy/free market basket, but where the culture, society, and political system seem unsupportive of democracy at least in the short term? Finally, and as hinted at above, one may strongly disagree—as in the case of Haiti on Pakistan—over the situation of human rights in that country, over its causes, and over what should be done about it. Thus, although there is widespread bipartisan consensus on human rights policy, and though the policy now claims universal applicability, there may still be sharp disagreements over the precise human rights situation in a given country, what the United States should do about it, and what should be the trade-off between human rights and other issues of importance in U.S. foreign policy.

CONCLUSION

Since the 1960s the promotion of human rights and democracy has become an integral part of U.S. foreign policy. The policy is now far more realistic and pragmatic than it was when earlier proposed; the human rights policy has helped resolve the long dispute between idealism and realism in foreign policy and has made many significant contributions to American successes in recent years—not the least being the fall of the Soviet Union whose legitimacy was in part undermined by human rights considerations. The policy enjoys bipartisan and near-universal consensus; there is no longer any dissent from it.

Human rights is now seen as part of a broader strategy of promoting democracy and economic growth through free markets. Free political systems and free economies—that is what America stands for. Human rights and democratization thus serve *concrete* American *interests.* The institutional machinery in support of democracy and human rights has now grown up, and the United States is now far more sophisticated and successful in the implementation of the policy than in earlier years. By this time human rights/democratization has emerged from its earlier regional focus (Latin America primarily) to become a truly global concern.

The end of the Cold War gave even greater importance to the democracy/human rights agenda. With the historic enemy, the Soviet Union, in tatters, human rights and democratization achieved even greater significance than in the past. In the nonwar, noncrisis, nonthreatening situation of the 1990s, such "new agenda" items as human rights and democratization emerged at the forefront of foreign policy concerns. The war on terrorism, however, introduced new tensions in the human rights/security trade-off.

There remain, nevertheless, many unresolved issues in implementing an effective human rights/democracy policy. Policy makers, including military officials, need to understand these harder issues, which are at the heart of a rights/democracy policy. Policy makers also need to comprehend the different, often culturally based interpretations, meanings, and priorities of human rights in different societies (again, the ethnocentrism problem), while also holding fast to an emerging legal and political consensus on global standards of human rights/democratization. On this more enlightened, realistic basis, a strong human rights/democracy policy can go forward on a foundation that is not only morally correct but also serves American interests. The United States armed forces, as well as civilian agencies, can and will have significant roles to play in the implementation of this policy.

NOTES

1. Walter LaFeber, *Liberty and Power: U.S. Diplomatic History, 1750–1943* (Washington, DC: American Historical Association, 1991).

2. The quote has been attributed to John Foster Dulles.

3. A careful, balanced treatment is Larman C. Wilson, "Human Rights in United States Foreign Policy," in Don C. Piper and Ronald J. Terchek, eds., *Interaction: Foreign Policy and Public Policy* (Washington, DC: American Enterprise Institute for Public Policy Research 1983), 178–208.

4. See my assessment in Howard J. Wiarda, *The Democratic Revolution in Latin America* (New York: A Twentieth Century Fund Book, Holmes and Meier, 1990).

5. Anthony Lake, *Somoza Falling* (Boston: Houghton Mifflin, 1989).

6. Robert E. Osgood, "The Carter Policy in Perspective," *SAIS Review* I (Winter 1981): 11–22; Terry L. Deibel, "Jimmy Carter, Denial of Power and the Quest for Values," ch. 3 in *Presidents, Public Opinion, and Power* (New York: Foreign Policy Association, 1987); and Stanley Hoffman, "Requiem," *Foreign Policy* 42 (Spring 1981): 3–26.

7. Daniel Pipes and Adam Garfinkle, eds., *Friendly Tyrants: An American Dilemma* (New York: St. Martin's, 1991).

8. See Howard J. Wiarda, *Human Rights and U.S. Human Rights Policy* (Washington, DC: American Enterprise Institute for Public Policy Research, 1982).

9. Tamar Jacoby, "The Reagan Turnaround on Human Rights," *Foreign Affairs* (Summer 1986): 1066–86.

10. A full examination is in Wiarda, *Democratic Revolution*.

11. Seymour Martin Lipset, *Political Man* (Garden City, NY: Doubleday, 1960); W. W. Rostow, *The Stages of Economic Growth* (Cambridge: Cambridge University Press, 1960); Larry Diamond et al., *Democracy in Developing Countries*, 4 vols. (Boulder, CO: Rienner, 1980s).

Chapter Nine

Friendly Tyrants
and American Interests

What should the U.S. government do if a foreign country has a nondemocratic regime that is friendly to the United States but abusive of human rights? What if that regime faces a serious guerrilla insurgency, yet remains unable or unwilling to reach accommodation with moderate or democratic forces? What if it is a terrorist state or harbors terrorists? What should be done if the country suffers a polarization and breakdown, threatening a crisis or even an anti-American takeover?

Of all the foreign policy dilemmas that the United States has faced over the past three or four decades, the problem of the friendly tyrant has been among the most persistent and thorny. It has confronted the U.S. government repeatedly, usually bringing in its wake acute crises.

Unfortunately, though many of America's experiences with friendly tyrants were prominent chapters in America's postwar foreign affairs, they never raised the generic issue of U.S. policy in these cases to the level of abstraction it deserves. Policy makers have treated each embroilment as sui generis and seem not to have sought lessons from the past that might now be of use in dealing with today's problem cases: Egypt, Saudi Arabia, Pakistan, and others. In academe, too, the monographic and comparative literature on which to base sound policy judgments in this field is still lacking. Comparative studies have emerged on the transition from authoritarianism to democracy,[1] but there are no broadly comparative studies of U.S. policies toward friendly tyrants.

Our quandaries about dealing with authoritarian allies multiply if we try simultaneously to think about left-wing dictatorships—"unfriendly tyrannies"—such as China, Cuba, North Korea, perhaps Iran. How do they resemble friendly tyrannies and how to they differ? What are American interests toward them and U.S. obligations, if any, to their populations? In light of policy toward friendly tyrants, can one justify pressing human rights issues upon regimes that like us (or need us, or use us), while ignoring even more egregious situations in anti-American regimes, only because we lack leverage over them?

Even without considering unfriendly tyrannies, we have problems enough. Should security interests prevail above all else, or do human rights and morality matter most? Should we see authoritarian regimes primarily as allies in the struggle against terrorism or to contain greater, totalitarian evils, or as oppressors of their own people? Do we reward authoritarian regimes for their helpfulness in keeping the lid on terrorists or punish them for violating human rights? Do we accept such regimes as friends and collaborators, regardless of the nature of their internal policies, or do we ostracize them, treat them as pariahs, and cast them out from the community of civilized states? Or, as George W. Bush expressed, do we try to convert them into democracies?

Striking a balance between the contending arguments is hard, but unavoidable; policy makers cannot turn the other cheek when these problems arise. For purposes of making policy, the problem of American dealings with friendly tyrants contains two parts, one analytic and one prescriptive. The key analytic question is: how does one gauge when an authoritarian regime may be susceptible to an overthrow or to internal changes that will damage U.S. interests? Such a judgment, of course, turns on a definition of what damage to U.S. interests really means, a contentious issue in itself that raises the question of America's mission and meaning. A further and unavoidable question arises from this realization: how do dealings with this or that friendly tyrant enter U.S. domestic politics? To answer this question, we also need to know the extent to which the United States is directly or indirectly involved in the regime's maintenance during "normal" times. Another way of putting this is: to what extent is the threat to U.S. interests in a falling tyrant a function of past U.S. policies, and to what extent does it inhere in the strategic location of the country per se? Saudi Arabia (oil) and Pakistan (an ally in the war on terrorism) are prime cases of this dilemma. Then comes the second problem—the prescriptive one. Once a friendly tyrant is judged to be faltering and U.S. interests are affected, a choice emerges: does one demand its reform, facilitate its removal, defend it anyway for lack of a better alternative, or disengage from it and let the chips fall where they may?

This chapter concentrates on the analytic question seen historically. It suggests a systematic way to evaluate policy choices made in years past in the hope that such evaluations may also be relevant to current and future troubles. It ends with a few reflections on changes within the U.S. domestic political context that suggest no end to the friendly tyrants dilemma. Indeed, the war on terrorism has added new dimensions.

THE NEED FOR COMPROMISE

The question of America's proper response to authoritarian regimes once again prompts two answers: the idealist and the realpolitik. The dichotomy between them reflects a long-term division over the place of human rights and democracy in U.S. foreign policy.

The pure idealist position would have the United States sever relations with all friendly tyrants. It argues that the United States—a special nation, the paragon of democracy—should not associate with authoritarian regimes, for these violate its standards of political behavior. Such regimes should be punished for their abuses, not coddled or rewarded. As to the proposition that such alliances sometimes enhance U.S. security, and Americans must accept the allies they can get, the idealist answers that repressive regimes detract from American security more than they enhance it. Idealists argue that instead of serving during the Cold War as bulwarks against the Soviet Union, dictatorships prepared the soil for anti-American sentiments to thrive.[2]

Realists have taken the opposite tack, arguing that the United States should pay attention to the internal politics of a regime only when these impinge on the national interest of the United States. If a regime opposed the Soviet Union during the Cold War, so the argument has run, or is good nowadays at clamping down on terrorists, such as Egypt or Pakistan, Washington should not undermine it, no matter how unpleasant its actions. Cutting such regimes off from the United States may salve moral consciences but leaves the United States without an instrument to push that regime in a democratic direction or the means to influence the postauthoritarian government. Thus, a policy of disengagement (such as was adopted at times toward Cuba, Argentina under military rule, and Somoza's Nicaragua) may lead to greater harm to U.S. strategic interests and be no more politically moral to boot.

Which choice better serves America's long-term interests? Whenever theory or ideology confronts reality, something has to give; the pure idealist and realpolitik positions are too extreme. Were the United States to sever relations with all the world's authoritarian regimes, it would cut itself off from one half of the countries on the globe. Ties to all authoritarian regimes cannot be immediately abandoned, despite a distaste for their nondemocratic character and human rights abuses, for too many vital interests are involved. The United States cannot afford a foreign policy that focuses only on the human rights/democracy agenda and expect to remain a great power for very long.

But pure realpolitik arguments are also problematic. The U.S. government cannot ignore the nature of the nefarious regimes with which it must deal or the plight of those who live under them. If the realist's arguments were taken to their logical conclusions, they would have argued for indifference to the

Jews of the Soviet Union who wish to emigrate, and to Christians and others in Iraq or the Sudan who wish only to practice their religion. Pure realism would have denied concern for the plight of South African blacks, for the cries of nuns and peasants in Central America, and for the pleas of harassed democratic oppositions in authoritarian regimes. The United States of America simply cannot conduct foreign policy without working for human rights and democracy. For Americans (and perhaps for Americans alone), pure realism is not realistic. Even the apostles of realpolitik have come to recognize this, as the earlier policies of pressure toward the Philippines, Haiti, Paraguay, Chile, South Korea, and South Africa made clear, and now toward Saudi Arabia, Egypt, and other tyrannies.

The American people want a foreign policy that protects the country's security interests *and* works for democracy and human rights. They want both things strongly, and at times contradictorily. That implies that compromises must be made and balances struck. How is this to be done?

To begin with, it is clear that authoritarian regimes are not all the same. Some states (such as Saudi Arabia) have overwhelming strategic importance; others (like Zimbabwe) have only marginal importance. Some authoritarian regimes are fresh, new, and full of vigor; others are wobbly and on their last legs (and that is usually when they become major concerns for U.S. policy). Some, particularly if they are wobbly, face strong internal challenges from guerrilla movements or terrorists; others do not. Plainly, strategically significant states—China, Egypt, Saudi Arabia, Pakistan—will tend to be of greater concern to U.S. policy makers and, unless they face imminent trouble, it is probably best not to tamper with their internal political structure. States that matter less tend to offer more leeway for American action. Without judging here the skill with which policy was pursued, this logical calculus is what led the U.S. policy eventually to pressure Nicaraguan dictator Anastasio Somoza Debayle over human rights issues, but not the shah of Iran, because the administration thought that Nicaragua did not matter much strategically, nor could it ever, while it knew that Iran did and always would.

Authoritarian regimes also vary greatly in the degree of their popular support. Many Americans find it hard to believe, but attitudes toward authority vary widely throughout the world. Many authoritarian regimes receive warm welcomes and genuine admiration from their people because they provide order, coherence, and stability in chronically unstable countries. Such regimes are often populist, at once nationalistic and paternalistic, and enjoy widespread public backing, at least during certain stages of their tenure. Perón's Argentina, Franco's Spain, and Chávez's Venezuela come quickly to mind, maybe even Saddam Hussein's Iraq; but many other examples exist as well. Local standards must be taken into account; authoritarian regimes fit into their own cultural contexts first, and must not be seen simply according to American or West European criteria. However distasteful to Americans, in their own cultural context such regimes can even be revered.

It is probably not appropriate, no matter how pure one's democratic motives, to try to unseat populist-authoritarian regimes if doing so would be contrary to the wishes of the people living under them. The cases below demonstrate that U.S. judgment on this score has been inconsistent. The regimes—Hitler's, Pol Pot's, Bokassa's, Idi Amin's—that go so far beyond all decency that they deserve condemnation from any point of view, even if apparently popular, are few in number. In the less extreme authoritarian regimes that constitute the vast majority of cases, indigenous standards, as well as universal ones, must be carefully considered.

Some authoritarian conditions are episodes within a generally democratic experience; for example, Greece's colonels, Turkey's interludes of military rule, and military regimes in Chile or Uruguay. Also, some regimes may seek to be authoritarian but lack the power to pull it off effectively—the Republic of Vietnam is perhaps the best example.

Authoritarian regimes change and evolve, too. Most get old, ossified, and out of touch. As they do, they also tend to develop ever more repressive methods of control to keep themselves in power. For the United States, the challenge is to recognize when an authoritarian regime that has held power for a long time, and may have enjoyed considerable popularity early on, weakens and slips toward greater repression. At that point, it usually becomes increasingly unpopular, and no longer acceptable—either by our standards or those of its own people.

This process describes the evolution of the most notorious of authoritarian regimes: Batista in Cuba, Trujillo in the Dominican Republic, Somoza in Nicaragua, Salazar in Portugal, the shah in Iran, Duvalier in Haiti, Marcos in the Philippines, Saddam in Iraq. Each started as an authoritarian figure with a considerable mandate, often as a populist, or even as a "savior" of his country. A few were even elected to power. But each gravitated toward such repression, corruption, and brutality that he became a full-fledged or quasi-totalitarian dictator, attempting to control ever more of his people's existence and frequently succeeding. As the ruler became more brutal and greedy, he became less acceptable to his population. As his base of support dwindled, the question invariably arose: how long could the United States ally itself to such an unpopular regime?

This is, in a sense, a new twist on the older, political science distinction between authoritarianism and totalitarianism,[3] elevated to foreign policy significance through the writings of Jeane J. Kirkpatrick.[4] However similar traditional authoritarianism and communist totalitarianism may be for their unfortunate victims, Kirkpatrick argued, American foreign policy should prefer the former if those are the only choices available.

Authoritarian regimes may be reformable or even amenable to a democratic future. They tend to be less permanent, too, than those of the totalitarian variety. And during their existence, authoritarian regimes tend to do less harm to broader U.S. interests. Unless, of course, they also harbor terrorists or warehouse weapons of mass destruction.

Of course, traditional authoritarians may evolve in the opposite direction, too, away from democracy and toward full-scale, right-wing totalitarianism—with disastrous consequences both for the country and for U.S. policy.[5] That was the route taken by some of the most notorious and difficult cases with which the U.S. government has had to deal. Consider these examples.

Fulgencia Batista was a populist and a nationalist when he first came to power in the 1930s. Even his second coup d'état in 1952 was welcomed by most Cubans as a harbinger of stability after the corruption and chaos of the previous eight years. But as Batista became more bloody and repressive from the mid-1950s on, he lost virtually all support. Washington could influence, but not fully control, the post-Batista transition that produced the Marxist-Leninist regime of Fidel Castro, who has been a thorn in the side of the United States now for over forty-five years.[6]

The Dominican Republic's Rafael Trujillo also began with considerable popular backing in the 1930s as the "savior" and "benefactor" of his nation. But by the late 1950s, his was such a cruel regime that it had alienated all of its support and verged on totalitarianism. Though the situation nearly got out of hand on several occasions, the United States did manage ultimately to shape and guide the post-Trujillo transition.[7]

The elder Anastasio Somoza, who founded the family dynasty in Nicaragua, was an authoritarian and a dictator, but not an excessively brutal one by the standards of his own society. His elder son Luís even accommodated the regime somewhat to the requirements of the Alliance for Progress. It was his second son, Anastasio, Jr., who became so corrupt and repressive that he brought the whole house of cards down on his head and, like Batista, cleared the way for a Marxist takeover.[8]

The shah of Iran, Mohammad Reza Pahlavi, was similarly popular in his early days. He became an effective if autocratic modernizer of his country through the White Revolution. But American politicians failed to recognize how, with time, his political base narrowed and his secret police became all-pervasive and technologically proficient (a hallmark of rising totalitarianism). And they failed to see how he had squandered his popularity through corruption and ostentatious displays of wealth, particularly in the aftermath of the oil price boom.[9] The regime came tumbling down in the 1979 revolution, which turned ugly and anti-American.

The elder François Duvalier had been a country physician who built up a political base in Haiti by helping his patients, but in office he proved dictatorial. His son Jean-Claude (dubbed "Baby Doc," though not a physician) was even worse, being at the same time less selectively brutal and much less efficient.

Ferdinand Marcos also enjoyed considerable initial popularity by bringing order and coherence to the Philippines; and let it not be forgotten that he was elected fairly to his office. But he became corrupt and brutal, lost his people's backing, and eventually had to flee.

Many Chileans welcomed Pinochet for providing order after the upheavals of the Allende years. But the mass killings that followed his rise to power shocked his country and led to an erosion of domestic support and to Chile's worldwide status as a pariah state—and great difficulties for U.S. foreign policy.

When Saddam Hussein first came to power in Iraq, he was seen as a wily tyrant who could keep order. His Baathist Party was viewed as progressive, a combination of Arab socialism and nationalism. Hussein managed to keep the separatist religious, ethnic, and tribal groups in check and the country from disintegrating. But over time he became more brutal, dictatorial, even pathological. The United States thought he harbored terrorists and weapons of mass destruction.

In all these regimes the pattern is clear. A disorganized and usually moderate prior regime is replaced by an authoritarian regime that at first wins a welcome, largely because it stands for peace and stability. As the regime ages, however, it gradually loses popularity and turns to totalitarian tactics to keep itself in power. In the most difficult cases, the unpopular dictator faces not just a democratic opposition but also an internal or military insurgency.

Since authoritarian regimes evolve, it clearly will not do simply to issue a formulaic condemnation of all authoritarian regimes as unacceptable to the United States. Degrees of unacceptability must be recognized, as well as the regime's age, its wobbliness and potential for losing power, its level of popular support, its strategic location, its chances for postauthoritarian democracy (or pluralism, locally defined), and the chances of a hostile or terrorist takeover.

WHEN TO CUT THE TIES

Should the United States continue to support a once-popular regime that has served as a bastion against communist or terrorist influence? Should it disassociate from that regime and, if so, how and when? How does one weigh the risks—alienating the government, losing control of the situation, losing the country to unfriendly forces, frightening other dependent allies—of such a step?

To systematize the patterns of the past to better understand the present and to plan for the future, a scale can be devised to help gauge the logical point when the United States should disassociate itself from tired or hostile authoritarians.[10] (Of course, the scale must be seen as an aid to general analysis, not as a policy blueprint.) This measure starts from the premise that the U.S. government cannot act against all the world's authoritarian regimes, for that would mean simultaneous conflict with approximately 50 percent of the world's governments.[11] Authoritarian rulers per se are often less a problem for U.S. policy than their imminent demise. The critical moment is when an unreformable authoritarian regime begins to weaken, verges toward totalitarianism, loses its backing, provides refuge for terrorists, and runs the risk of being superseded by unfriendly forces. When this process begins, the time has come for the United States to abandon the sinking ship and move toward a new policy. Numerous case studies show that the United States has often done (or tried to do) precisely this.

A number of factors help gauge when a tolerable (which is not to say desirable) authoritarian regime becomes intolerable to its population and when an ally (or former ally) threatens U.S. interests. By looking at the scale in both positive and negative dimensions, as it were, it can measure both authoritarian slippage toward totalitarianism or movement toward democracy, and fluctuations between the two.

- When graft, traditionally in the range of 5 to 7 percent and constituting more or less acceptable patronage, soars to 25 to 30 percent and becomes institutionalized bribery. That is a sign of future instability.
- When opportunities for legal opposition are snuffed out. Authoritarian regimes typically permit some opposition, but totalitarian regimes permit none.
- When institutional checks and balances are eliminated. Authoritarian regimes typically allow some limited institutional checks through a congress or the courts; totalitarian regimes do not.
- When freedom of speech, press, and assembly, always repressed in an authoritarian regime, are wiped out.
- When self-government at local levels is subordinated to an all-powerful central state.
- When social and political pluralism, always limited in an authoritarian regime, is eliminated.[12]
- When jailings and exile are replaced by terror and technologically proficient torture.

- When economic development and social justice are sacrificed to dictatorial megalomania and the regime's self-enrichment.
- When human rights are systematically abrogated.
- When government policy changes from paternalistic and beneficent to mean-spirited and selfish.
- When freedom from arbitrary and capricious authority is lost.
- When the regime's representative and participatory character (formal or informal, ethnic, functional, or corporative representation as this may be) is lost.
- When the regime loses flexibility and popular support, and appears indecisive as a consequence.
- When the regime supports terrorism, or harbors terrorists, or seeks to launch violent movements against the United States.

Here, thus, we have fourteen criteria that help us measure the differences between authoritarianism and totalitarianism. The scale also enables us to systematically gauge, by assigning numerical measures to each criteria and then applying them to real-life countries and situations, when a regime is behaving so badly that it has become unacceptable to its own population, or when it represents a danger to U.S. interests and therefore when U.S. policy needs to change. Had this scale been applied in Iran in 1976 or 1977, for example, just before the revolution, it might have been able to predict the fall of the shah and the dire consequences for U.S. policy (and the U.S. Embassy personnel who were captured and then humiliated by the Iranian revolutionaries) that followed.

In short, social scientists can predict, with some degree of accuracy, when a previously rather "sleepy," lethargic, old-fashioned authoritarian regime becomes so brutal and oppressive that it may set in motion the very revolutionary overthrow it seeks to snuff out. That moment becomes a critical one for U.S. policy to recognize; if it is missed and the United States stays loyal to what is a fading, human rights-abusing regime, it is likely to be faulted by the succeeding government. The United States may then be discredited by that government and anti-Americanism may flourish. In the worst of circumstances, retribution may be taken against U.S. interests and terrorist groups may flourish. The "friendly tyrant" regime is toppled and a violently anti-American one takes its place.

THE DOMESTIC DIMENSION

The preceding analysis rests on a "rational-actor model" of foreign policy-making. That is, it assumes the U.S. government will logically work out the best foreign policy and then apply it. But as the cases below make clear, the rational-actor model cannot be directly or easily applied to the workings of the U.S. government.

Other models should be factored in. The "bureaucratic model," we have seen earlier, focuses on differences between the agencies of the U.S. government and the resultant policy incoherence it can cause. The "organizational process model" holds that policy outcomes are deeply affected by organizational plans and procedures—for example, that Department of Defense contingency plans for various military operations are normally implemented more quickly than decision making in the State Department.[13] The "political process model," finally, suggests that foreign policy decisions involve a complex process of interaction with *domestic* political considerations.[14]

By focusing on decision processes rather than rational judgments, the bureaucratic and organizational models help explain why problems that ought to be seen together end up being compartmentalized. They also explain some of the pitfalls of bureaucratic clientalism and why intelligence rarely reaches the right people. The political process model helps explain how issues that ought to be discrete are thrown together with other matters. This last aid to understanding has special importance in understanding policy toward friendly tyrants.

Foreign policy and domestic policy have always been intertwined, and not just over matters having to do with friendly tyrants. Some of the cases discussed earlier, such as those of Batista and Trujillo, were clearly not played out on a pure rational-actor model. Bureaucratic dynamics had a role, as always; so did domestic politics, though a relatively minor one in these cases. Individual Americans did have a strong interest in the outcome of Cuban and Dominican events and sought to make their influence felt, but private interests could not dominate the policymaking process or determine its outcome. Above all, unlike many more recent friendly tyrants cases, these earlier episodes did not generate intense public debate and mass political mobilization in the United States.

After the war in Vietnam, the connections between foreign policy processes and domestic politics have became more numerous and complex.[15] In some cases, such as the Philippines, South Africa, Nicaragua, Haiti, and Iraq, domestic political considerations threatened to overwhelm the few attempts to arrange American options rationally. Not only are domestic considerations more significant, but they also feed other factors leading to the increasing disarray and even sclerosis of U.S. foreign policy.[16] This matter has special importance for the future of American foreign policymaking, and it goes beyond the issue of dealing with friendly tyrants. It may already have become a permanent debilitating feature of the U.S. foreign policymaking system: witness the intense and virtually constant debate over what the United States should do vis-à-vis Saudi Arabia, Egypt, or Pakistan.

Why has this change taken place? The Vietnam War is probably the first and most important factor, a critical turning point in U.S. foreign policy. There exists a persistent fear among many Americans that U.S. government support for embattled allies will again result in the United States being dragged into a distant conflict that will take the lives of young Americans, tear the country apart, and do irreparable damage to U.S. foreign policy. Witness Iraq.

Congress and the increasing politicalization of U.S. foreign policy constitute a second factor. Politics no longer "stop at the water's edge"; foreign policy is now politicized in much the same way that domestic issues are. Individual members of Congress play a far greater role in foreign policymaking. When former congressman Stephen Solarz (Democrat of New York) went to the Philippines to negotiate with the Marcos regime and its opposition, he acted in effect as Congress's secretary of state. Congress makes its views known in many other ways, too: the War Powers Act, the Boland Amendments, the human rights certifications required for countries like Guatemala and El Salvador, the biyearly Cyprus Report, the close scrutiny of presidential appointments in the foreign policy area, the budget debate over funding the war in Iraq, and the virtually nonstop and polemicized congressional hearings on difficult foreign policy issues.[17] No matter who occupies the White House, he tends to look upon these congressional initiatives as unwarranted interferences. But in the wake of Vietnam, Watergate, the Iran-Contra affair, and presidential mistakes in Iraq, Congress feels it cannot fully trust the executive branch.[18]

Television is a third factor. Even color television portrays only the blacks and whites of political issues, cutting out all nuance. And nuance is, after all, the essence of most friendly tyrant conundrums. But problems created by television transcend the biases and oversimplifications of that medium.[19] Its capacity to capture a particular controversy takes it out of the hands of foreign policy makers (who approach matters from the viewpoint of U.S. national interests), and brings it, as it were, into the streets.[20] Congresspersons soon follow, having mastered the art of the thirty-second instant analysis designed to get them on the evening news. This, unfortunately, now passes all too often for foreign policy discussion in the United States.

Further, television covers—and, hence, popularizes—issues concerning U.S. relations with right-wing dictators far more extensively than in the past. By inserting editorial views on these matters into the newscasts, television journalists can push a topic to the fore; they create issues rather than cover them. One can argue that television coverage of Marcos stealing the February

1986 Philippine election, or the revelation about Imelda's three thousand pairs of shoes, had more impact on U.S. attitudes and policy toward the Philippines than did Philippine public opinion itself. Similarly, television coverage of events in South Africa and South Korea has, on occasion, gone far beyond mere reportage, but has constituted a driving factor in moving events along—and U.S. policy with it. The violence of the Iraq War portrayed on television undoubtedly affected U.S. policy.

Fourth, the domestication and politicization of foreign policy have been aided by the emergence of new interest groups playing highly visible and active roles. Religious groups, human rights lobbies, associations of writers and actors, and others, receive little scholarly attention,[21] but their role is important and growing. They had access to the Carter administration through the executive branch; under Reagan they were effective in working through Congress. Both Clinton and George W. Bush calculated foreign policy moves on the basis of the interest group balance. With regard to Latin America, for example, the constant lobbying by these groups in the corridors of Congress, op-ed pieces in the major newspapers, testimony before congressional committees, and presentation of firsthand witnesses succeeded in making the abuses of various Latin American governments vivid to the American public. Human rights abuses of the Chilean or Paraguayan regimes under Pinochet and Stroessner, and the continuing human rights problems in El Salvador or Guatemala, were brought into living rooms and made a matter of American domestic politics. U.S. policy, especially toward Chile during the Reagan administration, was undoubtedly influenced by these activities.[22] The lobbies' relative silence about human rights abuses in Marxist Cuba or Nicaragua also affected policy toward the regimes of those countries.

Public opinion, the fifth factor, divides into two aspects. In the early stage of a discussion about a weakened friendly tyrant, the debate between those focusing on national interests and those advancing humanitarian concerns tends to be fairly even, and more often mixes these considerations together in various proportions. Arguments based more on interests than human rights usually prevails, for they represent the status quo and usually obviate the need to take risks.

But once the country—be it South Africa, the Philippines, South Korea, or Saudi Arabia—becomes a matter of intense public scrutiny and is regularly covered on the network news, human rights considerations tend to predominate. The shift may be ascribed to the biases in the media noted earlier, or simply to the fact that riots and bloody corpses make good television. The shift becomes more likely if an epic crisis occurs in the midst of the coverage— like the killing of Benigno Aquino on the tarmac in Manila practically in front of the television cameras, electoral fraud so obvious one can see the ballot boxes being carried away, the gruesome murder of Chilean leftists on the streets of Santiago, nightly police beatings on the streets of Seoul, or terrorists operating in Pakistan or Saudi Arabia. When such crises occur, decision making regarding authoritarian regimes virtually leaves the executive branch. U.S. policy makers must scramble to catch up to events.

In effect, the U.S. government is often left responding to events and hoping for the best. That was what happened in the Philippines during the final stages of the crisis: Marcos left and Corazon Aquino took power at least in part because of the events on U.S. television and the shift in U.S. public opinion. Fortunately, this is not always the case. While the public's capacity for outrage is high, it does not always go tromping off in anger; despite the horror stories and vivid television footage from Seoul before and during the 1988 Olympics, public opinion did not turn against South Korea, indicating at least some ability to think through issues in a moderately sophisticated way. In Saudi Arabia, of course, we need to think about the consequences for our entire economy if that regime were to be destabilized by some overzealous democratizing efforts.

The final factor is a shift in the *structural* context of U.S. foreign policy-making since the 1960s. Partisan politics and divisions did for the most part stop at the water's edge until then, but the United States is now a more divided, more fragmented, more ideologically diffuse nation. These polarizations have been reflected in—and sometimes led by—conflicts over foreign policy issues. These, in turn, have led to structural changes in the foreign policy system. Beyond the obvious, like the War Powers Act and the Boland Amendments, there is the effect of the Budget Act of 1974, which greatly increases the congressional power of the purse in foreign policy matters, the erosion of party seniority and control, and sometimes suffocating congressional intelligence oversight. Such changes lie at the core of U.S. foreign policy sclerosis and the consequent temptation to circumvent the system, so much the heart of the Iran-Contra affair, where such temptation was tragically indulged. Accordingly, it was unfair for some commentators to speak of the "Reagan Junta" and the imperial uses of the National Security Council system;[23] the executive branch would be much less tempted to circumvent the Constitution had its strictures not been altered by the legislative branch and other forces in American society. Under President George W. Bush Congress and the White House have been almost constantly "at war" over Iraq and other issues.

If the rational-actor model of foreign policymaking ever applied in dealing with friendly tyrants or other issues, that time has now passed. Each succeeding crisis noted above seems to revolve ever more tightly around domestic political considerations. It is domestic politics that now drives most foreign policy, rather than national calculations of the national interest.

CONCLUSION

It is neither prudent nor wise for the United States to divorce itself from all friendly tyrants. They differ widely in age, character, and wobbliness; some are genuinely popular; alternatives may be far worse, some hold important strategic assets for America; and there are simply too many of them for disengagement to work. Far too many factors need to be considered for the United States to follow a pure and idealistic policy of having no relations at all with the globe's numerous tyrannical regimes Left and Right. On the other hand, it may be wise to put some distance between the United States and the tyrants who would befriend us—a cool handshake rather than a warm *abrazo*—but deliberate divorce should take place only under unusual circumstances: when the dictator starts to totter; when terrorists or weapons of mass destruction are present; when a viable alternative exists; when the security situation is still relaxed enough to allow room for maneuver; when the United States has the means and capacity to influence, if not control, the postauthoritarian transition. Only a few dictators are so offensive that Americans will wish to have nothing to do with them. Since that is the case, some old advice is still good advice: *pas de zéle*.

A centrist position between the pure idealist and the pure realpolitik positions is generally the most sensible and realistic U.S. policy toward friendly tyrants. Americans cannot and should not seek to unseat all the world's authoritarian governments—no one would be well served by such a bull-in-the-china-shop approach. But it is critical to note when regimes cross the fine line between authoritarianism that is more or less tolerable by the country's own standards and unacceptable totalitarianism that not only damages the country but may also endanger U.S. interests. At this point, Washington may wish to get off the dictatorial government's bandwagon or even facilitate its ouster.

But policy questions may also arise before the end of an authoritarian regime. "Timely daring," as one colleague called it, is sometimes called for. Different U.S. responses ought to be advanced at different stages in the life cycle of friendly authoritarian regimes.[24] It is usually better to get an authoritarian regime like Pakistan or Saudi Arabia to reform itself than to preside over its burial. But this presents an exceedingly difficult challenge, in part because politicians prefer to put out brush fires rather than create them; and, in part, because it is hardly ever clear that friendly authoritarians are definitely entering a downward spiral. One never wants to undermine a foreign asset on the basis of false pessimism.[25]

This said, it is wise to pursue a policy that, at the very least, keeps a constant watch over friendly tyrants. The U.S. government should let it be clearly known, first, that it stands unequivocally for democracy and human rights; that represents a moral stance. Further, democratic governments serve U.S. interests best. They are less bellicose, tend to interfere less in the internal affairs of their neighbors, are more pragmatic and centrist, and do not harbor terrorists. Such an emphasis also smooths the domestic politics of U.S. foreign policy.

Second, at a pretottering stage, the U.S. government may take limited actions to urge movement toward democracy, or, failing that, to put some very public distance between itself and the dictatorship. Policy toward Paraguay during the Reagan administration provides a good example of this, or maybe policy now toward Egypt.

Third, at the tottering stage, the major danger seems to be complacency, an unwillingness to recognize that the risks of doing nothing can outweigh the risks of acting. Here the scale presented above may be of special use.

Fourth, in the stage of crisis, when the regime is actually collapsing, Washington must do what it can to manage and possibly control the postauthoritarian transition. This stage requires a variety of policy responses, including the use of force under some circumstances, and possibly quite different ones from those employed at earlier stages.[26] Diplomatic ultimata instead of suggestions, threats of military intervention instead of aid cutoffs, making public instead of private démarches, supporting opposition groups instead of merely maintaining liaison with them are all pertinent examples. For if the United States fails to act in a timely fashion, it may be faced by a hostile regime, by one that provides sanctuary to terrorists, or that is even taken over by terrorist elements.

The changed domestic political situation in the United States enters a new factor in these considerations. Domestic considerations may be so polarized that nothing can be decided until the situation in the foreign country gets out of hand. Timely daring may be impossible. Changes in the United States make it far more difficult to carry out a coherent and long-term policy toward authoritarian regimes.

The United States needs a cautious and realistic approach toward friendly tyrants. A review of the main cases does not offer much reason for optimism. Of the key cases, three (South Vietnam, Iran, and Nicaragua) were disasters for the United States, and to this one could add Cuba à la 1959–1960. Of the cases that worked out tolerably well, only those concerning Haiti and the Philippines were due even in part to U.S. actions. Things worked out in Greece, Turkey, and Argentina almost regardless of what the United States did. In short, in the past, successes that had little to do with U.S. policy and failures add up to more than two thirds of the cases. And that is without counting today's difficult cases—Afghanistan, Iraq, Pakistan, Egypt, Saudi Arabia, China, Syria, the Palestinian Authority—for whom it is still too soon to reach definitive conclusions.

This record should give Americans pause about rushing in pell-mell to unseat authoritarian regimes, and about U.S. capacity to build democracy. And even if the capacity were not limited, American comprehension of these countries certainly is. Events can be influenced, but many actions should not even be attempted. Rational foreign policy calculations are essential but crusades need to be avoided.

NOTES

1. For example, Hans Binnendijk, ed., *Authoritarian Regimes in Transition* (Washington, DC: U.S. Department of State, 1987); Guillermo O'Donnell, Philippe Schmitter, and Lawrence Whitehead, eds., *Transition from Authoritarian Rule: Prospects for Democracy* (Baltimore, MD: Johns Hopkins University Press, 1987).

2. See Barry Rubin, *Modern Dictators* (New York: McGraw-Hill, 1987).

3. See, for example, Carl J. Friedrich and Zbigniew Brzezinski, *Totalitarian Dictatorship and Autocracy* (New York: Praeger, 1962).

4. Jeane J. Kirkpatrick, "Dictatorships and Double Standards," *Commentary* (November 1979).

5. Howard J. Wiarda, *Dictatorship and Development* (Gainesville: University of Florida Press, 1968).

6. Hugh Thomas, "Cuba: The United States and Batista, 1952–58," *World Affairs* (Spring 1987): 169–75.

7. Robert D. Crassweller, *Trujillo* (New York: Macmillan, 1966).

8. Richard Millett, *Guardians of the Dynasty* (New York: Orbis, 1977).

9. Gary Sick, *All Fall Down: America's Tragic Encounter with Iran* (New York: Random House, 1985).

10. An earlier version of this scale was presented in Howard J. Wiarda, ed., *The Continuing Struggle for Democracy in Latin America* (Boulder, CO: Westview, 1980), conclusion.

11. See Roy C. Macridis, *Modern Political Regimes* (Boston: Little, Brown, 1986).

12. On the concept of limited pluralism in authoritarian regimes, see Juan Linz, "An Authoritarian Regime: Spain," in E. Allardt and S. Rokkan, eds., *Mass Politics* (New York: Free Press, 1970).

13. On these models, see the pioneering analysis of Graham Allison, *Essence of Decision: Explaining the Cuban Missile Crisis* (Boston: Little, Brown, 1971).

14. Roger Hilsman, *The Politics of Policy Making in Defense and Foreign Affairs: Conceptual Models and Bureaucratic Politics* (Englewood Cliffs, NJ: Prentice-Hall, 1987); also Howard J. Wiarda, *Foreign Policy without Illusion* (Chicago, IL: Scott Foresman, 1990).

15. Don C. Piper and Ronald J. Terchek, eds., *Interaction: Foreign Policy and Public Policy* (Washington, DC: American Enterprise Institute for Public Policy Research, 1983).

16. Howard J. Wiarda, "The Paralysis of Policy: Current Dilemmas of U.S. Foreign Policy-Making," *World Affairs* (Summer 1986): 15–21.

17. For a detailed example, see Mark Falcoff, *A Tale of Two Policies: U.S. Relations with the Argentine Junta, 1976–1982* (Philadelphia: Foreign Policy Research Institute, 1989), 31–35.

18. I. M. Destler, Leslie H. Gelb, and Anthony Lake, *Our Own Worst Enemy: The Unmaking of American Foreign Policy* (New York: Simon & Schuster, 1984), esp. chapter 3, "Congress and the Press: The New Irresponsibility."

19. S. Robert Lichter, Stanley Rothman, and Linda S. Lichner, *The Media Elite: America's New Powerbrokers* (Bethesda, MD: Adler and Adler, 1986).

20. For a conceptual overview, see Merle Kling, "Violence and Politics in Latin America," *Sociological Review* 2 (1967): 119–32.

21. An exception is Adam Garfinkle, *The Politics of the Nuclear Freeze* (Philadelphia: Foreign Policy Research Institute, 1984).

22. Joshua Muravchik, *The Uncertain Crusade: Jimmy Carter and the Dilemmas of Human Rights Policy* (Lanham, MD: Hamilton Press, 1986).

23. See, in particular, Theodor Draper, "The Reagan Junta," *New York Review of Books*, January 29, 1987.

24. The analysis here is indebted to oral commentary presented by Richard Haass at the Foreign Policy Research Institute's May–June 1987 conference on friendly tyrants in Philadelphia, PA.

25. Precisely such questions developed at a certain stage in the Iranian and Philippine cases.

26. See, for example, John B. Martin, *Overtaken by Events: The Dominican Crisis—From the Fall of Trujillo to the Civil War* (Garden City, NY: Doubleday, 1966); but see also Howard J. Wiarda, *Dictatorship, Development, and Disintegration: Politics and Social Change in the Dominican Republic* (Ann Arbor, MI: Monograph Series of Xerox University Microfilms, 1975).

Chapter Ten

Globalization and Its Critics

One of the hot new issues today is globalization. Globalization carries immense implications for the U.S. economy as well as for U.S. foreign policy. But people mean different things by globalization, and the concept and results of the process have been strongly attacked by antiglobalization protesters. In this chapter we examine the concept of globalization, weigh the claims of globalization advocates as well as critics, and explore the implications of globalization for U.S. policy.

Globalization has been with us for a very long time, indeed since the dawn of time. If Sub-Saharan Africa was the locus of the first human beings, then the gradual dispersion of the human species to the far corners of the earth was the first globalization. The domestication of animals, the development of agriculture, and the invention of primitive tools like the wedge or the wheel, and the spread of these beyond the places where they were invented are all hallmarks in the history of globalization. So are steam engines, the invention of printing, telephone and telegraph, radio and television, computers, and the Internet.

Confucianism, Hinduism, Buddhism, Christianity, and Islam—the world's great religions—have all been agencies of globalization as well as, sometimes, in conflict with each other. Greek civilization, the Roman Empire (which spread the use of a single language, law, sociology, and politics), and the Roman Catholic Church, which spread Christianity throughout Europe were also instruments of globalization. So were such great military conquerors as Alexander the Great, Darius of Persia, Philip of Macedonia, and Genghis Khan. Globalization can, it must be said, take violent as well as peaceful forms.

Moving into the modern age, the Renaissance, the Enlightenment, the Scientific Revolution, and the Industrial Revolution were all agencies of globalization. So was the age of European expansion in the sixteenth and seventeenth centuries, which enormously increased mankind's knowledge of the rest of the world and brought European ideas and institutions to far-flung regions, what we would now call the Third World. But this Europeanization and Westernization of the globe, while clearly beneficial in some major respects, was also sometimes devastating in its impact on local cultures and indigenous peoples.

What we so far know about globalization is:

- Globalization is not new; it has always been with us; it is part of world history and the process by which things change.
- Globalization takes many different forms: cultural, social, economic, military, religious, technological, political.
- Globalization is always contested, controversial; there are always going to be winners and losers.
- Globalization is ubiquitous, always present; it cannot be stopped (though it may be modified), nor is it likely to be reversed, nor would most of us want to do so.
- Globalization is most often peaceful, but it can also be disruptive, violent.
- Some countries and/or cultures are able to handle globalization better than others, absorbing its useful features while rejecting the rest; but other countries and cultures, generally smaller and weaker ones, may be overwhelmed by it.

Globalization is thus a complex, ambiguous, and mixed concept. It carries many different meanings. As a concept, it subsumes many different forces, which need to be carefully sorted out. Globalization can be good or bad, depending on one's priorities, values, and morals. Above all, globalization is always with us, so we need to be careful what we mean by the term, to sort out its many, often overlapping aspects, and only then can we draw balanced conclusions about it.

GLOBALIZATION IN THE PRESENT CONTEXT

In the present context, globalization takes a variety of forms and carries a variety of meanings. In their most controversial aspects, these include:

1. *Culture.* Particularly *American* culture is pervasive on a global basis. The elements of culture that have spread to the rest of the world include blue

jeans, rock music, and McDonald's. Also, consumerism; big, fast cars; movies; and entertainment. But also American ideas of justice, freedom, human rights, and democracy.

Almost every country in the world now has McDonald's restaurants—often dozens or hundreds of them. Many of these have become hangouts for young people, an opportunity to get away from their parents or stifling authority, a place to meet their girlfriends or boyfriends, a liberating refuge in an otherwise authoritarian society. Similarly with rock music and its message of liberation (from parents, school, government) and "do your own thing"; in a rigid authoritarian or Islamic regime, that message can be extremely subversive of established authority and even of governments, which is why authoritarian regimes seek to censor it. The same applies to the movies: movies can teach young people how to escape from their parents; they also teach sexual liberation and codes of conduct that are particularly American; and movies of the Arnold Schwarzenegger/Bruce Willis (the *Diehard* series) kind probably promote anti-Americanism and a perverted vision of America through their portrayal of excessive and gratuitous violence. Americans are often used to all these messages and partly inoculated against taking them too seriously, but in other countries the power of American culture can be overwhelming, subversive, and potentially destabilizing. And that helps explain why it can be both loved as well as resented.

Some countries and some people have reacted against this heavy American cultural influence. But television, VCRs, radio, disks, tapes, and the Internet enable people in these countries to bypass the censorship and, often, to rally against the regime in power. Most of us would consider these forms of globalization to be good things, liberating, democratic.

Among Western countries, France has been the one that has sought most assiduously to defend its own culture and keep out what it thinks of as an American onslaught. It has tried to put limits on American movies, American television, and the use of the American language. It fights vigorously and constantly to maintain the use of French as an official international language on a par with English. It seeks to maintain the purity of the French language while banning such Americanisms as *sandwich*, *lunch*, *French fries*, and other such "perversions." A French farmer, José Bove, became a national hero for a time when he rammed his farm tractor into a McDonald's restaurant; but later he went to jail and lost his luster when it was revealed that he held some truly crazy ideas. It is also the French who most often use the terms *hegemony*, *behemoth*, and *bully* to describe America. Yet the power of the American cultural influence is so great that even France has been forced to back off on many of these restrictions; and while the French language and culture are quite glorious, they cannot keep the American influence from rising. Furthermore, while the French elite is often resentful of American influence, public opinion surveys show that the French public likes American movies, television, and music and is quite level-headed in its views.

2. *Language.* Forty or more years ago, French was still considered the universal language of politics, international relations, and social interchange. Now it is English. In Europe, almost every educated person speaks English as a second, third, or fourth language; in much of the rest of the world, English has now replaced French, German, or Russian as the language that young people learn. In many countries, street signs are in English as well as the native language; television and radio are often heavily dominated by English-language expressions and even broadcasts; airports, airlines, and other modes of transportation use English as their official language; and in most museums and other facilities that attract international visitors, English is the main foreign language used.

While the globalization of the English language is great for American officials operating, or tourists traveling, abroad, it also means, because seemingly everyone else speaks English, that Americans are even less inclined to learn other languages than they were in the past. This breeds resentment throughout the world, because many feel that Americans expect everyone else to speak their language while only rarely do they learn other peoples' languages. Of course, the ability to use your own language abroad while others have to struggle to keep up in their often-still-imperfect English gives you enormous advantage in any business transaction or diplomatic negotiation being carried out. Recall also that in foreign countries people are also quite literally being bombarded constantly with English-language music, commercials, and political messages.

3. *Technology.* In many areas, but not all, American technology is the best in the world. One thinks of computers, software, biomedicine, the Internet, special effects in the entertainment industry, prescription drugs, food processing, and many other areas. One can get statistics on numbers of patents, Nobel laureates, and copyrights—all overwhelmingly dominated by the United States. For a time in the 1980s, it was thought that Japan or perhaps other nations might surpass the United States, and in certain technologies (television sets, VCRs, maybe even luxury automobiles—Acura, Lexus) they do. But the *overwhelming majority* of new or enhanced technologies in the world are dominated by the United States. Even in those industries—such as steel—once thought moribund, new technologies have been used to revive and make competitive a flagging U.S. industry.

The technological gap is especially large in the military sphere. There, U.S. military technology has become so advanced that it has not only left America with no serious rivals in the world, but it has left U.S. allies behind as well.

An enemy country would be foolhardy these days to seriously challenge the United States militarily, as Iraq after its 1990s invasion of Kuwait, the Serbs in Bosnia and Kosovo, and the Taliban in Afghanistan quickly found out. But the gap also produces tensions with U.S. allies because America is now so large that it feels it can wage war, if it has to, better and more effectively by itself than in concert with erstwhile allies. The allies often resent this and criticize the United States for its "unilateralism," even while relying on the United States to do global peacekeeping chores and relieving themselves from spending the money to keep pace with U.S. military technology. In many fields, civilian as well as military, the technological gap between the United States and other countries breeds resentment, jealousy, and sometimes anger.

4. *Economics.* The United States has the most powerful economy in the world—by far. There are no other rivals at present, nor any on the horizon. The U.S. gross national product is two or three times that of its nearest rivals, Japan, China, and Germany, and the country has a living standard that is, or among, the highest in the world. Not only is it big: the American economy is also one of the wonders of the world in terms of its dynamism, innovation, and ability to create jobs.

As the world's biggest and most powerful economy, with no serious rivals presently or on the horizon, America's economic power and ability to dominate others sometimes breeds resentments. Among those countries that lie on or close to U.S. borders (Canada, Mexico, Central America, and the Caribbean) the fear is often powerful that the strength and reach of the American economy will simply suck them up into the American orbit whether they or we wish it or not. In some quarters that may be called "imperialism," but it is also the inevitable consequence of a huge, dynamic, globalized economy located right next to smaller, weaker economies: not only is such dominance characteristic of the United States and its neighbors but also powerful Germany in relation to the weaker, poorer Eastern European countries, or Japan and China in relation to their smaller Asian neighbors.

In the developing countries generally, there is often great fear of American economic power and the ability of U.S.-based companies or multinationals to take advantage of local conditions, to pressure (or bribe) government officials to get what they want, to exploit local resources, and to "rip off" the country. After all, many of these companies have bigger budgets, have better Wall Street connections, can mobilize more lawyers, and have more influence, plus have the enormous power of the U.S. government behind them, than do most of the countries in which they operate. These inequities, this imbalance, this asymmetry has given rise to the theory of "dependency," which suggests that the poorer countries will always be subservient to and "dependencies" of the bigger countries. But the smaller countries often have strengths and the ability to manipulate the bigger countries. Hence, most scholars, while recognizing that dependency is a fact of life (big, powerful countries tend to dominate smaller, weaker ones), also emphasize *interde-pendence,* the complex relationship that suggests both big and small countries can benefit from trade, investment, and commerce.

In the developed countries there is also resentment of U.S. economic superiority. Many European countries are envious and therefore often resentful of the ability of the U.S. economy to create jobs, adapt to new circumstances, and recover from recession better than their own economies can. At the same time, they often resent the United States bragging about its accomplishments and presuming to tell the Europeans how to do things better. Most of the European economies, in response to constituency political pressures, have, in fact, opted to protect their so-called social economies, which means elaborate and expensive social welfare provisions, rigid labor markets that make it difficult to fire anyone, taxes roughly double those of the United States, and considerably higher state involvement in the economy than is true in the United States, in exchange for slower economic growth. That is their choice, and it is a trade-off many if not most Europeans have accepted, but it *does* mean slower growth and a less-flexible economy than America's.

Resentment is also directed at the large international lending (World Bank, International Monetary Fund [IMF]) and trade agencies (World Trade Organization [WTO]), which the United States is presumed to dominate. Both the World Bank and the IMF are often insensitive politically; they frequently advocate a one-size-fits-all lending policy that is not appropriate for all countries; and it *is* true that the United States is the most influential voice in their deliberations. But both agencies have become more flexible and politically conscious over the years, allowing for exceptions; being willing to postpone austerity in crisis times; and, while advocating privatization and free markets, being flexible about them and allowing state subsidies of such essentials as rice, gasoline, and cooking oil to continue. Still, they believe that Third World countries can't fundamentally alter the laws of economics, that they have an obligation to pay back their loans, and that they do need to put their economic houses in order. The U.S. government has used its influence to advocate *both* the orthodox and the flexible sides of the international lending agencies' policies. Similarly with the WTO: it stands for free trade but it is also flexible, adaptable, and not insensitive to the needs of the unfortunate whose jobs and livelihoods are sometimes sacrificed as free trade comes to dominate.

5. *Politics and International Affairs.* The United States is at this stage the only surviving superpower. It is a *hegemon,* to use the French term. The Soviet Union has collapsed; Japan has economic but not strategic might; Europe is only in the beginning stages of developing a common defense capability;

and China, still a Third World country, is not there yet. The United States therefore stands alone in the world as the only country with economic, political, military, and cultural ("soft") power—and with the ability to project ("to touch someone," as the Pentagon puts it) that power to all corners of the earth.

The overwhelming dominance of the United States inherently breeds resentment, hostility, and jealousy mixed with envy on the part of those not so richly endowed. Moreover, in international relations theory, whenever there is a "unipolar [one country-dominant] moment," other countries tend not only to pick on the dominant country but also to gang up to do so.

The resentments engendered by this overwhelming U.S. dominance take a variety of forms. U.S. allies are often resentful of its power and they may seek, as in France or Germany with their refusal to go along with the United States on a war strategy toward Iraq, to try to change or undermine the policy. Potential rivals like China refuse officially to recognize U.S. superiority and insist on being treated as equals. Because the United States is so powerful and its culture so pervasive, it also offers a tempting target to terrorist groups that may try to bring it down. Many Third World countries are resentful of U.S. dominance but prudence dictates that they cooperate in their own interests. Among the proverbial men (and women) in the street, attitudes are often mixed: admiration for the United States and its successes but often at the same time resentment of its power, occasional arrogance, and even lifestyle.[1]

The United States is often resented not just for what it does but also, often more importantly, for what it *is*. Of course, it is sometimes disliked for its policies, with which other countries or people may disagree. But equally important, the United States is often resented for what it is: a big, rich, powerful, and *successful* country (in contrast to so many others) both economically and politically. If America were only resented for its policies (such as in the Middle East), the problem would be easy to fix: change or modify the policies. But it is far harder for it to change what it *is*, and indeed most of the public and, by reflection, U.S. politicians, would not want to change that anyway. In other words, some of these resentments can be altered, but the more deep-seated roots of anti-Americanism—based on who Americans are as a people and what they stand for—will not go away and are likely to be with us for a long time. One country's success breeds other countries' resentments. And, as with the tradition Russian peasantry, if one person (or country) does better than the others and gets a little "uppity," then the others gang up to bring him down.

6. *Preachiness.* As many foreigners see it, if the United States were only bigger, richer, and more powerful, that would be one thing; but, in addition, as a "beacon on a hill" and a "missionary nation" in the Woodrow Wilson–Jimmy

Carter tradition, it seems compelled to want to bring the benefits of its obviously "superior" economic and political institutions to other poor, "benighted" people throughout the Third World. In these respects, the United States is often seen as preachy, patronizing, and condescending, and such attitudes are often deeply resented abroad. The trouble is, Americans really believe, often with good reason, in the superiority of their political (democracy) and economic (immense prosperity) institutions. And Americans feel they have an *obligation* to teach others how to achieve their successes: by imitating and following their country and its institutions. Such preachiness is not usually a result of arrogance, much less a desire to dominate the world, but an American belief that the conditions of the Third World will be vastly improved if it imitates us and our institutions.

So we have the National Endowment for Democracy to teach American-style democracy abroad; the Center for International Private Enterprise (CIPE), to say nothing of a host of private U.S. businesses and corporations, to teach American-style capitalism abroad; and a variety of other quasi-private, quasi-official agencies to teach American-style local government, American-style public administration, American-style family planning, American-style land reform, American-style central planning, American-style property law, American-style legal training, American-style justice, American-style elections (never mind the controversial year 2000 election!), American-style legislative staff work, American-style executive staff work, and so on, and so on. Often ignored are the facts that America's own institutions are seldom perfect in these regards, and that other countries have different ways of doing things—American institutions may not always be desired, appropriate, or even workable in other cultures and countries. It is small wonder that these U.S. efforts often breed resentment abroad, and that the United States is often disliked for its constant preaching and often heavy-handed meddling in the internal affairs of other nations.

Most countries, however, eventually go along with such U.S. efforts, in part because they have little choice (foreign aid and investment funds often depend on agreeing to such reforms), because their own institutions are not working well, and in part because they also believe the U.S. institutions and ways of doing things to be superior. In today's world, given such immense U.S. power and no real alternative to it, most prudent governments will eventually come around to doing pretty much what the United States wants them to do. To oppose America, beyond mild criticism, is imprudent—and there are serious consequences. That is why, after the initial inaction, private misgivings, and even criticism by some governments, a number of U.S. allies came around to supporting President George W. Bush's war efforts against Iraq. To do otherwise is foolish; you do not want in this day and age to antagonize the

United States. Better to go along with it on this issue in the expectation that will help you win points on the next issue, which may be more important to you than is Iraq. It sounds cynical, but that is the way it works. In the present-day world, with the United States as the only superpower, it makes no sense to cross it.

It is clear from this analysis that globalization takes many different forms—ideological, technological, economic, political, cultural, military. It is clear that many if not most of the globalizing changes underway emanate from the United States. While globalization is not quite synonymous with Americanization, it comes close to being so. That helps explain why so many of the antiglobalization demonstrations also carry anti-American messages. The United States is the chief advocate for, agent of, *and* beneficiary of these new global currents. And in some quarters that provokes a vigorous response and even outcry.

THE INSTITUTIONS OF GLOBALIZATION

Globalization is all around us. It is almost literally in the air we breathe (pollution, acid rain—now both globalized) and the words we speak—particularly if these go out over telephones, fax machines, e-mail, radio, television, or the Internet. Who among us, in the name of antiglobalization, would want to shut down any of these?

Hollywood and the film industry are institutions of globalization. So are CNN, MSNBC, FOX News, ABC, CBS, and NBC. But then, so are the British Broadcasting Corporation (BBC), Sky News (also British), and the Italian, French, Spanish, and German international broadcasting agencies, to say nothing of Al Jazeera, the international Arab news channel. All airlines that fly internationally are agencies of globalization; so are the international hotel chains, banks, and restaurants that cater to travelers. The Ford, General Motors, and Chrysler automobile companies, as well as BMW, Volkswagen, Volvo, Toyota, Honda, Nissan, and Hyundai, are all institutions of globalization. So are the English, French, German, Portuguese, Spanish, and Chinese languages, among others. Every company that either buys abroad or sells abroad (up to 30 percent of the U.S. economy now depends on foreign sales), and in the process creates jobs, provides goods and services, keeps prices low, and raises standards of living, is also an agency of globalization.

The points are obvious: globalization is all around us; most of us benefit enormously from globalization; almost everything we do has global implications; globalization is woven into our culture and lifestyles; we are all parts of a global society whether we wish it or not, and few of us would want to give up the benefits we receive from globalization. So if all this is true, where lies the problem?

The fact is that none of us, including the protestors, is totally against globalization. We receive too many benefits from it, and we could no longer live without it. And those countries that have tried to completely insulate themselves from globalization's effects—North Korea, Vietnam, Cambodia, Cuba—are quite dismal places to live, but even they found they could not entirely shut themselves off from the outside world, nor do they wish entirely to do so. The question therefore, is not whether we are for or against globalization but which aspects of it we oppose and which we favor, and which of its many agencies and institutions we favor and which we oppose.

In actual fact, protests against globalization have come to center on only a handful of institutions: multilateral corporations, the World Bank and the IMF, and the WTO. Let us see what the complaints are.

Multinational Corporations (MNCs)

Multinational corporations are frequently accused of polluting the environment, running sweatshops in Third World countries, exploiting these countries, and putting profits ahead of people.

One ought to begin by distinguishing between the Marxian critique of all MNCs, because they are a part of international and world capitalism, as inherently bad and evil, *and* the more reasonable (and responsible) critique that says that MNCs, like all human institutions, sometimes make mistakes, are self-serving, sometimes try to cheat or skirt the law then try to cover up these mistakes, and, in general, act in their own self-interest. The Marxian critique is a minority one, except perhaps on some college campuses and among some radical groups of protestors; "true believers" of this position are usually immune from rational, reasoned persuasion to any other point of view because, for them, Marxism is like a religious faith that is not subject to empirical verification. Here we focus on the more reasonable critique that *is* subject to the marshaling of evidence and, hence, a more balanced view.

Let us face the facts: MNCs do muck around in the internal affairs of other nations (less now than in earlier eras), *do* have profit as their primary motive (that, after all, is why they are in business), and do sometimes (but now rarely) engage in nefarious, illegal activities. But let us balance this view with the fact that (1) most MNCs try, in *their own* interests, to be good neighbors in the countries where they may locate; (2) generally providing higher salaries and better benefits than do local firms, and often housing, health care, and meals to their workers; (3) fearing the consequences (nationalization of their properties), most MNCs scrupulously obey the laws of their host countries and try to accommodate to local norms, which may also involve payoffs and bribery, but then, "everybody does it"); (4) Most importantly, MNCs provide sorely needed investment, jobs, and a stimulus to the economy that almost all Third World countries are desperate to receive.

The issue therefore is not that all MNCs are evil and all developing-nation governments are always right and pure of motive. Rather, the issue is one of balance. The largest MNCs can mobilize more influence and political connections than can many Third World countries; that gives them immense bargaining power. On the other hand, skillful Third World countries, including small ones, can also have considerable influence in the negotiations that take place. They have the resources and primary products the MNCs want, the expanding middle-class markets, labor supplies, favorable tax advantages, and *knowledge* that MNCs wish to come into their country. Plus they wield the ultimate threat: the possibility of nationalizing the company, or its technology, that invests in their country—although most Third World countries nowadays are so desperate for capital that they don't want to risk future investment by nationalization.

These advantages show that developing countries are not without influence in dealing with big companies. The result is usually a genuine bargaining situation, one of *interdependence* as well as dependence, in which both the country and the company negotiate to get more of what they want. It is true, of course, that companies try to get the best deal possible out of these negotiations, but then so do the countries involved. A country with a skilled, adept leadership can often get much of what it wants from these negotiations; and in most cases, it becomes a *partnership* based on mutual interest that emerges, not a one-way street where one party holds all the best cards.

So, is there a "race to the bottom," as some have alleged? Do MNCs "shop around" to find the country with the lowest wage rates and then go there—but only until they find a country with an even lower wage scale? The answer is, not really. There are a few cases of this, and recently we have seen a handful of MNCs in Mexico move to Southeast Asia because environmental laws, labor laws, and wage rates are lower or less enforced there. But many things go into a company's decision to locate, including proximity to the big U.S. market, transportation costs, banking and financial institutions, and honest government and future stability, as well as wage rates. Plus, most MNCs, once invested in a country in the form of a factory or assembly plant, have a huge stake there and cannot just pull up and relocate elsewhere on short notice. While there is a tendency for companies to go to the places that offer them the most advantages, that also involves a bargaining process with the Third World governments that are not without their own advantages in these talks. Once established in a particular country, most companies are reluctant to leave and would only do so under extreme circumstances: political instability in the country involved, severe economic pressures, such high levels of corruption that it proves impossible to generate revenue there, or a complete breakdown in the dialogue with the host country. The picture is thus not black or white; instead, the image we should have of most MNC–Third World country relations is one of constant, ongoing bargaining and negotiations.

The World Bank and the International Monetary Fund

Both the World Bank and the IMF were established after World War II to maintain the global economy and the world's economic systems. In many quarters it was feared that World War II would be followed by a severe economic downturn just as World War I had been followed by the Great Depression, and the Bank and the IMF were designed to prevent that from happening. The Bank was established to function rather like a global central bank (or like the Federal Reserve in the United States) to oversee global economic trends and perhaps, in limited ways in a world of sovereign states, make modest correctives or adjustments to them, while the IMF was intended to be a lender of last resort if a country got into desperate financial trouble. Initially, the Bank and the IMF were meant to monitor the economies of the developed countries, but since the 1960s and the large number of new and poor nations in the world, these sister institutions have come to focus on loans and programs for the Third World. Instead of being lenders of "last resort," they have become the primary agencies providing aid funds to the developing nations.

Voting and influence in both of these global institutions is weighted, according to the amount of donations that a country makes to them. As the largest donor by far, the United States has the biggest voice in how and where these institutions spend their money. That means that the U.S. view of development, foreign aid, and lending almost always prevails, although other major countries also have influence; and, as with MNCs, Third World countries are not without their own bargaining power in dealing with the Bank and visiting IMF missions. Informally, the Bank is always headed by an American while the IMF is headed by a European, although with an American subdirector.

As with MNCs, these are not inherently evil institutions, as many of the protestors claim, aimed at exploiting the Third World. Often misguided or mistaken, yes; but "evil," no. Let us explain.

First, the overwhelming American influence means that both institutions adhere to essentially the American or Western model of development, a model fashioned over fifty years ago and, by now, woefully out-of-date—even though still followed by the U.S. government and its aid agencies. That model was patterned after the American and European experiences with development, is terribly ethnocentric, and has limited relevance to the Third World. Although the model has had different emphases over the years, it has been remarkably consistent in emphasizing raw economic development over considerations of social, cultural, and political conditions. It is an economic determinist approach, paying little attention to whether a country is honest or corrupt, democratic or authoritarian, civilian or military-led. Emphasizing economics and economic growth above all else means the Bank and IMF gave loans to a number of bloody, authoritarian, corrupt, human rights–abusing regimes, which often pocketed the money rather than using it for honest, worthwhile development purposes.

The model followed by the big lending agencies assumes that sheer investment or "pump-priming" is the sole, virtually only factor in development, without taking into account the nature of the regime in power or the many cultural differences in the world. It *assumed* that the American model of economically driven technocratic change devoid of all political, societal, and cultural considerations could simply be transplanted to the Third World, where, of course, the conditions were quite different. The model was not based on any empirical knowledge of the Third World but on the historical record of the United States and Western Europe whose experiences and processes of development were thought to be both inevitable and universal. But that model does not fit the Third World very well, as the experience of the last fifty years has taught us; nevertheless, with only modest adjustments, that is still the model that the Bank and IMF try to impose on the Third World.

Second, and reflecting the first point, the Bank and IMF are overwhelmingly staffed by economists and financial officials, not by anthropologists, sociologists, and political scientists. Quite naturally, by training and background, these officials see economics as the main driving force in development, again ignoring the cultural, sociological, and political differences among nations. They argue that cultural and political conditions cannot repeal the "laws" of economics, which is, of course, true but ignores that those laws need often to be adjusted to fit the situation and culture of the affected country. The World Bank/IMF formula is thus a rigid, "one-size-fits-all" model that fails to take individual histories, cultures, values, or politics into account. But that is an indefensible position; one would think that after half a century the Bank and IMF would have learned something about the distinct countries where they operate. However, unfortunately, they have not, or very little. I find these institutions still holding to an outdated, narrowly focused, discredited development model that has seldom helped the Third World and often hindered it.[2]

The third consideration is of Bank/IMF missions to developing countries to assess their credit worthiness, *and* the *conditions* ("conditionality") that these missions place on their loans. Almost always, these conditions involve belt-tightening on the part of the applicant countries: fiscal austerity, a balanced budget, inflation under control (no printing of worthless paper money), cutbacks in social services (to achieve that balanced budget), and state shrinkage or the privatization of usually inefficient, patronage-bloated, state-owned firms. While this is the formula (and "one-size-fits-all"), I have found these IMF missions to be increasingly flexible and, surprisingly, more politically sensitive over the years. In other words, as with MNCs and the issue of private investment, these relations, between an IMF mission and a host-country government, are increasingly driven by bargaining and negotiations, and not by the Bank or IMF simply dictating economic policy.

Here is what happens. An IMF mission comes into a country, usually for a brief two- or three-day visit. It is wined and dined by the host-country government, which floods it with data and reports and seeks to put its best foot forward. The IMF then puts forward its one-size-fits-all model involving austerity, privatization, reduction of subsidies, and so on. The host government then responds, "Of course, you are correct at the macrolevel and in the long term. But in the short term, if we remove subsidies on gasoline and the price goes up, buses and public transportation will have to raise fares and people cannot get to work [few working people have cars in the Third World]; if we remove subsidies on rice and beans [the staple diet of the poor], we will have food riots, looting, and mass starvation; if we remove subsidies on kerosene, people cannot cook; if we privatize electricity, rates will go up and poor people cannot afford it." And so on, and so on. In the days of the Cold War, Third World governments would argue additionally that, if they did all these things, there would be revolution and the "commies" would take over, which proved often to be an effective argument; nowadays they say democracy will be reversed—also an effective argument but not as effective as the "communist" one.

In other words, when faced with one of these IMF visitations, Third World governments are not without their own influence and bargaining power. Because no World Bank or IMF mission, let alone the U.S. government, wants to see the countries they are responsible for destabilize or have democracy overthrown. And that gives developing countries considerable leverage. Whether they use that leverage wisely and cleverly is, of course, up to them. But the point is, as with MNCs, this is a bargaining relationship, not a wholly one-way process of the IMF "dictating" policy for the Third World. The relationship may still be uneven, but a clever Third World country can often get much of what it wants out of this bargaining. We may still conclude that the IMF and World Bank sometimes follow misguided, ethnocentric policies; but it is also true that Third World countries have considerable leverage in these negotiations. One therefore should see this as a political relationship of give-

and-take and not simply one where the IMF or World Bank can impose entirely inappropriate solutions on the countries involved.

The World Trade Organization

Created in 1995 and headquartered in Geneva, Switzerland, the WTO is the youngest and least well known of these international organizations. It has just under 150 members, or approximately three quarters of the nations in the world. Just as the IMF and World Bank were charged with maintaining global economic probity and stability, the WTO has as its mission regulating, normalizing, and *expanding* global trade. Trade has a multiplier effect on economic development: for every $1.00 invested in international trade, a country gets back approximately $2.00 in income. That is why so many countries want to join the WTO: trade is in everyone's interest: the rising tide of free trade tends to lift all boats, to expand *all countries'* economies.

As compared with the World Bank and the IMF, the WTO is still a relatively small organization. It was created because earlier efforts to expand and regulate global trade were done largely on an ad hoc basis, usually at brief meetings of developed countries' economic ministers and trade negotiators; it was thought that having a permanent organization with a central office and director would help institutionalize the trade regime. It was also seen as a way to bring Third World nations into the process. But while the WTO has a certain life of its own and some degree of independence, it remains, like the international lending agencies, largely a creation of the wealthier, bigger, more powerful nations. That means mainly, again, the United States, which provides most of the funds, chooses the organization's president (an American), and has the biggest say.

Negotiating trade policy is detailed, slow, often boring, slogging work, which helps explain why few people know much about the WTO or pay it serious attention. In this age of globalization and vastly expanded international trade, it is also extremely important, which helps explain why so many of our foreign policy officials (Warren Christopher, Sandy Berger, Charlene Barshefsky) are trade lawyers. But trade policy is seldom dramatic or on national television like war with Iraq or North Korea's nuclear program, and yet most of us know in the back of our minds how important it is, affecting jobs and the overall international economy. Moreover, most WTO agreements are reached in private, secretly, opaquely, which to some makes it an object of suspicion. The WTO's very secretiveness is what has aroused the interest of globalization protestors who believe that decisions affecting the core of people's lives—food safety, environmental concerns, jobs—are being made behind closed doors.

Everyone agrees that the WTO needs to be more transparent, but getting to that point has proved to be more difficult than expected. Both the legal briefs submitted by the parties to dispute and the follow-up oral arguments are kept secret (the United States is one of the few countries that releases these to the public), and the trade judges' decisions are also kept private, usually for several months. The counterargument is that if the hearings, briefs, and opinions were publicized, they would invite a flood of interest-group activity, lobbying, and lawsuits, and thus overwhelm the (still) small WTO bureaucracy. Small, poor, Third World countries also fear that, in an open environment, they will be either embarrassed by revelations of corruption or incompetence, or overwhelmed by the lawyers and powerful interest lobbies of the developed countries.

But a strong case can be made that greater openness is beneficial to all parties in the long run, even while recognizing that some of the horse-trading that goes into any trade agreement can best be done in private. Negotiations *do* need to be insulated somewhat from private lobbying in order to hammer out mutually productive deals, but the current system carries secrecy too far. The best analogy may be to a parliament where positions are staked out publicly but often finally negotiated privately; similarly, in parliamentary bodies, private interest group input is often beneficial to the process so long as it is the broader *public interest* that gets served in the end. Anything less than that only provokes suspicion on the part of member nations and hostility on the part of antiglobalization protestors who (usually falsely) assume that secretive deals are being hatched that are prejudicial against the poor and against Third World nations.[3]

SUCCESSES AND FAILURES OF GLOBALIZATION

Globalization has been with us since, really, the dawn of humankind. We cannot stop globalization, nor would we want to do so since globalization brings us many of the things that make our lives enjoyable and worthwhile: television, movies, the Internet, cell phones, computers, VCRs, food supplies, automobiles, technology, cheap prices, a high standard of living. Stopping globalization is not an option; instead, the only question is whether we can ameliorate some of globalization's harmful effects. Trying to stop globalization would be like trying to stop the world, and that cannot be done. Globalization is with us, around us, a part of us; the only question remaining is whether we adjust to it well or badly.

Under the impact of modern communications, technology, and transportation, globalization's pace has now accelerated. That is why it is so much in the news recently. We are more aware of globalization and its profound impact than were earlier generations. Our awareness of globalization has grown precisely because of the very technologies listed above that are among the strongest agents of globalization: television, movies, the Internet, and so on.

Globalization sets loose powerful cultural, social, economic, and political forces, and inevitably as part of such a powerful global movement of change it produces both winners and losers. Most of us benefit enormously from globalization and, frankly, could not live without it (which is why so many countries wish to join the WTO); but we need to recognize that there are losers in the process and that we need to pay attention to them also. Here we try to sort out the relevant positive *and* negative things about globalization, and to draw a balance. First, the positive:

1. Globalization increases international trade, and for almost all countries and peoples that's a good thing.
2. Globalization increases international prosperity.
3. Globalization makes our lives richer: television, movies, computers, automobiles, foods, flowers, etc., etc.
4. Globalization promotes diversity, multiculturalism, and international understanding, through immigration, the media, and cultural exchanges.
5. Globalization assists the Third World through international trade and, hence, greater prosperity; globalization lifts (almost) all boats.
6. Globalization undermines authoritarian regimes and advances democracy and human rights because democracy is now the only legitimate system of government, and countries that violate those norms are subject to severe sanctions and ostracism.
7. Globalization keeps prices low for almost everything and provides us with a great diversity of products.
8. Globalization helped defeat the Soviet Union and enabled the United States to win the Cold War.
9. Globalization benefits working people by creating new products, technologies, and, hence, jobs and higher living standards.
10. Globalization is synonymous with development, modernization, and the future. Those who oppose it prefer the world to stop so they can get off, but we know that is impossible. In Tom Friedman's terms, globalization is a Lexus; those who oppose it prefer a world of taking siestas under an olive (or coffee or banana) tree.[4]

But globalization also produces losers—mainly people who cannot adapt to new currents and therefore get left behind. To be truthful, no one knows what to do for those left behind, although doubtless politicians will come up with

[handwritten margin note: positive aspects of globalization]

palliatives that may partially relieve their plight. It may sound a bit heartless, but the fact is one either adjusts and adapts to globalization or one gets left behind, and for those left behind the choices are not bright: retraining, subsidies, or early retirement. Who, then, are the big losers in this process?

1. *Indigenous peoples.* The lands, villages, and cultures of indigenous peoples are being encroached upon by the forces of globalization. We can try to protect them, establish special preserves for them, and use the police or army to keep out interlopers. But all these steps are hard to enforce, and inevitably the march of modernization is going to force indigenous peoples to adapt or be swallowed up by the larger society.

2. *Traditional cultures.* Traditional cultures are often harmed by globalization. It would be nice if all traditional cultures, their native costumes, and often quaint ways could survive. But many of us have a romantic and false picture of traditional cultures: "happy" peasants dancing gaily in the streets, living in a lush, green countryside, and taking long siestas in large hammocks under the coconut trees. The nonromantic reality, however, is usually poverty, disease, bloated bellies (from malnutrition) in the children, and hopelessness. Some societies (more on this below) will be able to preserve, hopefully, the best aspects of their traditional culture in the face of globalization; in others, traditional culture will fade or disappear—except as it reappears in homogenized forms for the benefit of junketeering tourists—and maybe that's not all bad!

3. *Small farmers.* While globalization *tends* to lift all boats in the long run, in the short run many small farmers, who cannot compete with the large, globalized agri-industrial concerns, must either change their crops or go out of business. A third option, increasingly followed in the Third World, is to migrate to the cities or abroad.

4. *Small shopkeepers.* The Third World is dotted with tiny "mom-and-pop" stores that cannot compete with the Wal-Mart's or Targets of this world. Their options, like those of small farmers, are to find a new specialty, migrate, or go out of business. None of these is a very happy alternative.

5. *Older workers.* In much of the industrialized world, old industries (textiles, shoes, steel) are noncompetitive and going out of business. The solution most often suggested is to retrain the workers whose jobs are lost in new technologies. But can you take a fifty-five-year-old worker and retrain her/him in new computer skills able to compete with those of a young eighteen-year-old? Not likely. The other options are to subsidize the noncompetitive industry involved (usually a dinosaur) so it can survive for a time, or offer early retirement to its workers—both expensive and unattractive.

6. *Unionized workers.* Today's globalized economies require flexible, adaptable workers who may have to change jobs many times in their life-

times. But that flies in the face of a unionized shop whose primary interest is in job permanence and security. The unwillingness or inability of unionized shops to adapt to these new, more flexible job markets helps explain the decline of union membership in almost all industrialized societies.

7. *Third World workers.* Third World workers *of all kinds* are particularly vulnerable. They are mainly nonunionized, do not enjoy the protections or social safety nets of workers in developed countries, and are subject to the whims (factory closings, new product lines, moves to another country) of MNCs. While precarious, however, their lives and opportunities would be *far worse* if there were no MNCs or globalization.

8. *The poorest countries.* The poorest countries tend not to reap the benefits of globalization. The following "law" generally holds: the poorer the country, the less it benefits from globalization. The poorest of the poor countries tend not to have the resources, infrastructure, products, skilled workers, or trade negotiators to take advantage of globalization. But their sad plight is not the result of globalization per se; rather, it is a product of the more general vicious circles of underdevelopment in which these nations are caught. Globalization would undoubtedly help these poor countries—if only they could become a part of it.

9. *The environment.* The environment undoubtedly suffers as a result of the greater crowding, pollution, and environmental degradation brought on by globalization. But what are the options: going back to the "sleepier," nonmodern, nonindustrialized nineteenth century? Preventing the Third World from industrializing (and thus remaining backward) so they don't pollute as much as the First World did and does? Both of these are untenable positions. We cannot tell Brazil or any other Third World country that it must refrain from industrialization, not participate in globalization, and thus remain poor so that we in the wealthy countries can enjoy the pure oxygen generated by a roadless, undeveloped, factory-free Amazon rain forest. No, the solution must come from elsewhere (clean factories, scrubbers on chimneys, automobile and truck emission controls) and not from telling the Third World to stay poor so that we in the rich North can enjoy clean air.

The conclusions that stand out from this analysis are obvious:

1. *On balance,* globalization is a good thing.
2. It *tends* to improve living standards worldwide and to benefit peoples and countries in both the First and the Third Worlds.
3. The losers from globalization tend to be those peoples and institutions that would be disadvantaged by *any* modernizing changes: indigenous peoples, small farmers and shopkeepers, older and unionized workers, traditional cultures, and the poorest countries.

4. Society or the international community needs to find ways to help these marginalized sectors or countries, but opposing globalization or trying to turn back the clock will not do it.

THE ANTIGLOBALISTS

In recent years, meetings of the World Bank, IMF, and WTO, as well as those of high-level business and finance ministers, have been the subject of headline-grabbing protests in such cities as Seattle, Washington; Davos, Switzerland; Prague, Czech Republic; Nice, France; Gothenburg, Sweden; Salzburg, Austria; Genoa, Italy; and Washington, D.C. The protests have nowhere been able to close down these meetings, but they are disruptive as well as expensive in terms of the police overtime and cleanup required. The protesters tend to be small in numbers, but they reflect a broader, popular unease with globalization.

At one level there are serious issues involved (see below), but at another these rallies are like campus protests that occur according to the seasons, usually in the spring. They provide an opportunity to take a break from classes, have a lark, demonstrate against the establishment, and sow some wild oats, seemingly without penalty except, perhaps, for brief arrest and a small fine. Many of the leaders involved are professional protestors who float breezily from issue to issue; some have been doing this for years, even *decades*, going back to the Vietnam War. Protesting is often viewed as fun, a chance to meet other young people, and at the same time in the name of a cause. One is tempted to say to the protestors (and government and bank officials often do): "Get a life!"

But the issues and makeup of the protest groups are more complicated than that. The groups are diverse, as always consisting of some serious persons and others who are frivolous. In the United States the groups tend to consist of both the Old and the New Left: Marxists, old Vietnam War protestors, radical student leaders, activists and liberals who can be mobilized around specific issues, "Trotskyites" (whatever that means these days), and anarchists. In Europe the protestors tend to come more out of political party ranks: Greens, Socialists, Social-Democrats, and Communists, but also with Trotskyites and Anarchists thrown in. Most of the protestors are young, in their twenties, and still in college or graduate school; in Europe many of them are young and working class, fearful of losing jobs to foreign competition. Most are peaceful, but some use violent methods, a faction that is usually known and often condoned by the organizers.

The protests have brought together others from even more diverse backgrounds and made "strange bedfellows" out of otherwise opposed groups. The groups include environmentalists, anticapitalists (a new name for Marxists?), radicals, labor groups, "sovereigntists" (the new name for those opposed to lifting trade and immigration barriers), human rights activists, and others who feel aggrieved or injured by the sheer growth of modern business and international trade. The "strange bedfellows" opposed to globalization include conservative, nationalist Pat Buchanan on the Right, and another former (minority party) presidential candidate, Ralph Nader, on the Left.

While the antics of the antiglobalization forces are often comic opera and not very effective, it would be a mistake to dismiss them too quickly. Surveys show that, while they have little sympathy for the mainly upper-middle-class and sometimes violent young protestors, the American public is deeply suspicious of globalization.[5] The protestors are thus only the most visible presence of what is an often vague sense of unease on the part of the public. Depending on the survey, a large plurality and sometimes a majority of Americans are opposed to further trade liberalization, additional immigration, and globalization in general. These same surveys show that Americans understand the benefits of free trade, but they tend to see the costs in loss of jobs and lower wages as outweighing the benefits. Similarly, in the Third World various publics understand the advantages of lower trade barriers but are opposed to privatizations, removal of subsidies, and government belt-tightening that adversely affects their living standards.

Democrats, women, union members, and African Americans tend to be more opposed to globalization than other groups. The reasons for this are twofold: these are the groups whose jobs are most threatened by globalization (either by the competition from immigrant labor or by the fleeing of American factories to countries of lower labor costs) or, if they are employed, have seen their wages stagnate on a long-term basis. Perhaps the most striking finding of these surveys is that attitudes toward globalization are closely correlated with the skill and educational level of the respondents: the better educated and most skilled among the public tend to favor globalization (they are the ones who benefit from it), while the less skilled and less well educated—precisely those groups noted above—are most opposed. It is likely that *both* these groups are correct in assessing their own self-interest: those better educated and better skilled who benefit from globalization tend to support it, while those less skilled and less well educated and thus most threatened by it tend to be opposed.

While that may be an accurate reflection of divided public opinion on this issue, most professional economists see it differently. They say that, when total wages and benefits are calculated, the wages of almost all American workers have not been stagnant but have increased over the last twenty years. In addition, the jobs of only about 3 percent of American workers are threatened by foreign competition; plus, the number of jobs created from increased U.S. exports through globalization *significantly* outnumbers the job losses from imports. Their conclusion: globalization has a net positive impact both on wages and jobs. And, as part of the multiplier effect of trade, globalization also creates jobs, higher wages, and economic growth in the Third World. In other words, people's *fears* about the effects of globalization are out of line with the economic benefits. But then, in politics, what people believe is frequently more important than what actually is.

It is not clear that the (mostly) young, (often) radical protestors represent public opinion on these issues. No one elected them to organize protests or to serve as spokespersons about globalization; most of those who have doubts about globalization would be appalled at the (sometimes) violent street tactics used; and the radical ideology and often the lifestyles of the protestors are way outside the mainstream of American politics. On the other hand, the protestors have undoubtedly tapped into the widespread unease that exists among the public, especially on issues such as jobs and wages. And it is clear the World Bank, IMF, and WTO all recognize this because they have responded to the protestors far more positively than the latter's small numbers would merit. These international agencies have invited the protestors in for discussions; listened to their complaints; issued news releases also expressing their concern for indigenous peoples, the environment, and the poor; and have modified their policies accordingly. It is interesting that these agencies, which claim to be completely nonpolitical, are, in fact, reacting to the protests in completely political ways.

For there *are* important issues out there: pollution; acid rain; global warming; the environment; labor rights; the deleterious effects of globalization on indigenous peoples, small farmers, and the lower classes in the Third World. All these issues need to be dealt with at both the national and the international levels. The question is, in a democracy, whether the protestors have either the technical expertise or the public legitimacy and representativeness to speak for the country and the world on these issues.

CONCLUSION

This chapter has emphasized that globalization has *always* been with us; it takes many different forms (cultural, technical, economic, religious, political, strategic); and it cannot be stopped, nor the clock turned back, nor would we want to do so. Very few of us would want to turn in our foreign cars, our cell phones, our computers, our televisions, our VCRs—all of which are part of globalization. Nor would we want to sacrifice our relatively inexpensive gasoline, high living standards, abundant goods, and low prices for most things—which are similarly the result of globalization. It is telling that even the protestors mainly use the instruments of globalization—the Internet and cell phones—to organize their antiglobalization networks.

Globalization is here to stay and, *on balance*, most of us benefit enormously from it. The issue is not rejecting globalization or seeking to return to an earlier, "sleepier" time, but whether we can adjust to globalization and amplify its beneficial effects. *Of course*, we need to protect the environment, but being against globalization will not do that. *Of course*, we need to worry about indigenous peoples, small farmers and shopkeepers, and working-class persons in the Third World, but opposing globalization will not solve those problems either—and since it is globalization that creates jobs, raises wages, and lifts the standard of living in the Third World, stopping it will make these people worse rather than better off. The question is not whether we can turn back globalization—we cannot—but whether we can adjust its powerful forces to benefit more people rather than fewer.

Much the same applies to countries as to individuals. There are some countries that are so poor, so underinstitutionalized, so underdeveloped that they are unable to take advantage of the investment, growth, and development opportunities that globalization provides. Some countries (often the same ones) have such weak and fragile cultures that they are *overwhelmed* by globalization rather than able to selectively borrow from and adjust to it.

In contrast, such countries as Japan, China, India, Iran, Mexico, Brazil, and others besides have strong indigenous cultures and ways of doing things and are able to selectively borrow from Western-led globalization even while preserving their own customs and traditions—the preferred way to deal with such changes. Look especially at Japan: it is one of the most modern, industrialized, and prosperous nations in the world, and yet by *selectively borrowing* from the West and from globalizing influences, it has maintained its special Japanese character; no one visiting Japan for the first time would think she/he was in Chicago, London, Paris, or Berlin. And yet, many poor countries that lack the strength of a powerful culture like that of the Japanese are likely not to be able to take advantage of globalization but to be overwhelmed, maybe even smothered, by it. Those countries, just like the unfortunate peoples mentioned earlier who have been left behind by globalization, need special assistance, consideration, and help. There are signs that even the World Bank, IMF, and WTO now recognize that fact.

NOTES

1. Many foreigners have never been to the United States but nevertheless have strong opinions about it, mainly shaped by the unreal images of television and the movies: the lavish lifestyles portrayed in *Dallas* or *Beverly Hills 90210*, or violent films like those of Bruce Willis, Clint Eastwood, or Arnold Schwarzenegger. When I lived in Europe and lectured widely on U.S. foreign policy, I was repeatedly asked questions about capital punishment, which Europe has abolished and now feels morally superior about. Unfortunately, when I studied international relations, I never thought I'd have to respond to questions about capital punishment, about which I have no expertise.

2. In the interest of truth in packaging, and also because the story illustrates well the point made, I must say that I was once interviewed for a World Bank position. The Bank mistakenly thought I was an economist. When I told them that I was a political scientist, they said, "Oh no, we cannot take political considerations into account when making loans." That is, in fact, forbidden by the Bank's charter, but what is meant by that prohibition is that the Bank is not supposed to take *partisan* considerations into account. In other words, the Bank could not distinguish between *partisan considerations* (Republican or Democrat) and my work as a *political scientist* in assessing whether a particular government was creditworthy (honest, democratic, and dedicated to genuine development rather than just the private enrichment of its own officials) or not, or in weighing the political *effects* of Bank loans on the receiving country. That interview took place in the 1980s; I have since learned that the Bank has more recently hired a handful of anthropologists (because it belatedly "discovered" its policies often had effects on indigenous peoples) and even a "couple" of political scientists to judge democracy/human rights issues—a tardy step in the right direction but not nearly enough.

3. *Washington Post* (December 26, 2002), A-38.

4. Thomas Friedman, *The Lexus and the Olive Tree: Understanding Globalization* (New York: Farrar, Straus & Giroux, 1999).

5. See the analyses in *International Herald Tribune* (March 16, 2001), 15, and (July 6, 2001), 4; and in *Washington Post* (September 5, 2001), B-1.

Part Three

REGIONAL RESPONSES

Chapter Eleven

Asia and the Effort to Grow Civil Society

Asia is one of the most complex areas in the world in terms of U.S. foreign policy. Here we have more nuclear powers (Russia, China, India, Pakistan, probably both North and South Korea, potentially Japan) than in any other world area. Here we have at least four already or soon-to-be global powers (Russia, China, Japan, India). Here we have well over half the world's population, with over one billion each in both China and India. It is in Asia that we have some of the world's greatest economic success stories, together with some of the world's poorest nations. And here it is also that we have some of the greatest potential conflict (India–Pakistan, China–Russia, the two Koreas, Japan–China). Clearly, Asia is one of the most important regions in the world for U.S. policy.

But in this chapter we focus on another issue: the effort to grow civil society and, hence, democracy, in Asia. The United States sees democracy and civil society as the best way to solve the other problems above: civil society is good for democracy; civil society helps development; civil society serves to prevent war. However, this area illustrates as well the immense problems discussed earlier in the book to which the effort to build civil society gives rise: the problems of culture clash, ethnocentrism, U.S. interference in the internal affairs of other nations and the nationalistic reactions to which it gives rise. Obviously, we cannot deal with all of Asia's issues in one chapter, but the civil society focus provides us with a fascinating window through which to think about this important aspect of U.S. policy.

East Asia has some of the world's most dynamic economies and societies. Japan has the second largest economy (after the United States) in the world and is among the world's most prosperous countries with a high standard of living. South Korea, Hong Kong, Singapore, and Taiwan have also experienced miraculous economic growth over the last four decades, beginning in the 1960s as still Third World countries but then *leapfrogging* over other countries (relatively rare in the rank ordering of the wealth of nations, which has stayed quite constant over the last hundred years) to take their place among what the World Bank calls high-income countries. Although somewhat less dramatically and impressively, Malaysia, Thailand, the Philippines, Indonesia, and now China, Vietnam, and Myanmar have also experienced impressive but irregular economic growth, and despite U.S. efforts to help expand Asian civil society.

One would expect such vibrant economies to also have developed vibrant civil societies, and to some extent they have. But as compared to Western Europe or North America, especially relative to their level of socioeconomic development, East Asia for the most part still has weak civil society. "Strong states [in the sense of authoritative, bureaucratic, centralized decision making], weak societies" is the catchphrase that is generally employed to summarize the situation.[1] The question we wrestle with here is why East Asian civil society remains weak despite the area's impressive, even phenomenal, economic growth.

SOCIOECONOMIC DATA

East Asia has some of the most developed, most dynamic economies in the world. Table 11.1 provides some basic data on the region's economies, their levels of social modernization, and their rank ordering among the world's nations.

One would expect, from development theory, that countries with such high socioeconomic rankings would also have well-developed civil societies. Because these are countries—at least those at the top ranks—that have a sizable middle class, high literacy, high urbanization, low unemployment, low income inequalities, regular elections, and a functioning democracy. The theory of development, at least as articulated in the West and based on the Western model, leads us to expect that such countries will also have strong civil societies.

But that is not the case. In fact, East Asia has a notoriously weak civil society. Or, put in developmental terms, relative to its level of socioeconomic development, East Asia has a relatively weakly developed civil society.

ELEMENTS OF POLITICAL CULTURE

East Asia, unlike the United States, has no history of civil society in the Tocquevillian or Madisonian sense, denoting webs of popular or grassroots asso-

Table 11.1. East Asian Indicators of Socioeconomic Development*

Per Country	GNP	GNP Per Capita	Life Expectancy		Literacy		Urban- ization	GNP Per Capita Rank
			Male	Female	Male	Female		
Japan	4,078.9	32,230	77	84	100		79	6
Singapore	95.4	29,610	75	79	96	88	100	9
Hong Kong	161.7	23,520						20
South Korea	397.9	8,490	74	80	99	96	81	51
Taiwan	160.0	8,400	74	80	99	93	80	52
Malaysia	77.3	3,400	70	75	91	82	57	72
Thailand	121.0	1,960	46	48	83	64	21	102
Philippines	78.0	1,020	67	71	95	95	58	131
China	980.2	780	68	72	91	75	32	140
Indonesia	119.5	580	64	67	91	80	40	150
Myanmar (formerly Burma)		755 or lower**	58	62	89	79	27	
Vietnam	28.2	370	66	71	95	91	20	167
Cambodia	3.0	260	52	55	57	20	16	186

*Countries listed in declining order of per capita income.
**World Bank estimate.

Source: World Bank, *World Development Report 2000–2001*.

ciability. Most of the East Asian countries surveyed here are remarkably *civil*, in terms of absence of crime, absence of direct confrontation, and quiet, non-conflictual interpersonal relations; but civil society in the sense of vast networks of independent associations standing between the individual and the state and serving as a check on governmental authority is largely absent.[2]

Let us begin at the beginning, with language.[3] Most of Asia has no language equivalents for such key concepts as "public" (as in "public interest"), "civil," or even "society." The standard translation for *public* in Japan is *kç*, derived from a Chinese character (which therefore means it has approximately the same meaning throughout East Asia) that suggests "government" or "ruling authority" more than it does "public." Most Japanese, when they hear the word *kç*, assume it means *government* or *state*, or more specifically *state bureaucracy*, not so much *public* or *popular* or *grassroots*. The concept of "public" in the Western sense is still not very familiar in Japan. The obvious implication is that, for the Japanese and other East Asians, state interests tend to dominate over public interests, with largely negative consequences for civil society. We return to this theme shortly.

Much the same applies to "civil" and "society." The term *civil* in East Asia tends to refer to "proper," age-old, and accustomed interpersonal relations and Asian expectations of appropriate behavior, which are deferential, submissive, and hierarchically derived, not so much implying "civic" or popular participation in governmental affairs. Similarly with *society*, for which there is no equivalent Japanese translation either. Whereas *kç* is a concept implying vertical, hierarchical, and top-down (or state) relationships, "society," which suggests a horizontal and even spontaneous association of individuals, is also a foreign concept in the East Asian tradition. A wide variety of words and phrases were tried before *shakai* came to be commonly used as the standard rendering of *society*. The absence of Japanese and, in general, East Asian equivalents for such terms as *public*, *civil*, and *society* is symbolic. Most Americans and, of course, all civil society advocates think of the modern democratic state as founded on a strong civil society base where the concept of "public" or "public interest" is indispensable. But in Confucian, top-down, hierarchical, authoritarian East Asia, such fundamental terms have either been absent historically or they carry different meanings than in the American or Western context.

The reasons these terms are absent or unfamiliar in East Asia is that democracy itself, and its necessary accompanying notions of grassroots or popular participation, has long been absent from the area and is a relatively new, and perhaps not yet deeply imbedded, concept. The tradition historically in East Asia is instead one of respect for authority and disdain for the masses. Neither in Confucian nor in Buddhist theory is there a concept of "the people" or of "civil society" or even of democracy. Instead the assumption at least in the past is of the overwhelming superiority of "the state," the state bureaucracy, or officialdom. Decisions were authoritatively, if not authoritarianly, made from the top down, not from the bottom up. The assumption was (and still is) that the government alone is best able to judge what is in the public interest. The Confucian concept is thus close to the Rousseauian tradition in the West, wherein the ruler knows the "general will" and need not necessarily check with the public or electorate about his decisions, and civil society as the West knows it is neither present nor desirable.[4]

In such a top-down context, any attempt to understand East Asia in the light of "civil society" is bound to be frustrating. Under the East Asian bureaucratic or authoritarian state, the government represents the *whole* and is *the* authority embodying the public, while the people are simply considered subordinate parts of that larger system, perhaps pursuing their private interests but even then under official or state authority. Until these deeply held cultural beliefs in the superiority of authority and disdain for the public is overcome, and until the belief is widespread that the people themselves are worthy of respect and have individual as well as group value, a strong civil society and a strong democracy are unlikely to emerge.[5]

All of the East and Southeast Asian cultures have devolved elaborate rules for conducting interpersonal relationships, including between government and governed, but almost all of these are defined in hierarchical rather than egalitarian terms.[6] Formality and correctness are expected but not necessarily equality. Superior–inferior relationships are designed to glorify the dignity of the superior and to ensure that the inferior knows and stays in his/her place. Superiors are especially sensitive to real or perceived slights or challenges to their status. The political effect therefore is to reinforce authoritarian norms and retard the development of interest-group or civil-society bargaining and give-and-take that are essential to democracy. This is changing, of course, as democracy has come to the area, but the *form* of democracy that is practiced still tends to be top-down, bureaucratic, and state-centric.

Instead of civil society in the Western sense, much of East and Southeast Asia is dominated by networking or patron–client ties of greater or lesser complexity. In Japan, interpersonal ties are based on the concepts of *ou* and *giri*, which entail a powerful sense of obligation, indebtedness, and reciprocity. The Chinese system is that of *quanxi*, or personal connections, which is a firmly structured, institutionalized arrangement for ensuring and perpetuating mutual obligation. Both Indonesia and the Philippines have elaborate systems of patron–client relations that reach all the way from local to national levels and back down again. Burma (now Myanmar) and Thailand also have patronage networks—in a sense these are the functional equivalents of civil society—but they are less elaborately structured and often involve little more than norms of civility, without elaborate networking and top-to-bottom patronage channels. Tribe, ethnicity, and regionalism are also components of civil society. The line between patronage and outright corruption is often obscure.

An examination of these East and Southeast Asian patron–client systems reveals a number of interesting conclusions. First, in contrast to the Western attitude that in such systems patrons have all the advantages and clients are always exploited, in Asia it is often the clients who *force* their patrons to take risks in order to gain more power and influence so that the clients may also benefit from the advantages gained. Second, there are few signs that this Asian system is giving way, as is the presumption in the West whether from liberal, Marxist, or bureaucratic perspectives, under the impact of modernization. Indeed, third, many Asian figures—Lee Kuan Yew, Mohammed Mathitir—touted their model of a strong state and weak society as essential to Asian development, a model that is not only successful but reflects Asian values and indigenous traditions more closely than does the American system of civil society based on conflictual interest-group bargaining. Fourth, as Asian society does modernize and takes on the institutional accoutrements imported from the United States or the West, such as political parties, interest groups, and civil society, these so-called modern institutions remain heavily infused with some patron–client relations of the past, now updated and given Western dress.[7]

In much of Asia, whether in "communist" or "democratic" systems, it is still mainly the state and the state bureaucracy that govern, still in a top-down and authoritative rather than a grassroots, liberal, and popular/participatory way. The legitimation of group or individual interests separate from the state or community has been quite slow in coming and even now is not well established.[8] Private interests and individual personalities, apart from the group, firm, or government agency, are still viewed as shameful expressions of selfishness and greed.[9] Behind the glitter of the recent East Asian economic miracles, hence, is not so much a system of liberal, democratic capitalism and competition but an often more sordid system of special favoritism, bribery, and indistinct lines between public and private entrepreneurship.

The United States' foremost Asia specialist, Lucian Pye, argues that East and Southeast Asian societies are not deficient in norms of civility, social capital, or even some forms of civil society.[10] Rather, he says, they have been combined in ways that are very different from those of the West. Asian cultures, he argues, are particularistic, resistant to a universalist formula, or else *selectively* incorporate those institutions of the West that can best be adapted to Asian ways of doing things. For example, in Singapore, Malaysia, China, and other societies to a somewhat lesser degree, the "community" is identified with the state and state policy, so that any pressure from civil society in opposition to state policy is viewed as both an affront to the community and, dangerously, a subversive activity inviting retribution.

In the most developed Asian countries—Japan, Singapore, Taiwan, South Korea—what passes for "civil society" is so intertwined with government/bureaucratic/administrative agencies and state decision making as to be all but inseparable from them. Throughout Asia, what we call "state–society relations" or "civil society" is played out at a much lower level than American or European interest-group theory would suggest, at the level of the family, the clan, the neighborhood, and the immediate, face-to-face community. Even when the figures show a quantum increase in recent years in civil society groups in Japan and other countries, that does not mean necessarily an increase in American-style pluralism, interest-group competition, or grassroots democracy. But that also means that there is still a *huge* space between these lower-level, often local or neighborhood associations and the state, with relatively little civil society in between. And that absence of strong intermediary associations makes both democracy and stability in much of the region quite tenuous.

STRUCTURAL CHANGE AND
ASIAN STATE–SOCIETY RELATIONS

As long as Asia remained relatively underdeveloped, traditionalist (Confucianist), and plagued by both internal (disorder) and external (Cold War) issues, it was relatively easy to maintain a closed, top-down, state-centric, bureaucratic-authoritarian political system. But as Asian society modernized, as globalization had its cultural and social effects, and then as the Cold War ended, new openings, new space for civil society, began to emerge. Peter Moody calls this new era in Asia "post-Confucian."[11]

Japan, South Korea, and Taiwan—along with Singapore, the most developed countries in Asia—are the primary cases. In all three, à la W. W. Rostow, the patterns were similar—and, of course, South Korea and Taiwan had the earlier Japanese model to look to. In all three, economic development was initially, and for a considerable period, given priority over political development, or democratization. That is, in all three countries it was seen as necessary first to stimulate economic growth and to establish the conditions for economic growth—order, stability, a climate favorable to investment and export-led growth—before the "dangerous" pluralism and freedom of democracy could be permitted. That meant strong, centralized decision making, a powerful and effective state-bureaucratic structure, concentrated economic power, and close interconnections between business and the state, as well as strict controls and limits (of a quasi-corporatist kind) on human rights; freedom of association, speech, and assembly; pluralism; and especially student and labor union activity. Only after stability had been achieved, a strong economy developed, a sizable middle class emerged, and the internal and external threats ended could genuine freedom and pluralism be permitted.

And that is generally the pattern followed. Japan led the way with export-led economic growth beginning in the 1950s and 1960s, achieved "miracle" growth rates in the 1960s and 1970s, and emerged by the 1980s as the second most powerful economy in the world (after only the United States) and with one of the world's highest standards of living. South Korea and Taiwan followed (also Hong Kong and Singapore, but they are essentially city-states with special circumstances and thus somewhat distinct cases) utilizing the Japanese model, and perhaps applying it even more strictly than did Japan: strong, even authoritarian government, centralized decision making, close collaboration between the bureaucratic state and the entrepreneurial sector, and tight control on freedom and group activity. By the late 1960s Japan was called the economic "tiger" of Asia; by the late 1970s the other four were referred to as the "little tigers." Their economic growth rates were not only spectacular but also virtually unprecedented in world history, vaulting them over other countries, from poverty to affluence, from Third World to First World.

Democratization, however, lagged behind. Japan had a democratic constitution and had been occupied and was closely monitored by the United States so that authoritarianism and human rights abuses were limited; but it remained essentially a one-party state that limited civil liberties, maintained strict order and uniformity, and kept close control over pluralist group activities. South Korea and Taiwan, both flashpoints in the Cold War, maintained authoritarian, or "bureaucratic-authoritarian," one-party systems, where the army was either in power or so close to the surface of power as to be inseparable from it, and employed repressive controls and violence against student, labor, and opposition groups.[12] The Philippines (Ferdinand Marcos) and Indonesia (Raden Suharto) maintained military-authoritarian regimes that for a long time paid not even lip service to democracy. Singapore was an especially interesting case (and an exception to the general pattern) in that it maintained authoritarian controls and restrictions on civil liberties even *after* economic growth had been achieved, a strong middle class had emerged, and the internal (potential for ethnic conflict, civil, gang warfare) and external threats had largely disappeared.

It was only in the 1980s and 1990s, after the security issues had been mainly settled, significant development had been achieved, a middle class consolidated, and a consensus established on future social and political directions, that South Korea and Taiwan—both following somewhat separate routes—determined they could move toward greater pluralism and political democracy. Greater press freedom was allowed; opposition political parties were permitted that eventually even won elections; and, especially important for this study's purposes, greater freedom of association, assembly, and group activity was, somewhat grudgingly, authorized. In other words, it was only *after* significant economic growth had been achieved and social and political stability established that South Korea and Taiwan concluded they could afford the *luxury* of genuinely free, pluralist, and competitive civil society.[13]

But all this was achieved only with great anguish, reluctance on the part of government authorities, and struggle on the part of opposition groups. It was by no means automatic, according to some universal or global model of change, nor so antiseptic as presented in the preceding paragraph. Rather, it was the result of struggle and constant pressure on the part of student, labor, and other opposition groups; clash and contradiction between them and governing authorities; and sometimes violence and bloodshed. "Civil society" is not something, like Venus emerging fully formed from the sea, that springs up automatically, spontaneously, universally, or through the good offices and best intentions of civil society advocates; rather, it is the result of struggle, pressure, clash, and conflict.

The first issue, for our purposes, was the language problem: how to find a terminology for "civil society," "pluralism," and even "public interest" that overcame the absence of such ideas and concepts in historic Asian thought. This is essentially a problem of finding new meaning in old terms and is thus a problem of political culture. We have said that in traditional Japanese and in other Asian languages, there are no real equivalents of these key terms; and even when linguists, societal actors, and politicians began to search for such equivalents as, for example, in the Japanese term *kÇeki* for *public interest*, the emphasis was still overwhelmingly on the official or government or state-centered interpretation of this term rather than the societal or "public." But gradually over the last twenty years, we have witnessed a wrestling with this issue and an evolution of language to accommodate these new understandings—even while actual official and even popular usage still lags behind, putting emphasis even now on the state or top-down side more than on the bottom-up or civil society side.[14]

A second issue was the use of public-interest issues in Japan and East Asia more generally during the 1980s and 1990s that mobilized citizens' participation and led to a dramatic rise in civil society activism. Quite a number of these new movements arose in response to, or as a result of, large-scale economic, social, and political transformations that had occurred over the preceding thirty years and were still unfolding. The most significant of these were the democracy and people's movements in South Korea, Taiwan, the Philippines, and later Indonesia as well, although in the latter country what might be termed "premature democratization" seemed to be producing fragmentation and possibly national disintegration and ungovernability rather than happy, democratic, civil society. These movements pushed for genuine democracy, real opposition political parties that would have a chance at winning, and more "Western" or at least updated conceptions of human rights, including not just the classic freedoms but also individual rights as well as the historic group rights.

In Japan, which had had regular elections for some time and was at least a formal democracy, the changes were less dramatic in terms of capturing headlines but perhaps equally significant in long-range terms. There, the mobilization of a historically deferential (to the state as well as to superiors) people around such issues as opposition to the building of a new airport outside Tokyo, environmental and pollution controls on major industries, park projects in large cities that were built without consulting the residents, and rescue and relief projects in Kobe after the 1995 earthquake showed that private nongovernmental organizations (NGOs) and nonprofit organizations (NPOs) were far quicker and more effective at responding to popular needs than governmental agencies, and led to a major proliferation of civil society groups throughout Japan.[15]

In Japan, and to a somewhat lesser extent in the other countries, there has been a veritable groundswell in the growth of civil society. The rise of "public" consciousness on a variety of issues has gone hand in hand with greater citizens' activism and, hence, in the growth of civil society. As of 1996, over eighty-five thousand groups were registered as NGOs or NPOs involved in a wide range of activities from welfare and education to human rights, peace, the environment, even garbage collection. In the realm of international cooperation, Japan had only seven groups registered at the end of the 1960s, thirty-three at the end of the 1970s, one hundred thirty-two at the end of the 1980s, and over two hundred by the turn of the millennium. Volunteerism, another mark of an emerging civil society, is also up significantly: 1.3 million people were mobilized to assist with relief activities after the Kobe earthquake and 270,000 workers were mobilized to save coastal areas when a Russian tanker carrying crude oil ran ashore on the Japanese coast in 1997. There has been, in other words, a tremendous growth in the last twenty years in Asian democratic groups, people's movements, and civil society.[16] But remember that many of these are still only temporary, organized only at the local level, and are not really national interest groups or civil society in the American sense.

While this growth, even with the qualifications noted, is encouraging to civil society advocates, the situation in East and Southeast Asia is still far from the unfettered interest group pluralism, diversity, and competition of U.S. or European democracy. Rather, the system is still one of predominantly state-structured interest group activity, or corporatism, combined with some elements of free associability as well, as sometimes informal, sometimes violent street action. In Japan, for example, the concept of "public interest corporation" now exists in the law and civil code, but confirmation of an organization's "public interest" orientation by central government authorities is still the condition for authorization of its legal status. The power to grant such legal status, however, is also the power to deny or delay it, thus depriving the group of all-important legitimacy before the law. Moreover, even after incorporation, these groups remain under the guidance and supervision of the state and its ministries; there is no automatic human right of free associability. Furthermore, of the twenty-six thousand public interest corporations registered in Japan, a sizable percentage are aimed at providing postretirement employment for the country's legion career civil servants, thus reinforcing once again the old public-equals-official structure. Civil society has clearly grown in Japan but there is less there than meets the eye, and much of what does exist is still controlled, regulated, or absorbed into the state in corporatist, not necessarily liberal, fashion.

Japan is, of course, the most developed of the Asian countries, and perhaps the most "democratic," which may or may not be saying much. In countries that are less developed than Japan, and where civil society is less advanced, the balance may still be powerfully on the side of the state and less so on the side of civil society. For example, while South Korea and Taiwan have both taken some enormous strides toward democracy in the last decade, that process is still incomplete; civil society is still weak and often tenuous; and such fundamental pluralist groups as students, labor, and political parties may still be subject to government harassment, controls, regulation, and conceivably even, in the worst of circumstances, elimination. Proceeding further south to the Philippines, Indonesia, and Southeast Asia, the situation of civil society may be even more perilous because the state or the army not only possesses great power but also the ability literally to dissolve, repress, and eliminate civil society. In addition, in countries such as Indonesia and several of the others mentioned, "civil society" often means tribal, local, ethnic, or regional power; and the devolution of decision making to these groups may result in the breaking or disintegration of the *national* political system. Not only is civil society thus often perilous or on shaky grounds throughout the region, but there is a fairly close correlation between development and the health of civil society, with Japan (even with all its limits) on the top, followed by South Korea and Taiwan, and other societies with considerably weaker societies. And even there, as Shin'icki Yoshida has written, the entire political process represents even now a competition between the public-equals-official society and the forces for freedom from the fetters of that society.[17]

THE INTERNATIONAL CONTEXT

The more developed nations in East Asia—Japan, now South Korea, Taiwan, and Singapore—have *not* been the subject of major focus by international civil society groups. These countries have not been in the headlines recently as major democracy or human rights violators; moreover, they are often viewed by the international NGO/civil society community as being sufficiently developed economically and successful politically that they have "graduated" from the list of countries to aid or even to be concerned about.

Within these countries, furthermore, the focus of concern is often not so much the encouragement of more civil society per se or as a bulwark of liberal democracy in the American mode, but rather how to create civil society organizations that will make them *look* more acceptable to the international community or, in the case of often isolated Taiwan, that will assist in their forging international connections that will bolster their foreign policy, which is frequently hampered by the Mainland's (Peoples' Republic of China) insistence that Taiwan be isolated and not aided by *any* international group. In both Japan and South Korea civil society groups are often created by the state as a way of making them look good to the outside world or to Westerners—the "imitation of the West" affect. In Taiwan, NGOs are strongly encouraged not for their own sake but as a way of improving the appearance of Taiwanese democracy, which is seen as its primary diplomatic resource, and as a way, through their international activities, of enhancing the island's diplomatic presence abroad and breaking out of its international isolation. Since Taiwan's official representation in other countries and international agencies is often limited by Beijing's refusal to allow it, Taiwan's usually quasi-official NGOs provide an alternative channel.[18] But this is, of course, far from what most advocates of civil society have in mind.

When we get to the less-developed areas of Asia—the Philippines, Indonesia, Southeast Asia—even more serious problems emerge. In the Philippines, while there was a massive mobilization of civil society in the mid-1980s, first against the dictatorship of Ferdinand Marcos and then *for* the "peoples' movement" election of Corazon Aquino, after that crisis-of-the-moment civil society went into decline. Civil society was mobilized again in opposition to later president Joseph Estrada, but one could arguably make the case that was as much *destructive* of democracy, stability, and national unity as it was an expression of some degree of popular will. In Indonesia, civil society was encouraged by Western agencies as a way of undermining the dictatorship of Raden Suharto and encouraging democracy; but with the decline and possible disintegration of Indonesia, in part because of this effort, into strife, fragmentation, religious conflict, and separatism, one would be hard-pressed to say that it is a shining example of successful civil society accomplishment. Finally, in Southeast Asia (Cambodia, Laos, Myanmar, Thailand, Vietnam), where the international community has made a substantial effort to support civil society, relatively little democratization or development has as yet resulted.

The situation in the two key, transitional countries of Indonesia and the Philippines is especially complex. First, in both countries there has been in recent years, associated with the transitions to democracy, a proliferation of new civil society groups dedicated to such causes as human rights, greater freedom, the environment, honesty in government, the advancement of women, judicial reform, and democratization. Second and at the same time, the government has moved, corporatist style, to co-opt these groups or to create parallel organizations that it can more easily control. Third and again simultaneously, there are a variety of new public–private partnerships, what are sometimes called (contradictorily) governmental-nongovernmental organizations (GNGOs), that represent efforts to bridge the gap between the historic statism of these countries and the rise of a more dynamic private sector. Finally and again simultaneously, we have the problem that to the extent civil society comes to focus on such issues as Islamic fundamentalism or the aspirations of separatist movements in Mindanao (the Philippines) or Aceh (Indonesia), it may contribute to nondemocratic outcomes in the first instance or the disintegration of the central state itself in the second.

CONCLUSION

A number of conclusions stand out from this analysis:

1. With their strong Confucian and non-Western traditions, many Asian societies have had a hard time conceiving of civil society or even finding the proper words to describe it.
2. When they do, they tend to think of public, group, and state actions as distinct from the Western conception of private, individual, and grassroots activities.
3. This orientation leads often to state-centered and state-controlled (or corporatist) systems of civil society.
4. Nevertheless, civil society and associational life have flourished in Japan, South Korea, and Taiwan, recently in Indonesia and the Philippines (less so in other countries), mainly around local environmental and other less overtly political issues—that is, issues that are "safe" and do not challenge the state in its essentials.
5. There remains a strong emphasis on creating civil society, not for its own sake but in order to imitate and look good to outside observers.
6. The growth of civil society is correlated closely with socioeconomic development, especially in South Korea and Taiwan. As development occurred, ruling elites felt they could allow greater space for civil society. But that is still within the limits of predominantly statist systems.
7. Civil society is often associated with crises or transitions, such as postauthoritarian transitions to democracy; once the crisis is over, civil society tends to decline.
8. Civil society has not been an unmitigated success: it can lead to instability as in the Philippines or to fragmentation and possible disintegration as in Indonesia.

9. Even in the present era of rapid change and democratization, civil society in Asia remains weak, underdeveloped, and centered mainly on local or nonthreatening (to the state) issues. Meanwhile, state, bureaucratic, and private/public administrative agencies remain overwhelmingly dominant.

10. The growth of civil society is not inevitable or unilinear; under the threat of war, terrorism, ethnic strife, political instability, or Islamic fundamentalism, some hitherto increasingly democratic states (e.g., Singapore) may decide to restrict civil society activities.

11. The situation in many countries represents a mix of new, more democratic civil society, statist or corporatist tendencies, new public–private partnerships, civil society that is not necessarily democratic, and separatist movements that may lead to national disintegration.

12. Civil society development therefore yields a mixed bag in Asia both in terms of its contribution to democracy and in terms of its ability to solve any of Asia's major international issues.

NOTES

1. For background, W. T. DeBary, *Asian Values and Human Rights: A Confucian Communitarian Perspective* (Cambridge, MA: Harvard University Press, 1998); Gerald Curtis, *The Logic of Japanese Politics: Leaders, Institutions, and the Limits of Change* (New York: Columbia University Press, 1999); Peter Moody, *Political Opposition in Post-Confucian Society* (New York: Praeger, 1988); also Lionel Jensen, *Manufacturing Confucianism: Chinese Traditions and Universal Civilization* (Durham, NC: Duke University Press, 1997).

2. The best source is Yamamoto Tadashi, ed., *Deciding the Public Good: Governance and Civil Society in Japan* (Tokyo: Japan Center for Educational Exchange, 1999).

3. Yoshida Shin'icki, "Rethinking the Public Interest in Japan: Civil Society in the Making," in Tadashi, *Deciding*, 13–50.

4. Peter Moody, *Tradition and Modernization in China and Japan* (Belmont, CA: Wadsworth, 1995).

5. Iokibe Makoto, "Japan's Civil Society: An Historical Overview," in Tadashi, *Deciding*, 51–96.

6. Lucian W. Pye, "Civility, Social Capital, and Civil Society: Three Powerful Concepts for Explaining Asia," *Journal of Interdisciplinary History* 29 (Spring 1999): 763–82.

7. Pye, "Civility."

8. Pye, "Civility," 779.

9. During my research in China, my guide, a graduate student in political science in Beijing who later came to the United States to study, told me that she was "working on developing [her] individual personality." Such a comment sounds strange to

Western ears since we assume all of us since babyhood have individual personalities, but in China with its communalist tradition one has to *work* at developing such individualism.

10. Pye, "Civility"; also Pye, *Asian Power and Politics: The Cultural Dimensions of Authority* (Cambridge, MA: Harvard University Press, 1985).

11. Peter Moody, "East Asia: The Confucian Tradition and Modernization," in Howard J. Wiarda (ed.), *Non-Western Theories of Development* (Fort Worth, TX: Harcourt Brace, 1999), 20–43.

12. Daniel Pipes and Adam Garfinkle, eds., *Friendly Tyrants: An American Dilemma* (New York: St. Martin's, 1991).

13. Moody, *Tradition and Modernization*.

14. Tadashi, *Deciding the Public Good*.

15. Shin'icki, "Rethinking the Public Interest."

16. Makoto, "Japan's Civil Society."

17. Shin'icki, "Rethinking the Public Interest," 48.

18. Ksunhyuk Kim, "Civil Society in South Korea: From Grand Democracy Movements to Petty Interest Groups," *Journal of Northeast Asian Studies* (Summer 1996): 81–97; Baogang He, "The Ideas of Civil Society in Mainland China and Taiwan," *Issues and Studies* (June 1995): 24–64; Yang May-sing, "NGOs Promote a Civil Society," *Taipei Journal* (October 27, 2000), 7.

Chapter Twelve

Democracy and Development in Sub-Saharan Africa

Sub-Saharan Africa is the world's *least*-developed area. It is plagued by disease, misery, economic underdevelopment, high illiteracy, unstable and often repressive governments, civil war and conflict, absence of strong national institutions, lack of social safety nets, failed states, inadequate health care and doctors, ungovernability, weak institutions, mass starvation, and absence of hope.[1] Virtually every problem that one can think of associated with the vicious circle of underdevelopment is present in Africa. It also has, and as a correlate of the above, the weakest civil society of all global areas.

What should the United States do? Is the United States threatened in any way by what occurs in Africa? Are there any of its resources that are essential to our economy (as with oil from the Middle East)? Do we owe a moral obligation (because of past slave trading) to Africa? Are there terrorist cells in Africa that are dangerous to the United States? Should we intervene there to prevent mass starvation? Genocide? Civil war? To relieve AIDS? Or should we focus, not on the short-term issues, but on long-term economic growth, infrastructure development, and democratization? We cannot answer all of these questions here, but since it is key to the discussion in this book, we focus in this chapter particularly on the issues of development and democratization in Africa's future.

SOCIOECONOMIC INDICATORS

When the World Bank and other agencies talk about the poorest of the poor, those hundreds of millions of people who earn under $1.00 per day and live in abject poverty, it is largely Sub-Saharan Africa that they are speaking of.

Many countries of the area, as table 12.1 shows, have an average yearly income of about $300 per person. That puts them at a level of about one *one-hundredth* of the per capita income of the wealthy countries of North America, Western Europe, or Japan. Much of the meager wealth that does exist is squandered, terribly unevenly distributed, or finds its way into the private accounts of corrupt government and military officials.

The poverty and misery of Sub-Saharan Africa—and part of the reason for the absence of stability and democracy—may be gleaned from table 12.1. Note that the gross national product of South Africa is overwhelmingly superior to that of all other countries in the area—and roughly equivalent to all the other countries combined. On a per person basis, only Botswana, Gabon, Mauritius, South Africa, and the Seychelles have *begun* to lift themselves out of poverty. Life expectancy in Sub-Saharan Africa is mainly in the forty- to fifty-year range compared to seventy to eighty years in the developed countries. Literacy rates are similarly low but show considerable variation between countries. And most Sub-Saharan African countries are still predominantly rural and agricultural as compared with the more developed countries that are predominantly urban. Poverty, high illiteracy, low life expectancy, subsistence agriculture—none of these conditions is propitious for the growth of stability and democracy. Nor do we see in Sub-Saharan Africa, of the forty-two countries listed, more than four (only 10 percent) that have had the kind of economic growth and social modernization necessary to stimulate the rise of civil society that would lead to greater pluralism and democracy.

Because of the incredible poverty and underdevelopment, the system of civil society and democracy in Sub-Saharan Africa is generally weak, unstable, inadequately organized, and generally ineffective.[2] Of course, one must distinguish between countries, with some (Senegal, Ivory Coast, Kenya, Botswana, South Africa) having stronger civil society than others. But overall, the picture is a bleak one. Moreover, the kind of civil society that does exist is often ethnically or tribally based, a kind of organization that is usually viewed as "traditional" and is therefore rejected by most international aid donors. My own orientation, in contrast, is to see in these organizations a measure of hope in what seems an oftentimes hopeless local situation, a way of delivering some, however limited, services (social, educational, police, justice) in a context where other civil society agencies are weak or nonexistent, and perhaps the basis for an indigenous or homegrown system of civil society.

But the orientation of most civil society advocates as well as many African intellectuals and officials is to denigrate tribally based civil society as "backward," presumably to be replaced by more modern institutions. Not only is civil society weak, therefore, but many Westerners and Africans alike are not sure they like or want the form (tribal, ethnic) of civil society that does exist.

Table 12.1. Socioeconomic Indicators, Sub-Saharan Africa

Country	GNP	GNP Per Capita	Life Expectancy		Literacy		% Urban	GNP Per Capita Rank
			Male	Female	Male	Female		
South Africa	133.2	3,160	61	66	85	84	52	86
Angola	2.7	220	45	48			34	194
Benin	2.3	381	52	55	54	23	42	165
Botswana	5.1	3,240	45	47	73	78	50	84
Burkina Faso	2.6	240	43	45	32	13	18	190
Burundi	0.8	120	41	44	55	37	9	204
Cameroon	8.5	580	53	56	80	67	48	150
Central Af. Repub.	1.0	290	43	46	49	31	23	181
Comoros	0.2	350	60		58			
Congo, Dem. Rep.	1.9	670	49	52	71	47	30	147
Côte d'Ivoire	10.4	710	46	47	53	36	46	146
Eritrea	0.8	200	49	52	66	38	18	196
Ethiopia	6.6	100	42	44	42	30	17	206
Gabon	4.0	3,350	53					
Gambia	0.4	340	53		35			
Ghana	7.4	390	58	62	78	60	38	164
Guinea	3.7	510	46	47			32	155
Guinea-Bissau	0.2	160	44		37			
Kenya	10.6	360	50	52	88	73	32	170
Lesotho	1.2	550	54	57	71	93	27	152
Liberia			47		51			
Madagascar	3.7	250	56	59	72	58	29	187
Malawi	2.0	190	42	42	73	44	24	199
Mali	2.6	240	49	52	46	31	29	190
Mauritania	1.0	380	52	55	52	31	56	165
Mauritius	4.2	3,590	71		84			
Mozambique	3.9	230	44	47	58	27	39	193
Niger	2.0	190	44	48	22	7	20	199
Nigeria	37.9	310	52	55	70	52	43	179
Rwanda	2.1	250	40	42	71	57	6	187
São Tomé & Principe	0.04	270	64					
Senegal	4.7	510	51	54	45	26	47	155
Seychelles	0.5	6,540	72					
Sierra Leone	0.7	130	36	39			36	203
Somalia		755 or less*	48					
Sudan	9.4	330	55		56			
Tanzania	8.0	240	46	48	83	64	32	190
Togo	1.5	320	47	50	72	38	33	176
Uganda	6.8	320	42	41	76	54	14	176
Zambia	3.2	320	43	43	84	69	40	176
Zimbabwe	6.1	520	50	52	92	83	35	154

*Estimates by World Bank.

Source: World Bank, *World Development Report 2000–2001*. The data for some countries is missing or incomplete.

And, to the extent that civil society is tribally or ethnically based, it may also be a sign of a weak or a failed state and thus not necessarily a hopeful sign of democracy. In much of the world, and certainly in the theoretical literature, civil society and democracy are closely correlated; but in Sub-Saharan Africa, with its weak, corrupt, and ineffective states, coupled with ethnically and even gang-based civil society, the correlation between democracy and civil society may be negative.[3]

ANALYSIS AND CASE STUDIES

There are two basic problems of civil society in Sub-Saharan Africa. The first, already alluded to, is the low level of social and economic development in the area, which makes the institutionalization and consolidation of *any* viable form of democracy difficult at best. Sub-Saharan Africa simply lacks the educational base, literacy, communications grids, mobilized and organized populations, webs of association life at grassroots levels, interest group and political party systems, and governmental infrastructure, funding support, and public policy implementing capability to develop a healthy, vibrant civil society. Civil society grows with difficulty in developed countries; its emergence is far more difficult in less-developed countries that lack the socioeconomic underpinnings and prerequisites for it to grow.

The second reason for civil society's weakness in Sub-Saharan Africa is political: the weakness, tribulations, and *absence* in many countries of democracy.[4] Of the forty-eight countries in Sub-Saharan Africa, only eight (Botswana, Malawi, Mali, Namibia, Nigeria, Senegal, South Africa, Tanzania) embrace pluralism, are democracies, or are making a transition to democracy. Civil society, of course, thrives best under democracy in open countries, but in most of Africa authoritarian regimes limit, co-opt, weaken, or destroy all civil society groups that they cannot themselves control. Or they create official civil society groups—the corporatism phenomenon—by which they dominate potentially dangerous, oppositionist grassroots organizations. Civil society is unable to hold governments accountable—one of the prime purposes of civil society—if their only two alternatives are suppression or co-optation. In addition, about half the states in Sub-Saharan Africa are engaged in war, conflict, or armed disputes, both domestically and internationally. Ethnic and religious strife is also rampant, producing, especially in Central Africa, some of the world's worst cases of genocide. None of this is propitious for the growth of civil society.

In Latin America, civil society often emerged *during* an authoritarian interlude and was a prime force in stimulating opposition to the ruling dictatorship and in the subsequent transition to democracy. But in Latin America: (1) civil society is generally stronger than it is in Sub-Saharan Africa, and (2) there was a *preexisting* civil society in Latin America that could then be revived in the transition to democracy. In Sub-Saharan Africa, however, the base for civil society is weak and there is no or little preexisting civil society on which to build. The model that grew out of the Latin American transitions therefore is sadly not applicable to Sub-Saharan Africa.

In recent years events in Sub-Saharan Africa have produced both hope and despair, often simultaneously. The early 1960s were a time of hope and optimism for these new nations, followed in the later 1960s and 1970s by a huge wave of corrupt, authoritarian governments. For a time in the 1980s it was thought, or hoped, that Africa would follow Latin America in transitioning to democracy, but those hopes were dashed, too. In the early 1990s African economies were growing at only 2 percent a year—in other words, going backward as compared to population increases—but by the late 1990s the earlier figure had doubled. The Clinton administration seized upon that growth and some limited democratization to proclaim an "African renaissance"; Assistant Secretary for African Affairs Susan Rice indicated optimistically that in countries "across the continent" legislators were being trained, independent judiciaries fostered, and cooperative work with churches, universities, and newspapers increased so as to build a strong civil society.[5]

But in recent years these optimistic projections have again been unrealized: war in the Congo enmeshing all its neighbors, new or renewed dictatorships, AIDS, economic downturn, greater joblessness, lowered life expectancy. Africa faces a bleaker future than at anytime in the past, according to a U.S. National Intelligence Estimate for the area; Sub-Saharan Africa is backsliding on every front. Stephen Morrison, the director of African Studies at the Center for Strategic and International Studies (CSIS), says, "The number of simultaneous, multiple crises that the continent faces right now is unprecedented." He goes on, "Africa is in worse condition than ever before. And it's only going to get worse over the next generation." Chimes in Pauline Baker, an Africa expert and director of the Fund for Peace, "Even if you hold a free election in a collapsed state and elect a saint like Nelson Mandela, he'll be doomed to failure if there's no government structure." Particularly apropos this discussion of democracy, Baker concludes, "One man alone can't rule without institutions, many of which have eroded since independence."[6]

One needs, of course, to distinguish carefully between countries, to appreciate the differences between them and the hopeful signs that still exist in some places but that would require a far more detailed analysis than is possible here. A few illustrations, however, serve to indicate the variety of situations that exist and where civil society and democracy are sufficiently strong to hold out hope for the future. For example, the four most democratic governments in West Africa today—Benin, Ghana, Mali, and Senegal—all have flourishing private talk-radio stations, and an independent communications system is one of the hallmarks of civil society. Ghana itself, previously under the dictatorship of the charismatic Jerry Rawling, has recently witnessed its first-ever peaceful transition from one elected civilian government to another. If one asks why Senegal has been more successful than others in combating the HIV infection, the answer lies in large part in its (relatively) strong civil society and community-based institutions that have produced a web of homegrown self-help responses.[7]

In Zimbabwe, the Democratic Republic of the Congo, Kenya, Nigeria, Tanzania, and Rwanda, Christian missionaries and support groups, both Catholic and Protestant, have helped create some of the only civil society groups that exist—schools, hospitals, teacher training programs, social service and development agencies—but they are often beset by woefully inadequate funding, shortages of personnel, and the inability to organize these programs on a national basis. In addition, the chaos of the surrounding society, rising crime, civil and international war, genocide, mammoth corruption, and recently the often violent challenge of close-by fundamentalist Islamic groups (an alternative expression of "civil society," or its antithesis?) have made these groups' activities more dangerous and more precarious, in some cases to the extent of forcing the Christian groups to abandon their useful projects.[8]

Nigeria is an especially important test case. With 120 million people, it is Africa's biggest country and its second largest (after South Africa) economy. It is the world's sixth largest exporter of oil. Potentially it is one of the richest countries in Africa, but actually it is one of the poorest and rapidly *losing* ground. When President (and former general) Olusegun Obasanjo returned to power in 1999 through democratic elections, hopes were high both for democracy and for civil society in Nigeria. But the country is deeply torn by ethnic, tribal, and religious strife. Corruption and violent crime are omnipresent. Even with all that oil and a creative population, the economy is stagnant or shrinking. President Obasanjo, though elected democratically, has moved in authoritarian directions and is ominously making the familiar arguments that all authoritarians make: that in the absence of strong institutions and a strong civil society, strongman rule is necessary. Many Nigerians as well as international advisers fear that Sub-Saharan Africa's biggest and potentially richest country is fragmenting, falling apart. Civil society (what is left of it) seems on the verge of disintegrating.[9]

Nigeria is Africa's second largest economy, but what is the situation in the continent's largest economy, South Africa? Especially with the end of apartheid and the election of Nelson Mandela in 1994, South Africa seemed to have turned a corner. But since then South Africa has disappeared from the headlines and received little international attention. The world tends to assume that, as apartheid ended, South Africa's problems would also end. But that has not occurred. Crime, violence, corruption, civil conflict, AIDS—all the problems associated with the rest of the continent—now afflict South Africa, too. Political fragmentation is also occurring there and civil society in both the black and white communities, many will be surprised to hear, is disintegrating. Let us proceed to the more detailed South Africa case study now.

SOUTH AFRICA

South Africa was supposed to be the exception to the general—and generally discouraging—pattern in Sub-Saharan Africa. First, under apartheid South Africa had been the last bastion in the world of legal, constitutional discrimination, and its destruction lent moral authority and purpose to the building of democracy and civil society there. Second, South Africa, with a per capita income of $3,160 per year, is considerably richer than virtually all other countries in the area, is considered a "middle-income" country by the World Bank, and is *ten times* wealthier on a per person basis than most of its neighbors and as "close" as one-tenth (as compared with one-hundredth for the others—about the level of Botswana or Panama but considerably below Argentina, Brazil, Chile, Mexico, or Venezuela) of the level of the world's wealthier countries.

Third, South Africa has a quite well-developed infrastructure not only of industry and commerce but also of institutions; its total gross national product marks it as the only industrialized country in Africa. Fourth, South Africa had in 1994, for the first time, a truly democratic election that brought heroic Nelson Mandela to power and seemed to offer hope for the country's overall prospects and the future of democracy there. Mandela's charisma, grace, and moderation helped bring the ruling African National Congress (ANC), formerly Marxist, back toward the center, and also made it harder for his successors to depart from the democratic course that he set. And fifth, South Africa became for a time the darling of the international community, a recipient of major foreign aid and advice (wanted or unwanted) and *the* locus of a great deal of generous, foreign-sponsored and influenced nongovernmental organization (NGO) and civil society activity in southern Africa. The sense was widespread, although usually unspoken, that if South Africa, given its wealth, resources, and advantages, could not establish democracy and a functioning civil society, no African state could. South Africa was thus not only important in its own right but also as a hoped-for model and test case for other African states.

South Africa has vast mineral resources, well-developed industry, good and productive agriculture, and an overall standard of living higher than that of most of its neighbors. But within this generally favorable picture there are vast problems. First, wealth is terribly unevenly distributed, with the top 5–10 percent of the population enjoying an overwhelming preponderance. Second, unemployment is high at 35–40 percent; another 25–30 percent may be underemployed, the total reaching 70 percent of the population. Third, the distribution of wealth and income follows clear racial lines, with most of the wealth, land, mines, and industry in the hands of the white population and most of the poverty and unemployment concentrated among the black population. Fourth, there is a disconnect between where political power is concentrated in the country and the holders of economic power: blacks now control the political structure and government through the ANC and its affiliated organizations/subsidiaries, while whites are still overwhelmingly dominant in the economy.

Fifth, racism is still a powerful force: most whites in the business, intellectual, and university-educated communities have accepted the post-apartheid changes and want the present black-controlled regime to succeed (they have no other options), but many nonuniversity, working-class whites remain resentful of the changes and are particularly hurt by the black regime's affirmative action programs that leave them out in the cold in terms of civil service, government, and even private employment—although few of these go so far as to advocate or act on the idea of toppling the ANC-controlled government. Meanwhile, many blacks remain resentful of white affluence and privilege, which helps explain spiraling crime and violence directed against whites; refuse to speak the Afrikaner language, which is associated with the old apartheid regime; and are at times motivated by efforts to gain revenge against whites.

Sixth, with the transfer of power to the ANC, black expectations were raised that they would immediately become better off; but that has not happened; frustration is therefore rising among the black population; and there are well-founded fears both of white recalcitrance to refuse to share the wealth more equitably and of blacks taking the law into their own hands and seizing white property violently, as in neighboring Zimbabwe. Tensions are thus rising along class and racial lines; meanwhile, the political, social, economic, and institutional infrastructure of the country shows signs of decay and the potential for future breakdown.[10] We return to this point later in the discussion.

Elements of Political Culture

South Africa was settled and colonized mainly by the Dutch in the seventeenth century. As with the British and French in North America, the Spanish and Portuguese in Latin America, and the French, Belgians, Germans, and British elsewhere in Africa, the Dutch carried with them to their colonies the language, institutions, and values of their home country of that particular time. Once established, these values and institutions gradually became locked in place and continued to reflect the time period of the initial discovery and settlement. Over time, colonies and mother countries evolved in different paths, with the colonies often representing "fragments" of the mother countries set down in new places and circumstances, adapting to local conditions, and gradually distancing themselves from or losing track of the main currents of European civilization—even while trying desperately from these distant places to stay in touch with their roots.[11]

The Dutch in South Africa were shaped powerfully by their Calvinist and entrepreneurial heritage. In part, that belief system was used to justify a two-class society and the separation of the races. Equally important was the South African Dutch Calvinists' identification with the Old Testament, the story of a people, like themselves, set down in a wilderness, isolated and alone, a people of God, outnumbered by huge ratios, facing severe dangers and hardships, with enemies all around, quasi-paranoid, and heroically struggling and surviving against the odds. It is within this biblical conception, this "siege mentality," that the later system of apartheid was born.[12] Black, "colored," English, Indian, and Moslem South Africans would, of course, see the issue quite differently.

While the Dutch gradually moved into the interior to clear fields, develop farming, and worship God in their own tradition, urban and coastal areas were gradually colonized and taken over by the British. Indian and Islamic settlers added to the diversity of the population. In the Boer War at the end of the nineteenth century, the Dutch and the British fought each other for control of the colony, with the Dutch, defeated, "trekking" or moving even farther into the interior (from whence the famous song came, "We Are Marching to Pretoria") and developing an even more advanced case of paranoia as God's people, now isolated and alone, under siege, and abandoned eventually even by their own home government in The Netherlands. Recall also how different their situation was from whites in America: in the United States, whites outnumbered blacks by about ten to one, which made it relatively easy to contemplate racial integration, whereas in South Africa the ratios were exactly reversed: 90 percent black and colored and about 10 percent white, which meant that full racial integration and the enfranchisement of blacks would *automatically*, *immediately*, and *permanently* mean the loss of power for whites.

These numbers are critical, as much as white racial attitudes, in explaining the apartheid system of racial separation. The whites, both Dutch and British, thought of themselves as representatives of a superior civilization. They created a top-down or "pillared" society that favored whites over blacks, meanwhile locking the social structure in place and preventing change. Afrikaner "civil society" aimed to establish a separate political community controlling all areas of social life. They thought of the blacks as animist, primitive, backward, and pagan whom they, missionary-style, would educate, Christianize, "civilize" in European ways, and assimilate.

Although there was cruelty in the dominance of blacks by whites, white attitudes were generally more patronizing than hateful. Blacks were viewed as "children" who would have to be converted, trained, and assimilated into Christianity and Westernness. Given the numbers of blacks and their low level of education, this process would require generations, maybe centuries, not just years. But this process came to be seen as much too slow for the black population. In addition, it was assumed, in South Africa as elsewhere, that white, Western, European civilization was superior, more advanced, and had to lead and educate others; this was not a situation of equality and cultural relativism. And, given the numbers and the siege mentality, once blacks began mobilizing and demanding their rights, the response was a hardening of the shell of enforced racial separation into the apartheid system—although within both the Dutch and the British communities this was not by any means a unanimous view. Many whites, including in the Dutch Calvinist churches, came to favor a more liberal, integrated community.

The result in South Africa was the absence of a single, national, political culture. Instead, political culture was divided, organized around class, racial, and ethnic lines. There was an upper-class political culture and a lower-class political culture, and eventually a middle-class one. There was a white political culture and a black, African political culture. But within these categories there were further divisions. Among white groups were Dutch, British, Jewish, and European immigrants of various nationalities and political cultures; within each of these were further distinctions based on politics, religion, ethnicity, ideology, identity, and a wide range of perspectives. Among blacks there was a rising political consciousness that would eventually lead to a successful challenge of the apartheid system, but within the black community, if that term could even be used, were wide differences depending on location, income, ideology, ethnicity, class, and social and political orientation. Nor should we forget the quite separate political cultures of the Indian, Islamic, colored (a mix of black and white), and other minority communities.[13]

South Africa was a mosaic, not a monolith; but it was also marked by the absence of a single, national political culture on which all could agree.

Civil Society and State–Society Relations

South Africa's system of civil society both reflects and reinforces the political-cultural foundations of which we have been speaking.[14] It also reflects racial, developmental, and socioeconomic differences within the society.

First, within white culture, civil society is not very much different from what it is in other Dutch, British, or European societies throughout the First World. There are clubs, churches, associations of many kinds, sports teams, and professional and business groups to which one belongs and/or gives allegiance. They provide a vast web of associability and a firm foundation for civil society. The trouble is that these groups were, for the most part, discriminatory and limited to the white population, and exclusionary toward blacks. In addition, since the end of apartheid and the growing fear and isolation of the white population, this kind of rich, thick, European-like civil society has gone into considerable decline. No longer having access to public funds that long-time control of the government provided has also hurt Afrikaner civil society.

There is (or was) also the more oppressive form of civil society associated specifically with apartheid and the long-dominant Afrikaner National Party (ANP). The party had branches for everyone—youth, women, business-men—who supported it and who, like the parent organization, became more militant over the years. Such groups are not unusual in political parties and especially those with European roots; in addition, political parties and their ancillary organizations are generally considered a part of civil society, which we support. However, in the case of the National Party, as it faced increasing challenges including terrorism, a national liberation movement supported by the ANC and the South African Communist Party, and urban violence coming out of the black townships, it constructed a considerable web of secret, secretive, and often illegal counterterrorist groups, private militias, secret police units, and spy networks to counter the rising violence. Rather like skinheads, the Klan, or private militias in other societies, these groups were often called "fascist" and are not what we have in mind when we talk about civil society. Since the collapse of the apartheid regime, however, and the ouster of the ANP as the governing party, most of these groups and their activities have gone underground or else out of existence—although similar fringe groups are still out there operating in the private sector, perhaps even augmented as whites feel increasingly under siege.

In the black community, civil society is also facing severe problems. As militancy and opposition to the apartheid system increased in the 1980s, blacks organized a number of civic organizations—popularly known as "civics"—in the townships that played a key role in challenging and undermining the apartheid government. The civics were widely and favorably portrayed in the Western media, with the image being of "little David," armed only with stones and a smile, taking on the "Goliath" of the South African armed state. At the time it was thought that the civics, which were pictured benignly but were often the manipulated instruments of the ANC, the Communist Party, or terrorist groups, would form the basis for a vibrant, black, post-apartheid civil society.[15]

But it has not quite worked out that way. First, once the epic anti-apartheid struggle was won, black African civil society in general, no longer with a clear moral purpose, focus, or unambiguous goal, atrophied, became marginalized, and went into decline; there are now simply fewer, less enthused, less participatory groups, with no special claim to moral authority, than during the great struggle of the early 1990s. Many civic groups that once seemed to hold great promise have either closed down or been forced to radically curtail their activities—precisely the opposite of what was supposed to happen once apartheid ended and democracy was established.

Second, among the civics specifically, there have been severe adjustment problems in going from "comrade" to "citizen"—that is, of adjusting to pluralism instead of a monolithic crusade, accommodation rather than confrontation, and democratic give-and-take rather than revolutionary street action. The civics movements were often trained in the ideology of Soviet and Third World Marxism and in the revolutionary, often violent tactics of Third World liberation movements; they have had a hard time abandoning these strategies and adjusting to the requirements of genuine liberalism and democracy.[16]

Third, since the end of apartheid, while there has been some flowering of civil society, there has also been tightened control by the ANC over its ancillary organizations: labor unions, youth groups, peasant groups, women's groups, and so on. Party and government have come closer together and almost merged into one. The ANC has sought to turn these civil society organizations into agencies of the ANC government, often at the cost of their autonomy and freedom. An independent and autonomous civil society now exists alongside an increasingly ANC or state-dominated civil society.

Fourth and almost contradictorily, in the absence of much new investment and employment, some post-apartheid "civic" groups have been transformed into criminal gangs, drug or prostitution cartels, and even terrorist organizations taking the law on land reform or worker participation into their own hands. This has led both to an appalling increase in crime and violence and to an acceleration of "white flight," which means the wholesale, accelerating exodus of the professional, trained, intellectual, technical, entrepreneurial class whose departure South Africa cannot afford and which threatens potentially to turn the country into "just another" poor, miserable, African country.[17]

Fifth is the corporatism phenomenon: in some cases the black-controlled government has granted a virtual monopoly to certain favored black civic groups (sometimes called "associational socialism") so that they are able to dominate an entire sector of society. In other cases, such as with black farmers, the government has almost literally created a "civil society" group from scratch in order to fill a certain organizational space—or to prevent other groups, usually nongovernmental, from occupying it. In still others, which perhaps reflects the continuing Leninist orientation of some political leaders, the government has begun to use the fledgling civil society groups as top-down instruments of state control rather than as nascent grassroots organizations exercising influence from below. The government at times seems to favor not so much democratic, pluralist civil society but instead "democratic centralism," civil society of a particular or corporatist kind, that which supports the government or which it can control and co-opt.

Sixth and even more ominously, there is a considerable fear among objective observers in South Africa that the governing ANC, whose history has not always been democratic, may tire of the often cumbersome and time-consuming democratic process, declare a one-party state as in Zimbabwe, incorporate those groups favorable to itself as associated organizations under party hegemony, and move to undercut or destroy all independent civil society groups, keeping only those who are already branches of the ANC or which it can control by corporatist carrots and sticks. It is already using coercion and authoritarian measures to displace some groups and impose others in not very democratic fashion, or to blame some civil society groups—that is, the business community in this case—for neither fostering sufficient economic growth nor engendering black empowerment within the economy.

A neglected feature of the discussion of South African civil society is the degree to which it remains tribally dominated. Fully one-third of South Africa's blacks still live—even in this, the most modern and developed of African states—under tribal organization. Mostly rural, some of these ethnic groups live almost a completely separate and autonomous existence; others have been converted into "modern" political parties or interest groups independent of and often opposed to the ANC government. Chieftaincy is still the predominant way of choosing leaders within these groups.

Tribalism is usually identified with traditionalism and "backwardness." Some groups are largely self-governing, and the ANC government has tried by various means to get these tribal communities to adopt a secular, mayoral–town council form of government, which the ANC, of course, will certainly dominate. But so far that campaign has not been successful as many tribal entities prefer their own ways and leaders. At one level, tribalism may be considered traditional and unmodern, but at another it is also indigenous; and if we take seriously the notion that civil society, to be lasting, has to be built upon indigenous, homegrown roots, then in the African context—even South Africa—we must take tribalism seriously.[18]

The overall result of the overthrow of apartheid and the establishment of black-controlled government has thus not been the expected blossoming of civil society in the post-apartheid era but rather its atrophy, apathy, and even withering away. Now that the epic anti-apartheid battle is over, many former civil society members ask, what is the logic of continued involvement? Significantly, civil society's post-apartheid decline may be found in both the white and the black communities. And, increasingly, there is a trend toward greater corporatist civil society and perhaps a monolithic statist system, rather than away from it toward real, lasting pluralism and democratic civic involvement. Moreover, the civil society that continues to exist outside the state is increasingly divided and fragmented, and may not be very representative. Violence and intimidation are increasing, not decreasing; separatism of white, black, and colored communities remains a fact of life. Observers are agreed there are many dangers lurking and not a happy situation of democratic, Tocquevillian associational life. Some scholars have gone so far as to say there is as yet no genuinely South African civil society, and that to the extent civil society there continues to reflect sharp ethnic lines, it is not conducive to democratic politics.[19]

The International Context

While the anti-apartheid struggle was ongoing, many international civil society groups were involved in South Africa. These included religious groups, human rights organizations, black and Afro-American groups, official U.S. government organizations (the National Endowment for Democracy—NED; the U.S. Institute of Peace—USIP, etc.) and many others. There was a cause to support; the cause seemed righteous; and a multivariegated American and international civil society plunged into the task.

But since then a number of things have happened. The "cause" has been accomplished; apartheid has been eliminated; and majority rule was established. International interest in South Africa has therefore subsided and so have the activities of the civil society groups earlier involved. The withdrawal of the outside funding, technical support, and personnel is, in fact, one of the key reasons for the decline and destabilization of the South African NGO community and of civil society in general. Many South African civil society groups now must make it on their own; the large number of those that have fallen by the wayside reflects the fact that they may have been in large measure creations of the international community to begin with and lack a strong indigenous base. Meanwhile, large numbers of persons who once formed the backbone of civil society have abandoned that sector and taken more lucrative, often patronage-based jobs in the government and civil service.

In addition, once apartheid was abolished and democracy established, foreign assistance shifted away from supporting civil society and toward economic development and good governance projects. And with the euphoria of victory in the anti-apartheid struggle now giving way to the sober realities of hard political and economic choices, quite a number of civil society groups are being used as scapegoats, blamed by the government either for the lack of progress or—in the case of AIDS or declining business investment—for failure to conform to government policy. At the same time the government's attitude toward AIDS—seeing it as a Western plot and failing to acknowledge the medical science that goes into its detection and cures—has discredited it in the eyes of much of the international NGO community. In turn, the decline in aid and attention from the international community demonstrates how fickle and unreliable that community can be, while the decline in so many areas of South African civil society shows how weak civil society remains.

CONCLUSION

We began this chapter by presenting the general conditions in Sub-Saharan Africa and the low level of development throughout the continent. There are, obviously, issues of great immediate concern—poverty, violence, AIDS, civil strife, failed states, mass malnourishment—that require our attention, as well as long-term issues like development and democratization that need to be dealt with. We chose here to focus on the long-term issues and eventually narrowed the discussion down to the cases of Nigeria and, especially, South Africa. But even in South Africa, the continent's wealthiest country, we found severe problems in building and sustaining democracy and its essential underpinning, civil society.

As political scientists Hennie Kotze and Pierre Du Toit conclude from their survey research, South Africa is not now a "happy" or liberal democracy based on a strong civil society.[20] After all, illiberal and inegalitarian forms have a deep heritage in South Africa in both the black and the white communities, and there is a strikingly low level of political tolerance. Instead, they find a weak and divided civil society and a regime uncertain what to do about

it or even its own future directions. The society has become increasingly polarized rather than consensual and peaceful.

They find a multiply divided society, one that is still violent, plagued by financial and organizational problems, with civil society groups serving as antagonists in a divided country, a government that has had and is having a hard
time adjusting to pluralism, civic bodies that are strongly associated with partisan political groups that engage one another in conflicts that are highly un-
civil, a fundamentally polarized society, and one that runs the risk of being
torn apart at the seams. Moreover, persistent ethnic conflict and tension serve
to undermine existing civil society further and prevent the emergence of new
groups. They agree that a genuine civil society (liberal, pluralist, autonomous,
democratic) has yet to be built in South Africa and until that is done, both
state and regime in South Africa will remain undemocratic. Clearly in the
South Africa case, the most-developed country in Africa, the cliché that civil
society is not a panacea rings true; indeed, the situation is by now far worse
than that and actually quite desperate.

None of this was supposed to happen, and it may come as a shock to those
who believed that once the apartheid regime fell and blacks were in power,
democracy and civil society would certainly flower. But, in fact, tensions are
as high now as ever and South Africa could rather easily degenerate into violence, a one-party state, and/or civil war. The withdrawal of so many of the
international NGOs once the overriding goal—black power—had been
achieved and the fact they were no longer paying such close attention to the
country help explain why they are now shocked to discover how tense and deteriorating the situation is. Racial tension and confrontations are again rising;
public services are breaking down; the economy is deteriorating; crime and
corruption are rampant; unemployment and violence are increasing; investment has slowed significantly; and both capital and whites are fleeing.[21] Both
democracy and civil society are under siege.

If we now move, as a final comment, back to the other, far less-developed
countries of Africa, we find an at least equally interesting, but if anything even
less hopeful, situation of democracy and civil society. First, we find a number
of civil society groups that are largely the reflection of American or Western
foreign aid agencies, that lack indigenous roots, that are often created specifically for the purpose of looking good to the foreign donors and attracting
their money, but that have no prospects or intentions of blossoming into genuinely homegrown, grassroots, democratic organizations. Second, we have a
large number of religious or historically missionary or church-connected civil
society groups that *are* often democracy and development oriented but that are
extremely fragile, underfunded, and often under attack by state authorities or
Islamic fundamentalists.[22] Third, we have government-created or corporatist
civil society groups that are often similarly in it for the money, to serve as

props of authoritarian regimes, or to give the appearance of democracy without affording it real substance. Finally, we have genuine and indigenous civil society groups, often in the form of ethnic or tribal organizations that *do* provide a measure of social services, socialization, police and judicial protection but are often denounced as "primitive" or "traditional" and frequently undermined by both their own governments and by international aid donors and civil society groups. The situation of civil society in Sub-Saharan Africa is not healthy, and it may be getting worse rather than better.[23]

The overall conclusion here agrees with that of Stephen Orvis. In Sub-Saharan Africa civil society has been defined too narrowly, largely to echo Western concepts; at the same time, too much (a new basis for democracy and development) has been asked of it. An accurate portrayal of Sub-Saharan African civil society would have to include patron–client relations, traditional authorities (chiefs, others), ethnic or tribal organizations, and maybe even criminal groups and rival militias or fighting forces. It is clear that not all of these groups or agencies are democratic. On the other hand, they *do* constitute elements of a Sub-Saharan system of civil society. We may therefore conclude, as does Orvis, that civil society has a stronger basis in Sub-Saharan Africa than we have often thought; on the other hand, it may not serve as the basis for peaceful, pluralist democracy that we might wish.[24] U.S. and other foreign aid agencies as well as the U.S. government more generally need to be aware of these fundamental differences and to adjust their policies accordingly if they are to be successful in stimulating African development and democracy.

NOTES

1. For the general background see Basil Davidson, *The Black Man's Burden: Africa and the Curse of the Nation State* (New York: New York Times Books, 1992); Ali A. Mazrui, *The Africans: A Triple Heritage* (London: BBC Publications, 1986); Naomi Chazan et al., *Politics and Society in Contemporary Africa* (Boulder, CO: Rienner, 1992); John W. Harbeson et al., *Civil Society and the State in Africa* (Boulder, CO: Rienner, 1994).

2. *South Africa: A Country Study* (Washington, DC: Government Printing Office, 1981); Crawford Young, *The African Colonial State in Comparative Perspective* (New Haven, CT: Yale University Press, 1994); Michael Bratton and Nicolas van de Welle, *Democratic Experiments in Africa: Regime Transitions in Comparative Perspective* (Cambridge: Cambridge University Press, 1997).

3. Jannie Gagiano and Pierre Du Toit, "Consolidating Democracy in South Africa: The Role of Civil Society," in Hennie Kotze, ed., *Consolidating Democracy: What Role for Civil Society in South Africa* (Stellenbosch, South Africa: University of Stellenbosch Press, 1996), 47–73.

4. Tracy Kuperus, "Building Democracy: An Examination of Religious Associations in South Africa and Zimbabwe," *Journal of Modern African Studies* 37, 4 (1999): 643–68.

5. Geneva Overholser, "Africa's Growing Pains," *Washington Post* (October 17, 1998), A21.

6. The quotes are from Robin Wright, "Africa Faces Crises, Bleak Future," *Los Angeles Times* (August 27, 2000).

7. Thomas L. Friedman, columns in *New York Times* (April 28, 2001) and (May 2, 2001).

8. Kuperus, "Building Democracy."

9. *Financial Times Survey*, "Nigeria," April 9, 2002.

10. Pierre Du Toit, *South Africa's Brittle Peace: The Problem of Post-Settlement Violence* (London: Macmillan, 2001).

11. Louis Hartz, ed., *The Founding of New Societies* (New York: Harcourt Brace Jovanovich, 1964).

12. T. Dunbar Moody, *The Rise of Afrikanerdom: Power, Apartheid, and the Afrikaner Civil Religion* (Berkeley: University of California Press, 1975).

13. Pierre Du Toit, *State-Building and Democracy in Southern Africa: Botswana, Zimbabwe, and South Africa* (Washington, DC: United States Institute of Peace Press, 1995).

14. Wilmot James and Daria Caliguire, "Renewing Civil Society," *Journal of Democracy* 7 (January 1996): 56–66; Daryl Glaser, "South Africa and the Limits of Civil Society," *Journal of Southern African Studies* 23 (March 1997): 5–25; more generally Marina Ottaway, *Africa's New Leaders: Democracy or State Reconstruction?* (Washington, DC: Carnegie Endowment, 1999).

15. Glenn Adler and Jonny Steinberg, *From Comrades to Citizens: The South African Civics Movement and the Transition to Democracy* (London: Macmillan, 2000).

16. Adler and Steinberg, *From Comrades to Citizens*.

17. Du Toit, *South Africa's Brittle Peace*.

18. Jon Jeter, "Tribal Ways vs. Modern Government: South Africa's Ruling Party in Conflict with Age-Old Tradition," *Washington Post* (December 18, 2000), A-1; also Pierre Du Toit and Jannie Gagiano, "Strongmen on the Cape Flats," *Africa Insight* 23, 2 (1993): 102–11.

19. Hennie Kotze and Pierre Du Toit, "The State, Civil Society, and Democratic Transition in South Africa," *Journal of Conflict Resolution* 39 (March 1995): 27–48.

20. Kotze and Du Toit, "The State."

21. Clarence Page, "After Apartheid," syndicated column, *New Bern* (NC) *Sun Journal* (July 19, 2000), A-6.

22. Kuperus, "Building Democracy."

23. Richard Cornwell, "The Collapse of the African State," in Jakkie Cilliers and Peggy Mason, eds., *Peace, Profit, or Plunder? The Privatization of Security in War-Torn African Societies* (Pretoria, SA: Institute for Security Studies, 1999), 61–80.

24. Stephen Orvis, "Civil Society in Africa or African Civil Society?" *Journal of Asian and African Studies* 36 (February 2001): 1–29.

Chapter Thirteen

Benign Neglect: American Foreign Policy in Latin America in the Post–Cold War Era

Benign Neglect? It has a certain logic as a basis for policy, especially in the post–Cold War era. From a realist or national self-interest point of view, the logic is: if the Soviet Union (now Russia) or other hostile outside powers are not interested in Latin America, or in other Third World areas where U.S. interests are limited, then why should the United States bother to pay them serious attention? And since there is little terrorism in Latin America, this logic may be even more compelling now that the United States has committed itself to the "war on terrorism" as its main and virtually only foreign policy priority.

Moreover, there is a long history of U.S. benign neglect in Latin America and in other Third World areas. As James Reston, the long-time *New York Times* foreign affairs columnist, once put it, "the United States will do anything [aid, investment, political pressure, military intervention] for Latin America except read about it."[1] At many points in U.S. history, benign neglect has alternated with dramatic, desperate, usually not-so-benign interventions, often of the military kind: Guatemala in 1954, Cuba in 1961, the Dominican Republic in 1965, Chile in 1970, Grenada in 1983, Panama in 1989, and Haiti in 1994. The United States blows both hot and cold on Latin America—often at the same time, depending on which agency or part of the U.S. government is speaking.[2]

Benign neglect is closely in accord with other notable features of U.S. policy in Latin America that have waxed and waned—and often waxed again over the years. Thus, when the Pentagon speaks of "economy of force," it means that Latin America can be dealt with with a minimum of attention so that U.S. military forces can be concentrated in other, presumably more important, areas: Germany and along the Iron Curtain, Korea and Japan, Vietnam for a time, now Central Asia and the Middle East. The doctrine (of Lyndon B.

Johnson) of "no second Cubas" was a means to simplify the complexities of Latin American politics, and U.S. policy there, by ruling out, for the most part, Marxist, to say nothing of Marxist-Leninist, regimes. Similarly, with "the lesser evil doctrine": when faced with a choice between an authoritarian regime (Somoza, Trujillo, Batista, Stroessner, Pinochet, the Brazilian generals, and others) that was also steadfastly anticommunist, and a (usually) wobbly democratic regime that allowed freedom even for communists, the United States almost always opted for the authoritarian. This, too, simplified our policy conundrums.[3]

The literature is vast,[4] so let us briefly simply stipulate some truths, fortunate or unfortunate, about U.S. policy in Latin America:

1. The United States pays little serious attention to Latin America.
2. The region is low on our list of priorities, behind Europe, Asia, the Middle East, Russia, China, maybe even India, certainly now the war on terrorism.
3. The United States pays attention to the area mainly in times of crisis; seldom have we had a mature, sustained policy in Latin America.
4. Almost no one at high policy levels (Cabinet or above) has an interest or extensive experience in Latin America (Jeane Kirkpatrick, who wrote her PhD thesis on Argentina, and George W. Bush, from Texas, are the only two who come to mind).
5. The United States is unwilling to study or read about Latin America or take it seriously or on its own terms.
6. U.S. attitudes tend to be condescending and patronizing; we treat Latin Americans as "little children" who must be educated and "taught" by the United States. As President Woodrow Wilson once put it, "we will teach Latin America how to elect good men"; similarly, in U.S. democracy and economic development programs, it is *we* who will teach *them*.
7. Even more basically, the United States (and other societies) harbors deep-seated but usually unspoken prejudices about Latin America as Roman Catholic, a product of Spain and the Inquisition, racially impure, unsuccessful economically and socially, unable to govern itself, a grouping of "banana republics."
8. U.S. policy in Latin America (and elsewhere) is exceedingly ethnocentric: we will send *our* brand of democracy, governance, and free markets to Latin America whether they fit or are appropriate, or not. The attitude is: we are superior, you are inferior; therefore, you must learn from us.[5]
9. For diplomats and military officials (Southcom), being assigned to Latin America is usually considered a career-ender, a dead end, low priority, so top officials tend to avoid the area.

10. Latin America is sufficiently unimportant—and expendable—that new administrations often feel they can turn it over as a political patronage plum to their more radical, often highly ideological constituencies: the human rights, environmental, Black or Hispanic lobbies in the case of Democratic administrations; ideological conservatives or the Cuban-American National Foundation in the case of Republicans.

11. Since it doesn't count for or matter much, we frequently use Latin America as a guinea pig or experimental research laboratory for social and political programs that we would never dare to try out in our own or other high-priority areas: radical agrarian reform, national family planning, full transparency, pure forms of capitalism, and democracy.

12. Americans and American politicians can frequently say or do stupid, offensive, things about Latin America, or Hispanics, that they would never say or do about other people or areas (such as Israel or the Middle East) because, until recently, there were no costs for doing so.

13. Because of Latin America's low priority, it is even more subjected to the play of domestic political interests than are other, more critical areas.

14. Latin America is still seen as "our" sphere of influence, our area of responsibility. This means, still, that outside actors (European, Asian) are not particularly welcome in Latin America unless they support U.S. policy; that Latin America should continue to orient itself toward the United States; and that the United States should be the leader, model, beacon, and director of Latin America's future development. The Monroe Doctrine is not yet dead after all.

Thus, the picture is not a pretty one. The United States often *means well* for Latin America, and occasionally its policies have been more or less enlightened. But given the strong prejudices toward the area historically, the condescension, the ethnocentrism, we should not expect a great deal from U.S. policy. Having battled these strong prejudices and stereotypes and butted our heads against the walls of ignorance and ethnocentrism for nearly half a century by now, few of us see the fundamentals of policy changing anytime soon. My suspicion is that many of these attitudes apply toward Sub-Saharan Africa, the Middle East, and South and Southeast Asia as well—indeed, throughout the developing world.

But as we conclude this introduction, let me introduce three complexities into this otherwise inglorious picture. First, one could make a strong case that Latin America could do worse, even far worse, than a U.S. policy based on benign neglect. If your hope is for a consistent, enlightened, wise, mature, progressive U.S. policy in Latin America (which I see, given the preceding discussion, as unlikely anytime soon, or even ever), then you are bound to be disappointed with benign neglect. If, on the other hand, the realistic alternatives are military interventions, constant CIA machinations, or U.S. embassies playing a meddling, proconsular role, then benign neglect—letting Latin America, as Frank Sinatra famously put it, do it "their way"—is not such a bad policy. That, after all, is what the so-called Good Neighbor Policy of Franklin Roosevelt was all about in the 1930s and 1940s.

Second, even if U.S. *policy* in Latin America has often been unenlightened, the *facts on the ground* in both the United States and Latin America are changing, which will eventually *force* a change in policy. On the one side, the United States is, through immigration, increasingly becoming a Hispanic country and increasingly *interdependent* with Latin America on a host of major issues: immigration, investment, trade, oil and natural gas, tourism, banking, water supplies, drugs, labor supplies, the environment, democracy, human rights, and economic reform. At the same time, Latin America is changing radically in ways that will eventually make U.S. relations with it easier and more realistic if not necessarily always more enlightened: more democratic, more developed, more middle class, more integrated into the global economy, with a much better human rights situation. These facts "on the ground" will surely do more to affect U.S. policy in the area, and to draw the United States into a closer relationship with Latin America, than any wishful thinking we may express.[6]

Third, it may be that "benign neglect" is not a correct way to describe the policy. While Latin America is currently low on the United States' list of priorities and receives little high-level attention from Washington, at other levels U.S. policy in Latin America is vigorous and activist. To begin, a great deal of American foreign policy is taking place at lower policy levels, below the White House and Cabinet, often out of sight of media and popular attention, within the foreign policymaking bureaucracies at the assistant secretary and country-desk levels, on trade and other critical issues. Arguably, this is the most effective locus of U.S. policymaking since there is a great deal of information and expertise at these levels, whereas once an issue or country is at such a crisis condition that it reaches White House or Cabinet levels, the most amount of "politics" and least amount of expertise are brought to bear.[7]

In addition, much of the policy is carried out at local, county, state, and regional levels, on such important issues as drugs, immigration, water rights, the environment—what in the literature is called "local foreign policy." Furthermore, despite the lack of high-level attention, U.S. officials at *all levels* remain committed to and vigorously engaged in pursuing the "golden triad" of the so-called Washington Consensus (more on this below): democracy, free trade, and open markets—itself an activist agenda. Plus, while official Washington may be paying less attention to Latin America, in the field, in

U.S. embassies throughout the region, activist, even "pro-consular," often only slightly reduced from Cold War days policies are still being pursued by energetic U.S. officials. And finally, while official Washington may be less engaged in Latin America, the private sector, chiefly U.S. private businesses, capital, and foreign direct investment (FDI), but also including NGOs and civil society actors, have stepped into this vacuum; furthermore, this shift from public to private attention was part of a conscious U.S. strategy and does not signal any decline in U.S. interest in the area, only a shift in means and agencies. Overall, this does not add up to a policy of benign neglect toward Latin America.

THE DOMESTIC BACKGROUND

All American presidents from John F. Kennedy on have proclaimed, shortly after taking office, that they "really care" about Latin America. At one level, this is a sop to Latin American public opinion, which, among Third World areas, is the most "Western" (albeit reflecting a traditional, premodern Iberian/Southern European variant of the Western developmental model) and therefore likes to feel itself, by aspiration if not always reality, closest to the United States and to the developed Western world. At another level, these expressions of interest and brotherhood are often a cover for underlying Cold War/strategic concerns and, presently, for considerable confusion and uncertainty about Latin America's place in U.S. thinking.

President George W. Bush is no exception to this rule. After the hyperactivity (in more ways than one) of the Bill Clinton years, Bush was elected as an amiable fellow, a regular guy, marginally less boring and painful than Al Gore, who would return the country to nonactivist "normalcy" and presumably concentrate, now that the Soviet Union had been vanquished and the United States as the lone surviving superpower had few serious enemies, on domestic social and economic issues. Mr. Bush had little experience in or knowledge about foreign affairs, had never lived abroad, had traveled only to Mexico and, like many Texans, presumed to know Latin America based on his knowledge of Hispanics in Texas and cross-border excursions into Mexico.

Latin America was touted as the one foreign policy area that Mr. Bush understood and "knew." He speaks Spanish and has Mexican Americans in his family. During the 2000 campaign he promised that Latin America would not be an "afterthought" (benign neglect) of his foreign policy but would constitute a "fundamental commitment." Once inaugurated, he met with a steady procession of Latin American leaders, took his first presidential trip abroad to Mexico, promised support for the Free Trade Agreement of the Americas during the Hemisphere summit in Quebec City, and entertained Mexican president Vicente Fox at his first White House state dinner.

President Bush's key foreign policy advisers, including the vice president, secretary of state, secretary of defense, national security advisor, and CIA director, did not share his view of the importance of Latin America. First, they tended to come out of the realist school of international relations, which relegates Latin America to a low priority. Second, examining their careers closely reveals that, to a person, their backgrounds and priorities were forged, not on Latin America, but on U.S.–Soviet relations, NATO, Eastern Europe, and the Cold War. Those were all, of course, issues that were at least ten years old by the time Bush came to power. In addition, no one at high levels in the Bush team had any interest in Latin America or viewed it as important, seeing it rather as a "second order" foreign policy issue, which means it got no attention at all and was often viewed disparagingly. Experienced in foreign policy these advisers were but, by this time, they were out of date and certainly not a team that could boast of knowledge or experience anywhere in the Third World. Alone among high-level officials, only President Bush had a strong interest in Latin America, and one would have to go to a lower (undersecretary) tier of officials even to find any that had a long-term interest and experience in Asia or the Middle East.

Latin America issues at the "grand policy" level were therefore by default, handled by lower-level, often more ideological officials at the National Security Council, the Department of State, the Department of Defense, and the CIA. Recruited mainly from the conservative think tanks, they tended to see Latin America in stark either-or terms left over from the Cold War. Thus, Venezuela's Populist president Hugo Chávez had to be opposed and gotten rid of; Fidel Castro was still viewed as evil incarnate and there could be no relaxation of the embargo; and Luiz Ignacio "Lula" da Silva in Brazil was at first seen as a threat to the entire hemisphere. The rhetoric was overheated and often overwrought, fueled by the fact that of the thirteen or so officials handling Latin America at the assistant or deputy assistant secretary level, roughly half came out of the Cuban exile community. While this ethnicity is not a determining factor in explaining their policy views, it may help us understand some of their policy attitudes. This situation is not necessarily unusual, if nevertheless often destructive, in American politics: as with Sub-Saharan Africa or the Middle East, policymaking has been largely turned over to the very ethnic/political group that has a particular vested interest in its outcome.

Another political consideration enters into the equation, and that is the appointment of key Latin America ambassadorships on a political basis. As is well known, President Bush's electoral mandate in 2000 was less than overwhelming and, as a result, his political advisers in the White House were determined not to allow that to happen again in 2004. One of their targets therefore became the U.S. Hispanic community, a rising group, now the largest minority voting bloc in the United States, and believed to be within grasp of Republican appeals. Hence, appointments to ambassadorships and other key positions were filled by targeting the Hispanic community hoping thereby to secure their votes in 2004. In short, White House domestic political advisers, headed by Karl Rove, began to take a strong role in foreign policymaking as well.[8]

But policymaking is more nuanced than the preceding analysis suggests. First, at even lower levels in the foreign policy bureaucracies, policy on free trade and numerous other concrete issues continued to be hammered out and advanced by competent, professional civil servants, largely devoid of ideological or high-level political interference. Second, a process is already underway by which professional foreign service officers at the State Department and career officials at the Department of Defense, Treasury, CIA, and other agencies gradually "recaptured" policymaking from the ideologues and political appointees who accompany a new president into office and usually dominate the headlines in a new administration's early months. Third, there is a learning process that occurs in the White House and among appointed high government officials—unfortunately in the American system this on-the-job learning occurs *after* a new administration is inaugurated—as to what can and cannot reasonably be done in the realm of policy.

Meanwhile, other important shifts in policy were taking place out of sight of the usual media coverage. One of these was the post–Cold War shift away from strategic, political, and diplomatic issues in U.S. relations with Latin America (and elsewhere) and toward economic issues. That also meant, pre-9/11, a shift in power, resources, and budgets away from the traditional foreign policy bureaucracies (Department of State, Department of Defense, Central Intelligence Agency) and increasingly toward such economic agencies as the Treasury Department, Commerce Department, and Office of the Trade Representative. Another related shift involved an evolution away from public foreign aid and toward private FDI, of which Latin America is the largest recipient. This trend had been occurring for much of the last decade and was accelerated, for ideological reasons, by Republican administrations. FDI was viewed as both more effective *and* cheaper than public foreign aid in a time when aid was decreasing. These trends help explain some of the more fundamental shifts in emphasis in U.S. policy.

THE WASHINGTON CONSENSUS—IN CRISIS!

The dominant paradigm in U.S.–Latin American relations in the post–Cold War era has been termed "The Washington Consensus." Initially everyone in political Washington shared this consensus, and it enjoys widespread bipartisan support. Business, labor, think tanks, religious groups, human rights lobbies, the media, Republicans, Democrats, all the foreign affairs bureaucracies–all share in this consensus. Latin America bought into it as well as the United States, albeit not always enthusiastically or unanimously; but since the Americans wanted it so badly and Latin America saw no other options, it went along. Since the consensus is, or was, so widely shared, it will be very difficult politically and bureaucratically to change it.

The Washington Consensus consists of three pillars: free trade, open markets, and democratization. All of these parts are assumed to be closely interrelated. Thus, free trade helps stimulate open markets (and vice versa), which give rise to greater prosperity, a larger middle class, and a more stable democracy. One could argue that the sequence works the other way as well, that democracy gives rise to a desire for greater economic freedom and that free trade helps strengthen both; but generally it has been the economic motor forces that have been seen as driving the dynamic. The Washington Consensus sounds remarkably like the Alliance for Progress of John F. Kennedy in the early 1960s and, intellectually, derives from the same supposedly universal, inevitable, economic determinist school of W. W. Rostow (*The Stages of Economic Growth*)[9] and the U.S. foreign aid (Agency for International Development–AID) program. One size, one formula fits all. Have we learned nothing over the last forty years?

Before discussing the three main points of the Consensus, we should point out that there are two glaring omissions in it. First, there is no mention of foreign aid. Foreign aid has been declining significantly over the decades—so much so that most Latin American countries now think of it as a relatively small, even insignificant part of their overall national budgets, and it no longer gives the United States much leverage over their policy preferences. For another, as compared with Sub-Saharan Africa and other poor areas, most of Latin America is now "transitional" or "intermediary" on most economic indices, and many of the countries from the region have "graduated" from eligibility for most (except in emergencies) U.S. foreign aid programs. A third reason for the lack of attention in the Consensus to foreign aid is that for the last twenty-five years, since the first Reagan administration, all but eight of these under Republican administrations, the sense and ideology have been strong, à la Peter Bauer,[10] that foreign aid does little, keeps countries in a dependent status, prolongs their sense of "victimhood," and does little to help them break out of poverty. Far better, the argument has been, to use direct investment, free markets, and capitalism rather than foreign aid.

Nor does the Washington Consensus talk much about security issues. That has been left to the Pentagon; civilians in Washington tend not to see the subject as important or to shy away from it. Among other things, the Soviet

Union had been vanquished; the Cold War was over; the guerrilla movements in Latin America had been diminished or had joined the political process as political parties; the communist parties evidenced little popular support; and the Cuban Revolution, except perhaps in Venezuela, had run out of steam and no longer served as a beacon for Latin American revolutionaries. Therefore, until the war on terrorism, there seemed to be little reason to be preoccupied with security issues in Latin America.[11]

The "problems," as distinct from "threats," that did exist—drugs, immigration, border patrol, refugees, "boat people"—appeared to be of a lower-order character than the threat of thousands of Soviet missiles aimed at the United States, and only with some reluctance—and out of fear of its budget being reduced—did the Pentagon come to think of them as security issues. Certain specific countries were also seen as potential dangers, even threats— Haiti, Colombia, Venezuela, perhaps Mexico—but not in any conventional sense, only as countries whose potential for instability and drug exporting would affect the United States domestically. But if there was no real threat from Latin America, why pay attention to the area at all? Why not revert to benign neglect or, strategically, economy of force? Absent the Soviet threat, the post–Cold War logic in the United States was: if "Paraguay" wants to "go communist" at this stage, why should we care? Of course, the United States would care and would not carry this logic to its obvious conclusion, but the point was clear: with the Cold War over, and other than the above-mentioned problem areas, why pay serious attention to Latin America at all?

That left the Washington Consensus and its three pillars of free trade, open markets, and democracy. At first, in the early 1990s, there was widespread agreement on these priorities. The Consensus encompassed, for the most part, not only the two major American political parties, the several foreign policy-making bureaucracies, the think tanks, and all the major interest groups, but also both the United States and Latin America. The Washington Consensus was not forced upon Latin America but was widely seen there, at least by the elites, as constituting, since the bankruptcy of the earlier Import Substitution Industrialization (ISI) model, the only route for the Hemisphere to follow.

Governmental and business elites in Latin America saw clearly that, for their countries to survive and thrive in the new globalized economy, they could no longer hide behind protectionist barriers or rely on foreign aid but would have to become competitive in world markets. And that meant democracy, transparency, rule of law, judicial reform, efficiency, streamlining, government reform, economic reform, and an end to corrupt patronage-dominated politics. In addition (but that would have to be the subject of a separate work), I am convinced that Latin American intellectuals like Guillermo O'Donnell[12] and his collaborators in the "transitions to democracy" school also led Latin

America astray by naively arguing that one could ignore Latin American history, political culture, and sociology and concentrate only on institutional variables because, as the argument went, if you got the institutions right, that is all that mattered, everything else would fall into place, and no other variables would need to be taken into account. Professor O'Donnell has since admitted his interpretation was erroneous,[13] but meantime Latin America had been victimized again by what proved to be a less than successful policy.

More recently, the failures of the policy have been emphasized and the successes given less attention. The 1990s, in fact, have witnessed a gradual decline in support for the main pillars of the policy, and the trend is continuing today. The movement toward a free trade area of the Americas, first articulated by George H. W. Bush, has slowed considerably, as much due to protectionist pressures in the United States as to reluctance by Latin America to enter this intensely competitive global environment. The movement toward open markets has been slowed by the fact that Latin American history and institutions have been more statist and mercantilist and even today lack some of the essential institutions of a market economy. And while nineteen of the twenty countries are at least formally democratic, they are often viewed as limited, partial, incomplete democracies—"democracy with adjectives." Let us review briefly the assumptions on which all three of these pillars are based, not providing a complete analysis but only some key reasons why the so-called Consensus seems currently to be breaking down.[14]

First, free trade. While the United States has long been committed to a free trade agenda, in Latin America that commitment found expression recently in the North American Free Trade Agreement (NAFTA), the Central American Free Trade Agreement (CAFTA), and the Free Trade Area of the Americas (FTAA). In part, the FTAA was designed to counter the European Union as well as what were perceived to be Japanese efforts in Asia to create their own trade zones restricting U.S. trade, by creating a U.S. free trade zone of its own with our "natural partner" in Latin America. In part also, the FTAA and NAFTA were aimed at stabilizing Latin America, particularly neighboring Mexico in a time of crisis, and at shifting responsibility for that high priority from the public to the private sphere. In other words, NAFTA, CAFTA, and the FTAA are at least as much about U.S. political and security interests in Latin America as they are about economics and trade.

Though reluctant at first, a number of Latin American countries (Chile is the best example) have embraced the free trade agenda. They have reduced tariffs, opened their markets, and sought to become more competitive. It is fashionable these days to say that, because of political and protectionist pressures, it is the United States that stands in the way of free trade, not Latin America. There is some truth in that assertion but not the whole truth. In fact, quietly, unspectacularly, at low levels, and hopefully without making political waves, the FTAA negotiations continue to go forward, with the United States still leading the way, broadening the agreement, and hoping to draw the other Latin American countries along. Provision for "fast trade" authority has also been passed by Congress. Of course, as by far the largest and most dynamic economy in the area, the United States is in the best position to take advantage of a free trade regime; and there are increasing doubts if Latin America can effectively compete with the world's high-flying economies in this arena, and if a commitment to free trade is still viable politically in most Latin American countries whose economics are stagnant and where political pressures against free trade are building.

Second, open markets. Latin America has a long history of statism; its economic model is that of the French physiocrats, mercantilism, most recently expressed as ISI.[15] ISI was discredited by the economic and political failures of the 1970s and 1980s; hence, despite considerable opposition and skepticism from the defenders of statism, a free market ideology was officially embraced in the 1990s. There is considerable doubt as to just how much in fact Latin America warmed to free markets or if that was mainly a sop to U.S. pressures; nor is it clear that Latin America has sufficiently made the economic reforms— transparency, privatization, efficiency, accountability—necessary for a free market system to operate effectively. In addition, the effective functioning of a free market system is based on a large number of assumptions that in most Latin American countries are quite shaky; among them:

- a dynamic, independent entrepreneurial class
- functioning, dynamic markets not hemmed in by statism
- banks and credit agencies that actually encourage entrepreneurship and free markets
- a political, bureaucratic, and cultural infrastructure that is conducive to open markets
- a social system allowing the benefits of free markets to be widely shared instead of concentrated in the pockets of the elites

Given these and other weaknesses in the Latin American economies, one needs to think, rather as in Russia, that real economic reform and development will take three to four generations, not three to four years—if it can be accomplished at all.

Third, democracy. Democracy is in trouble in Latin America—and this is in a continent that has a long, or path-dependency, history of and aspiration for Western-style republicanism, democracy, and human rights. Throughout the hemisphere support for democracy as a *system* is at 60–65 percent, down 25–30 points from a decade ago.[16] Support for democracy's essential institutions and pluralist structures (political parties, parliaments, labor unions) is even lower, often in the 10–20 percent range. In some countries support for democracy is below 40 percent and trails behind its great "evil" alternative, "strong government," which suggests an authoritarian "out" or solution. Democracy is widely perceived to be not working very well, to be ineffective, not providing the economic and social advances that people had come to expect from it. Similarly with "civil society": instead of a dynamic, pluralist Tocquevillian civil society undergirding democracy, what we are increasingly getting, as in other developing areas previously discussed, is state regulation, control, manipulation, limits on, and co-optation of civil society—in other words, a new form of corporatism or public–private partnerships that are often antidemocratic.

In short, in the political as in the economic sphere in the Washington Consensus, the United States has projected its own preferred values, models, institutions, and preferences (free trade, open markets, democracy) on Latin America, whether those fit or are appropriate or not, and with the support of important sectors within Latin America. U.S. policy in Latin America needs to come to grips better and more realistically with the realities of the area, which may include compromises with such not-so-attractive and often nondemocratic, non-free market features as corporatism, organicism, elitism, patrimonialism, statism, and often a strong dose of authoritarianism.[17]

In practice, in the cases of such quasi authoritarians as Alberto Fujimori in Peru, Carlos Menem in Argentina, Joaquín Balaguer in the Dominican Republic, or the Mexican Revolutionary Institutional Party (PRI), the United States regularly makes such pragmatic compromises, even while the three legs of the Washington Consensus remain the official, rhetorical policy. In most cases, the gap between the lofty rhetoric and the more pragmatic practice can be managed quite well, but occasionally the practice becomes too much a prisoner of the rhetoric and then the policy may get in trouble. Meanwhile, there is almost no serious examination of the fundamental assumptions of the policy and whether the full agenda of the Washington Consensus of free trade, open markets, and full, participatory democracy may be, as one Latin American ambassador to the United States put it, a "little too rich" for Latin American palates. The issue is not, therefore, activism or benign neglect, for the United States seems always to be activist albeit at different levels; the question is whether it is activist for the correct or most appropriate purposes.

President George W. Bush was the heir to these policies rather than the initiator of them. He has largely followed the Washington Consensus even while adding to them such initiatives as the *possibilities* of new immigration standards, the freer flow of labor, and better relations with a democratic Mexico. However, since there is currently little terrorist threat from Latin America, and since that is presently almost the only focus of the president and his Cabinet, most of these issues have been temporarily set aside or dropped, while the policy continues to be carried out mainly at other or lower levels. It remains an activist policy rather than one of benign neglect, but it is activist not at a level where it receives major media attention in Washington or in the rest of the world.

POLICY INITIATIVES

American policy and its relations with Latin America have become increasingly complex over the decades. At one level is the hemispheric policy—the Washington Consensus—partly for rhetorical purposes but also meant to provide guidelines and purpose to the diverse foreign policy bureaucracies involved. At a second level is bilateral relations—the main focus of this section—with *all* the countries, with some countries obviously more important than others and with the bilateral relations increasingly taking priority over a broad but vague hemispheric position. A third level of policy is global, on such issues as the environment, human rights, drugs, sustainable development, terrorism, and democracy, and where Latin America, fits (or doesn't fit, with terrorism) into those larger policy issues. Still a fourth level involves the proliferation of private interest lobbies—human rights groups, business groups, democracy groups, ethnic lobbies, varieties of civil society groups—and their place in shaping policy, or even carrying out parts of the policy in the absence, or abdication, of much official U.S. government activity.

Among the bilateral relations, Mexico occupies a special place and has become one of the most important countries in the *world* from the standpoint of U.S. policy. It is not that Mexico is a security threat in any traditional sense; rather, the issue is one of interdependence and the ability of Mexico to impact the United States at a host of levels: immigration, trade, water supplies, drugs, tourism, investment, labor supplies, pollution and the environment, oil and natural gas, and, not least, the potential for instability. It was the latter possibility, either economic or political, and the prospect that even the slightest hint of instability would send millions of Mexicans across the border into the United States, thus putting enormous, inordinate pressure on U.S. schools, housing, social services, and law enforcement, that prompted President George H. W. Bush to enact NAFTA and for every recent American president to be sensitive to Mexican issues and to periodically bail out Mexico with massive aid packages. Of course, the Mexicans realize that for purely self-interest reasons the United States cannot afford to let Mexico destabilize, which thereby removes most incentives for cooperation and reform. The United States and Mexico are interdependent at so many levels and on so many issues that it is difficult to see their relations ever being characterized as benign neglect.

Colombia similarly comes close to constituting a "threat" in the modern, post–Cold War sense through its large-scale export of drugs to the United States. Colombia also has some of the last Marxist and Marxist-Leninist guerrilla movements in Latin America, but with the end of the Cold War and ongoing fears by domestic lobbying groups and some in Congress of "another Vietnam," the United States has been reluctant to get too deeply involved in internal Colombian affairs. However, since the guerrillas have also gone heavily into the drug trade, perhaps as their principal activity, the line between counternarcotics and counterguerrilla activities has blurred; hence, Plan Colombia, which garnered considerable bipartisan support and is now official U.S. government policy.

Argentina is unloved by both the United States and the rest of Latin America for a variety of political, historical, and cultural reasons; it is also far from the United States and therefore not "interdependent" in the same way that Mexico is. Hence, Argentina cannot expect either great sympathy from the rest of the Americas in its present depressed condition, nor consistent, large-scale bailouts from the United States or the international lending agencies.

Venezuela is a fascinating case because, from the U.S. point of view, it has "everything": strategic importance (oil, location), political importance (a faltering democracy), economic importance (oil again, a major trading partner), and ideological importance (a populist, quasi-Marxist president who befriends Fidel Castro, journeys to pariahs Iraq and Libya, undermines business, and rails against the United States). "Traditional" and "modern" security interests thus merge in a particularly volatile mix. Even if the United States did not have a hand in the aborted coup against mercurial Hugo Chávez, some of the more ideological persons in the Bush administration privately cheered his ouster—only to see the coup reversed and Chávez returned to power more boisterous than ever. The United States meanwhile straddles the line between intervention at several levels and allowing the Chávez phenomenon to run its course, meanwhile exhausting itself in the process.

Big, important Brazil has not been a priority for U.S. policy, but now with the election of Luiz Ignacio ("Lula") da Silva it is becoming so. Brazil is the fifth largest country in the world, sixth in population, eighth in gross national product, and a candidate for a permanent seat on the UN Security Council. Its diplomatic and strategic importance should be self-evident. Yet as a struggling democracy in sometimes dangerous economic difficulties, and with leftist, populist Lula and his even more radical advisers in the presidency, Brazil, like Venezuela, is worrisome and plays into the ideological orientations of conservatives in the Bush administration as well. Meanwhile, rising nationalism and anti-Americanism in Brazil make the relationship tenser still.

Haiti is the case par excellence in the circum-Caribbean of a failed state. As a predominantly African American country, it resonates strongly in U.S. domestic politics; there is a long and often tortured history of U.S. involvement, which still carries political consequences for all parties; and Haitian boat people frequently arrive, dead or alive, on South Florida beaches inconveniently during the tourist season. However, as long as Haiti is a "democracy" (which means Haitians cannot by definition be political refugees), U.S. law gives immigration authorities the power to return the boat people to Haiti. As a poor, underdeveloped, uninstitutionalized country, now also a major transshipment point in the drug trade, and with these special connections in U.S. domestic politics, Haiti will continue to be a subject of concern to U.S. policy.

Cuba is a fascinating case for all the known reasons and more: the embargo, the last surviving Marxist-Leninist state in the Americas (and one of the last in the world), a country only ninety miles from the United States, the politics of the Cuban exile community, the dismal economic and human rights record of the revolution, still pending claims of nationalized U.S. companies against the regime, anger and hatred on the part of many U.S. officials against Cuba, drug trafficking, aid and/or sanctuary for terrorists. At the same time, Fidel Castro is aging; would-be successors, like sharks, are circling in the water; the Atlantic Fleet continuously circumnavigates the island; and the United States will certainly seek to influence and manage the post-Castro transition. Although the United States would clearly prefer a peaceful transition to democracy and free markets, one can also envision future scenarios that include insurrection in some of Cuba's provinces, revolt, conflict, civil war, and U.S. military intervention.

Other countries are also important to the United States, for different reasons. Nevertheless, the picture that emerges even from this brief survey is one of active engagement and not of benign neglect. But let us make several points about the kind of active engagement involved.

First, as indicated, it is at relatively low policy and bureaucratic levels. Other than the president himself, presently preoccupied with Iraq, Iran, North Korea, and the war on terrorism, no one at high policy levels has expertise or special interest in Latin America.

Second, if one knows the politics of American foreign policymaking at high levels, this is not altogether bad. At low levels is where the expertise is;

in addition, the policy can often be quite rationally managed without much overt outside political interference from the top. Third, important policy initiatives are being carried out at these subordinate levels, especially dealing with trade, human rights and democratization, border conflicts, drugs, immigration, and such "second tier" reforms as transparency, education, governance, civil society, and judicial reform.

But fourth, without high-level guidance from the top, there is little consistency in the policy, an absence of priorities, little follow-through, absence of sustained effort, and often amateurish or mistaken efforts. Fifth, and again without high-level direction, there is almost no rethinking of the (perhaps fatally) flawed assumptions of the Washington Consensus. Instead, the policy simply continues as a "given" despite the fact that many of its aspects are not working.

Sixth, as the war on terrorism perhaps begins to wind down or fade from our consciousness, a more balanced, nuanced, and updated policy may begin to emerge. Alternatively, some countries—Colombia, Mexico, Haiti, Paraguay, Cuba—have either become havens of various and usually limited kinds of terrorism, or have learned to manipulate the terrorist issue to attract more attention and/or aid for themselves. But unlike the Middle East and some other areas, Latin America has not become a major terrorist haven, which provides one more reason for benign neglect. Hence, I would anticipate few changes in the basics of the policy, and also that Latin America would continue to be viewed as low priority, a "secondary area" in the U.S. rank-ordering of regional geopolitics.

CONCLUSION

It is too simple to characterize U.S. policy in Latin America as "benign neglect." There may be, because of the war on terrorism, benign neglect at high policy levels but not at lower levels within the bureaucracy; among activist human rights, democracy, business, and civil society groups; and at local, state, and regional levels where there is a great deal of activity. The policies pursued may be outdated or, in the case of the Washington Consensus, based on flawed assumptions, but benign neglect is not an accurate way to describe it.

Rather, the policy remains one of engagement and activism, but usually at lower, subcabinet levels. As part of this activist approach, U.S. cultural, political, economic, and strategic hegemony in the region will continue. U.S. hegemony has actually increased rather than decreased in the last decade, particularly economically, by the virtual withdrawal of other European actors (except Spain) from the area. In turn, Latin America recognizes that it is dependent on the United States, that the United States is "the only game in town."

In these respects, U.S. policy in the George W. Bush administration is not much different from that of past administrations. That means a low priority accorded Latin America, minimum attention at high levels, economy of both force and focus. And, with the increasing emphasis on foreign direct investment, the prevailing sentiment is "let the private sector do it."

Meanwhile, the lack of high-level U.S. attention, U.S. arrogance as well as hegemony, the condescension shown, and pro-consular meddling, as well as the failed promises of the Washington Consensus are leading to rising alienation and anti-Americanism in Latin America. Anti-Americanism is palpable (though seldom violent) and at a level seldom observed before. But at the same time, thoughtful Latin Americans understand that for the foreseeable future no one else will come to their rescue; they have nowhere else to turn beside the United States; they have no choice but to reach their accommodation with the United States.

Meanwhile, the facts "on the ground" keep changing. Hispanics are now the largest U.S. minority; in some areas the United States is becoming a "Latin American country"; the United States and Latin America are increasingly interdependent on a whole host of issues—just as is Western Europe and its "near abroad" of Central and Eastern Europe, Southeast Europe (including Turkey), and North Africa. Over time, it is these *facts*, rather than any wishful thinking on our part, that will slowly, eventually, but inexorably alter the posture and priorities of foreign policy.

NOTES

1. The statement was coined by Reston in the early 1960s when writing about John F. Kennedy's Alliance for Progress. It continues to have relevance today.

2. A solid treatment is Michael J. Kryzanek, *U.S.–Latin American Relations* (New York: Praeger, 1996).

3. Karl E. Meyer, "The Lesser Evil Doctrine," *The New Leader* XLVI (October 14, 1963): 14.

4. See again Kryzanek as well as my own writings: *The Democratic Revolution in Latin America: History, Politics, and U.S. Policy* (New York: Holmes and Meier, 1990); *American Foreign Policy toward Latin America in the 80s and 90s* (New York: New York University Press, 1992); *Democracy and Its Discontents: Development, Interdependence, and U.S. Policy in Latin America* (Lanham, MD: Rowman & Littlefield, 1995).

5. Howard J. Wiarda, *Ethnocentrism in Foreign Policy: Can We Understand the Third World?* (Washington, DC: American Enterprise Institute for Public Policy Research, 1985).

6. Abraham Lowenthal, *Partners in Conflict: The United States and Latin America* (Baltimore, MD: Johns Hopkins University Press, 1987); Lowenthal and Gregory F. Treverton (eds.), *Latin America in a New World* (Boulder, CO: Westview, 1994).

7. For an analysis of the domestic bases of U.S. policy, see Howard J. Wiarda, *American Foreign Policy: Actors and Processes* (New York: HarperCollins, 1996).

8. *The New York Times* (September 7, 2002), 1.

9. W. W. Rostow, *The Stages of Economic Growth* (Cambridge: Cambridge University Press, 1960).

10. Bauer, *Dissent on Development* (London: Weidenfeld and Nicolson, 1971).

11. L. Erik Kjonnerod, ed., *Evolving U.S. Strategy in Latin America* (Washington, DC: National Defense University Press, 1992).

12. O'Donnell et al., eds., *Transitions from Authoritarian Rule* (Baltimore, MD: Johns Hopkins University Press, 1985).

13. At the 2000 International Political Science Association Meeting in Quebec City, Canada.

14. Howard J. Wiarda, *Cracks in the Consensus: Debating the Democracy Agenda in U.S. Foreign Policy* (Westport, CT: Praeger/CSIS, 1997).

15. William Glade, *The Latin American Economies: A Study of Their Institutional Evolution* (New York: American Book, 1969).

16. The best survey data are from *Latinobarómetro*, as published in *Journal of Democracy*.

17. Howard J. Wiarda, *The Soul of Latin America: The Cultural and Political Tradition* (New Haven, CT: Yale University Press, 2001).

Chapter Fourteen

The Middle East and Islamic Society

Of all the world's areas, the Middle East has been the most disappointing in terms of economic and social development, democratization, and the growth of civil society. Note we said "most disappointing," not "least successful"; the latter dubious designation belongs to Sub-Saharan Africa. The Middle East is the most disappointing in the sense that, given its resources (mainly oil wealth), proximity to other wealthy areas (the European Union), population, and potential, it should be more developed than it is. It should be up there with East Asia or Latin America as an emerging, increasingly affluent, more democratic set of nations with strong civil society. But, in fact, most countries of the area lag behind. Their lack of success, most analysts agree, is a key reason for the anger, bitterness, frustration, anti-Americanism, and even the terrorism that we associate with the area.

Look at the figures in table 14.1. Almost all the countries are at the low end of the scale in terms of per capita income, life expectancy, literacy (especially for women), percent urbanized, and overall ranking. *Nowhere* in the region do we see any big emerging markets (BEMs) such as Argentina, Brazil, Chile, China, India, Indonesia, Mexico, South Korea, or Taiwan (note all these are from Latin America or Asia). Israel is the only developed country in the region; it is also the only non-Islamic country. *None* of the Middle Eastern countries—again excepting Israel—is a democracy or has a democratic, pluralist, participatory civil society.

The questions are why and whether the sad situation of democracy and underdevelopment in the Middle East is likely to change any time soon and can the United States and other outside powers (the EU) do anything to change the situation? Among the competing explanations are Islamic political culture, on the one hand: is there something in Islamic political culture that tends

Table 14.1. Middle East/Islamic Indicators of Socioeconomic Development

Country	GNP	GNP Per Capita	Life Expectancy Men	Life Expectancy Women	Literacy Men	Literacy Women	% Urban	GNP Capita Rank
Afghanistan	46.5	775 or less*	69	46	76	35	60	Low income / 101
Algeria**		1,550		72				Upper middle income / 127
Bahrain		2,996–9,265*		73	86			95
Egypt	87.5	1,400	65	68	65	42	45	
Iran	110.5	1,760	70	72	82	67	61	Lower middle income
Iraq		756–2,995*		59	54			
Israel		9,266 or more*	76	80	98	94	91	124
Jordan	7.0	1,500	69	73	94	83	74	
Kuwait		9,266 or more*	74	80	78	10	97	76
Lebanon	15.8	3,700	68	72	91	79	89	
Libya		2,996–9,265*		70	78			Upper middle income / 131
Morocco	33.8	1,200	65	69	60	34	55	
Oman		2,996–9,265*		73	69			Upper middle income / 159
Pakistan	64.0	470	61	63	58	29	36	
Qatar		9,226 or more*		74	80			High income / 59
Saudi Arabia	15.2	2,996–9,265*	70	74	83	64	85	139
Syria	19.9	970	67	72	87	58	54	91
Tunisia	20.9? 2,100	2,100	70	74	79	58	65	134
Turkey	186.3	2,900	67	72	93	75	74	
United Arab Emirates		9,266 or more*		75	75			High income / 197
Yemen	5.9	350	55	56	66	23	24	

*Estimates by World Bank.
**Following custom, the Islamic countries of North Africa are included in the "Middle East" category.

Source: World Bank, *World Development Report, 2000–2001.*

to discourage or retard democracy and civil society? On the other hand, is it the low level of socioeconomic development? If the latter is the key factor, then presumably once development occurs, democracy and civil society would also spring forth. A third possible explanation is the class structure and antiquated, two-class social system of the Middle East. And finally there are what are called "dependency factors": the Middle East's position on the periphery of the world's more affluent areas, its dependent position in the world economy, and its location as a center of Cold War conflicts, Arab–Israeli hatreds, terrorism, and internecine warfare.[1] As we go through the following discussion, we will seek to analyze these competing explanations and sort out which offers the more cogent explanation.

SOCIOECONOMIC DATA

The data presented in table 14.1 show that the countries of the Middle East, with a few exceptions, are among the world's poorest, least developed countries. They are not as poor as those in Africa, which often rank below the $1,000 per capita per year income level and have lower levels of life expectancy, literacy, and urbanization. But they are below the level of the emerging Latin American countries and *far below* the rapidly developing countries of East Asia and Central/Eastern Europe. Lebanon is the only (non-oil) country that approaches the $4,000 per person per year level (about one-tenth of the world's richest countries); most of the countries of the area are in the $1,000–$2,000 range. Bahrain, Oman, Qatar, Kuwait, Saudi Arabia, and the United Arab Emirates are anomalies: because they almost literally float on oil they have comparatively higher per capita income levels even while retaining antiquated social structures that are not conducive to democracy or democratic civil society. Turkey's relatively higher level of development is explainable by its proximity to wealthy Europe, its sizable resources and population, its internal modernization, and hence the growth of a more modern secular state and its increased integration into European markets and the EU. Nevertheless, Israel remains the only country in the area that is developed and fully democratic, and has a pluralist and democratic civil society.

We all understand that U.S. policy in the Middle East at the highest levels is preoccupied with Iraq, Iran, Afghanistan, and the Israel–Palestinian conflict. The war on terrorism has taken center stage as the main and seemingly virtually only issue in U.S.–Middle East policy. But we need to be careful here not to lose sight of other policy initiatives presently underway. While the president, his Cabinet, and the media are, quite understandably, focused on the Iraq War and the overall war on terrorism, at lower levels of policymaking, as the previous chapter on Latin America also indicated, a variety of other initiatives toward the Middle East are being developed. These include programs to stimulate the economies of the area and, most importantly for the purpose of this discussion, to assist in the development of civil society and democracy in the area. Democracy is viewed, in the long tradition of U.S. foreign policy, as an end in itself; but it is also a means to an end because democracies are not supposed to start wars or engage in terrorism.

The main question for us is, as the Middle East develops both economically and sociologically (becoming more urban, literate, and prosperous), will it also become more democratic and a stronger civil society? The answer is, probably yes. The fact is that some countries of the region (Algeria, Egypt, Jordan, Lebanon, Morocco, Pakistan, Tunisia), as they have developed, have also introduced some, often limited or sporadic democratic reforms and openings, such as greater respect for human rights, elections, a parliament. Generally, these are the more prosperous countries as well, so there *is* a correlation in the Middle East (as elsewhere) between development and democracy. But the correlation is not strong and there may be (as in several of the countries listed) reversions to more authoritarian practices.

No country of the area (except Israel, obviously a special case) has become fully democratic. Nor do we have a single country in the Middle East like South Korea or Taiwan, where economic development became so strong that it almost *forced* an existing, authoritarian regime to democratize. In addition, we have countries like Algeria, Iran, Iraq, Libya, Syria, and others where economic and social development failed to spawn democracy, instead producing only stronger authoritarian governments or Islamicist regimes hostile to democracy. Meanwhile, countries like Afghanistan and Yemen, both low (close to Haiti) in the per capita income rankings and also with almost no background or bases for democracy, have shown little progress either economically or politically.

ELEMENTS OF POLITICAL CULTURE

Islamic political culture has not historically been strongly supportive of democracy and civil society. Reinforced by and often themselves manipulating the political culture for their own private political or personal ends, governments of the region have not usually been very tolerant either of opposition political movements or of a pluralistic associational life outside of their control. They have moved to quash both opposition political parties as well as interest organizations that they could not dominate. Within the region only Israel has consistently maintained its democratic character; Turkey has moved in that direction; Pakistan has practiced democracy sporadically, while in Jordan and Kuwait some limited steps have been taken to open up the political system even while keeping the opposition under tight control. Intimidation often coupled, in the best of circumstances, with co-optation has been the main system of control.

Neither the Koran nor the Shariah (holy law) offers much justification for democracy or civil society. Instead, there is abundant rationalization of top-down, authoritarian, male-dominated decision making. Just as Allah is God and all things are subordinated to that fundamental principle, so the family, the essential and basic unit of society, is headed by the father/husband, the tribe or clan is similarly dominated by authoritarian leadership, and political authority at the state level is also concentrated, centralized, and top-down. *Nowhere* is there grounds for grassroots participation from below, although the leader, whether in the family, the tribe, or the nation-state, is supposed to consult broadly with society.[2]

For example, in Saudi Arabia, King Fahd would regularly pack his tent, assemble his entourage, and head out into the desert to consult with the bedouin chiefs. He would also find time to take petitions from humble people. If possible, he or his staff would take care of the problem on the spot; if that was not possible, the issue would be dealt with by appropriate government agencies immediately upon returning to Riyadh. This is obviously not Western-style democracy, but it does provide for some degree of consultation and participation. Petitions may be granted but the manner and system of doing so serves to reinforce the clientelistic, hierarchical, and authoritarian elements in the society.

It is clear that to the extent the Koran and Shariah talk about governance at all (not a great deal), they tend to justify authoritarian rule. It is also clear that authoritarian leaders have learned to take advantage of these holy injunctions for their own advantage. Between the God-given justifications for authoritarianism, on the one hand, and its long practice, on the other, authoritarianism is by now so deeply imprinted in Islamic society that it is part of the political culture, the normal way of doing things. And once it is *that* deeply a part of the political culture, the harder—almost impossible—it becomes to change. On the other hand, as Anwar Syed points out, *nowhere* in the Koran or Shariah is there any express prohibition against democracy.[3] That fact opens the possibility for democracy and elections in the future as we have seen even in such Muslim cleric-dominated societies as Iran where more-or-less democratic elections have recently been held.

Much the same applies to human rights. Human rights in the Western sense have not often been rigorously observed in Islamic society; on the contrary, the Muslim countries are known—and condemned—for the excesses (stoning to

death), cruelty (cutting off the hands of robbers), and arbitrariness of their criminal law, itself shaped powerfully by Islamic precepts. The religious-cultural-
historical setting has not been conducive to democracy and human rights.

Most regimes in the area have not been supportive of democracy, have seldom opened up to democracy, and have been suspicious of civil society. What
civil society exists has been weak and frail. Governments have sought to regulate it closely, control it, and keep it from posing potentially a threat to the
regime in power. These regimes, in the Middle East as well as in East Asia
and Latin America, have been almost inherently top-down and corporatist.

The civil society that is present has been all but exclusively limited to the
male portion of the population. Women have been subordinated: in the home
and in family affairs, they are influential, but not in the public sphere where
women's groups are largely nonexistent or very small in numbers. Moreover,
there is here as elsewhere in the Third World a class bias in civil society; most
civil society groups are composed of upper- and upper-middle-class elements.
In contrast, labor, peasant, bedouin, and urban slum-dweller groups are seldom organized, or, if they are, they are tightly regulated by the government.

Clientelism and patrimonialism tend to pervade all levels of society, bureaucracy, and relations with state agencies. Clientelism, with its system of
supplicants, on the one hand, and patrons, on the other, is almost everywhere
inherently unequal and undemocratic. Everyone in one way or another is tied
into this top-to-bottom clientelistic system. Whom you know is more important than what you know. To those who do have the right connections, patronage may take the form of jobs, favors, special access, government contracts, whole programs, and even government ministries doled out to the
"deserving" in return for loyalty and support. As society becomes more organized and differentiated, the clientelistic system is extended to whole
groups in society (tribes, regions, religious factions) and no longer just individuals. Once again we are back to corporatism, for when a group's relations
with the state are grounded on a clientelistic, patronage-based, subordinate–superordinate basis, that is a formula for corporatism.

Some have argued that civil society in the Middle East should be seen as
not less developed than that of the West but only *different* from it, and we can
accept that argument—up to a point. Historically, civil society in the Middle
East has consisted of three main groups: the clergy (*ulema*), tribes and tribal
confederations, and traditional merchants (*bazaris*).[4] By Islamic law as well
as precedence, the king or ruler is obliged to consult with these groups, but
(1) this is an exceedingly narrow range of interests, rather like the three European estates (clergy, nobles, and common) of the Middle Ages; (2) it does
not take into consideration new and modernizing groups such as labor unions,
professionals, or women; and (3) such a system of personalistic, clientelistic

consultation provides little training or experience in the functioning of a modernizing democracy.

As civil society *has* begun to emerge in the Middle East, moreover, it has taken a form that most Westerners are quite uncomfortable with. For example, in a number of countries the claim has been put forward—often by military officers and their not-very-democratic civilian supporters—that the armed forces, which are at or near the surface of power in most Middle Eastern countries, should be considered a part—maybe *the* part—of civil society. A second candidate for civil society status is the family, meaning the extended family and usually implying (although seldom said publicly) the ruling family and its various hangers-on, clientelistic relations, sycophants, and bureaucratic interests. A third group is the tribe or clan, which in some writings is being elevated to the status of a modernizing agency because it delivers some, limited public goods and services; but, as in Africa, it is sometimes hard for objective observers to think of "tribe" as a modern, public-interested, civil society group.

But the most troubling debate revolves around the issue of Islamic fundamentalism. Many Islamic societies have been undergoing a religious revival of late, secularism that was once associated with modernization appears to be in decline, and the Islamic fundamentalist movements are being touted as the Muslim world's civil society, the Islamic answer and counterpart to the hated liberalism, secularism, and supposed moral degeneracy of the West. Islamic fundamentalism in Afghanistan, Iran, Algeria, Pakistan, and increasingly Egypt and other countries as well has now taken the form of a mass movement, mobilized millions of followers, toppled or threatened to topple a score of governments, and promised to install a strict Islamic regime hostile to other forms of worship, free speech, and Western liberal ideals. Islamic fundamentalism seems to fit almost all our definitions of civil society, yet in its illiberal views it is unacceptable to most Westerners. In this sense it is rather like the Ku Klux Klan, various American militias, or the German skinheads: undoubtedly a part of civil society but not exactly what most of us have in mind by that term and probably not a good basis for democracy. This case (and that of tribalism in Africa or caste associations in India) provides one of the acid tests of our cultural relativism and commitment to civil society in whatever form. Can we accept a form of civil society that most of us abhor, or does our adherence to Western values in this case take precedence over our commitment to civil society?[5]

The literature on Islamic fundamentalism, to say nothing of a prudent foreign policy, suggests that some further distinctions need to be made. We may, for example, accept the fact that an Islamic revival is occurring in the Muslim world without necessarily welcoming all the movements spawned by it. There are, after all, a variety of Islamic voices on these themes and not just a single monolithic voice. Specifically, we need to distinguish between Islamic fundamentalist movements that are peaceful, show promise of moderation and democracy, and live within constitutional limits, and those that employ terrorism and are violently opposed to Western liberal values. Clearly we can accommodate the former while rejecting the latter. For if in the United States and other Western societies we accept the idea that religious movements, churches, synagogues, and now mosques form one part of civil society, we should also be prepared to accept the idea of Islamic fundamentalism as a part of civil society in the Middle East.

It is useful, by making these distinctions, to remain hopeful both about Islamic democracy and the possibilities of a viable, homegrown civil society to undergird it, which also will undermine terrorist appeals. But we also need to be realistic: some of this hope may be grasping at straws. For the overwhelming weight of Islamic culture and history, so far, has not been supportive of democracy or of a liberal, pluralist civil society. Rather, virtually the whole of Islamic history and culture has been authoritarian, top-down, and elitist. Some favored groups are advantaged while others are left behind. Social and political structures tend to be feudal and sultanic rather than modern and democratic. The system of clientelism and patron–client relations that reaches from the lowest to highest levels is inherently undemocratic, and as the Middle East has gradually modernized and developed over the years, that clientelistic system has also modernized and become more institutionalized rather than being displaced by democracy. The weight of history, culture, and religion in the Middle East is therefore extremely heavy, maybe even weightier than in East Asia and Latin America, and *almost none* of this heavy hand is propitious for democracy or democratic civil society.[6]

SOCIOECONOMIC CHANGE AND CHANGING STATE–SOCIETY RELATIONS

The presumption is that once socioeconomic change in the developing world begins in earnest, it tends to give rise to a more diverse and broader-based civil society that in turn begets democracy. Economic growth, the argument runs, stimulates social differentiation and thereby vast social changes — a new business class, a middle class, organized labor, women's groups, others — that produce pluralism and thereby make democracy a necessity and not just a luxury. For only democracy and democratic pluralism, we now know, not Marxism-Leninism or authoritarianism, have the capacity and flexibility to handle the social changes brought on by modernization. Certainly that has been the pattern in South Korea and Taiwan, and increasingly in other Asian societies and Latin America as well: economic growth that stimulates social change that in turn makes democracy a pragmatic necessity.

But not in the Middle East. Or, to be more precise, not so much in the Middle East. There, not enough economic growth has occurred to trigger such vast social changes—the first step in the process of democratization. Recall those per capita income numbers from table 14.1: the overwhelming majority of the countries of the area remain very poor. Only a handful—Egypt, Lebanon, Turkey—have had the kind of sustained economic growth to stimulate the vast social changes talked of here, giving rise to eventual societal pluralism and democracy. And those countries that do have a higher per capita income—Kuwait, Oman, Qatar, Saudi Arabia, the United Arab Emirates—have such a distorted, even artificial-growth pattern under their feudal sultanates, most of which are probably doomed in long-range terms, that the normal, expected process of social differentiation and change has not occurred. Whether because of too little, too slow, or distorted growth, the Middle East has not seen yet the vast social transformation stimulating political pluralism and democratization that we saw in East Asia and Latin America.

Moreover, when they do begin to modernize socially, the form of civil society that emerges is generally corporatist rather than liberal and pluralist.[7] Egypt is perhaps the leading case study. Egypt is one of the most developed and most Westernized countries in the Middle East; it has also been the recipient of more U.S. foreign aid, aimed at stabilizing and democratizing it, than any other country in the world except Israel. Yet despite all this developmental assistance, which has now gone on for over three decades, Egypt remains an authoritarian state and not a liberal one, corporately organized, and increasingly a police state.[8]

As Egypt (and other Middle East states) began to modernize, tribal, bedouin, and other traditional civil society groups began to lose influence. In their place came new urban groups: associations of journalists, lawyers, physicians, engineers. While the state has legally recognized and legitimized *some* of these newer groups, allowing them to play a limited social and political role, it has failed to recognize others and even repressed them. In addition, most of these groups are politically innocuous, reluctant to challenge or "take on" the state and its leaders, and both unwilling and incapable of mounting any opposition against the state for fear of losing the few corporatist privileges granted them. And, because of the corporatist system of organization, the groups do not compete with each other horizontally as in the pluralist model but instead are organized vertically, which weakens their power, prevents alliances from forming, and ties them to a relationship of dependence to the state. As Kamrava and Mora conclude, the Middle Eastern states "have been able to maintain those corporatist arrangements through which they keep key social groups beholden to them."[9] So far at least, as modernization has proceeded, the Middle Eastern state has been able to keep its corporatist controls in place, even expanding them to encompass new groups, but seldom moving toward liberalism, let alone being overwhelmed by it.

A key actor in all these arrangements is organized labor. Labor and industrial relations have long been the anvil on which the shape and structure of the modern state have been pounded out.[10] But as an organized labor movement began to emerge in Egypt and other of the more developed Middle East countries, it was tied to the state and controlled by the state in corporatist rather than liberal-pluralist fashion. Organized labor was duly recognized by the state and received some benefits from it, but it also became a client (one among many) of the state and was carefully circumscribed in its activities. It was patronized by the state, kept subservient, sometimes roughed up by security forces, prevented from allying itself with other change-oriented groups, and severely limited (even outlawed at times) in its political activities. There are different interpretations of this phenomena: Louis Cantori emphasizes the corporatist control mechanisms,[11] while Marsha Pripstein Posusney argues that organized labor has been clever in achieving some limited benefits for its members even within these corporatist arrangements.[12] But everyone agrees that state–society relations in the Middle East are essentially corporatist ones rather than liberal-pluralist.

While this is the established and still ongoing structure of Egyptian state–society relations, a newer phenomenon (in the last thirty years) has been the rise of political Islam as an alternative form of civil society.[13] Egypt's grassroots Islamic movement, which is made up of lawyers, doctors, students, mullahs, and ordinary men and women, has grown enormously in recent years, penetrated the state, and increasingly challenged the government. One needs to distinguish between the armed revolutionary groups seeking to impose Islamic rule by force and which have gotten most of the publicity, and the "quieter," popular Islamic movements that are broad-based within the society. Particularly in the last decade the quieter Islamic activists have, mainly through democratic elections, taken over the key professional unions that represent hundreds of thousands of Egypt's educated, middle-class citizens. The Islamic groups have increasingly captured Egypt's corporately organized civil society groups, but they refuse to play by the old rules and are increasingly challenging the state itself and the Hosni Mubarak regime, which the United States has long supported as a bastion of stability and moderation in the region.

One conclusion that could be drawn from this is the need, for analytic and policy purposes, to distinguish between radical Islam, which is implacably hostile to the West, and more moderate Islam with which we can probably have good relations. A second conclusion is that the old corporatist system of controls on civil society is being increasingly challenged and transformed, at least in the more advanced countries. But still a third conclusion is that Egyptian (and other Middle Eastern) civil society is moving from corporatism to Islamicism, and that neither is particularly liberal-democratic or in accord with the Western idea of civil society. Nor is that likely to be good for U.S. policy.

As the Islamic challenge to the state has grown, the state itself has tended to become more repressive. The pattern sounds like that of Latin America in the 1960s and 1970s when a wave of military authoritarianism swept the area. Egypt has become more and more a police state. Mubarak stays in power in large part because the army and police keep him there. The National Assembly is largely a rubberstamp and elections are manipulated. The press is censored and the mass media controlled by the Information Ministry. Civil society and opposition groups are increasingly repressed. As the Islamist groups grow in strength, so does the government's willingness to violate civil liberties and use force against them. Democracy is increasingly seen as a sham; civil society is either being eliminated, suppressed, or taking intolerant directions.[14]

In looking at Egypt and the Middle East, one is reminded more of South Africa and the "bureaucratic authoritarianism" of Latin America of past decades than of recent successful civil society development and democratization. First, civil society is more often in decline than it is growing. Second, when it does emerge, it takes a form—corporatist, now increasingly Islamicist—that is not liberal, pluralist, tolerant, or democratic. Third, the state is inclined to use repression against it; meanwhile, the state itself may be disintegrating. It is not a pretty picture for those who favor democratic pluralism and a tolerant, autonomous, freewheeling, dynamic, competitive civil society. Nor is it hopeful from a U.S. policy viewpoint.

THE INTERNATIONAL CONTEXT

For the last quarter century, and particularly since President Anwar Sadat's 1979 decision to support the Middle Eastern peace process, Egypt has been the recipient of a mammoth international—mainly U.S.—foreign aid program. Now totaling over $52 billion, the amount of foreign aid given to Egypt is second only to that given Israel. The aid is mainly designed to ensure that peace endures at least from the Egyptian side and to demonstrate to the Egyptian public that avoiding war would improve their lives.[15]

The assistance is multipurpose, with much of it going to military equipment and training. On the civilian side, the aid has gone to a variety of developmental panaceas that have come and gone over the years, including family planning, basic human needs, sustainable development, and, most recently, civil society and democratization. Overall, one could say that the project has been successful in terms of its basic objectives: Egypt has not gone to war with Israel in recent decades; Mubarak has been a generally moderate voice in the Middle East; and Egyptian per capita income has slowly inched up from about $1,000 per year to approximately $1,500.

U.S. AID has done numerous long-term development projects in Egypt: schools, roads, agriculture, water resources, even mosques. By common consensus and keeping in mind the long term, a number of these programs have been successful. U.S. assistance has also sought to improve the performance of Egypt's governmental institutions: the courts, customs, tax collection, bureaucratic performance. U.S. AID has tried to instigate privatization, anticorruption, and state reduction programs, but the verdict is not yet in on most of these latter programs.

The aid program has also begun to focus on developing Egyptian civil society and democracy, but in this area the results have been even less successful. Without here going into the details of these programs, the "big picture" offers abundant reasons to be skeptical. First, Egypt is an authoritarian regime so that programs to improve elections, build political parties, and develop genuinely competitive democracy are seldom looked on with favor by the government. Second, when there is a clash between the security (Middle East peace) and the democratizing aspects of U.S. policy, the security argument always trumps all others, often to the detriment of democracy. Third, as civil society began to emerge in Egypt, it was usually co-opted by the government and organized in a corporatist fashion rather than a liberal-pluralist one. And fourth, if and when the foreign aid programs supported oppositionist "civil society" groups as a way, presumably, of building or strengthening democracy and pluralism, it ran up against the uncomfortable fact that most of these groups were Islamicist incorporating varying degrees of fundamentalism—not exactly what the United States wants to support. Moreover, a double negative whammy: supporting oppositionist groups might undermine the overall policy goal of securing a stable, peaceful Egypt; it might also strengthen the fundamentalists whose commitment to democracy is suspect and to whose policy goals many Americans object.

The policy mantra from most U.S. officials, journalists, and scholars who know the Middle East is as follows: (1) rising Islamic fundamentalism is a fact of life; (2) we need to deal with that fact realistically and not just ignore it or wish it away; (3) not all fundamentalist movements are the same nor are all of them anti-American and a threat to us; and (4) the United States therefore needs to get on the side of history by distinguishing between the violent and anti-American Islamic fundamentalist groups who want to create an Iran-like theocratic state or who support Osama bin Laden–like terrorism, *and* the more moderate, usually middle-class business and professional groups whose aims of religious revival and national modernization we can live with and even support.

But such a policy is fraught with difficulties: first, most Americans — including many public officials — do not acknowledge or recognize such a sharp distinction between the various Islamic fundamentalist groups; second, it runs up against the dilemma that U.S. policy in the Middle East is dominated by strategic considerations (peace, oil, Israel, stability) and less so by a democracy/civil society agenda; third, Congress and the U.S. government generally have trouble dealing with admittedly authoritarian regimes that are not very democratic and often violate human rights. Fourth, the United States tends not to understand well or empathize with Islamic societies and peoples, which may be enough to discourage major new initiatives in the area. Fifth, in a context of scarce foreign aid resources or attention to foreign affairs, attention to Middle Eastern civil society is not high on the list of priorities; and sixth, many Americans have concluded that Islam and democracy/civil society are incompatible so we should not put many resources into a hopeless situation.

CONCLUSION

There is considerable attention and ferment in the Middle East with regard to the idea of democracy and the concept of civil society. For one thing, the traditional civil society of the tribe, the clan, the bazaar is beginning to give way — to be replaced or supplemented by what? For another, new groups centered around new concepts such as the environment or human rights are beginning to organize. Third, new social movements of workers, women, and students are mobilizing in the Middle East, groups that have for a long time been organized under statist-corporatist auspices but are now pointing toward greater autonomy. Fourth, there is the phenomenon of Islamic fundamentalism and its place in "civil society"; alternatively, how does this new phenomenon of civil society fit or apply in an Islamic setting? And fifth, civil society has by now acquired a certain international cachet that makes it worthy of attention in this area not heretofore known for the strength of civil society. In his 2004 inaugural address and State of the Union speech, President George W. Bush spoke movingly of the need for democracy in the Middle East.

But in the Middle East the precise meaning and implications of democracy and civil society are still ambiguous. In Iran, for example, civil society has come to mean the "rule of law" and the "rule of the people"—not necessarily pluralism or countervailing interest groups as in the Western conception. In other countries "civil society" is used to advocate honest elections, greater power to the parliament, regional or ethnic group autonomy from the central state, or as a cover for oppositionist politics, including terrorism. Civil society groups in many of the area's autocratic regimes are often limited to such issues as the environment—issues that can be dealt with without (unlike opposition or human rights groups) threatening the regime in power. Some of my interviewees in the Middle East now use the term *GNGOs* (government-nongovernmental organizations), a contradiction in terms to American civil society advocates whose definition requires that civil society groups *not* be governmental, and which sounds like a new, more socially acceptable term for corporatism. In addition, in a variety of countries, opposition groups, including Islamic fundamentalists, are now organizing as "study groups" or "civic movements," using the umbrella of "civil society," to disguise or "front" their potentially destabilizing political activities. The concept of "civil society" by now carries so many meanings, gradations, and implications that the concept may have lost all precise meaning.

That many of these more-or-less autonomous organizations exist is certain; so is the fact of considerable attention to and ferment regarding civil society. Far less certain, however, is the viability of all these groups and their commitment to democracy. For one thing, civil society in the Middle East is still weak by Western standards. Second, it is often used and abused by regimes in power to put in place corporatist or GNGO systems that have little or no autonomy from the state. Third, as civil society has emerged, the strongest groups have frequently been those based on Islamic fundamentalism—not in accord with most Americans' conception of civil society. And fourth, there seems to be no correlation, so far, between the rise of civil society (by whatever definition) in the Middle East *and* democracy. Indeed, as Kamrava and Mora conclude, "if the latest democratic wave has been on a global march since the early to mid-1980s, it has either completely skipped the Middle East or has yet to make its introduction to the area."[16] So can democracy and civil society bring peace to the Middle East? The verdict is not yet in but the early signs are not encouraging, and it will be a very, *very* long road to travel.

NOTES

1. The issues are posed in *The Civil Society Debate in Middle Eastern Studies*, Near East Center Colloquium Series, with contributions by James Gelvin, Augustus Norton, Roger Gwen, and Diane Singerman.

2. Anwar H. Syed, "Islamic Models of Development," in Howard J. Wiarda, ed., *Non-Western Theories of Development* (Fort Worth, TX: Harcourt Brace, 1999), 99–115.

3. Anwar H. Syed, "Democracy and Islam: Are They Compatible?" in Howard J. Wiarda, ed., *Comparative Democracy and Democratization* (Fort Worth, TX: Harcourt Brace, 2001), 127–43.

4. Mahmood Monshipouri, "Islamism, Civil Society, and the Democracy Conundrum," *Muslim World* 57 (January 1997): 54–66.

5. Debbie Lovatt, "Islam, Secularism, and Civil Society," *World Today* (August/September 1997), 226–28.

6. Mehran Kamrava and Frank O. Mora, "Civil Society and Democratization in Comparative Perspective: Latin America and the Middle East," *Third World Quarterly* 19, 5 (1998): 893–915.

7. Louis Cantori, "Civil Society, Liberalism, and the Corporatist Alternative in the Middle East," *Middle East Studies Association Bulletin* 31, 1 (1997): 34–41.

8. Robert Bianchi, *Unruly Corporatism: Associational Life in Twentieth Century Egypt* (New York: Oxford University Press, 1989).

9. Kamrava and Mora, "Civil Society and Democratization," 894–95.

10. David Collier and Ruth Berins Collier, *Shaping the Political Arena: Critical Junctures, the Labor Movement, and Regime Dynamics in Latin America* (Princeton, NJ: Princeton University Press, 1991). This book has implications beyond its geographic focus.

11. Cantori, "Civil Society," 38.

12. Marsha Pripstein Posusney, *Labor and the State in Egypt* (New York: Columbia University Press, 1997).

13. Geneive Abdo, "How Moderate Islam Is Transforming Egypt," *Washington Post* (November 5, 2000), B-5; Diane Singerman, "Civil Society in the Shadow of the Egyptian State: The Role of Informal Networks in the Construction of Public Life," in Norton, *The Civil Society Debate*.

14. Thomas Cromwell, "Egypt Is a Police State," *International Herald Tribune* (May 29, 2001), 9.

15. *Washington Post* (December 26, 2000), A-1.

16. Kamrava and Mora, "Civil Society and Democratization," 893.

Conclusion

We have argued in this book that American foreign policy is in deep trouble. That the American political system is not working, or working effectively or as intended. That since the country is deeply divided, so are the parties, Congress, the executive branch departments, and the government as a whole. Polarization has set in. So have gridlock and paralysis, and not just on a short-term basis but long-term as well. Perhaps gridlock, paralysis, and ineffectiveness have become permanent features of the American system. But if that is so, how can the United States conduct a rational, coherent, effective foreign policy? The answer: only occasionally and with great difficulty.

But maybe things are not as bad as they sometimes seem. How else to explain that we still conduct a reasonable and enlightened foreign policy toward China, Russia, Japan, and other areas and countries as well? Is it crisis—9/11 and the war on terrorism—that forces us to focus and put aside for now at least some of the partisan and ideological battles? Is it possible that, even with all our strife and disagreements, the system still *does* work in the end? Have we been overly pessimistic? It is a subject to which we return later in this chapter.

SUMMARY AND ASSESSMENT

In part I of the book we looked at the main institutions of American foreign policymaking. Chapter 1 spelled out the paralysis and gridlock themes, showing how public opinion, the press, the parties, Congress, and other agencies are agents of, reflect, and help perpetuate the deep divisions in the American system. Chapter 2 analyzed the traditional sources of U.S. foreign policy, alternating between the global environment of issues and pressures in which U.S. foreign policy operates and the domestic institutional arrangements for dealing with these issues as they evolved after the Cold War and after 9/11. Chapter 3 focused on such key institutions as Congress, the presidency, the National Security Council, and the Defense, State, and other departments in the making of American foreign policy.

In chapter 4, on think tanks and foreign policy, we analyzed the role of these institutions as new and major actors in the political process and showed how they both reflect and reinforce the country's partisan and ideological divisions. Chapter 5, on Washington social life, has its light sides, but it also showed the degree to which self-interest, self-aggrandizement, and looking out for number one (oneself) has come to dominate politics and politicians in the nation's capital, rather than a broader focus on what's good for the country as a whole.

In part II of the book we looked at the hot global issues on the plates of U.S. policy makers. Chapter 6 dealt explicitly with the ethnocentrism issue: why it is so hard for the United States to understand and come to grips with other countries in their own terms and languages? This chapter sets the tone and provides the framework for the other chapters in this section. Thus, chapter 7 focused on U.S. efforts to export and spread democracy abroad. Chapter 8 did much the same for the issue of human rights. In chapter 9 we analyzed the ongoing dilemma of what to do about countries and "tyrannies" that are friendly to us but nevertheless are not democracies and have terrible human rights problems. Chapter 10 wrestled with the issue of globalization, what this hot topic does and means, and whether its critics are correct or not.

In part III of the book we tested out a number of these themes and issues in specific regional areas that are of special importance to the United States. Chapter 11 focused on the difficulties of transferring American ideas of civil society into the Asian context. Chapter 12 concentrated on the problems of development and democratization in Sub-Saharan Africa. In chapter 13, although Latin America is the main subject, the topic raised—Is the United States after 9/11 paying too little attention to other parts of the world ("benign neglect"?)—has relevance for other areas as well. Finally, in chapter 14 on the Islamic Middle East, we explore the difficulties of encouraging economic, social, and political reform in that area—not only for its own sake but because we assume such reform will also undermine the potential for violence and future terrorist attacks.

WHAT'S WRONG WITH
AMERICAN FOREIGN POLICYMAKING

There are many problems with American foreign policy. So is the system working? We leave it to our readers to make these critical judgments.

We start at the most general level. First, public opinion in the United States is deeply and bitterly divided, as shown in the 2000 and 2004 election campaigns. The country is almost exactly evenly divided between "Red" and "Blue" states. These divides reflect the bitter cultural wars that have been underway in the United States in the last two decades: not just Republican versus Democrat but also religious versus secular, elite versus mass, college educated versus noncollege educated, coastal areas versus the interior, North versus South, liberal versus conservative. If the country is that deeply divided, we should not expect our foreign policy to be any less so.

Second, let us look at some of our main institutions. The two main political parties, Republican and Democrat, have both become more ideological, more radical, more extreme. Both conservative Democrats and liberal Republicans have been forced to the margins. The dialogue has become nastier and more polarized. And all this is reflected in the U.S. Congress where the two parties barely speak to each other anymore, where the divisions in the country-at-large are reflected and amplified, and where the old idea of an agreed-upon, unified, bipartisan foreign policy has gone by the boards.

The interest group struggle similarly reflects and reinforces these divisions. Big labor and big business are at severe odds over immigration, trade agreements, globalization, and other major issues. Virtually all ethnic and racial groups in the United States have mobilized their constituencies for action in support of their individual countries or issues; identity politics, which frequently pits one ethnicity against another, is on the rise. At the same time, a host of new interest groups has mobilized around a variety of new issues—human rights, global warming, the Kyoto Treaty, anti–land mines, the international criminal court, antiglobalization, peace and reconciliation, nation building, genocide, conflict resolution, and many others. The mobilization of some groups on one side of these various conflicts seems to galvanize equally vociferous groups on the other, leading to rancorous debate and polarization between the extremes. The middle ground seems to be giving way.

The media, no longer just a neutral reporter of the news, reflects and reinforces by its coverage and its either-or talk shows the deep divisions, the shouting match that presently is American politics. Similarly with the think tanks: these are not just scholarly, academic, neutral research institutions; instead, they have also become highly partisan agencies, tied to the political parties and staking out sharply polarized positions on both domestic and foreign policy issues. In other words, those agencies that we count on to provide neutral, balanced, nonpartisan views—the media, think tanks, perhaps universities as well—have themselves become partisan and no more to be trusted than other, more overtly partisan bodies.

Within the government there are also deep divisions, which we frequently call "bureaucratic politics." The State Department can barely work with the

Defense Department (and vice versa) and both of them despise the CIA. All three of them resent the FBI and the Department of Homeland Security as naive, inexperienced newcomers to the foreign policy arena. At the same time, as the U.S. economy has become internationalized and globalized, such agencies as the Treasury and Commerce Departments and the Office of the Trade Representative (OTR) have become more influential in foreign policy, taking power away from the traditional foreign policy agencies.

Similarly, as such issues as drugs (Drug Enforcement Agency—DEA), immigration (Immigration and Naturalization Service—INS), global warming (Environmental Protection Agency—EPA), and terrorism (CIA, FBI, Homeland Security, Border Patrol, etc.) have become hot topics, the agencies responsible for these issues have also gained prominence and greater budgets, often at the expense of the more traditional agencies. This leads, again, to intense bureaucratic rivalry for money and influence among the departments involved: on drug issues, for instance, no less than forty-three agencies of the U.S. government are involved; on terrorism, even more. You can't have a coherent policy when that many competing, self-interested government agencies are involved.

Meanwhile, at the apex of the foreign policy, decision-making system, within the White House and the Oval Office itself, things are not much better. Almost none of our recent presidents (Ford, Carter, Reagan, Clinton, George W. Bush; George H. W. Bush was the sole exception) had any foreign policy experience before occupying the presidency. All of them had to learn on the job, a risky proposition in these dangerous times. Meanwhile, their personal foreign policy staffs, at the National Security Council, were more and more chosen for their personal and political loyalty to the president, and as representatives of the various feuding departments as discussed above, rather than for their foreign policy expertise.

It is not a pretty picture. It is a picture of a foreign policy system based increasingly on partisanship, on bureaucratic rivalries, on narrow ethnic considerations, on special interests having their way, rather than on competence and the bipartisan pursuit of U.S. *national* interests. It is a terribly flawed system that will not be fixed soon or easily.

THE ETHNOCENTRISM PROBLEM

The other main theme of this volume is ethnocentrism. Ethnocentrism refers to the inability of the United States to accept and understand other countries on their own terms, or even in their own languages. We are constantly trying to export, missionary-style, our institutions, including *our* concepts of democracy, human rights, civil society, and free markets to other countries. Moreover, we tend to do this with a condescending, patronizing, superior attitude that frequently results in our riding roughshod over other countries' institutions and cultures. This U.S. attitude is deeply resented by other countries; perhaps even worse, it seems to undermine other countries' institutions often before newer, more modern, or more democratic ones are created, thus helping to foster the very instability that our policies seek to prevent.

We argued that such ethnocentrism is deeply rooted in the American culture and people. We really believe ours are the best and most successful institutions and that other countries should follow our example, both politically (democracy) and economically (free markets). At a fundamental level, we said, such attitudes are embedded in our basic liberal arts education, in our History of Western Civilization courses, and in the way our entire educational system is structured.

With the rise of diversity and multiculturalism programs in our universities and our newfound attention to non-Western areas, however, some of these attitudes have begun to change. But among high policy makers it remains the case that only the Western model of democracy, human rights, and so forth is followed. To combat this pervasive ethnocentrism we advocated the study of Latin American, African, Asian, and Islamic alternative models of development, but to date it is the Western paradigm—whether on such issues as agrarian reform, civil society, government reform, economic reform—that is the main and still virtually only one used.

Our immediate foreign policy concerns are in combating the war on terrorism and dealing with problems in the Middle East. But that very focus serves to strengthen the argument advanced here. For how can we deal with terrorism and the problems of the Middle East if so few Americans, even at high policy levels, speak Arabic, have any experience of living in the Islamic world, and harbor such strongly negative views of Islamic culture and civilization? The answer, of course, is that we can't. That is why it is heartening to now suddenly find so many young Americans studying Arabic and taking courses on the Islamic world. But remember that is only the tip of an even bigger iceberg: we are equally ignorant, or almost so, about Africa, Asia, Latin America, even Europe from which so many of our ancestors came.

ONWARD

Much of the argument in this book has centered on the problems of American foreign policy. These include excessive partisanship, division, culture wars, conflict at various levels, bitter rivalries—to the extent of the system becoming dysfunctional. We even raised the question of whether the American system was still working effectively, as it was intended, and as most of us learned in our early social studies courses.

But if the system is not working, does that mean that the radical protesters are correct after all? That we must scrap our system entirely? That we must tear it down and begin all over again? That we must replace it with something else?

It is easy and perhaps tempting to answer "yes" to those questions. The system really is not working well; whether that means it is broken and needs to be completely replaced, however, is still another matter. Although, even for those who consider themselves moderates and middle-of-the-roaders, the point when we might decide to scrap the system seems to be coming closer.

Nevertheless, three arguments seem at this stage still persuasive. First, what would be the alternative? We might all agree that the American political system is or is becoming dysfunctional, but what other system would we substitute for it? The American system is not working well, but the alternative may be even worse. One is reminded of former British prime minister Winston Churchill's famous quip that "democracy is the worst form of government except for all the others." So before we scrap the political system that we have, we had better be certain that what might follow would not be even less attractive and workable than what is currently in place.

Second, even with all our problems as a country, we still manage to be *the* leader in the world, to enjoy an affluent and free lifestyle, and to maintain quite good relations with most countries in the world. Here we have in mind Japan, India, Russia, Eastern Europe, Canada, Great Britain, Australia, and numerous others. More than that, even with those countries with whom we may disagree, or have problems, or fail to understand—Western Europe, Latin America, parts of Asia, the Middle East, Africa—we nevertheless learn from our mistakes, try to adjust, and seek to improve our relations. For even if our democracy has flaws and even severe ones as argued here, it is *only* democracies like ours that have the capacity to adjust, change course, and move on. Such changes in a representative democracy take time but they do occur.

Finally, we find encouragement in the fact that our ethnocentrism is decreasing and our empathy with and understanding of other countries and peoples are increasing. Surely we are a much more diverse, multicultural, and pluralist country now than we were thirty years ago. Our universities now teach non-Western areas to an extent that was not present before; in addition to our Western Civ courses and the older, exclusively Western-oriented political theory canon, we now teach Confucian theory; Hindu and Buddhist theory; and even Islamic law, culture, and theory. We may have arrived late to the subject but the fact so many of our students are now studying Arabic, Chinese, Swahili, or Aymará has to be heartening.

Maybe not all is lost after all. Maybe, by fits and starts, often incompletely, and sometimes glacially, the system does respond and does change. But it is becoming a close call.

Suggested Readings

Adebajo, Adekeye. "Africa and America in an Age of Terror." *Journal of Asian and African Studies* 38, nos. 2–3 (2003): 175–91.

Allison, Graham. *Essence of Decision: Explaining the Cuban Missile Crisis.* Boston: Little, Brown, 1971.

——, and Samantha Power, *Realizing Human Rights: Moving from Inspiration to Impact.* New York: St. Martin's, 2003.

Asmus, Ronald. "Rebuilding the Transatlantic Alliance." *Foreign Affairs* 82, 5 (Sept./Oct. 2003).

Avineri, Shlomo, ed. *Karl Marx on Colonialism and Modernization.* Garden City, NY: Anchor, 1969.

Bauer, Peter. *Dissent on Development.* London: Weidenfeld and Nicolson, 1971.

Binnendijk, Hans, ed. *Authoritarian Regimes in Transition.* Washington, DC: U.S. Department of State, 1987.

Bratton, Michael, and Nicolas van de Welle. *Democratic Experiments in Africa: Regime Transitions in Comparative Perspective.* Cambridge: Cambridge University Press, 1997.

Chazan, Naomi, et al. *Politics and Society in Contemporary Africa.* Boulder, CO: Rienner, 1992.

Dallek, Robert. *American Style of Foreign Policy: Cultural Politics and Foreign Policy.* New York: Knopf, 1983.

Destler, I. M., Leslie H. Gelb, and Anthony Lake. *Our Own Worst Enemy: The Unmaking of American Foreign Policy.* New York: Simon & Schuster, 1984.

Friedman, Thomas. *The Lexus and the Olive Tree: Understanding Globalization.* New York: Farrar, Straus & Giroux, 1999.

Garfinkle, Adam. *The Politics of the Nuclear Freeze.* Philadelphia: Foreign Policy Research Institute, 1984.

Halperin, Morton, *Bureaucratic Politics and Foreign Policy.* Washington, DC: Brookings Institution, 1974.

Hartmann, Frederick H., and Robert L. Wendzel. *America's Foreign Policy in a Changing World*. New York: HarperCollins, 1994.

Hilsman, Roger. *The Politics of Policy Making in Defense and Foreign Affairs: Conceptual Models and Bureaucratic Politics*. Englewood Cliffs, NJ: Prentice Hall, 1987.

Hofstadter, Richard. *The Paranoid Style in American Politics*. New York: Vintage, 1967.

Hollander, Paul. *The Adversary Culture*. New Brunswick, NJ: Transaction, 1987.

Hook, Steven W. *U.S. Foreign Policy: The Paradox of American Power*. Washington, DC: CQ Press, 2005.

———, and John Spanier. *American Foreign Policy Since World War II*. Washington, DC: CQ Press, 2004.

Kagan, Robert, *Of Paradise and Power: America and Europe in the New World Order*. New York: Knopf, 2003.

Kegley, Charles W., and Eugene R. Wittkopf. *The Domestic Sources of American Foreign Policy*. New York: St. Martin's, 1988.

Krauthammer, Charles. "The Unipolar Moment Revisited." *National Interest* 70 (Winter 2002/2003): 5–17.

Kryzanek, Michael J. *U.S.–Latin American Relations*. New York: Praeger, 1996.

Lovell, John P. *The Challenge of American Foreign Policy*. New York: Macmillan, 1985.

McCormick, James M. *American Foreign Policy and Process*. 4th ed. Belmont, CA: Thomson Wadsworth, 2005.

Mead, Walter Russell. *Special Providence: American Foreign Policy and How It Changed the World*. New York: Knopf, 2001.

Melanson, Richard. *Reconstructing Consensus: American Foreign Policy since the Vietnam War*. New York: St. Martin's, 1991.

Muravchik, Joshua. *The Uncertain Crusade: Jimmy Carter and the Dilemmas of Human Rights Policy*. Lanham, MD: Hamilton Press, 1986.

Nathan, James A., and James K. Oliver. *Foreign Policy-Making and the American Political System*. 2nd ed. Boston: Little, Brown, 1986.

Nye, Joseph S., Jr. *The Paradox of American Power*. Oxford: Oxford University Press, 2002.

Ottaway, Marina, et al. (eds.). *Funding Virtue: Civil Society Aid and Democracy Promotion*. Washington, DC: Carnegie Endowment, 2000.

Packenham, Robert A. *Liberal America and the Third World*. Princeton, NJ: Princeton University Press, 1973.

Piper, Don C., and Ronald J. Terchek (eds.). *Interaction: Foreign Policy and Public Policy*. Washington, DC: American Enterprise Institute for Public Policy Research, 1983.

Pipes, Daniel, and Adam Garfinkle (eds.). *Friendly Tyrants: An American Dilemma*. New York: St. Martin's, 1991.

Reilly, John A., ed. *American Foreign Opinion and U.S. Foreign Policy 1991*. Chicago: Chicago Council on Foreign Relations, 1991.

Rosati, Jerel A. *The Politics of United States Foreign Policy*. Forth Worth, TX: Holt, Rinehart and Winston, 2004.

Sick, Gary. *All Fall Down: America's Tragic Encounter with Iran*. New York: Random House, 1985.

Snow, Donald M. *U.S. Foreign Policy: Politics beyond the Water's Edge*. 3rd ed. Belmont, CA: Thomson Wadsworth, 2005.

Wiarda, Howard J. *American Foreign Policy: Actors and Processes*. New York: HarperCollins, 1996.

——, *Cracks in the Consensus: Debating the Democracy Agenda in U.S. Foreign Policy*. Westport, CT: Praeger/CSIS, 1997.

——, *Foreign Policy without Illusion: How Foreign Policy Works and Doesn't Work in the United States*. New York: HarperCollins/Scott Foresman, 1990.

Wittkopf, Eugene, and James McCormick. *The Domestic Sources of American Foreign Policy*. New York: St. Martin's, 2004.

Index

Aceh (Indonesia), 255
acid rain, 46
AEI, 105
Afghanistan, 193, 213, 297, 298
Africa, 259
African Americans, 237
African National Congress (ANC), 265, 271
African renaissance, 263
Afrikaner National Party, 269
Agency for International Development (AID), 139, 194, 284, 306
aggressive multilateralism, 178
agricultural interest groups, 52
AID. *See* Agency for International Development
Albright, Madeleine, 177
Alexander the Great, 217
Algeria, 298
Allende, Salvador, 78
Alliance for Progress, 176, 185
alumni associations, 131
American Enterprise Institute for Public Policy Research (AEI), 105
American institutions, 2–6
American Israel Public Action Committee, 52
Amin, Idi, 203
Amnesty International, 53

ANC. *See* African National Congress
anti-Americanism, 293
antiglobalists, 236–38
anti–land mines, 313
apartheid, 179, 267, 272
Aquinas, Thomas, 143
Aquino, Benigno, 210
Aquino, Corazon, 254
Arabic, 315
Argentina, 213, 290
Aristide, Reverend Jean Bertrand, 45
armed forces, 301
Armed Services Committee, 55
Asia, 243
assertive multilateralism, 37
Augustine, 143
austerity, 230
authoritarian governments, 298
authoritarian regimes, 200
Aymará, 315

Bahrain, 297
Baker, Pauline, 263
Balaguer, Joaquín, 288
Bauer, Peter, 284
Batista, Fulgencia, 204
Bay of Pigs, 77
Beltway, 120
BEMs (big emerging markets), 295

benign neglect, 277
Benin, 264
Berlin Wall, 35
big emerging markets (BEMs), 295
bin Laden, Osama, 42
Black, C. E., 138
"boat people," 45
Boer War, 267
Bokassa, 203
border patrol, 314
Bosnia, 18, 178
Bosnia-Herzegovina, 20
Botswana, 262
Bove, José, 219
Brazil, 290
Brookings Institute, 103
Brzezinski, Zbigniew, 104
Buddhism, 217
bureaucratic-authoritarian, 250, 305
bureaucratic interests, 67
bureaucratic politics, 22, 55, 66–68, 313
Bush, George H. W., 29, 43, 51, 177,
    286, 289, 314
Bush, George W., 4, 6, 29, 54, 66, 74,
    175, 179, 200, 281, 293, 307, 314
Bush, George W., administration, 47, 48

Cable News Network (CNN), 53
CAFTA, 286
Califano, Joseph, 131
Canada, 46, 221
Cantori, Louis, 304
Caribbean, 221
Carter, Jimmy, 6, 88, 173, 176, 186, 314
Carter administration, 78
Casey, William, 76, 78
caste associations, 159
Catholic, 160
Cato Institute, 107
Center for American Progress, 104
Center for International Private
    Enterprise (CIPE), 224
Center for Strategic and International
    Studies (CSIS), 104–5
Central America, 221

Central American Free Trade Agreement
    (CAFTA), 286
Central Intelligence Agency (CIA), 5,
    67, 74–79, 195, 314
Chávez, Hugo, 290
checks and balances, 53
Cheney, Richard, 51
chieftaincy, 271
Chile, 78, 210, 286
China. *See* People's Republic of China
Chinese, 315
Christianity, 217
Christian missionaries, 263
Christopher, Warren, 177, 187
Church, Frank, 78
Churchill, Winston, 316
CIA. *See* Central Intelligence Agency
CIPE. *See* Center for International
    Private Enterprise
civics, 270
civil society, 243, 288, 300
class changes, 155
class structure, 297
Clay, Henry, 176
clergy, 300
Clergy and Laity Concerned, 180
clientelism, 300
Clifford, Clark, 130
Clinton, Bill, 6, 30, 177, 314
Clinton administration, 37
CNN, 53
Colby, William, 76, 78
Cold War, 7, 15–16, 32, 33, 49, 62, 73,
    195
Colombia, 43, 285, 290
commander in chief, 87
Commerce Department. *See* Department
    of Commerce
Company, The, 77. *See also* Central
    Intelligence Agency (CIA)
complex interdependence, 49
Comprehensive Test Ban Treaty, 54
Confucianism, 217, 249, 255
Congress, 5, 21–22, 30, 54, 59–66, 78,
    83, 209, 307

Constitution, 21, 62, 84
Coors, Joseph, 106
corporatism, 145, 252, 271, 288, 300
Council on Foreign Relations, 99
covert operation, 75
CSIS, 104–5
Cuba, 45, 72, 173, 199, 213, 291
Cuban American National Foundation, 52
cultural context, 149
culture, 218
culture wars, 315

Darius of Persia, 217
DEA. *See* Drug Enforcement Agency
Defense Department. *See* Department of Defense
Dellums, Ron, 185
democracy, 7, 49, 80, 84, 243, 260, 262, 285, 287, 307
democracy agenda, 171
"democracy with adjectives," 286
democratization, 250, 284
Democrats, 21, 237
Department of Agriculture, 52
Department of Commerce, 5, 52, 67, 79, 314
Department of Defense, 5, 37, 67, 70, 73, 195, 208, 314
Department of Homeland Security, 5, 42, 67, 79, 314
Department of Justice, 22, 67, 68, 79
Department of State, 5, 22, 55, 67, 68, 186, 195, 208, 313
Department of Treasury, 5, 67, 68, 79, 314
dependency factors, 297
Derian, Patt, 186
détente policy, 34
development, 151
Diamond, Larry, 36
divided government, 54
division, 315
domestic political considerations, 50, 208

domestic politics, 211
Dominican Republic, 77
domino theory, 49
Donovan, William "Wild Bill," 76
Drug Enforcement Agency (DEA), 22, 55, 314
drugs, 80
Duarte, José Napoleon, 180, 190
Dulles, Allen, 76
Durkheim, Emile, 149
Du Toit, Pierre, 273
Duvalier, François, 205

Eastern Europe, 35
economic interdependence, 40
economic issues, 283
economics, 154, 221
Egypt, 199, 202, 209, 213, 298, 303, 305
El Salvador, 173, 179, 210
energy security, 47
enlargement, 178
Enlightenment, 144, 218
environment, 45, 80, 223
Environmental Protection Agency (EPA), 5, 67, 79, 314
EPA. *See* Environmental Protection Agency
ethnic cleansing, 38
ethnocentrism, 7, 135, 314
EU, 49
Europeanization, 218
European Union (EU), 49
exceptionalism, 169
executive, 21–22
executive agreement, 62

Fahd, King, 299
family, 301
"fast-track" authority, 54
FBI. *See* Federal Bureau of Investigation
Federal Bureau of Investigation (FBI), 5, 68, 79, 314
"Foggy Bottom," 69

Ford, Gerald, 186, 314
foreign affairs, 99
foreign aid, 156
Foreign Policy Research Institute, 101
Foreign Relations Committee, 55
foreign service officers (FSOs), 69
Fox, Vicente, 282
France, 219, 223
"free associability," 252
free trade, 284
Free Trade Area of the Americas
    (FTAA), 286
friendly tyrant, 199
FSOs, 69
FTAA, 286
Fuentes, Carlos, 148
Fujimori, Alberto, 288

Galbraith, John Kenneth, 100, 138
Genghis Khan, 217
Georgetown dinner party, 125
Germany, 223
Ghana, 263
globalization, 39, 217
global warming, 313
GNGOs. *See* governmental-
    nongovernmental organizations
Good Neighbor Policy, 280
Gorbachev, Mikhail, 34
Gordon, Lincoln, 138
Gore, Al, 52
governmental-nongovernmental
    organizations (GNGOs), 255, 308
government reform, 285
Greece, 213
Greenpeace, 53
gridlock, 64
Guatemala, 210
Gulf of Tonkin Resolution, 85
Gulf War, 73

Haiti, 19, 38, 45, 178, 193, 213, 285, 291
Haliburton, 51
Harkin, Tom, 185
Helms, Richard, 76

Heritage Foundation, 106
Hinduism, 217
Hispanics, 293
Hitler, Adolf, 203
Hobbes, Thomas, 144
Hong Kong, 243
Hoover Institution on War, Revolution,
    and Peace, 102
Hudson Institute, 102
human rights, 7, 49, 80, 172, 313
human rights abuses, 210
human rights movement, 185
Huntington, Samuel P., 3
Hussein, Saddam, 42, 205

idealism, 36
idealist, 201
identity politics, 313
IMF. *See* International Monetary Fund
immigration, 44, 80
Immigration and Naturalization Service
    (INS), 5, 314
import-substitution industrialization, 181
India, 243
indigenous institutions, 164
Indonesia, 194, 244, 247, 250, 253, 254
Industrial Revolution, 218
INS. *See* Immigration and
    Naturalization Service
Institute for Foreign Policy Analysis,
    101
Institute for Policy Studies (IPS), 102
institutions, 313
interest groups, 4, 19–20, 51–53;
    agriculture, 52
interest group struggle, 313
"intermestic" (both international and
    domestic), 47
international community, 273
International Criminal Court (ICC), 313
International Monetary Fund (IMF),
    228–31
IPS, 102
Iran, 34, 199, 297, 298
Iran-Contra, 79

Iraq, 19, 37, 61, 72, 193, 209, 213, 297, 298
Iraq War, 210
"iron triangle," 131
Islam, 217
Islamic fundamentalism, 255, 301
Islamic fundamentalist groups, 264
Islamic political culture, 295, 298
Islamic regime, 219, 298
isolationism, 18, 31
Israel, 295, 297, 298

Jackson, Andrew, 176
Jackson, Henry ("Scoop"), 180
Jackson-Vanik amendment, 186
Japan, 243, 248, 249, 251, 252, 254
Joint Chiefs of Staff, 73
Jordan, 298
judicial reform, 285
Justice Department. *See* Department of Justice

Kahn, Herman, 102
Kennan, George, 184
Kennedy, John F., 33, 185
Keohane, Robert O., 49
Kerry, John, 66
Kirkpatrick, Jeane J., 175, 203–4, 278
Kissinger, Henry, 34, 36, 48, 104, 184
Kobe, 251
Kohl, Helmut, 181
Koran, 299
Korea, 33
Korea, North, 199, 243
Korea, South, 210, 243, 248, 249, 251, 253, 254
Kosovo, 38
Kotze, Hennie, 273
Krauthammer, Charles, 36, 49
Kuwait, 172, 297
Kyoto Treaty, 46, 313

Lake, Anthony, 177
language, 220
Latin America, 185, 277

League of Nations, 73
Lebanon, 297, 298, 303
Lefever, Ernest, 89, 189
"lesser evil doctrine," 173, 278
liberal arts education, 142
Libya, 298
Lipset, Seymour M., 138
Locke, John, 144

Machiavelli, 144
Mahan, Alfred Thayer, 72
Malawi, 262
Malaysia, 244
Mali, 262, 264
Mandela, Nelson, 265
Marcos, Ferdinand, 205, 254
Mariana, Juan de, 144
Marx, Karl, 144, 149
Mathitir, Mohammed, 247
McCaffrey, General Barry, 43
McDonald's, 219
McFarlane, Robert, 75
media, 4, 20–21, 51–53, 313
Menem, Carlos, 288
Mershon Center, 101
Metternich, Klemens, 148
Mexico, 45, 176, 178, 221, 285, 286, 288, 289
middle class, 159
Middle East, 84, 191, 295, 315
military coup, 160
Milosevic, Slobodan, 38
Mindanao, 255
MNCs. *See* multinational corporations
modernization, 145
Molina, Luis, 144
Monroe, President James, 31
Monroe Doctrine, 31, 176
Morgenthau, Hans, 48, 184
Morocco, 298
Morrison, Stephen, 263
Mubarak, Hosni, 304
multilateralists, 36
multinational corporations (MNCs), 226–28

multipolar, 49
Muravchik, Joshua, 36
Myanmar, 244, 247

NAFTA. *See* North American Free
  Trade Agreement
Namibia, 262
narcotics trade, 43
National Council of Churches, 53
National Endowment for Democracy
  (NED), 179, 224, 272
National Security Act, 77
National Security Council (NSC), 6, 70,
  81–83, 314
nation building, 70
NATO, 38
Neustadt, Richard, 91
news media. *See* media
NGOs. *See* nongovernmental
  organizations
Nicaragua, 187, 213
Nigeria, 262, 264
Nixon, Richard, 34, 186
nondemocratic regime, 199
nongovernmental organizations (NGOs),
  53
nonprofit organizations (NPOs), 252
Noriega, General Manuel, 43
North, Oliver, 79
North American Free Trade Agreement
  (NAFTA), 41, 45, 65, 88, 286, 289
North Atlantic Treaty Organization
  (NATO), 38
"no second Cubas" doctrine, 278
NPOs. *See* nonprofit organizations
NSC. *See* National Security Council
Nye, Joseph S., 49

O'Donnell, Guillermo, 285
Office of Strategic Services (OSS), 76
Office of the Secretary of Defense, 73
Office of the U.S. Trade Representative,
  5, 67, 80, 314
oil, 40
Oman, 297

OPEC. *See* Organization of Petroleum
  Exporting Countries
open markets, 284
organic-corporatist, 148
Organization of Petroleum Exporting
  Countries (OPEC), 40
organized labor, 52, 304
oval office, 6

PACs. *See* political action committees
Pahlavi, Mohammad Reza, 204
Pakistan, 199, 202, 209, 212, 213, 243,
  298, 299
Palestinian Authority, 213
Panama, 43, 176
Panama Canal, 65
Panama Canal treaties, 88
Paraguay, 210, 213
Parsons, Talcott, 151
partisan politics, 22–23
partisan posturing, 64
partisanship, 89, 315
patrimonialism, 300
patronage networks, 131
pattern variables, 151
Peace Corps, 7
peacekeeping, 70
Pearl Harbor, 32
Pentagon, 3, 57, 284
people's movements, 251
People's Republic of China, 32, 33, 174,
  195, 199, 202, 213, 223, 243, 244,
  254
Philip of Macedonia, 217
Philippines, 72, 194, 210, 244, 247, 250,
  251, 253, 254
Pinochet, 205
Plan Colombia, 290
plausible deniability, 75
pluralism, 56
pluralistic, 48
Podesta, John, 104
Poindexter, John, 75
Poland, 180
police state, 303

political action committees (PACs), 19
political culture, 3, 6, 16–17, 50–51,
    267–69
political economy, 154–57
political Islam, 304
political party, 4, 54
political process model, 208
political theory, 143–48
politicize, 91
"politics of blame," 65
Pol Pot, 203
Portugal, 97
Posusney, Marsha Pripstein, 304
poverty, 260
Powell, Colin, 57, 70
power, struggle for, 48
preachiness, 223
presidency, 83–91; bully pulpit, 90;
    inherent powers, 90; precedent, 85
president, 54
protectionist pressures, 286
Protestant reformation, 144
public-interest issues, 251
public opinion, 18–19, 50–51, 313
public pressures, 48
public-private partnerships, 288
Puerto Rico, 72

Qatar, 297

rational-actor model, 207
Reagan, Ronald, 6, 177, 314
Reagan administration, 65, 173,
    189
realism, 36
realpolitik, 201
recognition, 90
Renaissance, 218
Republicans, 21
Rice, Condoleezza, 70
rogue states, 29, 37
Roman Catholic Church, 217
Roman Empire, 217
Roosevelt, Franklin, 32
Roosevelt, Theodore, 32

Rostow, W. W., 138, 155, 181
Rove, Karl, 283
rule of law, 285
Russia, 178, 243
Rwanda, 38

SALT. *See* Strategic Arms Limitation
    Talks
Sandinistas, 187
Saudi Arabia, 172, 199, 202, 209, 210,
    212, 297
Scientific Revolution, 218
security issues, 284
Senate, 87, 88
"Senatorial courtesy," 89
Senegal, 262, 264
shah of Iran, 204
shakai, 246
Shariah, 299
Sierra Club, 53
Singapore, 243, 248, 249, 253, 256
Soares, Glaucio Ary Dillon, 161
social sciences, 142
socioeconomic development, 255,
    297
sociologists, 149
Solarz, Stephen, 209
Solidarity, 177, 180
Somalia, 19, 38, 193
Somoza, Anastasio, 204
SOPs, 67
Sorensen, Theodore, 89
Soros, George, 104
South Africa, 179, 210, 262, 264, 265
Southeast Asia, 253, 254
Soviet Union, 33, 34, 49, 174
Spain, 72
Spanish-American War, 31
stalemate, 54
standard operating procedures (SOPs),
    67
State Department. *See* Department of
    State
state-structured interest group, 252
statist, 272

Strategic Arms Limitation Talks
   (SALT), 34, 88
Strauss, Robert, 131
strong government, 288
Suárez, Francisco, 144
Sub-Saharan Africa, 295
Suharto, Raden, 254
Supreme Court, 85
sustainable development, 46
Swahili, 315
Syria, 213, 298

Taiwan, 243, 248, 249, 251, 253, 254
Talbott, Strobe, 104
Taliban, 42
Tanzania, 262
technology, 220
television, 209
terrorism, 41, 72, 80, 314
terrorist attacks, 3, 57
Thailand, 244
Thatcher, Margaret, 181
think tank, 5, 93–116; funding, 113;
   influence, 111
Third World, 77, 135
threat, 290
totalitarianism, 203
transparency, 285
Treasury Department. *See* Department
   of Treasury
treaties, 62
treaty making, 87
tribal, 159
tribalism, 271
tribes, 300
Trujillo, Rafael, 204
Tunisia, 298
Turkey, 213, 297, 298, 303
Turner, Stansfield, 78

unilateralists, 36
union members, 237
unipolar, 49
United Arab Emirates, 297
U.S. Institute of Peace (USIP), 272
USIP. *See* U.S. Institute of Peace

Vandenberg, Arthur, 2
Venezuela, 285, 290
Vietnam, 33, 61, 73, 244
Vietnam, South, 49, 213
Vietnam War, 209
Vitoria, 144

Walesa, Lech, 180
Waltz, Kenneth, 48
war, 86
"war on drugs," 43–44
war on terrorism, 47, 70, 84, 315
War Powers Act, 54, 85
Washington, D.C., 118–20; friendships,
   128–30; law firms, 130; social life,
   123–28
Washington Consensus, 181, 292
Westernization, 145, 218
White House, 21, 86
Wilsonian, 7
Wilsonian tradition, 175–79
women, 237
women's networks, 131
World Bank, 228–231
World Trade Center, 3, 57
World Trade Organization (WTO), 51,
   231–32
WTO. *See* World Trade Organization

Yemen, 298
Yew, Lee Kuan, 247
Yugoslavia, 38

About the Author

Howard J. Wiarda is Dean Rusk Professor of International Relations and head of the Department of International Affairs at the University of Georgia. Much of his career was spent as professor of political science and comparative labor relations and the Leonard J. Horwitz Professor of Iberian and Latin American Studies at the University of Massachusetts, Amherst; he also spent twenty years in the Washington think tank and policy-making worlds. He retains his positions as public policy scholar of the Woodrow Wilson International Center for Scholars, and senior associate at the Center for Strategic and International Studies (CSIS) in Washington, D.C. Professor Wiarda began his career as a scholar of Latin American politics, and his writings on Latin America, Spain, Portugal, and the developing nations are well known in the field. While continuing these research and writing interests, over the last twenty years his scholarly interests have broadened to include Russia, Asia, Europe, Sub-Saharan Africa, comparative democratization, civil society, and general comparative politics and American foreign policy. He is recognized as one of the country's leading authorities on foreign policy, comparative politics, and international affairs.